ALTERNATIVE STRATEGIES FOR ECONOMIC DEVELOPMENT

Keith Griffin

Distinguished Professor, Economics
University of California, Riverside

Second Edition

in association with
OECD DEVELOPMENT CENTRE

First published in Great Britain 1999 by
MACMILLAN PRESS LTD
Houndmills, Basingstoke, Hampshire RG21 6XS and London
Companies and representatives throughout the world

A catalogue record for this book is available from the British Library.

ISBN 0–333–74653–8 hardcover
ISBN 0–333–74654–6 paperback

First published in the United States of America 1999 by
ST. MARTIN'S PRESS, INC.,
Scholarly and Reference Division,
175 Fifth Avenue, New York, N.Y. 10010

ISBN 0–312–22339–0 (clothbound)
ISBN 0–312–22340–4 (paperback)

Library of Congress Cataloging-in-Publication Data
Griffin, Keith B.
Alternative strategies for economic development / Keith Griffin. –
– 2nd ed.
p.   cm.
Includes bibliographical references and index.
ISBN 0–312–22339–0 (cloth). — ISBN 0–312–22340–4 (pbk.)
1. Developing countries—Economic policy.   2. Developing
countries—Economic conditions.   3. Economic development.
I. Title.
HC59.7.G747   1999
338.9'009172'6—dc21
                                                         99–18657
                                                              CIP

This book is printed on paper suitable for recycling and made from fully managed and
sustained forest sources.

10   9   8   7   6   5   4   3   2   1
08   07   06   05   04   03   02   01   00   99

Printed and bound in Great Britain by
Antony Rowe Ltd, Chippenham, Wiltshire

To
JANICE and KIMBERLEY

CONTENTS

TABLES

FIGURES

FOREWORD

In the last ten years we have witnessed important changes in economic performance and policy. Indeed in both the industrialised and developing countries there have been profound reforms in financial, economic and social policies. These changes were largely initiated in the industrialised countries where inflation was declared public enemy number one and supply-side economics, with its procession of privatisation, deregulation and industrial restructuring became a new orthodoxy. In one sense the new orthodoxy has worked in that inflation has been reduced to very low levels in many countries, but of course there has been a price to pay. Unemployment, particularly in Europe, has been high and sustained; the level of investment, particularly public investment, has been low; and there has emerged a predominance of the monetary and financial economy over the real economy.

Low commodity prices, high real rates of interest and neo-protectionist tendencies in the OECD countries have in the 1980s played havoc with the economies of many developing countries. This economic downfall followed an extremely dynamic period of growth in much of the Third World in the 1960s and 1970s and the current reversal has caused acute hardship, particularly in Africa and Latin America. The new financial and economic orthodoxy of the OECD countries has spread to the developing countries where in recent years emphasis has been placed on adjustment programmes and other policies designed to reduce government expenditure substantially, on releasing private market forces and on eliminating bureaucratic controls. In common with the industrialised countries, the developing world has paid a price: higher levels of unemployment, more poverty, less public investment and cuts in education and health budgets. There has thus been a decline in the essential prerequisites for growth, namely in physical and human capital formation.

The new orthodoxy has brought into question the effectiveness of development policies and indeed of development assistance as these were pursued in the 1960s and 1970s. This questioning has occurred notwithstanding the average rate of economic growth of 5 per cent per annum that was achieved in the developing countries, partly presumably as a consequence of the policies adopted and the foreign assistance provided. The new orthodoxy, like all orthodoxies, is characterised by exclusiveness (or intolerance of competing views), comprehensiveness (or lack of selectivity) and by the tendency to become pervasive. The orthodoxy of the 1980s – with its emphasis on deregulation, privatisation, unregulated financial flows, market forces and (what is not the same thing) getting prices right – claims to be more effective in reaching the objectives of economic and social development than the policies pursued in the 1960s and 1970s.

The OECD Development Centre has a long tradition of pioneering research on controversial issues, of taking an objective view of international economic affairs and of seeking mutually beneficial solutions to economic problems. It should come as no surprise therefore that we decided to examine the different economic and social development strategies that have been adopted in the recent development history of the world. There are by now a sufficient number of countries that have pursued for a sufficiently long time a given set of policies for comparisons to become possible as to which policies have been relatively more effective in reaching specified development objectives within a reasonable period of time. The present publication is a first attempt to get a clearer view on this.

The author tries to avoid extremes and to present a balanced view. The essence of good policy often consists in striking the right balance: the balance between the role of the state and the role of market forces; the balance between the role of planning and of individual initiative; the balance between an emphasis on economic growth and on a redistribution of income, etc. This theme runs throughout the book and carries an important message.

The relationship between a country's development strategy and its political system also is considered. Again, the conclusion is undogmatic and the message important:

> "There is no best path to development and there is no close correspondence between development policy or development strategy on the one hand and the resulting political system on the other ... Nonetheless, we have argued that the strategy of economic development pursued by a country can predispose it towards authoritarianism or democracy although it seldom is the sole determining factor."

We were fortunate that Keith Griffin, the President of Magdalen College, Oxford, was willing and able to find the time to be with us at the OECD Development Centre in order to write this book and assist us in many other ways. Keith Griffin is an outstanding colleague and old friend. His experience and golden pen guarantee good quality, clarity, honesty and balance. I thank him for the effort he has put into this joint venture. I thank also the Macmillan Press Ltd. for having agreed to publish the book jointly with the OECD Development Centre.

Louis Emmerij
President, OECD Development Centre
August 1987

PREFACE

This is a volume reporting the findings of a major research effort on policy choices before the developing countries sponsored by the OECD Development Centre in Paris. I was invited by the President of the Development Centre, Louis Emmerij, to undertake this study and I wish to thank him for offering me such a stimulating and challenging assignment. Mr. Emmerij took an exceptionally active interest in the project and I am grateful to him for his constant support and encouragement.

Most of the research for this volume and almost all of the actual writing was done at the Development Centre while I was on leave from Magdalen College, Oxford. It is unusual for a President of Magdalen to be given leave of absence to undertake research and I am grateful to the Fellows for agreeing so readily to my request. It was perhaps ungracious of me to resign from the Presidency and move to my present post at the University of California, Riverside just a year after returning to Oxford from research leave.

The facilities provided at the Development Centre for research were superb. My research assistant was Ganeshan Wignaraja and he was exceptionally industrious in compiling data, producing bibliographies, criticising drafts of chapters and generally stimulating me to greater effort. I am much indebted to him. The three librarians, Isabelle Cornélis, Michèle Alkilic and Marian Ashworth went out of their way to be helpful and if a reference was not available in the Centre's library they made every effort to track it down in one of the other libraries in Paris. Michèle Fleury-Brousse provided excellent computer assistance. The speed and accuracy of her team greatly increased my own productivity.

Louis Emmerij commented upon and criticised every chapter. In addition I received many useful comments and suggestions from friends and colleagues. I would like to mention in particular James Boyce (Chapters 3, 5 and 6), Richard Conroy (Chapter 8), Charles Harvey (Chapters 1 and 4), Azizur Rahman Khan (Chapter 8), Angus Maddison (Chapter 1), Allan McHarg (Chapter 4), John Mellor (Chapter 6), Charles Oman (Chapter 5), Cranford Pratt (Chapters 1, 3, 4 and 9), Carl Riskin (Chapters 1, 3 and 8) and Axel Van Trotsenburg (Chapter 4). Their observations undoubtedly helped to raise the quality of the final product quite considerably.

My secretary, Christine Johnson, typed and re-typed seemingly innumerable drafts. She was amazingly fast and accurate and this volume would not have been completed as quickly as it was without her unstinting commitment to it. I am very grateful to her.

K.B.G.

INTRODUCTION TO THE SECOND EDITION

Much has happened in the world since the first edition of this book was published in 1989. Three events in particular have had a significant impact on thinking about strategies for economic development. First, a new approach to development problems has emerged – the human development approach – which has attracted much attention in academic circles and among international and national policymakers. Indeed the human development approach has become the intellectual framework for much advice given by the United Nations Development Programme to developing countries. Second, following the disintegration of the Soviet bloc in 1989–91 and the decision by almost all of the ex-socialist countries to adopt a market oriented economic system, there has been intense debate about how best to effect a transition from socialism to capitalism. Third, the spread of liberal economic policies in the developed countries, the creation of more open economies in the developing countries and the integration of the ex-socialist countries into the world economy has accelerated a process of globalisation that began shortly after the end of the Second World War. This process of globalisation has altered the context in which national development strategies are formulated and raises issues about the distribution of gains and losses associated with closer economic integration.

These are the three topics that are discussed in this Introduction. Each could well be the subject of a separate chapter, but that would make sense only if all of the original chapters were completely rewritten and that, alas, is not possible at present. I hope, however, that the relatively brief treatment each topic receives here will stimulate interest and encourage the reader to consult the wider literature.

The human development strategy

Development economics has largely been about material enrichment, that is expanding the volume of production of goods and services. It was usually assumed, explicitly or implicitly, that an increase in output, say, the growth of gross domestic product per capita, would reduce poverty and improve the general well being of the population. Indeed the connection between increased output and decreased poverty was thought to be so strong that many economists believed that a concentration on growth alone would suffice to achieve the goal of development. Growth, in other words, became not just the means for achieving development but the end of development itself. True, there were always dissenters, but the dissenters tended to qualify the emphasis on growth by underlining the importance of the distribution of the benefits of growth, rather than challenging the importance of growth as such. Debates about alternative development strategies often were debates about how best to accelerate the growth of production of goods and services.

The human development approach, in contrast, challenges the basic assumptions on which much of development economics rests. Above all, following the pathbreaking work of Amartya Sen, the process of development is seen as a process of expanding the "capabilities" of people.[1] That is, the objective of development is not to increase output but to enable people to increase their range of choice, to do more things, to live a long life, to escape avoidable illness, to have access to the world's stock of knowledge, and so forth. An increase in the supply of commodities in this formulation may help to increase human capabilities, but it does so indirectly and is not an end in itself. The human development approach, in other words, dethrones national product as the primary indicator of the level of development.

The human development approach also challenges the common assumption that the means to development is the accumulation of physical capital, that is investment in plant and equipment. Following the equally pathbreaking work of T.W. Schultz, emphasis is placed on the accumulation of human capital in the form of investment in education, basic health, nutrition, the generation of new knowledge and technology, and so on.[2] That is, investment in human beings is regarded as productive whether the objective is to increase GDP or expand human capabilities.

Taken together, the shift in the objective of development and the emphasis on human capital as the means to development, the new approach has far reaching implications for the overall strategy of development.[3] People are placed firmly in the centre of the stage: they are simultaneously the object of policy and a major instrument of their own development. A commodity-centred view of development is abandoned in favour of a people-centred view of development.

This new approach was first recognised by the United Nations system in the 1988 report of the Committee for Development Planning.[4] A year later, under the leadership of Mahbub ul Haq, the human development approach was endorsed by the United Nations Development Programme (UNDP),[5] and beginning in 1990 the UNDP issued an annual *Human Development Report* which expanded the concept of human development and attempted to show how the strategy could be translated into operational terms for policymakers.[6]

As part of the dethronement of GDP per capita as the primary indicator of development, the UNDP compiled a Human Development Index (HDI) which attempts to measure the level of human capabilities in a country. The HDI has four components, life expectancy at birth, the adult literacy rate, the combined enrolment ratio in primary, secondary and tertiary education and real income measured in purchasing power parity terms. Real income (in PPP$) is adjusted to take into account the diminishing contribution to human development of a rise in GDP per capita above the world average.[7]

One would expect that country rankings on the HDI would be broadly similar to country rankings in terms of per capita income, and indeed this is the case. In a surprising number of instances, however, there is a substantial diversion between rankings on the two indicators. In Table 1 below we include the HDI rank and the real GDP per capita rank (measured in PPP$) for 20 countries. These are the countries, out of a total of 175, in which the difference between the two rankings is 25 places or more. The countries are listed in order of their HDI rank.

Some countries evidently do much better in terms of human development than their income level would lead one to predict. Costa Rica, for example, ranks 33 on the HDI

Table 1 REAL GDP PER CAPITA AND HDI RANKING COMPARED FOR 20 COUNTRIES, 1994 (PPP$)

Country	HDI rank	Real GDP per capita rank	Real GDP per capita rank minus HDI rank
Luxembourg	27	1	-26
Costa Rica	33	60	27
Brunei	38	2	-36
Kuwait	53	6	-47
Qatar	55	22	-33
Mauritius	61	31	-30
Saudi Arabia	73	41	-32
Oman	88	39	-49
Botswana	93	63	-30
Georgia	105	136	31
Azerbaijan	106	131	25
Moldova	110	138	28
Tajikistan	115	150	35
Namibia	118	83	-35
Morocco	119	93	-26
Gabon	120	95	-25
Vietnam	121	147	26
Myanmar	131	157	25
Zaire	142	173	31
Senegal	160	134	-26

Source: UNDP, *Human Development Report 1997*, New York: Oxford University Press, 1997, Tables 2.10 and 2.11, pp. 44–5.

whereas in terms of per capita income it ranks only 60, a difference of 27. Similarly, Vietnam ranks 121 on the HDI whereas its per capita income rank is 147, a difference of 26. Six other countries in the table (Georgia, Azerbaijan, Moldova, Tajikistan, Myanmar and Zaire) have performed relatively better in terms of human development than in terms of their ability to produce the goods and services measured in GDP. A relatively low per capita income, in other words, has not prevented these eight countries from adopting policies which resulted in relatively high levels of human development.

The opposite also is true. Some countries, despite a high level of real income per head, have underperformed in terms of human development. Kuwait, for example, ranks sixth out of 175 countries in the world on a real GDP per capita scale, yet it ranks only 53 on the HDI scale, a difference of –47. Similarly, Mauritius ranks 31 in terms of real income as compared to 61 in terms of human development, a difference of –30. Ten other countries, from Luxembourg to Senegal, have performed very poorly on the HDI scale compared to the ranking on a real income scale. A high average income, in other words, is no guarantee of a high level of human development. If one accepts that an expansion of human capabilities should be the objective of development policy, the strategy of development will have to be broadened to include much more than the growth of GDP.

Turning to the means of development, recent evidence suggests that the contribution of human capital to growth is higher than that of either natural or physical capital, and perhaps more than the two combined.[8] This is especially true if one interprets growth to mean an increase in human development, since improvements in health and education contribute directly to human development as well as indirectly through their effects on increasing the growth of output and incomes.

Using data on 98 countries for the period 1960–85, Robert Barro finds that the growth rate of real GDP per capita is positively related to the initial stock of human capital as proxied by primary and secondary school enrolment rates.[9] Thus the larger is the stock of human capital and the more equitably distributed are educational opportunities, that is, the higher is the percentage of the population enrolled in primary and secondary schools, the higher is the growth rate of GDP. The effects on raising human development would be stronger still, because of the direct contribution of education to human development.

The microeconomic evidence supports these findings. Rati Ram estimates that the returns to schooling are 13 per cent on average for all countries, with a higher return in developing than in developed countries.[10] The evidence also indicates that the returns to education increase as one moves down the education pyramid from tertiary to secondary to primary education.[11] Given that tertiary education usually favours the elite, a more equal distribution of expenditure on education in developing countries would increase efficiency and growth as well as equity. Indeed George Psacharopoulos finds that in developing countries the rates of return on investments in primary education are more than 25 per cent, whereas they fall sharply at higher levels, namely, to 15–18 per cent at the secondary level and to 13–16 per cent at the tertiary level.[12]

It is sometimes thought that the benefits of education are confined mainly to the formal sector and that expenditures of education have low returns in agriculture. This is not true. Daniel Cotlear and others have shown that investing in education raises farm productivity.[13] This occurs in two ways. First, education is a complementary input in production, particularly in technologically more advanced agricultural regions, and the higher is the level of education, the higher is the level of farm output. Second, and perhaps more important, education facilitates the adoption of new and improved technology and thereby contributes to growth of agricultural output. The sectoral and microeconomic studies thus provide strong support for the human development strategy.

A recent study by the Asian Development Bank provides supporting macroeconomic evidence.[14] The study enables one to estimate the contribution of various factors to the difference in the rate of growth of per capita income in East and Southeast Asia during the period 1965–90, on the one hand, and three other regions during the same period, on the other hand. Consider the example of sub-Saharan Africa. During the twenty-five years under examination, the rate of growth of output per head in sub-Saharan Africa was four percentage points a year slower than in East and Southeast Asia. This difference of four percentage points can be decomposed as follows: 2.3 percentage points are due to differences in human capital (namely, "schooling" and "demography"), one percentage point is due to differences in natural capital (namely, "resources and geography") and 0.1 percentage point is due to differences in physical capital (specifically, "government savings rate"). The remaining 0.6 points are attributed to other factors. A broadly similar result was found in South Asia but not, curiously, in Latin America, where "initial conditions" and "openness" appear to have been much more important.

While such decomposition exercises must be treated with some scepticism, the Asian Development Bank study confirms the importance of human capital in accelerating economic growth and, in the cases of East and Southeast Asia and South Asia, suggests that human capital was more than twice as important as natural and physical capital combined in explaining differences in economic performance. These results are therefore consistent with other recent empirical findings. At the very least the evidence supports the efficacy of a redistributive strategy of development (as discussed in Chapter 7 below) and more ambitiously, it strengthens the case for the human development strategy.

Transition strategies in ex-socialist countries [15]

There are 29 countries with a combined population of 1,688 million people that have embarked on a transition from central planning to a more market oriented economic system. Eleven of the 29 countries are in Central and Eastern Europe and 12 are successor states to the former Soviet Union; in addition, there are the three Baltic States, plus China, Vietnam and Mongolia. All 29 countries are classified by the World Bank as either low- or medium-income economies. All of the countries, with the exception of China, began the push to a market economy in 1989–91; in China the reform process began a decade earlier, in late 1978.

There is considerable debate about the best strategy to adopt to complete the transition. On one side are those who advocate simultaneous reform across a broad front (popularly known as the big bang or shock therapy approach) while on the other side are the advocates of sequential reform (often called the gradual approach). The Soviet bloc countries, by and large, adopted a big bang approach whereas China and Vietnam pursued sequential reforms.

Let us consider these alternative reform strategies. There is general agreement that systemic transformation implies fundamental reforms in a great many areas. Seven sets of reforms are widely regarded as essential to the success of the transition process. I list them in approximate order of priority.

First in order of importance is the creation of domestic markets. This sounds obvious and simple, but it is not. Macroeconomic stability, particularly the absence of rapid price inflation, must be established so that markets produce clear and accurate signals. A legal framework must be created so that contracts can be enforced; property rights must be reasonably secure, whether for state, collective or private property; and market institutions must be created, and in particular a properly regulated, financially viable and efficient commercial banking system must be created.

Second, once domestic markets have been created and are functioning properly, liberalisation of international trade becomes an essential reform. Most transition economies are rather small and have little alternative to relying on international markets to exploit their comparative advantages. China and, possibly, Russia are the only exceptions.

Third, opportunities should be created for a private sector to emerge. New enterprises require access to land, raw materials, foreign exchange and bank credit; they must also be allowed to hire labour. In principle there are many activities that could attract private entrepreneurial initiative – personal services, domestic and foreign trading, small workshops and repair facilities, tourism, small scale farming, and so on – but administrative obstacles and controls must be removed so that private enterprise is not inhibited. New private sector activities have several features which make them especially attractive during the early stages of a transition: they usually are small in scale, widely dispersed and labour intensive, and hence the benefits of private sector activity contribute to employment creation and a relatively equal distribution of income. In addition, small scale activities usually have a relatively short gestation period and hence contribute quickly to increased output and incomes.

Reforming the existing state enterprises is the fourth essential reform. Irrespective of the system of ownership, the firm under a market economy operates very differently from the firm under a planned economy and it is unrealistic to suppose that state enterprises can flourish under a market economy without substantial adaptation. Indeed the alternative to adaptation often is bankruptcy or large losses which have to be financed by the state.

Fifth, reform of the state enterprises also implies reform of the system of taxation. This is especially important in those countries where state owned enterprises provide social services elsewhere provided by local and central government. It is very common for state enterprises to finance childcare and kindergarten facilities, supply housing for their workers, primary schooling, medical care and clinics, and even vacation facilities. The cost structure of state enterprises therefore reflects not only the costs of production but also the costs of providing basic social services. This cost structure cannot be sustained in a competitive market economy and hence alternative arrangements will have to be made to finance and provide social services. If this is not done, state enterprises will go out of business, or essential social services will disappear or state enterprises will run huge deficits which, if covered by the state, will contribute to rapid inflation. In many countries one can observe a combination of the three responses.

Privatisation of state owned enterprises is the sixth reform. Most analysts are in favour of the privatisation of small state enterprises; the debate centres on what to do with the medium and large state owned enterprises. Experience indicates that careful attention should be paid to the method of transfer of state owned assets (for example by voucher, by sale to the existing managers, by sale to the workers of the enterprise, by sale to the general public, by sale to foreigners) and to the effects on the distribution of income and wealth. Even in the best of cases one should not expect too much from privatisation: the benefits, if any, will arise primarily from a once-for-all improvement in the use of existing resources whereas the long term objective of the transition is continuing improvements arising from an acceleration in the rate of growth of output and incomes.

Finally, there is the question of liberalisation of the external capital account. It is natural that transition economies would wish to attract foreign capital to help restructure the economy and accelerate the pace of expansion. Foreign direct investment can be particularly useful, but it is doubtful that short term foreign borrowing or portfolio investments should be liberalised until the transition is completed, and particularly not until macroeconomic stability is achieved, the commercial banking system is reformed, markets are functioning well (including the market for foreign exchange) and the state owned enterprises have been reformed. Experience in Latin America, Southeast Asia and most recently in Russia has shown that the premature liberalisation of the capital account exposes a country to potentially highly destabilising movements of short term capital that can undermine the economic reform process.

Let us now compare performance under the two broad transition strategies indicated earlier: big bang versus sequential reform. In Table 2 we present data for the five largest transition countries, which between them account for nearly 90 per cent of the population living in the 29 transition economies. Three countries, namely, Poland, Russia and Ukraine attempted to adopt a big bang strategy, while the remaining two, China and Vietnam, adopted sequential reforms. Performance is evaluated in terms of five indicators.

Consider first the rate of growth during the period 1990–5. China and Vietnam enjoyed a very rapid increase in total output (8–13 per cent a year) whereas Russia and Ukraine experienced a very sharp decline in output and Poland, the most successful of the big bang countries, enjoyed only a moderate growth rate of 2.4 per cent a year during the period

Table 2 **PERFORMANCE INDICATORS FOR THE FIVE LARGEST TRANSITION ECONOMIES**

| | Big Bang Strategy | | | Sequential Reform | |
	Poland	Russia	Ukraine	China	Vietnam
Growth of GDP, 1990–5 (per cent per annum)	2.4	–9.8	–14.3	12.8	8.3
GDP deflator, 1993–5 (per cent per annum)	28.3	249.6	616.6	16.0	17.0
Income inequality, 1993 (Gini coefficient)	0.30	0.50	0.26[a]	0.45[b]	0.34
Change in male life expectancy, 1980–95 (years)	0	–4	–1	2	4
Change in crude death rate, 1980–95 (per thousand people)	0	+4	+3	+1	–1

Notes: a 1992
          b 1995

Sources: World Bank, *World Development Indicators 1997*, Washington, D.C.: World Bank, 1997; Azizur Rahman Khan and Carl Riskin, "Income and Inequality in China", *China Quarterly*, forthcoming; Keith Griffin, ed., *Economic Reform in Vietnam*, London: Macmillan 1998; Keith Griffin, "Economic Policy During the Transition to a Market Oriented Economy", report prepared for UNDP, 1998.

1990–5. The countries following a sequential reform strategy clearly performed better by this test than those which attempted to follow a big bang strategy.

Next, consider macroeconomic stability, as measured by the average annual rate of inflation of the GDP deflator during the period 1993–5. Again, China and Vietnam enjoyed greater stability than the other three countries. Inflation in the big bang countries varied between 28.3 per cent a year in Poland and 616.6 per cent a year in Ukraine, whereas it was only 16–17 per cent a year in China and Vietnam. Moreover, there is a clear association between macroeconomic stability and growth: the lower is the rate of inflation, the faster is the rate of growth.

Third, inequality appears to have increased in all five countries, but the degree of inequality as measured by the Gini coefficient does not seem to be affected in a systematic way by the transition strategy followed. In Russia and Ukraine, however, rising inequality occurred in a context of falling average incomes and hence the proportion of the population in poverty increased dramatically. In China and Vietnam, in contrast, rising inequality occurred in a context of rapidly rising incomes and hence the proportion of the population living in poverty tended to fall. Poland occupied an intermediate position between these extremes.

Shock therapy had severe demographic consequences, particularly for males of working age. Male life expectancy actually declined in Russia and Ukraine between 1980 and 1995 and remained unchanged in Poland; in China and Vietnam, again in contrast, male life expectancy rose. This fourth indicator strengthens the conclusion that the well being of the population worsened or remained static in the big bang countries and improved considerably in the two countries which adopted a sequential reform strategy. Finally, this conclusion receives further support from the data on changes in the crude death rate. Russia and Ukraine are conspicuous for the rise in the death rate as compared to rough constancy in Poland, China and Vietnam.

On balance, then, it seems pretty obvious that the big bang strategy or shock therapy was a relative failure. Many millions of people are worse off today than they were when their country followed a socialist strategy of development as described in Chapter 8. What went wrong?

The central idea behind shock therapy is that countries should effect the traverse from central planning to a market economy as quickly as possible by introducing market reforms simultaneously, in a big bang. This presupposes that the strategy is feasible; that it is possible to do everything at once. The danger, a real one as it turned out, is that an attempt to do everything quickly will result in little being done at all. It was of course recognised that a certain amount of "pain" would be suffered, but it was believed that the duration of pain would be brief and the subsequent gains would be considerable. These gains depended on creating a full set of markets and this, in turn, required well defined property rights, which was interpreted to mean private property rights.

In practice the big bang strategy was reduced to three components. First, state owned enterprises should be privatised and, in effect, a capitalist class created without the prior necessity of the private accumulation of capital. Second, all prices should be completely liberalised, domestic and foreign. Third, foreign capital should be used to ease the pain caused by falling output and incomes.

No country of course followed the big bang strategy in all its details. Indeed the strategy probably was not feasible in most countries, if any. Privatisation occurred in fits and starts, price liberalisation was never instantaneous or uniform across all sectors, and foreign capital failed to materialise in sufficient volume to prevent a sharp fall in output and incomes and a dramatic increase in poverty. Nevertheless the majority of countries in the former Soviet Union and in Central and Eastern Europe adopted what can best be described as shock therapy or the big bang approach and they were noticeably slow to implement the other reforms indicated above to be essential for the success of the transition, for example creating space for new private sector firms to emerge, reforming the state enterprises, restructuring the social services and creating a viable commercial banking system.

In retrospect it is clear that the big bang strategy was seriously flawed. Foreign capital was not integral to the strategy but was a *deus ex machina* introduced to temper the hardships caused by the failure of shock therapy (price liberalisation and privatisation) to be in fact therapeutic. Privatisation was even more problematic. Its role was largely political, namely, "to cut the government-controlled sector down to a size that would make a return to the totalitarian state and its central planning impossible."[16] In other words, privatisation was not necessary from an economic perspective to ensure the success of the transition. The big bang, as an economic strategy, thus becomes reduced to rapid price liberalisation and the evidence is now clear: price liberalisation by itself is unlikely to work well.

Price liberalisation is not limited to the ex-socialist countries; it has become a worldwide phenomenon. Since the end of the Second World War economic forces have been unleashed which are creating for the first time a global economic system which is regulated largely by market forces. Globalisation, as this phenomenon is called, is a consequence partly of policy changes, partly of technological changes which have reduced the costs of economic integration and partly of the disintegration of the European, Japanese and Russian empires which fragmented the world into separate spheres of influence.

These processes have transformed the world economy in a remarkably short period of time. World income and output between 1950 and 1995 grew about 3.8 per cent a year, faster than at any time in recorded history. World trade grew about 6.2 per cent a year, and individual countries became much more "open" to external influences. Foreign direct investment grew half again as fast as foreign trade and three times as fast as world output.

Sceptics might argue that only those ignorant of history could claim that globalisation is a new phenomenon. The present period of rapid integration, they might argue, should be seen as a return to the past, and particularly to the economic conditions that prevailed in the second half of the 19th century and the first 13 years of the 20th century. Prior to the First World War, international commerce was relatively free, overseas investment was commonplace and, unlike today, there was widespread international migration of labour. All of this was interrupted by the two world wars and the great depression of the 1930s. Globalisation today represents a resumption of an earlier trend of closer global economic integration.

While there is some truth to this sceptical view, there are several factors that suggest that the process of globalisation today is qualitatively different from the processes operating in the 19th century. We must not forget that a high proportion of the world's population participated only marginally in the global economy of the 19th century. Because of the high cost of transport and communications, countries experienced high levels of "natural" protection and the degree of economic integration necessarily was rather low. Moreover, a majority of the world's population lived under colonial regimes where trade and investment were regulated in the interests of the imperial power.

This situation began to change radically with decolonisation, starting in 1947 with the independence of India and Pakistan. When China began to open its economy in late 1978, another billion people – roughly one fifth of the world's population – became more closely integrated into the global economy. The process continued with the disintegration of the Soviet Union in 1991, when another 400 million people were added, not without great economic disruption, as we have seen.

On the conceptual plane, too, globalisation is much broader than ever before. Indeed it is virtually all-embracing.[18] The penetration of market forces to every corner of the globe is affecting everything: our social relations and politics, our culture, even our global climate. True, human activity in the past has altered micro-climates, reduced biological diversity and led to the extinction of certain species, but the effects usually were localised whereas now they often are generalised. Equally important, we lack institutions of global governance which even in principle could enable us to take collective action to correct or mitigate undesirable generalised effects of globalisation.

How did this state of affairs arise? Let us begin with policy-induced liberalisation. Since 1947 there have been eight rounds of global negotiations to reduce tariffs and other restrictions on international trade. The most recent negotiations were completed in 1993.

Initially trade liberalisation concentrated on manufactured goods and on trade among the rich countries. Indeed many developing countries adopted import substituting industrialisation as their strategy of development, as described in Chapter 5. The results of trade liberalisation among the rich countries, however, have been highly successful and tariffs on manufactured goods imported into rich countries are today only about 4 per cent on average. Furthermore, trade liberalisation has gradually been extended to cover agricultural products as well as services and to include the developing countries, so that trade liberalisation now is universal if not complete.

Restrictions on the international movement of capital were removed more slowly. The United States generally eschewed capital controls from the beginning, but elsewhere capital controls were not abolished until 1979 in Britain, 1980 in Japan and 1990 in France and Italy. Capital account liberalisation was even more gradual in the developing countries, but after 1982 the process accelerated dramatically, particularly in Latin America and sub-Saharan Africa where liberalisation was made a condition for international assistance to stabilisation and restructuring programmes.

There has not been a comparable liberalisation of the global labour market. On the contrary, policies have become less liberal in recent years. In this respect globalisation is moving backwards.

There was a time when international migration was massive and forced. In the 17th and 18th centuries the Atlantic slave trade led directly to the deaths of over 50 million Africans and to the importation of some 15 million slaves into North America, the Caribbean islands and Brazil. In the 19th century between 10 and 40 million indentured workers, mostly from China and India, were transported around the world, mostly to colonial territories where labour was scarce. In the second half of the 19th century and the first decades of the 20th century there was massive but free migration from Europe, when 60 million people left for the United States, Canada, Australia, New Zealand, South Africa and parts of Latin America.

Since the early 1970s, however, the global labour market has become less free. Controls over immigration have been tightened, the annual flows of immigrants into the rich countries have declined and a bias against the migration of low-skilled labour has been introduced. There is a fragmented global market for high-skilled workers, technicians and professionals but there is no real, legal global market for low-skilled workers. The result in the United States, for example, is that the foreign born account for a much smaller proportion of the US population today (9.3 per cent) than they did a century ago (about 15 per cent).

Technological changes have reinforced policy changes in trade and capital account liberalisation in fostering globalisation. The costs of freight and passenger transport, communications and computing have fallen dramatically and as a result the pattern of global production is changing beyond recognition. A product may be designed in one country, its components produced in a second, the parts assembled in a third and the final product exported to a fourth. Lower transport costs have reduced "natural" protection and this has permitted a much more dispersed location of production worldwide. Indeed labels of national origin on manufactured products are becoming meaningless.

Primary products, which are transport intensive, are of declining relative importance in world trade whereas trade in services and in manufactured goods has been growing very rapidly. Some services, for example computer software, can be "shipped" over a telephone line, and containerisation has greatly reduced the cost of shipping manufactured goods. New technologies have reduced both space and time. These new technologies also have helped to make globalisation irreversible. Electronic transfers of funds make it more difficult for governments to reimpose capital controls. The fax and e-mail make it more difficult to restrict flows of information services. The large volume of intra-firm trade within multinational corporations and the ability of multinational corporations to shift resources readily throughout the world make it more difficult to reimpose trade barriers. Globalisation and liberalisation will be with us for as far ahead as one can see.

Let us now consider the economic consequences of globalisation. Viewed from outer space, economic prosperity increased moderately during the period 1980–95. The world's per capita income increased about 1.1 per cent a year during that period.[19] By the standards of the last 50 years this is rather slow, but if one takes a longer historical perspective, this represents relatively rapid growth of the world economy. Angus Maddison, for example, estimates that between 1400 and 1820 world GDP per capita increased only 0.07 per cent a year.[20]

It is widely believed that globalisation has been accompanied by greater inequality in the distribution of the world's income. The facts are unclear and the causal relationships are not well understood, but one way of looking at the issue is to divide the world into three groups classified by average income per head. This is the convention that has been followed by the World Bank for many years, and is somewhat analogous to dividing society into three classes of low, middle and upper income groups. If we do this, it transpires that during the period 1980-95, average incomes in the low-income countries increased 4.4 per cent a year as compared to 2.1 per cent a year in the high-income countries; in the middle-income countries average income actually fell by 0.4 per cent a year. That is, growth rates were bimodally distributed across countries classified by level of per capita income. The poorest countries grew faster than the richest and, in this sense, global inequality diminished.[21]

This is slightly misleading, however, because inequality within the group of low-income countries increased dramatically. The countries of sub-Saharan Africa experienced a rapid decline in average incomes (–1.2 per cent a year) whereas the two largest and poor Asian countries, China and India, enjoyed much faster growth (9.8 and 3.4 per cent a year, respectively). This illustrates the more general point that growth has been distributed very unevenly among the major regions of the developing world. Growth rates were negative not only in sub-Saharan Africa but also in the Middle East and North Africa (–2.1 per cent a year) and, as we have seen, in the ex-socialist developing countries of Europe and Central Asia (–1.3 per cent a year). In Latin America and the Caribbean the rate of growth was positive but very low (0.3 per cent a year), whereas in South Asia (3.2 per cent a year) and in East Asia and the Pacific (7.0 per cent a year) growth was positive and rapid.

These large variations in growth rates cannot be attributed entirely to the process of global integration and liberalisation. National and regional growth rates also reflect national political events and the strategy of economic development pursued. For example, the decline in incomes in most of the ex-socialist countries arises in the first instance from the political collapse of the former Soviet Union. The transition from central planning to a more market oriented economic system and the way the Soviet bloc countries were reintegrated into the world economy often were handled poorly, but this has little to do with globalisation as such. China, as we have seen, handled the processes of transition and reintegration smoothly and experienced no fall in income. On the contrary, growth accelerated. The same is true in Vietnam.

Similarly, the steep decline in average incomes in the Middle East and North Africa reflects the political turmoil in the region (civil conflict in Algeria, wars in Iraq, Iran and Kuwait) at least as much as falling oil prices. Yet it is only the latter that is connected directly to globalisation. Falling incomes in sub-Saharan Africa and the near-stagnation of incomes in Latin America can more plausibly be linked to globalisation. The debt crisis of the 1980s hit these two regions particularly hard and the recovery from the crisis-induced depressions was slow and difficult. And in many parts of Africa, civil conflicts of various sorts greatly aggravated the region's economic difficulties.

At the other end of the spectrum, the best growth performance clearly was in East Asia. Indeed many commentators cite East Asia as evidence that globalisation is a powerful force for economic progress. But just as globalisation cannot be blamed entirely for a region's failure, so too it cannot be credited for another region's success. There is much more to East Asia's outstanding economic performance than trade liberalisation, low exchange rates and exploitation of its comparative advantage in labour intensive exports of manufactured goods.[22] Several countries of the region (China, South Korea, Taiwan) had major land reforms and several others (including Hong Kong and Singapore) began the development process with a reasonably equitable distribution of income. East Asia also emphasized human capital formation – notably basic education and health – and this contributed both to rapid growth and low inequality. Rates of physical capital formation were high and this investment was financed largely by domestic savings; foreign capital was relatively unimportant. In other words, "domestic" economic factors were at least as important as "global" factors in explaining East Asia's success.

The global economic forces that impinge on developing countries come down essentially to flows of international capital, particularly foreign direct investment, and international trade in goods and services. Consider first foreign direct investment (FDI).

Despite the liberalisation of global capital markets, FDI is rather small. In the rich countries, FDI accounts for only about 6 per cent of total investment. Most investment continues to be financed by domestic savings. Despite the great scarcity of capital in developing countries and its apparent abundance in the rich countries, the largest recipient of foreign direct investment is the United States. In fact, most foreign investment consists of one rich country investing in another rich country. Roughly 60 per cent of all FDI circulates among the small number of rich countries and only 40 per cent is directed to the large number of poor countries that account for 85 per cent of the world's population. Within this large group of developing countries, most FDI is directed to the middle-income countries. In 1995, for instance, the low-income countries received only 43.5 per cent of the FDI that was channelled to developing countries. Moreover, one country, China, received 86.4 per cent of all the foreign capital invested in low-income countries. In other words, most poor countries received virtually no foreign capital.[23]

Despite the liberalisation of the world's capital markets, foreign investment has not become an engine of growth in the poor countries. If anything, flows of foreign capital, because they are concentrated in the rich countries, have helped to widen global inequalities. Foreign investment does not flow to countries where capital is "scarce" in a physical sense, rather it flows to countries where expected profits are high. In the developing countries this implies that FDI is most likely to be attracted to countries that have rich mineral deposits (especially oil) or natural resources or to countries that have succeeded in achieving rapid growth of exports (particularly manufacturing exports)[24] or more generally to countries which already are enjoying a rapid rate of growth of total output and income.[25] Foreign direct investment, in other words, is not a cause of growth, it is a consequence of growth.

The same is true, broadly speaking, of foreign trade. Most of the world's trade consists of exports from one rich country to another. The high-income countries currently account for more than three-quarters of total world merchandise exports. The share of the developing countries is less than 24 per cent and the share of the low-income developing countries excluding China and India is a paltry 1.3 per cent. In other words, most of the very poor countries are out of the trade loop; they are effectively de-linked from the global economy.

During the first half of the 1990s the volume of world trade grew 6.0 per cent a year. Merchandise exports originating in the high-income countries grew somewhat less rapidly than this, namely, 5.4 per cent a year, indicating that the rest of the world was becoming more closely integrated into the global economy. This was especially true of East and South Asia, where exports increased 17.8 and 8.6 per cent a year, respectively. In sub-Saharan Africa and in the Middle East and North Africa, however, trade increased only about one per cent a year. These two regions are becoming increasingly marginalised.

Thus the forces propelling globalisation – trade and investment – have had a very uneven impact. The rich countries have participated fully in the process and the middle-income countries are becoming increasingly integrated into the global system, but among the low-income countries, only China has become a large recipient of foreign capital and a major trading nation. Most of the poor countries have benefited neither from a rapid growth of exports nor from a large inflow of foreign investment. The most important economic consequence of globalisation in these countries has been the exodus of much of their human capital through the emigration of professional, technical and managerial personnel.

None of this is intended to deny the potential benefits to developing countries of closer integration into the global economy. One should however be sceptical of the proposition that globalisation is sufficiently powerful by itself to raise living standards everywhere. This is a case where a rising tide may not lift all boats. National development strategies remain the key to reduced poverty and inequality and an expansion of human capabilities.

NOTES AND REFERENCES

1. Amartya Sen, "Development as Capability Expansion", in Keith Griffin and John Knight, eds, *Human Development and the International Development Strategy for the 1990s*, London: Macmillan, 1990.

2. See, for example, T.W. Schultz, "Capital Formation by Education", *Journal of Political Economy*, December 1960 and T.W Schultz, "Investment in Human Capital" *American Economic Review*, March 1961.

3. See Keith Griffin and Terry McKinley, *Implementing a Human Development Strategy*, London: Macmillan, 1994.

4. Committee for Development Planning, *Human Resources Development: A Neglected Dimension of Development Strategy*, New York: United Nations, 1989, Ch. III.

5. See Mahbub ul Haq, *Reflections on Human Development*, New York: Oxford University Press, 1995.

6. See UNDP *Human Development Report*, published annually since 1990 by Oxford University Press, New York.

7. The method of calculating the HDI has varied slightly from year to year. For the most recent methods used in computing the index see UNDP *Human Development Report 1997*, New York: Oxford University Press, 1997, Technical Note 2, p. 122.

8. Asian Development Bank. *Emerging Asia: Changes and Challenges*, Manila: Asian Development Bank, 1997; UNDP, *Human Development Report 1996*, New York. Oxford University Press, 1996; Keith Griffin, "Culture, Human Development and Economic Growth", UNRISD/UNESCO, Occasional Paper Series on Culture and Development, No. 3. 1997.

9. Robert Barro, "Economic Growth in a Cross Section of Countries", *Quarterly Journal of Economics*, Vol. 106, May 1991.

10. Rati Ram, "Level of Development and Returns to Schooling: Some Estimates from Multicountry Data", *Economic Development and Cultural Change*, Vol. 44, No. 4, 1996.

11. George Psacharopoulos, "Education and Development: A Review", *World Bank Research Observer*, Vol, 3, No. 1, 1989.

12. George Psacharopoulos, "Returns to Investment in Education: A Global Update", *World Development*, Vol. 22, 1994.

13. See Daniel Cotlear, "The Effects of Education on Farm Productivity", in Keith Griffin and John Knight, eds, *op. cit.*

14. Asian Development Bank, *op. cit.*, p. 80.

15. This section draws heavily on Keith Griffin, "Economic Policy During the Transition to a Market Oriented Economy", Unpublished report prepared for UNDP, 1998.

16. Axel Leijonhufvud and Christof Rühl, "Russian Dilemmas", *American Economic Review*, Vol. 87, No. 2, May 1997, p. 344.

17. This section draws heavily on Keith Griffin, "Globalization and the Shape of Things to Come", keynote address delivered to the Macalester International Round Table on Globalization and Economic Space, Macalester College, 8–10 October 1998.

18. This point is emphasized by Dharam Ghai in his "Globalization and Competitiveness: Implications for Human Security and Development Thinking", in Louis Emmerij, ed., *Economic and Social Development into the XXI Century*, Washington, D.C.: Johns Hopkins University Press for the Inter-American Development Bank, 1997, p. 168.

19. The growth estimates were compiled from data in World Bank, *World Development Report 1997*, New York: Oxford University Press, 1997.

20. Angus Maddison, "Economic Policy and Performance in Capitalist Europe", in Louis Emmerij, ed., *op. cit.*, Table 3.12, p. 295.

21. The UNDP comes to the opposite conclusion in a study covering the period 1960 to 1989. See UNDP, *Human Development Report 1992*, New York: Oxford University Press, 1992.

22. For a short statement of how East Asia's development strategy differed from the liberalisation strategy of the "Washington consensus" see Frances Stewart, "John Williamson and the Washington Consensus Revisited", in Louis Emmerij, ed., *op. cit.*, pp. 64–7.

23. See Overseas Development Institute, *Foreign Direct Investment Flows to Low-income Countries: A Review of the Evidence*, Briefing Paper. September 1997, Table 1, p. 2.

21. H. Singh and K.M. Jun, *Some New Evidence on Determinants of Foreign Direct Investment in Developing Countries*, Policy Research Working Paper No. 1531, Washington, D.C.: World Bank, 1995.

25. See, for example, A. Bhattacharya, P.J. Montiel and S. Sharma, *Private Capital Flows to Sub-Saharan Africa: An Overview of Trends and Determinants*, unpublished paper, World Bank, Washington, D.C., 1996.

Chapter 1

DEVELOPMENT IN HISTORICAL CONTEXT

It was once said by Sir William Arthur Lewis that the development of Third World countries "does not in the long run depend upon the existence of the developed countries, and their potential for growth would be unaffected even if all the developed countries were to sink under the sea"[1]. The developing countries have everything they need for growth. The potential is there. It is only necessary to exploit it. Lewis, it should be added, did not recommend that the developed countries should sink under the sea; he simply made the important point that the poor countries need not be dependent on the rich; they have the capacity for autonomous growth.

Some countries, of course, have exploited the potential for growth more effectively than others, although all countries have experienced relatively good times and bad. Even now, however, at the end of the twentieth century, there are countries which have yet to experience a sustained rise in income per head. At the other end of the spectrum are a few that embarked upon what Simon Kuznets calls modern economic growth[2] at the end of the eighteenth century and these early leaders were joined by many others by the end of the nineteenth century. One of the great puzzles in economic history is why growth began earlier in some countries than in others and why in general growth in the Third World lagged so far behind that in Western Europe and North America.

One view is that growth first sprung up in Great Britain and then in other parts of Western Europe, for reasons peculiar to that region, and spread gradually to the rest of the world. The mechanism of transmission was international trade, particularly during the long world economic boom that extended from 1850 to 1914. An alternative view is that growth was inhibited or retarded in the Third World by Western Europe, and particularly by the economic relations imposed upon it by the colonial and imperial powers. According to this view there was nothing particularly surprising about growth in Western Europe; what is surprising and hence needs to be explained is the absence of growth elsewhere. The second view regards underdevelopment in the Third World and the lack of growth or slowness of growth which usually accompanied it as closely connected to the development of Europe as a political and economic power. Authors in this intellectual tradition tend to focus on institutional factors, the social system (including the collaboration of the indigenous elite with the colonising power), the inequitable distribution of the benefits of foreign trade (sometimes called export-led exploitation) and the constraints imposed upon the choice of development strategy by the way the country was inserted into the world economy. Those

1

who adhere to the first view, in contrast, regard development in the Third World and specifically a rise in living standards as dependent upon growth in Europe and the trading opportunities created by growth. Thus according to this view, self-reliant, autonomous development was impossible in the Third World; the most a country could do would be to attach itself to the engine of growth represented by world trade.

Lloyd Reynolds has recently surveyed the vast qualitative and quantitative literature on world economic growth and his findings provide a useful starting point for analysis [3]. He begins by distinguishing between "extensive growth" (when population and production increase at about the same pace) and "intensive growth" (when per capita output begins to rise), and calls the period that separates them the "turning point". The question then becomes what causes the turning point, the switch from extensive to intensive growth. Reynolds himself argues that intensive growth begins when countries latch on to the spread effects emanating from the developed countries as transmitted by international commerce. He observes that few countries reached the turning point during the long depression of 1914-1945 while many did so during the booms of 1850-1914 and 1945-1973. He concludes from this that "the turning point is usually associated with a marked rise in exports" [4].

Even if exports are the key, as Reynolds claims, and without attaching too much importance to the specific dates identified as turning points, we must ask why, in the period before the First World War, some countries increased their exports and reached the turning point while others did not. No doubt the answer to this question is complex – one rarely finds a single cause of anything in history – but the political organisation of the world economy appears to have played a major role. In the case of Latin America, as Reynolds himself recognises, the "turning point dates in most cases mark the beginning of political stability after the prolonged civil wars which followed independence" [5]. True, many territories reached the turning point while they were still colonies. These include Korea in 1910, then a Japanese colony; Ghana and Nigeria in 1895 and Malaysia in 1850, British colonies; the Philippines in 1900, an American colony; and Algeria in 1880, a French possession. Most of these countries, however, were small and when put together accounted for a very small proportion of the population of the Third World. This does not mean that their historical experience is without significance, but it does suggest that growth during the colonial period was limited to a small range of products traded internationally, to a handful of countries and hence to a tiny proportion of the population of the Third World.

The Reynolds turning point was not reached in India, Pakistan, China, Egypt and Indonesia until somewhere between 1947 and 1965 (see Table 1.1). That is, in these five countries output per head did not begin to rise on a sustained basis until after they achieved independence or regained their full sovereignty. These five countries alone account for nearly two-thirds of the population of Asia and Africa, the two regions most strongly dominated by the then imperial powers. The countries of Latin America, which achieved their independence earlier, in the nineteenth century, also tended, as we have seen, to reach the Reynolds turning point earlier. Japan, too, never a colony, reached the turning point in the nineteenth century, in 1880. Thus the end of colonialism and imperialism coincided, for a large proportion of the people of Asia, Africa and Latin America with the period when the capacity to produce first began to rise appreciably faster than population.

There is nothing magical about full sovereignty and independence. Ethiopia and Liberia, after all, were independent countries but they failed to develop. Their ruling elites were exploitative of the majority of the population and the regimes can perhaps best be described as a form of internal colonialism. Governments can and do pursue policies which harm the well being of their people, sometimes severely, and Reynolds surely is right when he says that "the single most important explanatory variable is political organization and the administrative competence of government" [6]. But it helps if the government is not an alien one, is responsive to the needs of the governed and is free to adopt economic policies in pursuit of a development strategy of its own choice. Many colonial regimes, in fact, did possess good political organisation and administrative competence, but they lacked a commitment to develop their territories save as it would benefit the metropolitan power. Most independent regimes possess the last quality, but unfortunately some lack the first two. Freedom does not guarantee growth and prosperity – the evidence on that is painfully abundant – but the evidence also indicates that external domination by a colonial or imperial power is likely to retard material progress for those who are dominated. This is hardly surprising and only those who count countries rather than people will fail to see it. If, rather loosely, one identifies the developed countries as a whole with the imperial ones, then it may well be true that if the developed countries were "to sink under the sea", the rest of the world on balance would not just be unaffected, as Arthur Lewis speculates, but measurably better off. This, at least, may have been the situation in the past.

Table 1.1 **THE REYNOLDS TURNING POINT**
Selected countries

Latin America:	
Argentina	1860
Brazil	1850
Chile	1840
Colombia	1885
Mexico	1876
Peru	1880
Africa:	
Côte d'Ivoire	1895
Egypt	1952
Ghana	1895
Kenya	1895
Tanzania	1900
Asia:	
Bangladesh	
China	1949
India	1947
Indonesia	1965
Malaysia	1850
Pakistan	1947
Philippines	1900
Sri Lanka	1880

Source: Lloyd G. Reynolds, "The Spread of Economic Growth to the Third World: 1850-1980", *Journal of Economic Literature*, Vol XXI, No. 3, September 1983, Table 1, p. 958

Growth rates in the Third World, yesterday and today

The analysis so far has been wholly in qualitative terms and in many cases that is as far as one can go. In a few cases, however, brave attempts have been made to prepare quantitative estimates of growth rates in the Third World for the period before 1950 and it is worth while examining these data to see what they reveal. One must not, of course, place too much reliance on the accuracy of the estimates – indeed, even the figures for the period since 1950 often are suspect – but it may be possible to obtain one or two insights from the sparse amount of numerical information that exists. The reliability of the data is such that they cannot carry a heavy load of analysis, but they are not so unreliable as to be ignored.

3

In Table 1.2 we have assembled, for a selected number of countries, three pieces of information. First, there are the estimates prepared by Angus Maddison of the annual percentage rates of growth of gross domestic product per capita for the two periods 1870-1913 and 1913-1950 [7]. Second, where quantitative estimates are not available for these two early periods, we have used Lloyd Reynolds' dates for the turning points to indicate whether per capita growth was positive (+) or approximately zero (-) in the period concerned [8]. Third, there are estimates of the long-run rate of growth in the period since 1950 or, if independence or full sovereignty were achieved after that date, in the period since independence. We thus have an era of economic boom (1870-1913) followed by depression and world wars (1913-1950) followed by a period that included both a boom (1950-1973) and a recession (1973 onwards).

A number of interesting points arise from Table 1.2. First, insofar as it is possible to judge from the very limited quantitative evidence, the growth of output per head in the Third World in the recent period, or in the period since independence, is usually at least as rapid as it was in the boom years of 1870 to 1913. Argentina is an important exception: it grew 1.5 per cent a year in the early boom period as compared to 0.9 per cent during 1950 to 1984, a period which includes an early boom followed by a deep recession. Ghana also is an exception: it grew 0.9 per cent a year in the early period and –2.0 per cent in the period after independence. In India there appears to have been neither acceleration nor a slowing down of growth. In Pakistan and Bangladesh, however, performance since independence is two (Pakistan) or three (Bangladesh) times better than it was in the "golden age" of the late nineteenth and early twentieth centuries. There was also a dramatic acceleration in China and a more modest one in Mexico. Second, when one takes into account the qualitative information, it is evident that growth rates rose sharply in Egypt, which had not even reached the Reynolds turning point before the First World War. In other countries, too, it is highly likely that growth of income per head since independence has been significantly faster than it was in 1870-1913. This includes Côte d'Ivoire, Kenya and Tanzania in Africa and Malaysia, the Philippines and Sri Lanka in Asia. Moreover, where there was growth during the colonial era much of the rise in incomes associated with that growth probably accrued to expatriates and foreign-owned plantation, mining and other enterprises, so that the rise in income per head of the indigenous population was much less than the aggregate growth rates might suggest [9].

Third, turning to the period 1913 to 1950, it is noteworthy that several Third World countries did rather well. The two European civil wars and the depression triggered off by the financial collapse in the United States may have created opportunities in parts of the Third World which when grasped, enabled industrialisation to accelerate and average growth rates to be maintained or even to increase. The performance of several Latin American countries (Brazil, Peru, Colombia and Mexico) is striking, but Malaysia and Ghana also did well. On the other hand, the South Asian countries (India, Pakistan, Bangladesh and probably Sri Lanka too) experienced complete stagnation during this period. In China per capita GDP declined 0.4 per cent a year. The situation in Africa is unfortunately unclear, although in Egypt per capita output probably increased slightly.

The average growth rate for the fourteen countries for which we have data covering the period 1913-1950 is about 0.8 per cent per annum. This undoubtedly overstates the true position because of the low implicit weights given to China and the three large South Asian countries, India, Pakistan and Bangladesh. If the growth rates were weighted by size of population the average would be much lower. Even so, it would be wrong to think that the series of crises during this period in what are now the OECD countries created crises of

4

similar magnitude and duration throughout the Third World. A number of Third World countries prospered during this period and introduced significant structural change. This occurred particularly in those countries which managed to avoid becoming a battlefield in the world wars and which also were independent and thus were able to design their own development strategies.

Table 1.2 **GROWTH OF GDP PER CAPITA, 1870-1984**
Selected countries, per cent per annum

	(1)	(2)	(3)
	1870-1913	1913-50	1950-84
Latin America:			
Argentina	1.5	0.6	0.9
Brazil	1.2	1.6	1.8
Chile	(+)	0.6	0.4
Colombia	(+)	1.3	1.2
Mexico	0.8 a	1.7 b	1.3
Peru	(+)	2.2	0.3
Africa:			
Côte d'Ivoire	(+)	(+)	1.5 c
Egypt	(−)	0.2	1.3
Ghana	0.9	1.1	−2.0 d
Kenya	(+)	(+)	1.3 e
Tanzania	(+)	(+)	1.3 f
Asia:			
China	0.5	−0.4	2.2
India	0.6	−0.1	0.6
Pakistan	(0.6)	(−0.1)	1.4
Bangladesh	(0.6)	(−0.1)	2.1 g
Malaysia	(+)	2.2	2.8 d
Philippines	(+)	0.3	1.3
Sri Lanka	(+)	(+)	1.5

a) 1877/8-1910.   d) 1957-1984.   g) 1971-1984.
b) 1910-1950.   e) 1963-1984.
c) 1960-1984.   f) 1961-1984.

Note: Where quantitative estimates of growth rates are missing, a (+) in a column means that a country had reached the Reynolds turning point well before the end of that period and hence that its per capita growth rate was positive; a (−) means that it had not yet reached the turning point.

Sources: Columns (1) and (2): Angus Maddison, *Economic Progress and Policy in Developing Countries,* W.W. Norton, New York, 1970, Table I-4, p. 32 and Angus Maddison, "A Comparison of Levels of GDP Per Capita in Developed and Developing Countries, 1700-1980", *Journal of Economic History,* Vol. XLIII, No. 1, March 1983, Table 1, p. 28 (for the quantitative estimates); Lloyd Reynolds, "The Spread of Growth to the Third World: 1850-1980", *Journal of Economic Literature,* Vol. XXI, No. 3, September 1983, Table 1, p. 958 (for the qualitative estimates). Column (3): OECD Development Centre data files.

Finally, let us consider the most recent period, 1950-1984. All of the 18 countries in Table 1.2 except one, namely Ghana, experienced positive rates of growth of GDP per capita. The trend in Ghana since independence has been sharply negative and living standards have declined precipitously. In a number of Latin American countries – Mexico, Chile, Colombia and Peru – the trend rate of growth in the 34 years after 1950 was lower than in the 37 years before 1950. Evidently the crisis of the 1970s and 1980s has had a greater impact on growth rates in Latin America than did the long world depression that began in 1913-14. In fact some of the figures in column (3) of the Table, while they indicate accurately the average rate of growth, give a misleading picture of the trend. Peru, for example, grew very rapidly (2.5 per cent a year per capita) in the quarter century 1950-1975 and then collapsed into negative growth per head for the next 10 years. The growth rate in the Table, 0.3 per cent a year, is thus an average of two very distinct trends. The situation in Chile is similar [10].

Apart from these five countries it is clear from the Table that growth in the Third World has been faster, usually much faster, in the recent period than in the period before 1950. The unweighted average rate of growth of GDP per capita of the 18 countries in column (3) is 1.2 per cent a year. This, however, understates the true position because it fails to reflect properly the dramatic improvement in China and in South Asia. The average growth rate of the 18 countries weighted by size of population is 1.53 per cent a year. That is, since 1950 or since independence, whichever is more recent, growth in the Third World, on a conservative estimate, has been nearly twice as fast as it was in any period between 1870 and 1950. Despite famine, despite the debt crisis, despite the fall in primary commodity prices, despite political instability and widespread civil disorder and violence, growth in Third World countries in recent decades has been unprecedented in their history. Some countries have done much better than others, and we shall want to explore why this is so, but on average, growth performance in the Third World has been remarkably good. This should not be forgotten, for example, when contemplating the severe economic difficulties in parts of sub-Saharan Africa.

A comparison with the rich countries

If the poor countries are doing much better today than they did in the past, it is natural to ask how their performance compares with that of the rich countries in a broadly comparable phase of development. Some might imagine that development in the second half of the twentieth century is easier than it was in the late nineteenth century: the Third World can adopt and adapt technology from the advanced countries rather than invent their own, they can exploit opportunities created by a much more closely integrated world trading economy and they can obtain a substantial amount of capital from the rich countries on concessional terms to finance their investment projects. On the other hand, the newly independent countries of the Third World face far more competition in domestic and international markets than the early developers had to face, they suffer absolutely from a great shortage of skills and from the fact that differences in levels of skills between rich and poor countries are much greater now than they were a hundred years ago and, of course, they are attempting to develop long after the era of free international migration has come to an end.

One sometimes forgets the extent to which Europe exported her surplus labour to "empty lands" during the industrial revolution of the last century. If the poor were unable to earn a decent livelihood in Europe, they were free to leave – and millions did so. Between 1843 and 1913 emigration from the United Kingdom to the United States, the territories of the British Empire and to other countries was 1 882 000 [11]. In Sweden in the 1880s as much as 60 per cent of the natural increase of the population emigrated [12]. Net emigration from England, the richest part of the United Kingdom, was 23 per thousand in 1881-91 and even in 1901-11 it was as high as 15 per thousand [13]. In Germany, population pressure and the hardship accompanying technical change in small holding peasant agriculture accounted for the vast majority of the 726 000 migrants who sailed to America in the six years 1850-55 [14]. Indeed in the United States alone there landed from Europe 2 093 000 immigrants in the period 1849-54 [15]. Many more millions migrated to other countries. As a result, between 1870 and 1913, population growth in France, the United Kingdom, Italy, Norway and Sweden was less than one per cent a year; only in the United States did it exceed two per cent, where, of course, immigration was massive [16].

In most Third World countries today the poor are free to go, but unlike nineteenth century Europe, there is nowhere for them to go to. Most must stay at home. They have no choice. The United States has strict immigration quotas which favour migrants with valuable skills and people from other developed countries. Illegal immigration in the United States is common, particularly from Mexico, but the flow of migrants to that country is much smaller than it was in the last century. Migration to the United Kingdom and France from Third World countries which once formed part of their empires has been reduced to a trickle. The situation is no better in the other Western European countries and in Japan, apart from a few Koreans and Chinese, immigration is almost unknown. Thus there is no vent for surplus labour for the late developers and this is a major handicap for them. Or to put it another way, a vent for surplus labour, an escape valve for poverty and unemployment through migration, is one of the great advantages many of the rich countries enjoyed during the early decades of their development, and this undoubtedly contributed to the pace of their economic transformation.

Estimates of the rate of growth of GDP per capita in 16 OECD countries during the period 1870-1913 are contained in Table 1.3. These estimates, like the earlier ones we examined for the Third World, must be regarded as no more than rough approximations. Nevertheless, they are of considerable interest.

The fastest rate of growth achieved during the period was by the United States and Canada (which enjoyed abundant natural resources per head of population) and by Sweden. The growth rate in these three countries was 2 per cent per capita per annum. This is a slower rate of growth than that achieved by China (the world's largest developing country) during the period 1950-84 and is significantly slower than the rate of growth achieved by Malaysia (2.8 per cent) in the period since independence. That is, the best performances by the developing countries are as good as or better than those by the developed countries. On the other hand, no developed country in our sample performed as poorly as the least successful countries in our sample from the Third World.

More important, the average rate of growth in the two samples of countries is practically identical. The developed countries grew on average 1.4 per cent a year per head in the 43 years beginning in 1870, whereas the Third World countries grew on average 1.5 per cent a year per head in the 34 years beginning in 1950. This in itself is a remarkable achievement given the handicaps the late developers face. It is even more remarkable, however, when one recalls that the period 1870-1913 consisted of an uninterrupted boom whereas the period 1950-85 includes the worst economic crisis since the 1930s. Had the crisis years been excluded from our calculations, so that two periods of boom had been compared, growth performance in the Third World would have exceeded by a large margin the performance of the rich countries in their period of early industrialisation [17].

Social indicators of development

Accelerated growth of average incomes has not been the only change for the better in the Third World. There has also been remarkable social progress. Perhaps the best indicator

7

of this is the increase in life expectancy at birth since around 1950. In the poorest countries life expectancy at mid-century was between 30 and 40 years; today, in our sample of 20 countries, it is at least 50 years (for males in Tanzania and Bangladesh and for females in Pakistan) and rises to 70 or more for females in China, Malaysia, Sri Lanka, Chile and Argentina. The data in Table 1.4 suggest that on average life expectancy rose about 4.6 years per decade. This represents a very rapid increase in the well being of hundreds of millions of people in the Third World.

Table 1.3 **GROWTH OF GDP PER CAPITA IN 16 OECD COUNTRIES,**
1870-1913
Per cent per annum

Australia	0.6
Austria	1.5
Belgium	1.0
Canada	2.0
Denmark	1.6
Finland	1.7
France	1.5
Germany	1.6
Italy	0.8
Japan	1.5
Netherlands	0.9
Norway	1.3
Sweden	2.1
Switzerland	1.2
United Kingdom	1.0
United States	2.0
Unweighted average	1.4

Source: Angus Maddison, *Phases of Capitalist Development,* Oxford, Oxford University Press, 1982, Table 3.1, p. 44.

It is important to note that the correlation between per capita income and life expectancy is far from perfect. The people of China and Sri Lanka, countries with very low average incomes, enjoy a life expectancy higher than that of many upper middle-income developing countries such as Brazil, Mexico and Iran. Peru, on the other hand, has a lower life expectancy than the Philippines despite the fact that average incomes in Peru are half again as high as in the Philippines. Growth of output evidently is not sufficient to increase longevity: the pattern of growth, the strategy of development as reflected in public action also is vital [18]. Indeed, one of the lessons of recent history is that similar levels of social development can be achieved at very different levels of economic development.

The importance of the development strategy can be demonstrated in another way. In almost all countries women live longer than men. This seems to be the natural order of things. Yet in two of the 20 countries in the Table, namely, Pakistan and India, women have a shorter life expectancy than men. The same was true in an earlier period in Bangladesh and Sri Lanka as well, but those countries now conform to the general pattern. Thus Pakistan and India stand out as exceptions and this probably reflects a traditional social discrimination against females in South Asia that has persisted in those two countries despite the progress that has been achieved in other areas [19].

The data on infant mortality in Table 1.4 tell a similar story to that of life expectancy.

Table 1.4 SELECTED SOCIAL INDICATORS

	Life expectancy years				Infant mortality (deaths per 1 000 aged under one)		Primary school enrolment (% of age group)			Secondary school enrolment (% of age group)	
	1950		1984		1950	1984	1965	1983		1965	1983
	M	F	M	F				M	F		
Latin America:											
Argentina	57 a	62 a	67	74	70 a	34	101	107	107	28	60
Brazil	58 d	61 d	62	67	70 d	68	108	106	99	16	42
Chile	50 b	54 b	67	73	153	22	124	112	110	34	65
Colombia	44	46	63	67	124	48	84	119	122	17	49
Mexico	55 c	58 c	64	69	96	51	92	120	117	17	55
Peru	49 h	52 h	58	61	104	95	99	120	112	25	61
Africa:											
Botswana	46 h	49 h	55	61	108	72	65	89	102	3	21
Côte d'Ivoire	35 c		51	54	138 c	106	60	93	64	6	19
Egypt	52 d	54 d	59	62	130	94	75	101	76	26	58
Ghana	38 a	38 a	51	55	121	95	69	89	70	13	38
Kenya	43 h	46 h	52	56	113 h	92	54	104	97	4	19
Tanzania	35-40 e		50	53	170 f	111	32	91	84	2	3
Asia:											
Bangladesh	45 h	44 h	50	51	153 h	124	49	67	55	13	19
China	35		68	70	90 h	36	89	116	93	24	35
India	32	32	56	55	127	90	74	100	68	27	34
Indonesia	48 d	48 d	53	56	125 g	97	72	118	112	12	37
Malaysia	56 c	58 c	66	71	102	28	90	100	98	28	49
Pakistan	46 h	44 h	52	50	150 h	116	40	63	33	12	16
Philippines	49 f	53 f	61	65	102	49	113	115	113	41	63
Sri Lanka	56	55	68	72	82	37	93	103	99	35	56

a) 1948. e) 1945-49.
b) 1952. f) 1952.
c) 1956. g) 1956.
d) 1960. h) 1965.

Sources: U.N., *Demographic Yearbook*, various years; U.N., *Report on the World Social Situation*, 1975; IBRD, *World Development Report 1986*, Washington D.C., 1986.

There has been a decline everywhere and in some countries the decline has been dramatic, with the rate falling by 50 per cent or more. This is true in Latin America for Argentina, Chile and Colombia and in Asia for China, Malaysia, the Philippines and Sri Lanka. However, infant mortality rates remain very high, i.e., above 100 per 1000 infants less than one year old, in Bangladesh, Pakistan, Tanzania and Côte d'Ivoire. Once again, there is only a weak correspondence between infant mortality rates and average incomes. For example, the infant mortality rates in China and Sri Lanka are lower than the rate in Colombia, although per capita income in Colombia is roughly four times higher than in the two Asian countries. The relative social backwardness of Peru is again conspicuous: its infant mortality rate is higher than Kenya's, yet Kenya's income is less than one-third Peru's.

Turning now to primary education, one can see in the Table that this is one of the great success stories of the Third World, at least in quantitative terms. It is less certain that there have been improvements in the quality of education. School enrolments have expanded rapidly in the last 20 years and primary education for boys is universal or nearly so in 16 out of 20 countries in the Table. The position of girls is less good, but even so, in 13 countries over 90 per cent of girls attend primary school. Discrimination against educating young girls continues to be a problem, above all in Pakistan (where twice as many boys as girls attend school) but also in India, Bangladesh, Egypt and Côte d'Ivoire. Although illiteracy rates still are over 50 per cent in Africa and South Asia (apart from Sri Lanka), one can expect them to continue to fall as the proportion of the population with a primary school education continues to rise.

Secondary education also has grown rapidly, although often from a very small base. Still, between one- and two-thirds of the relevant age group attends a secondary school in 14 out of the 20 countries in Table 1.4, including the two largest countries in the sample, India and China. The third largest – Indonesia – has expanded its secondary school system very rapidly and has overtaken the two Asian giants. Serious shortcomings remain in Pakistan and Bangladesh (where expansion of the system has been slow) and in sub-Saharan Africa (where apart from Tanzania, expansion has been fast). Given the difficulties encountered in Asia and Africa at the time of independence, progress in secondary education has been remarkable.

Poverty and inequality

The historical evidence indicates that in the last 35 years or so the production of goods and services has increased faster than the population. In addition, great progress has been achieved in the fields of education and health. As a result, life expectancy has risen, illiteracy has fallen and in many other ways the quality of life has improved. Yet living standards in the Third World remain low and in some countries, including very large ones, the incidence of poverty remains high.

It is not easy to compare average incomes in one country with those in another, and it is even more difficult to compare the incidence of poverty across countries, since one must have accurate information not only on average incomes but also on the distribution of income. The usual way of making international comparisons of income per head is to convert incomes expressed in local currencies (pesos, rupees, yuan) into a common currency (usually the U.S. dollar) using the official exchange rate. This procedure, however, may produce misleading results. First, the official exchange rate may not be an equilibrium rate; it may be grossly overvalued or undervalued, or "distorted" by tariffs and quotas. Second, there may be no such thing as "an" official rate of exchange; the government may have introduced a multiple exchange rate system, applying different rates to different commodities (traditional versus new exports, luxury versus essential imports) or distinguishing between capital movements on the one hand and goods and services on the other. Third, even if there is a single rate of exchange and it happens to be in equilibrium, its use will produce misleading results because exchange rates do not accurately reflect the purchasing power of local currencies in different countries. Exchange rates reflect, at best, the relative prices of goods and services that enter into international commerce, i.e., exports and imports or, more generally, tradables. They leave out of account non-tradables, goods and services such as urban transport, electricity and housing and a wide range of personal services (haircuts, domestic services) which do not normally cross international boundaries.

There are reasons to believe that the relative price of tradables to non-tradables varies fairly systematically across countries, and in particular it is likely that the price of non-tradables is relatively higher in rich countries than in poor. For example, the relative price of a haircut, a shoeshine, a domestic servant – indeed, all non-traded, labour intensive goods and services – will increase as one moves from countries with low to high wages and per capita incomes. This being so, the use of exchange rates to convert incomes of different countries to a common currency will tend to understate the real incomes of poor countries and exaggerate the real incomes of rich countries.

What is needed is not an equilibrium exchange rate but an index which compares the real purchasing power of local currencies. In principle comparisons of purchasing power can be made and Irving Kravis and his associates have pioneered in this area, but the work involved is laborious, slow and expensive and as a result, purchasing power conversion ratios have been prepared for only a relatively few countries and for only a few years [20]. Still, we must use what we have.

In Table 1.5 we reproduce estimates of poverty originally calculated from World Bank data by Montek Ahluwalia, Nicholas Carter and Hollis Chenery [21]. The estimate for each country was prepared using the same poverty line, namely, "the income per head accruing to the forty-fifth percentile (approximately) of the Indian population" [22]. The estimates thus imply an Indian-centred view of the Third World. The standard that would be used for measuring poverty, the poverty line, in any particular country, say, Argentina, would almost certainly be different from the forty-fifth percentile of the Indian population. Indeed each country would have its own standard based on local conditions, aspirations, attitudes and possibilities. None the less, a perspective from India, the largest non-communist developing country, is an interesting one.

The Table contains, for each country, two estimates of the percentage of the population in poverty, one using Kravis adjustment factors and the other using official exchange rates. In almost every case (Indonesia is the exception) poverty estimates using the Kravis adjustment factors are higher than those using official exchange rates. This implies that, relative to India, official exchange rates tend to overstate real incomes in other Third World countries. Thus, for instance, in Kenya about 48 per cent of the population is below the poverty line when official exchange rates are used, but this rises to 55 per cent when Kravis adjustment factors are used. The average incidence of poverty in all 36 countries included in the original study was either 38 or 35 per cent depending on whether the Kravis or the exchange rate method of comparison was employed. The data refer to 1975, and the situation today is unlikely to be the same, but broad comparisons across continents remain valid.

It is clear from the Table that if one uses an absolute standard to measure poverty, the poorest countries are concentrated in South Asia (Pakistan, India and Bangladesh),

Table 1.5 **THE PERCENTAGE OF THE POPULATION IN POVERTY, 1975**

	Using Kravis adjustment factors	Using official exchange rates
Latin America:		
Argentina	5	3
Brazil	15	8
Chile	11	9
Colombia	19	14
Mexico	14	10
Peru	18	15
Africa:		
Côte d'Ivoire	25	14
Egypt	20	14
Ghana	25	19
Kenya	55	48
Tanzania	51	46
Asia:		
Bangladesh	64	60
India	46	46
Indonesia	59	62
Malaysia	12	8
Pakistan	43	34
Philippines	33	29
Sri Lanka	14	10

Source: Montek S. Ahluwalia, Nicholas G. Carter and Hollis B. Chenery, "Growth and Poverty in Developing Countries,"*Journal of Development Economics,* Vol. 6, No. 3, September 1979, Table 1, pp. 302-3.

Southeast Asia (specifically Indonesia) and parts of Africa (Kenya and Tanzania). China, too, should be included on this list, although comparable data do not exist for that country. Moreover, if one thinks not in terms of countries but in terms of the number of poor people, it is obvious that the problem of poverty is concentrated in about five very large Asian countries (China, India, Indonesia, Bangladesh and Pakistan). If one insists on adopting a global perspective one could almost ignore Latin America and Africa, the former because the incidence of poverty (by Indian standards) is relatively low and the latter because the number of poor people (compared to Asia) is relatively small.

This raises the question of whether, ultimately, it is appropriate to adopt an Indian centred view of the Third World, to use a universal standard in assessing deprivation, to take an absolutist view of poverty. Amartya Sen has argued persuasively "that ultimately poverty must be seen to be primarily an absolute notion" [23] and one hesitates to dissent from this judgement. It is of course true that there is "an irreducible absolutist core" [24] to the notion of poverty. If someone is starving, he is poor even if everyone else is starving too. But once one moves away from extreme cases it becomes much more difficult to make assertions that carry conviction or inspire confidence. For example, despite decades of work by nutritionists and physiologists we still do not know what is the minimum calorie intake necessary for adequate nutrition. More awkward for the absolutist position, we do not even know, as some claim [25], whether individuals really do have fixed requirements, i.e., whether the body is able to adjust to a persistent shortfall of calories and thereby in effect avoid "undernutrition".

In the eighteenth century Adam Smith made it clear that "necessities" were determined by "custom" and hence that poverty was relative. He said, "By necessities I understand not only the commodities which are indispensably necessary for the support of life, but whatever the custom of the country renders it indecent for creditable people, even of the lowest order, to be without" [26]. A similar view was taken in the following century by Thomas Carlyle. Writing in his *Chartism* in 1839, he asked "What constitutes the well-being of a man?" In part, he said, it is wages and the amount of bread his wages will buy, but he then goes on and brings in other considerations that make it evident that he regarded poverty as a relative phenomenon.

> "Can the labourer, by thrift and industry, hope to rise to mastership; or is such hope cut off from him? How is he related to his employer – by bonds of friendliness and mutual help, or by hostility, opposition and chains of mutual necessity alone?... With hunger preying on him, his contentment is likely to be small! But even with abundance, his discontent, his real misery may be great."

Across the channel, in France, a relativist position also was taken at about the same time by Théron de Montaugé who said bluntly that "poverty is measured by comparisons" [27]. It has nothing to do with the physiological need for calories.

The absolutist view of poverty, however, does not depend on the results of physiological research. It is much more sophisticated than that! Emphasis is placed not only on the absolute need for adequate nutrition but also on the need for decent shelter, to live without shame and to have self-respect. The needs for decency, self-respect and the avoidance of shame are absolute, but the commodity requirements to fulfil these socially defined needs rise with average prosperity. In this way absolute needs or capabilities are transformed into relative requirements for commodities and income [28].

Perhaps there is enough common ground here between relativists and absolutists to make further discussion unnecessary. But once it is accepted that needs, or at least some needs, are socially defined, we are very close to accepting that poverty itself is socially defined. That is, poverty is neither a relationship between a person and a bundle of commodities nor is it a relationship between a person and a bundle of (socially defined) needs and capabilities, it is a relationship between one person and another. This interpretation of the nature of poverty has emerged most forcefully from the research of Marshall Sahlins and others on the economies of extremely "primitive", "backward" and "poor" people such as the Bushmen of the Kalahari desert, hunter-gatherers in the forests of South America and the aboriginal Australians [29]. The economic anthropologists have shown that these "primitive" people do indeed have an objectively low standard of living. However they also have much leisure time, are generous in sharing their possessions with others, are essentially egalitarian, and most important of all, do not regard themselves, individually or collectively, as poor. As Sahlins says,

> "The world's most primitive people have few possessions, *but they are not poor*. Poverty is not a certain small amount of goods, nor is it just a relation between means and ends; above all, it is a relation between people. Poverty is a social status. As such it is the invention of civilization" [30].

If civilisation invented poverty and if social status defines it, presumably man in society, operating through the institutions he has created, or if necessary through new institutions, can abolish poverty. One dimension of poverty, on this reading of the evidence, is inequality in the distribution of income and wealth. If this is acknowledged, it follows that a *reduction* of inequality is likely to be a necessary condition for the *elimination* of poverty. It is not a sufficient condition, partly because of the irreducible absolutist core to the notion of poverty and partly because there is more to social status than differences in income, as Carlyle pointed out; but as long as great inequality persists, poverty will be present. Thus if a development strategy has as one of its objectives the reduction of poverty, it will have to address itself to the question of inequality.

The distribution of income

Data on the distribution of income in Third World countries are difficult to obtain and often unreliable. They must be handled with caution. The data on the 14 countries included in Table 1.6 below were collected by the World Bank and are the best estimates available; even so, some of the estimates go back to the late 1960s (Chile, Tanzania, Sri Lanka) and it is possible that conditions today may be different from what they were then. All of the data refer to the distribution of income among households uncorrected for differences in the size of households. If, as seems likely, there is a positive relationship between the level of income of a household and the number of persons comprising a household, the degree of inequality will tend to be overstated by our data. Larger households do of course enjoy some economies of scale, but this is unlikely to compensate for the disadvantage of more mouths to feed. It would be better to have data grouped by household per capita income.

Table 1.6 **THE DISTRIBUTION OF INCOME**
Percentage share of household income

	(1)	(2)	(3)	(4)	(5)	(6)
	Year	Poorest 20%	Middle 60%	Richest 20%	(4)/(2)	Gini coefficient
Latin America:						
Argentina	1970	4.4	45.3	50.3	11.4	0.43
Brazil	1972	2.0	31.4	66.6	33.3	0.60
Chile	1968	4.4	44.2	51.4	11.7	0.44
Mexico	1977	2.9	39.4	57.7	19.9	0.52
Peru	1972	1.9	37.1	61.0	32.1	0.56
Africa:						
Egypt	1974	5.8	46.2	48.0	8.3	0.40
Kenya	1976	2.6	37.0	60.4	23.2	0.55
Tanzania	1969	5.8	43.8	50.4	8.7	0.42
Asia:						
Bangladesh	1976-77	6.2	46.9	46.9	7.6	0.38
India	1975-76	7.0	43.6	49.4	7.1	0.40
Indonesia	1976	6.6	44.0	49.4	7.5	0.42
Malaysia	1973	3.5	40.4	56.1	16.0	0.49
Philippines	1970-71	5.2	40.8	54.0	10.4	0.45
Sri Lanka	1969-70	7.5	49.1	43.4	5.8	0.34

Source: Columns (1)-(4): IBRD, *World Development Report 1985*, New York, Oxford University Press, 1985, World Development Indicators, Table 28, pp. 228-9.

Three different indicators of inequality are presented in the Table. First, in columns (2) - (4) the distribution of income by quintiles is displayed. Column (2) contains the poorest 20 per cent of households, column (3) the middle 60 per cent and column (4) the richest 20 per cent. If one is interested in "the poor", perhaps column (2) is of greatest significance. In no country does the poorest 20 per cent of the population receive as much as 8 per cent of total household income. Sri Lanka comes closest with 7.5 per cent and Peru and Brazil are furthest away with an astonishingly low 1.9 and 2.0 per cent, respectively. The share of the poor seems to be highest in Asia and lowest in Latin America, with Africa coming somewhere in between. There are important exceptions, however: Malaysia, the Philippines and Kenya conform more closely to the Latin American pattern than to the pattern characteristic of their region.

Second, in column (5) we present the ratio of the share of income received by "the rich", i.e., the upper quintile, to that received by the poor. At one extreme are Peru and Brazil, where average incomes of the rich are 32 and 33 times those of the poor, respectively. At the other extreme is Sri Lanka, where rich households are less than six times better off than poor ones. The great range of the ratio (from 5.8 to 33.3) indicates clearly the extent to which inequality can vary from one country to another.

Third, estimates of Gini coefficients are presented in column (6). These give an overall measure of inequality although one must be careful about how they are interpreted. The lowest Gini coefficient is for Sri Lanka, viz:, 0.34, and one would expect Sri Lanka to have the lowest coefficient given that the share of the bottom quintile is the highest in that country and the ratio of the rich to the poor is the lowest. So far so good: the three indicators point in the same direction. In the case of Bangladesh, however, this is not true. Bangladesh has the second lowest Gini coefficient, viz., 0.38, suggesting that overall Bangladesh has the second most even distribution of income. But if one looks at the share of income received by the poor, one discovers that the share of the poor is higher in India and Indonesia (and of course in Sri Lanka) than it is in Bangladesh. Similarly, if one looks at the ratio of the rich to the poor, one finds the same thing: the ratio in Bangladesh is higher than that in Indonesia, India and Sri Lanka. The relatively low Gini coefficient for Bangladesh is due entirely to the fact that the upper quintile in that country receives a significantly lower share of total household income than is the case in India and Indonesia and the middle-income groups consequently receive a higher share. That is, it is differences in income at the upper tail of the distribution which account for Bangladesh's favourable ranking by the Gini coefficient. This is not uninteresting, but it has nothing to do with poverty.

An obvious omission from Table 1.6 is China, but unfortunately there are no directly comparable figures for that country. One can, however, cite rough calculations which give some idea of where China stands in relation to other countries. Thus in 1983, the bottom 20.7 per cent of peasants, classified by household income per capita, had an average income of 154.9 yuan. The top 29.5 per cent of staff and workers in cities had an average income of 678.8 yuan. Assuming the bottom quintile of the entire population consists of poor peasants and the top quintile of prosperous urban staff and workers, the ratio of the top to the bottom quintile in China is likely to be between 4.4 and 5.0 [31]. This is considerably lower than the ratio in Sri Lanka, the country with the lowest ratio of those reported in column (5) of Table 1.6. Similarly, the Gini coefficient for the distribution of household income per capita in China has been calculated to be about 0.33 [32]. If correct, this means that China has the most even distribution of income of the countries in our sample.

Ever since the famous articles by Arthur Lewis and Simon Kuznets in the mid-1950s, it has been assumed by many that economic development leads inevitably to greater inequality in the distribution of income, until relatively high levels of per capita income are attained [33]. The conventional view is well expressed by Lloyd Reynolds as follows:

15

"The initial effect of intensive growth is to wrench apart the country's income structure, and this effect may continue for a long time. Income disparities increase substantially" [34].

This "wrenching apart" of incomes is thought to occur as a result of the shift from agriculture to manufacturing or, not quite the same thing, a shift from traditional to modern sector activities. These shifts in the structure of production are likely to be accompanied by higher capital-labour ratios in the expanding sector and consequently by a rise in profits relative to wages. Moreover, within the wage-earning population income differentials are likely to widen because of a rapid growth of demand for skilled labour. Thus the overall distribution of income is expected to become more unequal.

Whatever the theoretical basis for the conjecture, a large number of cross-sectional studies of countries has been undertaken and these have been used to provide support for the hypothesis of growing inequality [35]. Moreover, a number of studies of individual countries, based on time-series data, has shown that inequality has increased along with a rise in average incomes. Indeed some authors have attempted to show that not only has inequality increased but that in some countries for quite long periods the absolute standard of living of some sections of the poor has declined [36].

The debate today is not over whether inequality has increased but whether it is inevitable. The balance of recent evidence suggests that the degree of inequality is not closely related to the level of income per head, as was once thought, but to factors dependent upon the strategy of development that is followed. These factors include the distribution of productive assets (particularly land), the distribution of educational opportunities, the employment intensity of the development path and the general policy stance of government. In other words, it is not growth as such that creates inequality but the particular pattern of growth a country chooses to adopt. What matters is the strategy of development. That is, it is possible to prevent large income disparities emerging and the income structure being "wrenched apart" by adopting a development strategy that places high priority on an equal distribution of agricultural land, universal access to primary and secondary education, labour-intensive methods of production and a pattern of international trade that reflects the relative availability of resources. If this is done, the disequalising factors can be counteracted. Inequality, far from increasing with rapid growth and development, can actually decline.

The lack of association between the level of development and the extent of inequality is readily visible in Figure 1.1. In that Figure we plot, for the 14 countries that particularly interest us, the share of the poorest 20 per cent of households against the level of per capita income (measured in 1981 U.S. dollars). One can see at a glance that in Chile and Argentine, for example, the extent of inequality is identical despite the fact that per capita income in Argentina is significantly higher than in Chile. Similarly, the extent of inequality in Kenya is much greater than in Tanzania although both are very poor countries. There is no discernible pattern in the scatter diagram. Moreover, the substitution of other measures of inequality, such as the Gini coefficient or the ratio of the top to the bottom quintile, does not alter the results.

Thus it is not inevitable that in poor countries the incomes of poor people should rise less rapidly than the incomes of rich, although this is precisely what has happened in many cases. Has the same pattern of inequality been reproduced on a world scale? That is, have the average incomes of poor countries risen less rapidly than those of rich countries? The short answer is yes, but a more complete answer is more complicated.

16

Figure 1.1. **THE SHARE OF THE POOR**

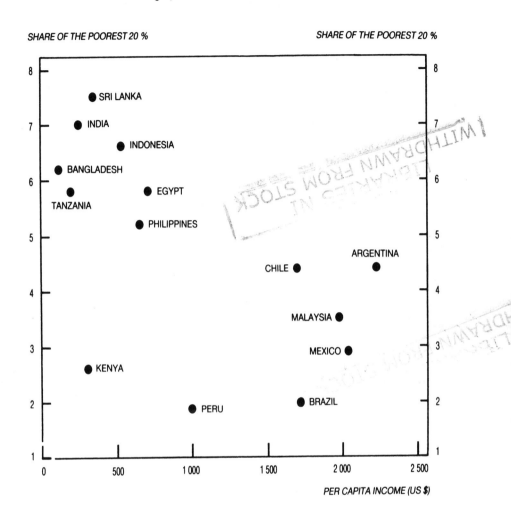

SHARE OF THE POOREST 20 %   *SHARE OF THE POOREST 20 %*

PER CAPITA INCOME (US $)

Simon Kuznets was perhaps the first to estimate the distribution of world population and income. His data indicate that in 1938 the three underdeveloped regions of the world (Latin America, Asia and Africa) accounted for 66.5 per cent of the world's population and 23.8 per cent of world income. By 1949 their share of the population had increased to 67.6 per cent while their share of income had fallen sharply to only 16.9 per cent [37]. World inequality evidently rose dramatically during that period. More recent work, covering the period 1950 to 1977, shows that the outcome depends on whether or not the socialist countries are included in the calculations [38].

If one excludes the socialist countries, the share of the poorest 20 per cent of the world's population fell from 1.5 per cent of total income in 1950 to 1.3 per cent in 1977. The Gini coefficient rose during the same period from 0.67 to 0.68. However, if one includes the socialist countries the share of the poor remained constant, at 1.7 per cent, as did the Gini coefficient, at 0.67. One country, China, because of its huge size, makes all the difference to the outcome. This can be seen more clearly if one considers World Bank data for an overlapping period, 1965-84. During that time the trend rate of growth of GNP per capita was as follows [39]:

All low-income economies	2.8
China	4.5
India	1.6
Other low-income	0.9
Lower middle-income	3.0
Upper middle-income	3.3
Industrial market economies	2.4

During the 19 years covered by the data, the Third World countries as a group grew noticeably faster than the annual rate of 2.4 per cent achieved by the rich industrial market economies. Moreover, each category of poor country (low-income, lower middle and upper middle-income) exceeded the rate of growth of the rich countries. By this measure world inequality must have decreased. Within the 96 Third World countries covered by the data, however, the less poor groups expanded more rapidly than the poorest groups and thus there was a tendency for the Third World countries themselves to become more differentiated and unequal. This tendency is especially marked if one sets China to one side. The average rate of growth of the low-income economies excluding China was only 1.3 per cent a year per capita from 1965 to 1984 and this was more than one percentage point slower than growth in the rich countries and 1.7 percentage points slower than growth in the lower middle-income countries. Thus the inhabitants of the poorest countries (excluding China) found themselves trailing further and further behind the rest of the world. In this restricted sense, too, world inequality has increased [40].

Building new nations

The modern nation-state as we know it today in Europe emerged gradually during a long period of political turbulence and violence. It was built up slowly through the amalgamation of smaller territorial units and a central authority, recognised and widely accepted, developed only on a step-by-step basis. The integration of disparate peoples was therefore slow and the consolidation of a sense of national identity among the people comprising a modern European nation was a relatively recent phenomenon. A majority of the people of France did not speak French as their mother tongue until sometime in the nineteenth century [41]. A large minority of the people of Northern Ireland give their allegiance to Eire rather than to the United Kingdom. The Basque region of Spain still insists upon its separate identity. And so on. Although the European case is distinctive, similar slow processes occurred in the cases of China and Japan. And in the United States a great civil war was fought to prevent the disintegration of the union.

In most parts of the Third World, however, nation-states were instant creations. This is as true of Brazil and the Spanish colonies of Latin America, which achieved independence mostly in the first quarter of the nineteenth century, as it is of South Asia, Indonesia and the Philippines, which achieved independence in the late 1940s, or of Malaysia and most of Africa, which became independent in the 1960s. The political entities we observe today in the Third World often are artificial constructions left behind by a defeated colonialism.

These new nations are poorly integrated and they lack territorial rationality and cultural cohesion. As a result, they are prone to violence, to both civil and international conflict.

Some indication of the extent of violence is given in Table 1.7. It should be emphasised, however, that the Table almost certainly understates the loss of life through violent conflict, if for no other reason than that we have no information on the number of deaths sustained by Egypt during the various confrontations in the Middle East in which she has been involved: the Suez invasion of 1956, the Six-day War with Israel in 1967, the war of attrition with Israel along the Suez canal in 1969-70 and the October War with Israel in 1973. But even excluding Egypt the figures are horrific; in approximately 35 years the 19 countries represented in the Table lost nearly four million lives as a result of national and international conflict.

In the world as a whole it is estimated that there have been 150 wars since 1945, many of them civil conflicts, and approximately 20 million people have been killed. There are now more than eight million refugees who have fled their country. About one country in four is engaged in one of the 50 current wars or conflicts, and most of these conflicts are located in the Third World [42]. The world has indeed become an "anarchical society" both nationally and internationally [43].

Table 1.7 **CIVILIAN AND MILITARY DEATHS IN NATIONAL AND INTERNATIONAL CONFLICTS, SELECTED COUNTRIES, 1950-1985**

	Civilian	Military	Total
Latin America:			
Argentina	14 000	5 000	19 000
Brazil	n.a.	n.a.	1 000
Chile	n.a.	n.a.	25 000
Colombia *a*	200 000	100 000	300 000
Mexico	n.a.	n.a.	n.a.
Peru	2 000	1 000	3 000
Africa:			
Botswana	n.a.	n.a.	n.a.
Côte d'Ivoire	n.a.	n.a.	n.a.
Egypt	n.a.	n.a.	n.a.
Ghana	n.a.	n.a.	1 000
Kenya	3 000	12 000	15 000
Tanzania	n.a.	n.a.	n.a.
Asia:			
Bangladesh	1 000 000	500 000	1 500 000
China	1 067 000 *b*	40 000 *b*	1 157 000
India	20 000	8 000	28 000
Indonesia	n.a.	n.a.	836 000
Malaysia	n.a.	n.a.	14 000
Pakistan	6 000	3 000	9 000
Philippines *c*	20 000	23 000	43 000
Sri Lanka	6 000	1 000	7 000

a)   1948-85.
b)   Excluding an estimated 50 000 civilian and military deaths during the cultural revolution.
c)   1946-85.
Source: South, August 1986, pp. 44-5.

The new nations of the Third World are struggling to establish their legitimacy, to persuade or compel their people to accept common rules for the peaceful resolution of political conflicts. Legitimacy, however, presupposes a minimum of political liberty and social justice. Where these are absent, legitimacy, the consent of the governed, often is withheld and the people, or at least some of them, may resort to direct violence. The great problem confronting statesmen in the Third World is that many governments lack legitimacy in the eyes of their own people. Equally, many people – those of different language, religion or ethnic origin – lack legitimacy in the eyes of their own government.

Part of the problem arises from the political inheritance of colonialism. Many countries have had their culture undermined and consequently the social bonds that hold a people together have been weakened. In some cases, as in French-speaking Africa, this is due to the deep cultural penetration of the former imperial power. In other cases, as in East Africa, it is due to the massive immigration of Asians that was encouraged by the British during the colonial era. The resulting social stratification and cultural heterogeneity made it difficult to create a sense of nationhood and shared destiny after the colonies became independent. The anarchy in Uganda, where the southern Bantu are in conflict with the northern Nilotic people and both resent the Asian community, is a good illustration of what can happen in such a situation.

Quite apart from cultural disintegration and heterogeneity is the structural violence that characterises many Third World countries [44]. This is the opposite of political liberty and social justice and frequently has its origins in a very unequal distribution of wealth, income, political power, civil rights and social status. Structural violence is a major reason why many people in, for example, Latin America, the Philippines and South Africa regard their governments as lacking legitimacy. It is also a major reason why "normal" political activity often is punctuated by open violence.

The inequalities that give rise to structural violence are associated with pronounced social stratification and this stratification, in turn, may be reflected in sharp class cleavages. Differences in class interests can readily give rise to class conflict, including violent confrontations between those who own property and those who do not. On the other hand one must not exaggerate class conflict as a source of violence in the Third World since there are many other sources of conflict too. There are, for example, conflicts among the "rich" (landowners versus industrialists versus importers) and these intra-class struggles often are a major determinant of the strategy of development that is pursued. Similarly, the "poor" comprise many different groups often with competing interests (small peasant landowners versus landless labourers versus urban wage workers) and they seldom are able to resolve their differences and take collective action. None the less, social stratification and class conflict increase the vulnerability of the nation-state to internal violence and add to the problems of legitimacy.

The list of governments suffering from problems of legitimacy is long and the source of discontent is varied. In the Sudan the problem is partly racial (Africans versus Arabs), partly religious (Christians and animists versus Islam) and partly cultural in a wider sense; the origin of the problem clearly goes back to the colonial period. In Sri Lanka the problem is partly religious (Hindus versus Buddhists), partly linguistic, partly ethnic. Although Tamils lived in Sri Lanka before the colonial period, there is no doubt that the problem was greatly aggravated by the British policy of importing Tamil workers from India to work on the foreign-owned rubber and tea plantations. In Ethiopia the problem is largely one of separate national groups (the Oromos, Tigreans and Eritreans) resisting the hegemony of Shoa, although here too there are religious and linguistic overtones.

In all of these cases, and in the many others that dot the landscape, contested legitimacy has led to a mixture of social conflict, civil war and military dictatorship. Moreover, the cheapness and abundance of the instruments of violence has exacerbated what is already an extremely difficult situation. Those who deny a government their support, those who contest its legitimacy, can confront authority directly thanks to the ready availability and low cost of explosives and small arms. Governments no longer have a monopoly of force.

It is in this context that the ideology of nationalism should be understood. In the Third World nationalism can be a constructive, integrating force. It is one of the few mobilising ideas available to a government whose legitimacy is open to question and whose monopoly of force has been broken. At its best it can widen the horizons of people and create a sense of community and solidarity where these did not exist before. At its worst, it can be destructive and disintegrating and set one group of people off against another. Much depends on the point from where one starts. Nationalism in the United Kingdom, for example vis-à-vis the European Community, represents a narrowing of political horizons. Similarly, the more nationalist, less internationalist posture of the United States (as seen for instance in its temporary withdrawal from the ILO, its withdrawal from UNESCO and its reduced financial contribution to the United Nations system as a whole) represents a retreat toward a more anarchical international society. Nationalism in India or Nigeria or Indonesia, in contrast, is a step forward, an attempt to embrace a larger political community, to break down narrow parochial allegiances and to widen the definition of those who count as "one of us".

Ideally, nation building and economic development should go hand-in-hand, each helping to create a greater sense of well being, of goals shared in common and a commitment to the established order. In some circumstances, however, economic policy may make the task of creating a political community more difficult. This may occur because policy fails to produce a rise in average living standards, or because it fails to correct and even accentuates inherited inequalities, or because it impoverishes or in other ways "marginalises" important groups in society, or because it results in the alienation of part of the polity and leads them to question the legitimacy of the government and perhaps even of the state. Thus the strategy of economic development matters, and just how it matters, in what ways it has mattered is the subject of this book.

NOTES AND REFERENCES

1. W. Arthur Lewis, *The Evolution of the International Economic Order,* Princeton University Press, p. 71, 1978.
2. See Simon Kuznets, *Modern Economic Growth: Rate, Structure and Spread,* New Haven and London, Yale University Press, 1966. A fascinating analysis of the different development strategies followed by the European countries in the wake of Great Britain's take-off is contained in Dieter Senghaas, *The European Experience: A Historical Critique of Development Theory,* translated from German by K. H. Kimmig, Leamington Spa, Berg, 1985.
3. Lloyd Reynolds, "The Spread of Economic Growth to the Third World: 1850-1980", *Journal of Economic Literature,* Vol. XXI, No. 3, September 1983. This article was later expanded into a book. See Lloyd Reynolds, *Economic Growth in the Third World, 1850-1980,* New Haven, Yale University Press, 1985. Our references will be to the original article.
4. *Ibid.,* p. 963.
5. *Ibid.,* p. 959.
6. *Ibid.,* p. 976.

7. Angus Maddison, *Economic Progress and Policy in Developing Copuntries*, New York, W.W. Norton, 1970, Table I-4, p. 32 and Angus Maddison, "A Comparison of Levels of GDP Per Capita in Developed and Developing Countries, 1700-1980", *Journal of Economic History*, Vol. XLIII, No. 1, March 1983, Table 1, p. 28.

8. Lloyd Reynolds, *op. cit.*, Table 1, p. 958.

9. See Keith Griffin and John Gurley, "Radical Analyses of Imperialism, The Third World and the Transition to Socialism: A Survey Article", *Journal of Economic Literature*, Vol. XXIII, September 1985, pp. 1105-1109 and the references cited.

10. This is apparent from the low R^2 s on the regression equation used to estimate the trend rates of growth of GDP per capita 1950-1984. In the case of Peru, $R^2 = 0.1935$ and in Chile, $R^2 = 0.3567$.

11. Brinley Thomas, *Migration and Economic Growth*, 2nd ed., Cambridge University Press, 1973, p. 57.

12. *Ibid.*, p. 168.

13. *Ibid.*, Table 35, p. 124.

14. *Ibid.*, p. 95.

15. *Ibid.*

16. Simon Kuznets, *op. cit.*, Table 6.6, pp. 352-3.

17. David Morawetz estimates that in the period 1950-75 the developing countries as a whole enjoyed a rate of growth of GNP per capita of 3.4 per cent per annum. See his *Twenty-five Years of Economic Development 1950 to 1975*, Washington, D.C., The World Bank, 1977, Table 1, p. 13.

18. See Amartya Sen, "Public Action and the Quality of Life in Developing Countries", *Oxford Bulletin of Economics and Statistics*, Vol. 43, 1981.

19. See Amartya Sen, *Resources, Values and Development*, Oxford, Blackwell, 1984, Chapter 15.

20. See Irving B. Kravis, Alan W. Heston and Robert Summers, "Real GDP Per Capita For More Than One Hundred Countries", *Economic Journal*, Vol. 88, No. 350, June 1978. In this article 16 countries were studied in detail and then short-cut methods of extrapolation were used to estimate real incomes in the rest. Also see Irving B. Kravis, "Comparative Studies of National Incomes and Prices", *Journal of Economic Literature*, Vol. XXII, March 1984. The OECD also has done work in this field and in 1985 published *Purchasing Power Parities and Real Expenditures* by Michael Ward which contains an important section on methodology. Subsequently, the OECD has regularly published figures for PPPs in its 24 Member countries.

21. Montek S. Ahluwalia, Nicholas G. Carter and Hollis B. Chenery, "Growth and Poverty in Developing Countries", *Journal of Development Economics*, Vol. 6, No. 3, September 1979.

22. *Ibid.*, p. 304. The forty-fifth percentile corresponds roughly to the proportion of the Indian population with total consumption expenditure sufficient to ensure a daily supply of 2 250 calories per person given the observed expenditure patterns of the population. This level of calory consumption is conventionally used to determine the poverty line.

23. Amartya Sen, "Poor, Relatively Speaking", *Oxford Economic Papers*, Vol. 35, No. 2, July 1983, p. 153.

24. *Ibid.*, p. 159.

25. The debate was started in India by P. Sukhatme. See his "Assessment of Adequacy of Diets at Different Income Levels", *Economic and Political Weekly*, Vol. 13, 1978; "On Measurement of Poverty", *Economic and Political Weekly*, Vol. 16, 8 August 1981; "On the Measurement of Undernutrition: A Comment", *Economic and Political Weekly*, Vol. 16, 6 June 1981 and "Measurement of Undernutrition", *Economic and Political Weekly*, Vol. 17, 11 December 1982.

26. Adam Smith, *The Wealth of Nations*, Book 5, Chapter 2, Part II.

27. Louis Théron de Montaugé, *L'agriculture et les classes rurales dans le pays toulousain depuis le milieu du XVIIIe siècle*, (1869) quoted in Eugen Weber, *Peasants into Frenchmen: The Modernization of Rural France, 1870-1914*, London, Chatto and Windus, 1977, p. 22.

28. See Amartya Sen, *op. cit.*, p. 163.

29. See Marshall Sahlins, *Stone Age Economics*, Chicago, Aldine-Atherton, 1972.

30. Marshall Sahlins, "The Original Affluent Society", *Development*, 1986:3, p. 22, emphasis in the original.

31. The source of the calculations is State Statistical Bureau, People's Republic of China, *Statistical Yearbook of China 1984*, Economic Information and Agency, Hong Kong, 1984, Table 1, p. 466; Table 2, p. 467; Tables 5 and 6, p. 473.

32. IBRD, *China: Socialist Economic Development*, Baltimore, Johns Hopkins University Press, 1983, p. 64.

33. W. Arthur Lewis, "Economic Development with Unlimited Supplies of Labour", *Manchester School*, Vol. 22, May 1954; Simon Kuznets, "Economic Growth and Income Inequality", *American Economic Review*, Vol. 49, March 1955.

34. Lloyd Reynolds, *op. cit.*, p. 956.

35. See, for example, Felix Paukert, "Income Distribution at Different Levels of Development: A Survey of Evidence", *International Labour Review*, Vol. CVIII, Nos. 2-3, August-September 1973; Montek S. Ahluwalia, "Inequality, Poverty and Development", *Journal of Development Economics*, Vol. 3, No. 3, September 1976.

36. Keith Griffin and Azizur Rahman Khan, "Poverty in the Third World: Ugly Facts and Fancy Models", *World Development*, Vol. 6, No. 3, March 1978; Irma Adelman and Cynthia Taft Morris, *Economic Growth and Social Equity in Developing Countries*, Stanford University Press, 1973.

37. Simon Kuznets, *Economic Growth and Structure: Selected Essays*, London, Heinemann, 1966, p. 144. The decline in the share of the Third World was concentrated in Asia, whose share of world income fell from 17.3 to 10.5 per cent.

38. Albert Berry, François Bourguignon and Christian Morrisson, "Changes in the World Distribution of Income Between 1950 and 1977", *Economic Journal*, Vol. 93, No. 370, June 1983, Table 1, p. 338 and Table 2, p. 341.

39. IBRD, *World Development Report 1986*, Washington, 1986, World Development Indicators, Table 1, pp. 180-1. The low-income economies are the 36 countries with a per capita income of less than $400 in 1984.

40. The point can be made in another way: 24 of the 28 low-income countries for which we have data grew less rapidly than the industrial market economy countries in the period 1965-84.

41. In 1983 about a quarter of the country's population, according to official figures, spoke no French. Moreover, "the Third Republic found a France in which French was a foreign language for half the citizens". (Eugen Weber, *Peasants into Frenchmen: The Modernization of Rural France 1870-1914*, London, Chatto and Windus, 1977, pp. 67 and 70.)

42. The numbers cited were reported in *South*, August 1986, pp. 39 ff.

43. See Hedley Bull, *The Anarchical Society: A Study of Order in World Politics*, London, Macmillan, 1977.

44. See for example Barrington Moore, Jr., *Social Origins of Dictatorship and Democracy: Lord and Peasant in the Making of the Modern World*, London, Allen Lane, 1967.

23

Chapter 2

MANY PATHS TO DEVELOPMENT

Most Third World countries have been independent for 25 to 40 years and some for much longer. Spanish and Portuguese speaking Latin America became independent in the nineteenth century, Asia in the 1940s and Africa in the 1960s. A few colonies remain, of which Namibia is perhaps the most important, but the significant fact to record is that the Third World consists today of more than a hundred countries which have acquired full responsibility for their economic destiny. The experience of economic development in these countries is varied and rich and it is possible to learn much from it, both analytically and in terms of economic policy. Already it is clear that there are many paths to development although some no doubt are more circuitous than others. Enough time has elapsed and enough data are available to make it possible to test the strengths and limitations of the most widely advocated strategies of economic development against the actual practice, as illuminated by empirical evidence, of countries which have followed a distinct path or strategy.

It should be said straight away that few countries have followed a distinct strategy of development. Those that have are distinguished from others by the coherent and internally consistent set of economic measures they have adopted, which at least in retrospect can be seen to have constituted an identifiable approach to the problems of development. Most countries, most of the time, are confused and inconsistent. They are eclectic, borrowing bits and pieces from a number of different strategies, and they are unsteadfast, chopping and changing with shifts of political opinion. Policy confusion, inconsistency, eclecticism and the reasons for lack of steadiness of purpose are themselves worthy topics for study by a political economist, but they are not our topic. We are interested in something rather different, namely, the economic consequences of adopting coherent development policies over a long period of time, say, a quarter of a century.

No country, of course, will in practice have followed a particular strategy consistently, without qualification, dilution or amendment. There are no pure cases, no controlled experiments in the real world. None the less, some countries have come reasonably close to being a model or key example of a particular strategy and careful study of their experience is likely to be especially valuable. This will be true even if, as sometimes happens, a country that has been cited as a model abandons that strategy and switches to another, for an analysis of the reasons for a change in direction may tell us a great deal about the advantages and disadvantages of particular lines of policy.

Even in the best of circumstances, the facts will never speak for themselves. First, there are never enough facts; information inevitably is incomplete and imperfect. Second, whatever facts exist can always be interpreted in more than one way. There usually are several hypotheses that are more or less equally plausible in accounting for economic events. Third, the failure of a strategy to produce the predicted results may reflect not a flaw in the strategy or the supporting theory, but a failure to implement the strategy fully and rigorously. Fourth, an economy's performance may be dominated by external or exogenous events that can neither be anticipated nor counteracted, and hence performance may have been little influenced by the development strategy pursued however efficacious that strategy might have been in the abstract. Judgement thus is indispensable in any evaluation of economic policy and caution must be exercised in drawing conclusions or lessons from history.

One danger in a study such as this is that preconceived opinions may obstruct the clarity of perception and blind one to important but possibly unexpected findings. Another is that the desire to achieve definitive results may lead one to claim more than the analysis can support, to overstate the findings when more qualified conclusions would be appropriate. Our intention is neither to overlook what is important nor to exaggerate what is discovered, but it must be recognised that in common with all observers of the human condition, we have our biases (which hamper objectivity) as well as our values (which determine the significance attached to both ends and means). The study of alternative strategies of economic development is broad in scope and comprehensive in terms of the social and political issues with which it is inevitably concerned. Hence it is more important than usual that the subject be approached with an open mind, with tolerance and humility, for even a cursory examination reveals that the benefits of a particular strategy are not always as great nor the disadvantages as severe as one sometimes imagines.

Moreover, it is helpful in a study such as this to try to envisage the situation of the planner and policymaker. No planner begins with a *tabula rasa*, a blank sheet of paper on which to outline his policies, projects and programmes, a green field on which to construct his vision of the ideal society. Policymakers are surrounded by constraints. These include the external environment, the scarcity of resources, ideological convictions and cultural conventions as shaped by history, social cleavages and conflicts, the strength or feebleness of political authority, the distribution of power and the administrative capacity of government. Policymakers are not free agents, but nor are their actions wholly determined. They are free to make choices, but their choices are heavily constrained, subject to great uncertainty and often taken in ignorance of their ultimate consequences. One must therefore not be too harsh a judge, while at the same time taking advantage of hindsight to advance our understanding of the complex process of economic development.

A classification of strategies

Government policies and programmes for development can be classified in a number of ways depending on the purpose of the analysis. The classification of strategies we shall use is based on three criteria:

i) The strategies refer to development in the round, to overall development, and not just to one aspect of development or to one sector. On the surface it may appear that some of the strategies are partial or sector specific favouring, say, foreign trade or agriculture, but they are classified as a general strategy of development because the activities singled out for special attention are regarded by the proponents of the

25

strategy as constituting a "leading sector" capable of propelling the economy as a whole onto a faster development trajectory;

ii) The strategies can readily be formulated in a way that makes them amenable to empirical testing, to measurement and quantification of at least some of the central variables. Although quantification *per se* seldom resolves a complex issue, it is important for the credibility of the conclusions that the research be empirically based. Logical reasoning, or theory, also is important of course to ensure that the interpretation of empirical evidence makes sense. The ideal is a judicious blend of theory, fact and history;

iii) The strategies correspond closely to formulations familiar to and often employed by policymakers in both the Third World and the OECD countries. By couching the research in the same terms, in the same vocabulary as that used by practitioners, it is hoped that it will be easier to conduct a dialogue with all interested parties (governments, non-governmental organisations, international agencies, academics, journalists, etc.) and to ensure that the conclusions of the research are accessible to a wide audience.

The hope thus is that research organised around such a classification will have direct and immediate relevance to the current widespread debate on development. At the same time it should be of more lasting value and interest to, say, scholars and university students.

Six distinct strategies of development have been identified. The first is called a Monetarist strategy. It is distinctive in that it concentrates on increasing the efficiency of market signals as a guide to an improved allocation of resources. In practice the strategy often is introduced during a period of crisis, when economic stabilisation and the adjustment of acute imbalances are of high priority, and consequently measures to improve relative prices usually are accompanied by measures to control the rate of increase in the general level of prices. Emphasis, then, is placed on monetary and fiscal policies and on financial reforms. Indeed it is for this reason that we label this approach to economic policy a monetarist strategy for developlment. It could perhaps be described equally well as a strategy of financial orthodoxy of a type fairly common in the 1930s, but monetarism is part of the vocabulary of the 1970s and 1980s and we shall stick to that term.

Monetarist strategies sometimes are said to be concerned only with short-run adjustment, with reducing inflation and restoring macroeconomic balance, after which longer term policies can be resumed. No doubt episodes can be found where such an approach has been adopted, but in general this is a misperception of what the advocates of monetarism believe. Monetarist strategies are deeply concerned with microeconomic issues, with getting markets to work properly, with removing distortions and establishing the correct set of relative prices that will permit efficient, long-run growth. The strategy has a microeconomic orientation, but it pursues macroeconomic objectives.

A major feature of the strategy, consistent with its microeconomic orientation, is the abundant space granted to the private business sector in which to operate. In the economically more advanced Third World countries the strategy implies placing reliance on private industry, although agriculture is of course equally free to grow. The crucial point, however, is that the private sector is regarded as the focus of development and takes on the role of the dynamic sector, responsible for generating backward and forward linkages with the rest of the economy. The role of the state is reduced to a minimum and in ideal circumstances is confined to providing a stable economic environment in which the private sector can flourish. Hence the importance of measures to maintain economic stability. That is, by using stabilisation policy the state attempts to reduce fluctuations of the economy as much as possible, thereby helping the private sector to make reliable forecasts and undertake accurate planning. Policies to denationalise or privatise state-owned enterprises (to increase efficiency and to avoid a crowding out of the private sector) and legislation to reduce trade union power may also be part of this strategy. In the extreme case, monetarist strategies approach *laissez faire*.

The objectives of monetarist strategies are, first, to stabilise the economy and produce well-functioning markets; second, to improve the allocation of resources and thereby raise the level of output and income and improve living standards; third, to achieve high levels of savings in order to raise the rate of growth of production; and fourth, to ensure a more efficient use of capital so that for any given rate of savings, the rate of growth of output is as rapid as possible. The strategy is non-interventionist in spirit and relies on individual initiative and entrepreneurship to move the economy forward. Measures to alter the market-determined distribution of income generally are avoided on grounds that such interventions inevitably introduce distortions and inefficiencies which ultimately are harmful to the poor.

The second distinct strategy is an outward-looking strategy of development which we shall call the Open Economy. The open economy shares some of the features of a monetarist strategy, but not all of them. It too relies on market forces to allocate resources and on the private sector to play a prominent role, but it differs from monetarism in part by placing special emphasis on policies that directly affect the foreign trade sector, i.e., exchange rate policy, tariff regulations, quotas and non-tariff barriers to trade and policies which regulate foreign investment and profit remittances.

Foreign trade, often supplemented by foreign private direct investment is seen as the leading sector or engine of growth. Particularly for small countries, the world market is regarded as a source of demand for exports of virtually infinite elasticity. Thus the constraints imposed by a small economy and domestic market – undiversified resource endowment, inability to exploit economies of scale – can be overcome by exporting. Particularly important are the supply side effects. Export-oriented strategies seek to exploit a country's international comparative advantage and in this way achieve an efficient use of resources. The pressure of international competition is thought to be vital because it provides a strong incentive to producers to keep costs low, to use capital and labour efficiently, to innovate, to improve quality standards and to sustain high rates of investment. These effects, it is believed, are unlikely to be confined to the export sectors but almost certainly will spread throughout the economy and provide a strong stimulus to overall development.

Indeed the open economy does not rely on just the static gains from comparative advantage. An outward-oriented strategy of development should raise not only the level of income but also the level of savings and possibly the rate of savings too. This, in turn, permits a faster rate of accumulation of capital and hence faster growth. In addition, the incentives to increase efficiency associated with export-led growth are likely to result in a more efficient pattern of investment and a lower incremental capital-output ratio. This will give a further stimulus to growth.

The open economy is open not just to foreign trade but also to international movements of the factors of production, capital and labour. Foreign direct investment, commercial lending by international banks and foreign aid all have a role to play, possibly a decisive one. The international transfer not just of capital but also of knowledge, technology and management skills is seen as increasing factor productivity in the Third World and thereby contributing to higher levels of output and a faster growth of incomes. Equally, the international migration of labour is welcomed, although possibly not the emigration of professional and highly skilled labour (sometimes known as brain drain). An exodus of unskilled labour, however, is seen as contributing to a reduction in unemployment, as helping to push up wage rates of those left behind and as providing a valuable flow of foreign exchange and income in the form of emigrants' remittances.

It is logically possible to separate an absence of discrimination against exports from absence of discrimination against foreign capital, and in practice countries often have been inconsistent in their treatment of the two, but it is better to regard both policies as belonging naturally to an open economy strategy. There are at least three reasons for this. First, if foreign direct investment is encouraged in a closed economy that is heavily protected against imports, the foreign capital imports may actually make the country worse off. This could happen, for example, if the prevailing set of policy induced incentives leads foreign businessmen to invest in industries which are profitable from a private point of view but which are socially unprofitable. Some protected industries in the Third World have been known to have negative value added, i.e., the value of material inputs exceeds the value of output when both are valued at world prices, and a foreign financed expansion of such industries actually lowers welfare. Second, assuming a country is interested in attracting foreign capital, it is likely to attract more such capital in the long run if it does not discriminate against exports. The reason for this is that in an open economy foreign capital can invest not only in activities serving the domestic market but also in activities geared for export. In other words, non-discrimination doubles the options for overseas investors. Third, if capital imports take the form of borrowing abroad from foreign banks, and if this is done by a country where protection is combined with an overvalued exchange rate, there is a grave danger that indebtedness will be incurred merely to finance "capital flight" rather than to add to the nation's stock of physical capital. Thus an "equilibrium" exchange rate, or more generally an absence of bias against exports, is important in helping to ensure that foreign loans are used productively.

Unlike a monetarist strategy, an outward-looking strategy of development normally implies an active role for the state. First, government policy is involved in the supply side orientation of the economy, particularly in removing obstacles restraining a country's capacity to export (e.g., inadequate infrastructure) and in promoting those activities which will increase exports. An export-oriented strategy relies for its justification in large part on the theory of comparative costs and on modern extensions to that theory, not on financial orthodoxy (as in the monetarist strategy) or on the particular advantages of certain sectors of production (industry or agriculture). Policy measures may include providing credit and tax incentives, financing training programmes, assisting in market research and in the provision of transport networks and power facilities. Second, the state is responsible for removing price distortions in the economy, possibly left over from previous inward-looking regimes which followed policies of import-substituting industrialisation. In general terms, the state is expected to be concerned with "getting prices right", in particular the key prices of the exchange rate, interest rates and wage rates. This is a feature it has in common with monetarist strategies.

The distribution of income under an open economy strategy depends partly on the commodity composition of exports. Conventional economic theory suggests that exports are likely to use rather intensively the factors of production in relative abundance. In a labour abundant economy this implies that an export-oriented strategy will be employment intensive and consequently the strategy should have a direct and positive impact on reducing poverty and inequality. In a raw materials abundant economy, however, factor shares will shift in favour of economic rents (e.g., in the petroleum or mining sectors) and the impact on poverty will depend on how the economic rents are used by those who receive them. In the first instance the rents will accrue as profit to the private or publicly-owned enterprises engaged in production and export, but some of the profit will be taxed away by the government or transferred to it by the state enterprises and much will depend on how the state chooses to spend its revenues. This choice, in turn, will reflect government priorities and the development strategy implicit in them. Finally, the effect of an export-oriented development strategy on the incidence of poverty also will depend on the nature of the linkages between the foreign trade sector and the rest of the economy. If the linkages are strong, an expanding export sector will generate activity throughout the entire economy, but if the linkages are weak, the export sector may be little more than a foreign enclave.

The third strategy is Industrialisation. The emphasis here, as with the previous strategy, is on growth but the vehicle for achieving growth is rapid expansion of the manufacturing sector. The significance of the strategy, however, is not so much its choice of sector as the instruments used by government to promote development. Unlike the monetarist strategy, the immediate concern is not short-run efficiency in the allocation of resources but an acceleration of the aggregate rate of growth of gross domestic product. This is achieved by a strategy of industrialisation typically in one of three ways: (*i*) by producing manufactured consumer goods largely for the domestic market, usually behind high tariff walls; (*ii*) by concentrating on the development of the capital goods industries, usually under the direction of the state; or (*iii*) by deliberately orienting the manufacturing sector towards exporting, usually under some combination of indicative planning and either direct or indirect subsidies.

Industrialisation strategies in practice tend to place much stress on raising the level of capital formation, on introducing modern technology (which often is highly capital intensive) and, by extension, on promoting the growth of a small number of large metropolitian areas. Urbanisation and the industrialisation strategy tend to go together. Government intervention in pursuit of its objectives usually is pervasive, although it takes different forms depending on which of the three variants of the strategy is adopted. *Laissez faire,* however, forms no part of the strategy. Indeed intervention is advocated and justified on the grounds that it will result in faster growth. It is acknowledged that there will be some losses due to static inefficiency, but these are tolerated because it is believed that the losses are only once-for-all and soon will be outweighed by the benefits arising from faster growth.

Intervention, in other words, is designed to increase production, not to increase allocative efficiency or alter the distribution of income and wealth in favour of low-income groups. On the contrary, where they occur, distributive interventions may actually be biased against the poor and in favour of what are sometimes called the saving classes. The underlying hypothesis is that the rate of saving is an increasing function of the level of household income and hence the greater the degree of inequality, the higher the aggregate level of savings. That is, the distribution of income under this strategy is regarded in instrumental terms and the objective is to shift the distribution of income toward those groups with high marginal propensities to save. In this way, it is argued, investment will be more readily financed and growth will accelerate. The poor eventually will benefit from this process when the fruits of growth spread or trickle down to them.

Fourth, there is the Green Revolution strategy. The focus under this strategy is not on aggregate growth rates, exports or industrialisation but on agricultural growth. One purpose of the strategy is to increase the supply of food, especially grains, the most important wage good. An abundant supply of grains will force down the relative price of food and this, in turn, will help to lower unit labour costs. Low unit costs will raise the general level of profits in non-agricultural activities and this should permit higher savings, more investment and a faster rate of growth overall. A second purpose of the strategy is to help industry directly – particularly those located in rural areas – by providing raw materials (for instance, for the textiles and food processing industries), by stimulating the demand for agricultural inputs, capital and intermediate goods (fertilizer, irrigation pumps, construction materials) and by creating a larger market for simple consumer goods consumed in the countryside (bicycles, radios). Many of these industries tend to be more labour intensive than the industries promoted under an industrialisation strategy and hence greater employment opportunities are created in both rural and urban areas.

In the rural areas, technical change is seen to be the key to accelerating agricultural growth and it is this of course that gives the strategy its name. Relatively little emphasis is placed on institutional change, tenure reforms, land redistribution or direct participation and mobilisation of the rural population. Instead the emphasis is on improved crop varieties, greater use of fertilizer and other modern inputs, investment in irrigation, transport and power, more agronomically based research and improved extension services and credit. Thus the approach is technocratic in its orientation.

The strategy is intended to alleviate mass poverty in several different ways. First, the poor are thought to benefit directly from a greater abundance of food. Second, because of the increased agricultural output, there will be greater employment in agriculture. Third, because of the high income elasticity of demand for non-food items of consumption, large numbers of jobs will be created in non-agricultural rural activities and in urban industry. Fourth, because of the high labour intensity of the strategy, real wages in both the cities and the countryside should rise and this is likely, finally, to result in a more equal distribution of income. The green revolution strategy thus is regarded by its advocates as fostering faster overall growth, a reduction in the incidence of poverty and a more equitable distribution of income.

Redistributive strategies of development start where the green revolution strategy finishes, namely, with a concern to improve the distribution of income and wealth. This is our fifth strategy of development. The strategy is designed to tackle head-on the problem of poverty by giving priority to measures which benefit directly low-income groups. There are three distinct strands which have shaped thinking about redistributive strategies. First, there are those who place great emphasis on creating more employment or more productive employment for the working poor. Second, there are those who advocate redistributing to the poor a part of the increment to total income that arises from growth. This can take the form either of consumption transfers or of a redirection of investment towards the poor. Third, there are those who urge that top priority should be given to the satisfaction of basic needs. These include the need for food, clothing and shelter as well as the provision by the state of primary health care programmes and universal primary and secondary education. Implicit within this third strand is greater economic and political power in the hands of the poor. This, it is thought, often requires a redistribution of the ownership of productive assets, and in particular a land reform. Greater political power for the poor can be achieved by decentralising the public administration and making government more accountable to local groups, by promoting greater participation by the poor in the institutions that affect their well being, by helping the poor to become organised into effective pressure groups and by exploiting more fully the numerous opportunities that exist for local resource mobilisation.

Interest in redistributive strategies arose as a reaction to what their proponents perceived as a failure of growth-oriented strategies to reduce significantly over a reasonable period of time the number of those living in poverty or to improve their well being. Unlike the other strategies outlined above, a redistributive strategy aims to improve the distribution of income and wealth through direct intervention by the state: its objective is to put the needs of the poor first and to create a more egalitarian society. This objective of policy does not necessarily imply a larger role for government (as measured, say, by the ratio of public expenditure to GDP) but it does imply a change in the composition of government expenditure and a qualitative transformation of the relationship between the governed and those who govern them.

A comprehensive redistributive strategy of development contains five central elements: (*i*) an initial redistribution of assets; (*ii*) creation of local institutions which permit people to participate in grass roots development; (*iii*) heavy investment in human capital; (*iv*) an employment intensive pattern of development, and (*v*) sustained rapid growth of per capita income. In contrast to monetarist and most industrialisation strategies, redistributive strategies of development are based on an assumption that there need be no conflict or trade-off between policies intended to produce a more even distribution of income and wealth and those intended to accelerate growth.

Finally, there are Socialist strategies of development. These strategies are distinctive in that private ownership of the means of production is of relatively little significance. Almost all large industrial enterprises are in the state sector, while medium and small-sized enterprises may be organised along co-operative principles; private ownership, where tolerated, often is limited to a few services and small workshops employing only a small number of people. In agriculture, state farms, collectives, co-operatives and communes predominate, although in some countries, notably in China, the collectively owned land is cultivated by individual peasant households.

State and collective ownership of productive assets usually is accompanied by central planning of most economic activities. Planning historically has been in physical terms, quotas and quantitative controls being the main policy instruments, but there have been a number of recent experiments in which prices rather than quantitative targets have been used to guide the economy. These prices, however, usually are planned prices and do not necessarily reflect the forces of supply and demand as understood in capitalist economies.

Socialist countries do of course differ from one another and one can identify four different approaches to economic development that have been adopted at various times by socialist regimes. These comprise (*i*) the classic Soviet (or Stalinist) model, in which agriculture is squeezed in order to finance rapid expansion of the intermediate and capital goods industries; (*ii*) the workers' self-management model of Yugoslavia, and the high degree of decentralisation that accompanies it; (*iii*) the Chinese (or Maoist) model, with its greater emphasis on rural development within a commune structure, and (*iv*) the North Korean model of self-reliance. Regardless of the variant adopted, however, socialist strategies of development seem to be characterised by high rates of capital formation. Indeed, it is not uncommon for investment to account for 30 per cent of domestic product or even more. The efficiency of investment sometimes is relatively low, but even so, rates of growth tend to be quite rapid. A high investment ratio implies a low ratio of consumption to national income, and within this compressed consumption ratio socialist countries tend to favour public consumption (health, education, public transport) at the expense of private. The result is a scarcity of personal services, a fairly uniform distribution of consumption goods among households and a relatively even spread of the benefits of growth.

These, then, are the six strategies of economic development that have been identified for the purposes of analysis. The strategies clearly are ideal types and as far as any particular country is concerned, the strategy followed becomes apparent only after the event, i.e., it is revealed *ex post*. No country announces in advance that it intends to follow such-and-such a strategy and then proceeds to do so, not even the socialist countries. Indeed, for the reasons indicated earlier, most countries do not follow any identifiable strategy, and certainly not for long.

The strategies do not constitute a typology. It is evident from what has been said that there is no intention of classifying each Third World country under one of the six strategies. Indeed, it would not be possible to do so. The attempt would be utterly futile. Instead the strategies can be viewed as points along a multi-dimensional spectrum, two of the strategies occupying the extreme ends of the spectrum (monetarism, socialism) and the others intermediate points of particular interest. The hundred or more Third World countries are scattered along this multi-dimensional spectrum and some adopt positions close to one or another of the six selected points. That is, a few Third World countries approximate in their economic policies to the six strategies that have been identified and these naturally are of special interest to us.

It is not our purpose ultimately to rank the strategies on a scale of better or worse, to list them in descending order in terms of their success in achieving development. This cannot be done objectively and it is better not to try. There are several reasons for this. First, governments have multiple objectives, not just one. The economic objectives could include rapid growth, the avoidance of economic instability in the level of output, high levels of consumption, a low rate of inflation, or a high rate of capital formation. Distributive objectives could include the alleviation of poverty, a reduction in income inequality, wider ownership of productive assets, or greater wage and income differentials to encourage initiative and entrepreneurship. The social objectives could include protection of the interests of minorities and their separate identities, or cultural assimilation, or the containment of religious, linguistic or ethnic conflict. The political objectives could include such things as safeguarding the power of certain groups (the property-owning classes, the dictatorship of the proletariat, the whites of South Africa, the indigenous population of Fiji), or reducing regional inequalities or strengthening national security.

Second, the values attached to these objectives may differ qualitatively from one country to another. In some countries the preservation of a plural society composed of several nationalities may be positively valued, while in others it may be negatively valued and instead a high value given to assimilation and the creation of a singular national identity. In some countries a positive value may be attached to reducing regional differences whereas in others zero value may be attached to this. Similarly, in some countries a high value may be given by government to preserving the monopoly of political power by certain groups whereas in other countries a negative value might be given to this, positive values given instead to the diffusion of political power and the creation of democratic institutions. Again, in some countries the development of a strong public sector may be positively valued and in others negatively valued.

Third, even if agreement can be reached on what is to be positively valued and hence on the goals of development, the weights attached to the various objectives will differ from country to country. Each country will have its own ranking of priorities, its own weighting of objectives, its own "social welfare function" which it attempts to maximise. An externally imposed set of weights not only is arbitrary, it is also unfair for it implies criteria for evaluation of strategies other than their own. Just as it is absurd to judge an airplane by how well it floats on water or a boat by how well it flies through the air, so too is it absurd to judge a strategy of development in terms of goals and priorities different from its own.

Fourth, the distinction between means and ends, goals and instruments is not as clear as some might imagine. Means as well as ends have values attached to them. Reliance on the market is thought by many to be "good"; coercion is "bad"; high taxation is "confiscatory"; abortion is "immoral"; to work is "good". Moreover, as is perhaps obvious by now, many things are valued not only as a means to an end but also as an end in themselves. Participation, for example, is thought by many people to be desirable in its own right as well as a way to achieve certain development goals. The emancipation of women is a goal in itself as well as a means to increase output. Abstaining from consuming alcohol is in some societies an objective; it may also be a way to increase the productivity of labour. Many other illustrations could be given. The essential point, however, is that strategies differ not only in their objectives but also in the means used to attain their objectives, and since the means as well as the ends are valued differently in different countries, it is impossible to rank strategies in an order of merit. Neither "development" nor "success" are unambiguous terms and consequently one seldom can award definitive marks to strategies for their success in achieving development. The most that one can aspire to achieve is to determine how well strategies perform in certain specific ways (growth, efficiency, equity, etc.) without attempting to sum up and produce an overall evaluation. This, at least, shall be our approach.

Each of the six strategies is analysed separately in the six chapters that follow. The strategies are defined in terms of policy instruments and developmental objectives, the theoretical underpinnings of the strategies are discussed and relevant empirical information is presented. In addition, most chapters contain fairly detailed case studies of countries whose policies have approximated quite closely to the ideal type under discussion. These case studies run like a thread throughout the book. For example, the strengths and weaknesses of the monetarist strategy are illustrated by the experience of Chile and Argentina. Strategies of industrialisation are illustrated with case studies of Brazil, India and South Korea. The Philippines is used to illustrate the green revolution. The chapter on redistributive strategies of development contains case studies of Taiwan and Sri Lanka, and the experience of socialist Third World countries is illustrated by case studies of China and North Korea. These case studies, it is hoped, will put some flesh on the bones of what otherwise might be a rather abstract analysis.

A second connecting thread also runs throughout much of the book. This takes the form of data on 19 Third World countries that are incorporated into the text whenever a wide perspective is thought to be desirable. The 19 countries are sufficiently small in number that information about them can be digested easily, yet they account for a sufficiently large proportion of the population of the Third World to enable reasonable generalisations to be made. The countries are listed in Table 2.1.

The countries were selected in part to provide regional balance. Thus there are seven countries from Asia, the most populous Third World region. These include China in East Asia, Malaysia and the Philippines in Southeast Asia and Bangladesh, India, Pakistan and Sri Lanka in South Asia. Six countries have been chosen from Africa: Kenya and Tanzania from East Africa, Ghana and Côte d'Ivoire from West Africa, Botswana from Southern Africa and Egypt from North Africa. Another six countries were selected from Latin America: Argentina, Brazil, Chile, Colombia, Mexico and Peru.

The countries differ enormously in terms of size of population. Indeed the largest, China (with a population of 1 060 million) is nearly a thousand times larger than the smallest, Botswana (with a population of only 1.1 million). Between them, however, the 19 countries account for 69 per cent of the entire population of the Third World. In three of the countries (Argentina, Chile and China) population growth rates are relatively low, less than 2 per cent a year, whereas in two of the African countries (Kenya and Côte d'Ivoire) they approach 4 per cent a year. The others fall somewhere in between these extremes.

Table 2.1 **POPULATION AND INCOME IN NINETEEN COUNTRIES**

	Population		GNP per capita	
	1985	Growth rate, 1960-85	1984	Growth rate, 1960-85
	(million)	(% per annum)	(U.S. dollars)	(% per annum)
Asia:				
Bangladesh	101.1	2.7	130	0.3
China	1 059.5	1.9	310	4.7
India	758.9	2.2	260	1.5
Malaysia	15.6	2.6	1 980	4.0
Pakistan	100.4	2.8	380	2.9
Philippines	54.5	2.7	660	2.3
Sri Lanka	16.2	2.0	360	2.7
Africa:				
Botswana	1.1	3.3	960	8.2
Côte d'Ivoire	9.8	3.9	610	1.7
Egypt	46.9	2.4	720	3.7
Ghana	13.6	2.8	350	-1.7
Kenya	20.6	3.8	310	2.3
Tanzania	22.5	3.2	210	1.5
Latin America:				
Argentina	30.6	1.6	2 230	0.9
Brazil	135.6	2.5	1 720	4.0
Chile	12.0	1.8	1 700	0.2
Colombia	28.7	2.5	1 390	2.4
Mexico	79.0	3.0	2 040	2.9
Peru	19.7	2.7	1 000	0.2

Sources: Population: UN, *World Population Prospects: Estimates and Projections as Assessed in 1984*, New York, United Nations, 1986. GNP per capita: IBRD, *World Development Report 1986*, New York, Oxford University Press, 1986. GNP per capita growth: IMF and OECD Development Centre data files.

The range of per capita income runs from $130 in the poorest country, Bangladesh, to $2 230 in the richest, Argentina. Eight of our countries are classified by the World Bank as low-income economies: Bangladesh, Tanzania, India, China, Kenya, Ghana, Sri Lanka and Pakistan. Five are in the upper middle-income category: Chile, Brazil, Malaysia, Mexico and Argentina. The remaining six are classified as lower middle-income economies. Growth rates also have varied considerably among the 19 countries. In Ghana the trend rate of growth of GNP per capita during the quarter century beginning in 1960 actually was negative. In Peru and Bangladesh it was very low (0.2 and 0.3 per cent a year, respectively) while in Brazil, Malaysia and China it was very rapid (4.0, 4.0 and 4.7 per cent, respectively).

The prize for the fastest grower, however, is won by Botswana, where GNP per head increased spectacularly by 8.2 per cent a year.

The sample of 19 countries includes several where economic policies approximate to one of our development strategies. Chile and Argentina followed monetarist strategies for a number of years; Botswana and Côte d'Ivoire adopted the open economy model; Brazil and India have emphasized industrialisation; the Philippines and more recently Bangladesh have adopted a green revolution strategy; Sri Lanka and Tanzania implemented parts of a redistributive strategy; China adopted a socialist strategy of development. A number of these countries, as previously indicated, have been selected as case studies in subsequent chapters and this should help to tie together the two threads of the analysis.

This volume is about alternative strategies of economic development. Its purpose is comparative and synthetic, to pick out the main features of each strategy in such a way that the differences and similarities among strategies can readily be visualised. This approach has obvious strengths, but it has equally obvious deficiencies. By concentrating on the period after the end of the Second World War, it neglects the long run, historical dimension of development and thereby runs a risk that secular continuities will be overlooked or mistakenly attributed to economic policy when in fact deep-seated cultural or social phenomena are the prime movers. A global comparative approach also discounts the geographical dimension of development. Countries of a particular region – Africa, Latin America, the Caribbean – often have a shared history and have evolved common cultural conventions, social structures and institutional arrangements. These regional particularities may impart to policy a distinctive "style" which in turn gives to development a pattern or shape which tends to become characteristic of all or most of the countries of the region[1]. Finally, a comparison of strategies inevitably plays down the uniqueness of countries. As Dudley Seers once said, "economics is about economies", and any study which is not firmly rooted in the details of a particular country is open to criticism for illegitimate generalisation.

Of course this study does contain some historical material, a considerable amount of data grouped on a regional basis and a large number of country case studies. But its strengths are cross-country comparisons and its global vision. Attempts are made to remedy the deficiencies of this approach in other volumes. Angus Maddison's volume on economic policy and performance covers nearly three-quarters of a century (1913-87) and gives an historical perspective to development in six, mostly rather large, Third World countries in Latin America and Asia, namely, Argentina, Brazil, Mexico, China, India and Korea. A second volume already has been published which contains essays by a number of economists examining development strategies essentially from a regional perspective: Latin America, Asia, sub-Saharan Africa and Eastern Europe and the Soviet Union[2].

NOTES AND REFERENCES

1. It is for this reason, of course, that universities offer courses in such things as "the economics of Latin America", "economic development in Asian perspective" and "African economic development".
2. Louis Emmerij, ed., *Development Policies and the Crisis of the 1980s*, Paris, OECD Development Centre, 1987.

Chapter 3

MONETARISM

One of the great intellectual triumphs of the 1930s was Keynesian economics. Looking back fifty years it is hard to appreciate the profound change in thought that occurred during that period of economic depression and political crisis. The orthodoxy of the time was *laissez faire*, the only respectable strategy of development was that advocated in Adam Smith's *Wealth of Nations*, and the only macroeconomic theory that was available was the laws of motion of capitalism as described in Karl Marx's *Capital* – a theory which had few supporters in the West and no policy implications. The "new economics" as it was called emerged in Sweden, in Poland through the work of Kalecki and in England through the work of Keynes and his close colleagues at Cambridge University. The new economics was not just a product of university research and of pure thought, however. Certainly the theorists made an important contribution, perhaps the most lasting contribution, but the application of Keynesian ideas before Keynes, especially in Argentina where Raul Prebisch was responsible for economic policy, demonstrated in concrete terms that there was an effective alternative to orthodox doctrines [1].

In place of Say's law, which implicitly assumed full employment and tried to demonstrate that markets always clear, the new economics showed that an unemployment equilibrium was possible. In place of the orthodox prescription of a balanced budget, the new view advocated functional finance: the doctrine that the budget should be used as an instrument of policy not as a symbol of moral rectitude. According to the new view it would be appropriate to run a deficit when an expansion of aggregate demand was needed and a surplus when the pressure of demand on available resources was excessive. The notion of aggregate demand was itself a novel concept and initially was hard to grasp, and the idea that governments could manipulate aggregate demand and thereby regulate the level of output and employment was revolutionary and encountered fierce resistance. In fact resistance never disappeared completely although for many years the critics were a small if vocal minority.

The depression of the 1930s was the midwife of fascism in Germany and Italy and threatened the survival of capitalism as an economic system. Keynesian macroeconomics, it can be argued, was one of the saviours of capitalism. In place of *laissez faire*, Keynesian economics envisaged a positive role for government; the nightwatchman state (a fiction of the imagination of liberal economists) was to be thrown into the dustbin of history and replaced by an interventionist state charged with the responsibility for overcoming depression and ensuring prosperity. The first task of the new economics was to try to reduce the massive unemployment in the United States and in much of Western Europe, an attempt that never wholly succeeded. The second was to provide the principles of public finance that would be needed during the Second World War. The third was to point the way, at the end of the War, toward the welfare state. This last task represented an extension of government's recently acquired responsibility for ensuring prosperity, an extension which began modestly but which grew rapidly. Starting with the provision of unemployment compensation, the welfare state soon expanded to include state pensions to provide economic security for the elderly, a national health service (in Europe but not in the United States) to protect the population against the consequences of disease and injury and a variety of benefit schemes whose purpose was to provide a safety net for families in danger of falling into poverty. Within three decades the number of benefits aimed at specific groups in need increased enormously.

Parallel to the provision of welfare services, the state also assumed responsibility for investment and growth. This led inevitably to the creation of a large state enterprise sector, formed partly by nationalising some private firms and partly by investing public funds in newly established state enterprises. In this way the mixed economy was born. State enterprises had not of course been unknown, even outside the socialist countries. Turkey had long relied on its state economic enterprises to promote industrialisation, several Latin American countries had public enterprises (e.g., oil in Mexico) and state owned development banks (as in Chile), and even some European countries had a few government owned enterprises. But prior to 1945 these were exceptions; the spirit of the age was against it; *laissez faire* was not compatible with a large public sector.

After 1945 the situation changed almost beyond recognition. In Western Europe state enterprises were dominant in transport (railways, airlines), energy (coal, oil, gas, electricity), finance (notably in France), broadcasting and telecommunications, and in the "commanding heights" of the manufacturing sector (steel, shipbuilding, and in some countries automobiles). In the United States the picture was rather different. There were few state enterprises as such, but private enterprise was subject to detailed regulation and supervision where there was a danger of monopolistic power being exploited (as in the railroad, airline, telephone, broadcasting and oil businesses) or where there was a large number of defence contractors involved (including those engaged in the space programme). Throughout the West, in one way or another, the state was in business in a big way, although perhaps not always on behalf of the general public.

A reaction was to be expected. The reaction began in the United States, where traditionally fewer welfare services are provided compared to Europe and where, as we have seen, state regulation of private industry is preferred to state ownership. It spread from the United States to the United Kingdom and from there to continental Western Europe. Having conquered the North, the reaction spread to the South and received a particularly warm welcome in parts of Latin America[2], the region of the Third World where the intellectual influence of the United States is strongest.

The reaction took the form of a simultaneous criticism of Keynesian economics, the welfare state and the mixed economy. The condemnation thus was sweeping, an attack on the political and economic system as it had evolved in the OECD countries during the last forty years or more. This attack occurred on three levels: there were technical criticisms of specific features of the political and economic system; there were more general criticisms of the way the economic system as a whole functioned and there were fundamental objections to the political doctrines which lie behind and provide justification for state intervention in the economy. Let us consider each of these levels of criticism in turn.

On a technical level it is claimed that the set of benefits provided by the welfare state constitutes a disincentive to work, to search for employment, and consequently the welfare state tends to perpetuate the very things it seeks to remedy, namely, unemployment and poverty. The solution, according to the critics, is sharply to reduce both the number of benefits provided and the generosity of benefits. It is unclear, however, just how strong is this technical criticism. It is known, for example, that a high proportion of the population does not claim benefits to which it is legally entitled. If people do not claim benefits, it is difficult to see how they can be a disincentive. Moreover, where pecuniary disincentive effects are very strong, e.g., where marginal tax and benefit rates are such that it doesn't "pay" an unemployed person to accept wage employment, it doesn't follow that this will strongly affect actual behaviour. Man is not motivated by pecuniary incentives alone and it may well be – indeed casual observation suggests that it is common – that people would prefer to have a job and the dignity, sense of participation and self-reliance that go with it, even if the net gains in income were marginal or even slightly negative. This is not a reason to be complacent, but it does suggest that where "poverty traps" exist the solution may be to reform the system of benefits rather than eliminate them.

A second technical criticism is that state enterprises in a mixed economy are not subject to a market test and for that reason tend to be inefficient, to be characterised by high costs (and hence high prices to the consumer), by substantial losses (which have to be covered by general government revenues at the expense of the taxpayer), and by low quality and poor service. All of this represents a gross misallocation of resources and hence a reduction in average incomes below what might otherwise be attained. The solution is to sell state enterprises to the private sector.

The solution is not without irony, however. First, many nationalised enterprises were taken over from the private sector because they were unprofitable and were in danger of closing down. Examples include the railways and coal mining. The governments responsible for nationalisation believed that closure of these industries was neither in the short-run national interest (because of the loss of thousands of jobs) nor in the long-run interest (because these industries supplied goods and services essential to other industries but for various reasons were unable to charge a price which covered their costs). Second, still other enterprises, e.g. steel, were nationalised in order to exploit economies of large scale production, to rationalize the industry, to cut costs, to become more competitive internationally and thus to improve the allocation of resources. The state sector in such cases was thought to be more efficient than the private sector, not less. Third, a number of industries, e.g. electricity and telecommunications, were incorporated into the state sector because they are "natural monopolies". It was feared that if such industries were allowed to remain in the private sector, they would behave in a typically monopolistic fashion, restricting output and raising prices (and profits) at the expense of their customers. Thus once again the case for nationalisation was based on criteria of efficiency in resource allocation. Of course it is conceivable that nationalisation made sense after the Second World War and privatisation (presumably with state regulation) makes sense today, but one ought not to jump to that conclusion hastily. It is not obvious, for example, that the coal, railway and steel industries in the United States (all of which are in the private sector) are more efficient than their European counterparts (most of which are in the state sector). For that matter, it isn't obvious that Pan American Airways is as efficient (or as profitable) as British Airways.

Profitability, in any case, is not a good yardstick with which to compare private and public sector enterprises. The latter, in principle, are concerned with social costs and benefits and these may well diverge from market costs and private profits. Externalities of various sorts are an obvious cause of divergence between private and social costs and benefits. Public investment in urban transport, for instance, helps to reduce the social costs of congestion and one would not expect, say, the Paris Metro to make a profit. Indeed if it did, that would almost certainly mean that prices were too high, the volume of sales of its services too low and consequently that it was operating inefficiently. A divergence of private from social costs and benefits does not in itself justify establishing a state enterprise – taxes, subsidies and government regulation of private firms could be used instead – but where state enterprises already exist, the mere fact that they may operate at a loss does not prove that they are not acting in accordance with the public interest, let alone that they should be sold.

None of this implies that all state enterprises are efficient. Clearly some of them are not. Before selling them to the private sector, however, one should consider whether it is possible to improve performance and reduce inefficiency by introducing rational pricing and investment criteria or through other administrative reforms. Assuming it is decided to sell, an issue then arises about the use to be made of the proceeds. If state assets are sold to the public to finance general government expenditure, this represents a transformation of private savings into public consumption. The public sector in effect consumes part of its capital. If the proceeds are used to reduce taxation, the outcome depends upon what private individuals decide to do with their higher after-tax incomes, but presumably some portion will be consumed and the rest saved. Reduced investment in the economy will occur to the extent that consumption increases. On the other hand, if the proceeds of asset sales are reinvested by the government in other state enterprises, this represents a change in the public sector's investment portfolio. The balance between the private and public sectors remains unchanged. Finally, if the proceeds are channelled into the financial markets, so that public sector savings are used to finance private sector investment, there will be a shift of the centre of gravity in favour of the private sector, and this shift will occur without any decapitalisation of the economy. Thus the recommendation to sell state enterprises is not as simple as it might seem and the consequences are not straightforward.

Behind the technical criticisms of the welfare state and the mixed economy lie a number of more general economic points. First, the critics claim that the use of government tax and expenditure policies to stabilize the economy and maintain a high level of output and employment in practice does not work; the policies actually destabilize the economy. Instead the critics tend to advocate a balanced budget combined with a slow, steady increase in the money supply. With the advantage of hindsight, this criticism seems rather odd. In fact the increase in economic instability in the 1970s and 1980s has been associated not with Keynesian policies but with a reversion to the orthodox financial and monetarist policies of the 1930s whereas the rapid growth and full employment of 1945-1973 was associated not with monetarist policies but particularly in Europe with the application of Keynesian macroeconomic policies and widespread government intervention. The monetarist position thus has not withstood the test of history.

A second criticism is that the application of Keynesian macroeconomic policies leads to inflation. The containment of inflation, in turn, requires the imposition of price controls (and possibly queuing and formal rationing) as well as controls over wages and incomes. Markets are not allowed to play their normal role, price signals become a poor guide to resource allocation and inefficiency tends to become widespread. It should be said straight away that there is some force to this criticism. Sustained full employment does tend to encourage wage-push inflation and this does lead to experimentation with incomes policies and administrative measures to restrain price increases. Inefficiency in factor and commodity markets does tend to increase. It is not obvious, however, that a tight monetary policy and deflation are more successful in combating inflation, unless one is prepared to contemplate high unemployment as a permanent feature of capitalist economies. Indeed inflation in the 1970s occurred in the absence of full employment. Furthermore, as we shall see below, it is not certain that markets always function in the way monetarist theory postulates.

Third, monetarists object to the high average tax rates common in advanced capitalist economies. Government current revenue is more than 40 per cent of GNP in many European countries, namely, in Ireland, Italy, Belgium, the Netherlands, France and Norway, whereas it is less than 20 per cent in the United States. The high level of taxation is seen as "crowding out" the private sector and since the private sector is thought to be more effficient than the public, this results in lower efficiency. Allied to this is a fourth criticism that high marginal tax rates on upper income groups act as a disincentive to entrepreneurship and business initiative. (In the United States, where taxes are relatively low, "crowding out" is said to result from large government budget deficits which raise interest rates and discourage private investment.)

The empirical evidence, however, does not provide much support for these arguments. There is no evidence, for example, that the productivity of labour is affected one way or another by the general level of taxation. Certainly one can find countries with a low incidence of taxation which have experienced a slow increase in labour productivity, and vice versa. In Canada and the United States, for instance, current government revenue was 20.0 and 19.7 per cent of GNP in 1983, respectively, but growth of GDP per member of the labour force increased only 0.2 and 0.7 per cent a year, respectively during the period 1973-1984. In West Germany and France, in contrast, the tax ratio was 29.3 and 41.7 per cent, respectively, and the increase in labour productivity in both countries was 1.2 per cent a year, i.e. several times higher than in North America. In other words, France and Germany, with a higher tax ratio, enjoyed a more rapid increase in output per man than did Canada and the United States, with low tax ratios. Thus if there is a connection between levels of taxation and efficiency, as the monetarists claim, it is not very strong or direct, as this simple illustration demonstrates.

There is however a related weakness of Keynesian economics that might have some substance. It is that societies vary in the level of personal taxation that they accept before there is a marked increase in evasion and illegal economic activities. At some point perceived high taxation may undermine respect for the law and induce people to cultivate what is sometimes called the black economy. The critical level of taxation varies from one country to another and, within countries, between different eras. The level of taxation that will be tolerated during times of war, for example, is higher than during peacetime. The variation in the critical level presumably is linked to the degree of national cohesion, ideological convictions and the sense of national purpose. However once tax rates exceed this psychological ceiling the consequences may be damaging. Thus insofar as Keynesian policies are associated with high average personal tax rates, monetarist criticisms are addressed to real issues.

The fundamental objection of the monetarists to Keynesian economics, the welfare state and the mixed economy is political and philosophical and ultimately has relatively little to do with an analysis of the way modern capitalist economies perform. This is not to say that questions of incentives, inefficiency and sub-optimal resource allocation are unimportant, but at the end of the day what is at stake are value judgements, not prices and quantities. The issue, as the monetarists see it, is freedom [3]. Hostility to the state and bureaucracy, a strong preference for the market mechanism and the private sector, reflect underlying value preferences. Individualism, self-reliance and competition are ends in themselves. If it can be shown that they promote growth and efficiency, so much the better, but if not, they are still prized. Moreover, economic freedom, *laissez faire,* also has an instrumental value because it is regarded as necessary for political freedom. Hence anything that erodes *laissez faire* – collective action, co-operation, social security, state intervention in the economy – is viewed as a threat to liberty and freedom and is opposed regardless of the economic consequences.

The concept of freedom on which the monetarist view rests is a highly restrictive one and has to compete with other visions which place more emphasis on considerations of equity and envisage a larger role for government [4]. Be that as it may, monetarist economics is now entrenched in many Western universities, has guided economic policy in the United States and the United Kingdom and has influenced policy on the continent of Europe. The international agencies, particularly the World Bank and the International Monetary Fund, have endorsed monetarist thinking and have done what they can to promote it in those Third World countries which have sought their assistance. The reception in the Third World has been mixed. Only a few countries have applied monetarism whole-heartedly, and then only for a short time, but many governments have implemented parts of the monetarist strategy and many others have been encouraged to do so. A study of the monetarist strategy of development is therefore important.

Price formation and economic efficiency

If there is one slogan that summarises the monetarist approach to economic policy it is "get your prices right" [5]. Free enterprise and the unhindered operation of market forces are advocated with scarcely a qualification because they are thought to produce efficiency and greater welfare. Indeed if two consenting adults enter into a transaction, then almost by definition it is thought to be mutually advantageous and to raise their welfare. This is Milton Friedman's "misleadingly simple" case for *laissez faire:* "if an exchange between two parties is voluntary, it will not take place unless both believe they will benefit from it" [6].

Of course their beliefs may be mistaken. They may be ignorant, lack information or judgement and hence be unable to make a well-informed choice. Many consumers when confronted with the array of goods produced in a modern economy are woefully ignorant of the characteristics of the commodities on offer. This is as true of soap powder and wine as it is of automobiles, stereophonic equipment and dishwashers. Producers also suffer from lack of information, be they bankers uncertain of the credit-worthiness of their borrowers, peasants ignorant of the health of a hired bullock or employers who lack knowledge of the capabilities of wage labourers.

Lack of information is so pervasive in an economy that it has led to the development of a specific body of theory to deal with it. Joseph Stiglitz has called this theory, rather grandly, the "imperfect information paradigm" [7] and its application in the Third World, even more grandly, the "new development economics" [8]. What the imperfect information paradigm shows is that, even assuming institutions adapt slowly to reduce the cost of acquiring information, at any particular moment in history the economy is most unlikely to be in a Pareto optimum. That is, the economy is likely to be inefficient. This implies that there exists in principle a set of government interventions – taxes and subsidies – which can make everyone better off. Of course the government may also lack information and hence be unable in practice to reduce inefficiency, but equally, it may have more information than those in the private sector and hence have a positive role to play.

Thus the rehabilitation of the public sector is one outcome of the imperfect information paradigm. The new theory represents a turning away from the excessive claims of those who advocate *laissez faire* and at the same time it can be seen as an exploration of the implications of Arrow and Debreu's demonstration [9] that market economies will be efficient only under exceptional conditions. These conditions include a complete set of markets (including futures markets) and perfect information by all actual and potential participants in the market. Needless to say, these conditions are not present in any economy, least of all an underdeveloped one. Thus while it may be important to "get prices right", there can be no presumption that the correct set of prices will be generated by unhindered market forces.

This conclusion is strengthened whenever competition is absent. The deliberate withholding of information by one party to a transaction is of course one form of monopoly power, but there are many other sources of monopolistic and oligopolistic competition and all of them result in departures from the conditions necessary for efficiency. The fact that an exchange may be voluntary does not imply that it increases efficiency. Moreover, paradoxically, voluntary exchange does not even imply that both parties to the exchange benefit.

It has been shown by Kaushik Basu that if one relaxes the assumption that markets are characterised by two-person (or dyad) relationships and instead includes the possibility of three-person (or triad) relationships, the weaker person in a transaction may be forced, voluntarily, to accept a deal from a more powerful person that makes him absolutely worse off [10]. Suppose, for example, that a landlord offers an agricultural labourer currently working for someone else a package of w rupees an hour for h hours, and accompanies it with a threat that if the offer is rejected he (the landlord) will ensure that a third person (say the village shopkeeper or moneylender) ceases to trade with him. If the landlord is sufficiently powerful, and his threat therefore credible, the labourer may accept the package offer (w, h) even though he ends up in a worse position than before. The deal in a sense is voluntary, and it is certainly the product of unhindered market forces, but the result for the labourer is a reduction in well being. He has been exploited, voluntarily.

The example from Kaushik Basu raises the question of how prices are formed. Monetarist theory relies on a universal auctioneer: the economy behaves as if all prices were set at an immense auction at which bids and offers are made until a market clearing price is established simultaneously in all spot and future markets. The auction occurs instantaneously, at zero transaction cost with perfect information. Relative prices consequently are highly flexible upwards and downwards, including of course the price of labour and other factors of production, and supply is responsive to price changes. In this frictionless world adjustments occur smoothly and quickly. Everybody is a price-taker.

An alternative world is a world of uncertainty, of lack of information and of great economic friction. This is a world of price-makers and price-leaders, of mark-up pricing, of fix-price [11]. Prices in this world are "sticky" and adjustments occur far from smoothly. In fix-price markets adjustment to a disturbance usually takes the form of a variation in quantity rather than a change in price. That is, output (including stocks) responds more rapidly to changes in demand than do prices. The market "clears" in the sense that production approximates to purchases by customers, but the volume of production tends to be sub-optimal. That is, at the prevailing price, the level of output is below that which maximises profits or minimises costs. The economy is inefficient.

Furthermore, if left to its own devices, a fix-price economy runs a risk of macroeconomic instability and high unemployment. It is easy to imagine how this could occur. Assume, for instance, that a low cost building material becomes available on the market which is a substitute for steel. The steel makers notice a falling off of demand, but they do not know whether it is temporary or permanent, a random fluctuation that quickly will be reversed or a structural change in their market. Consequently their initial reaction is to wait and see, to do nothing. The price of steel remains unaltered, production remains constant and the fall in demand is reflected entirely in a rapid build-up of unwanted stocks. This triggers a response in the next period, but the response in a fix-price world is to curtail production sharply in an attempt to bring the level of stocks back to its "normal" relationship to sales. Prices continue to remain unaltered, and the adjustment to the change in demand is now carried entirely by a reduction in the volume of output. Lower output, in turn, is likely to be accompanied by a reduction in employment, not in lower wages. If the world would stand still, no doubt steel prices and the wages of steel workers would begin to take some of the strain of adjustment, but of course the world never does stand still and, in our example, if the steel industry happens to be large, a contraction of output and employment there could set off a multiplier-accelerator interaction which amplifies the effects of the original disturbance. Unrestrained market forces in such a setting can be bad for the health of the economy. We will see just how bad they can be when monetarist stabilisation programmes are examined.

Some markets, however, do conform more closely to the model of the auctioneer and it is natural to think that these flex-price markets lead to an efficient allocation of resources. Prices rise quickly when there is excess demand and fall quickly when there is excess supply. Indeed some international primary commodity prices are highly volatile, especially in those markets where no attempt is made to regulate or stabilise prices, but it is not obvious that this price flexibility is of long-run benefit to those countries which are highly dependent on primary commodity exports to earn foreign exchange. Indeed changes in the relative price of petroleum (not a flex-price market) have helped to destabilise the world economy both when the relative price increased in 1973 and 1979 and when it fell in 1985-86. Nicholas Kaldor has often made the point that stable commodity prices would stimulate production and that in the long run this would result in lower average prices. "The working of flex-price markets is thus in fact very inefficient – it is attended by large fluctuations in prices which are not regular enough to be predictable in extent or timing, and which generate risks that act as a drag on production" [12].

Thus both fix-price and flex-price markets are inefficient but for different reasons. Inefficiency in fix-price markets arises from the fact that the response to a disturbance takes the form of quantity adjustments and this can lead in the short run to depressed output and unemployment. Inefficiency in the flex-price model arises from the fact that price volatility increases risk and in the long run this can lead to lower average output and higher average prices. These problems are inherent in a market economy and there is no obvious solution to them. It is for these reasons that the advice to countries to get your prices right is not very helpful for it is the very process of price formation, the mechanism by which correct prices are supposed to be generated, that produces some of the inefficiency the right prices are intended to eliminate.

Key prices and price distortions

Let us put to one side the issue of price formation. Nothing that has been said so far should be taken to imply that prices do not matter. On the contrary, they matter a great deal.

44

The monetarists surely are correct to emphasise the large price "distortions" that can be found in many Third World countries and the harmful effects these can have on resource allocation. It may not always be obvious what the right price is, and we have seen that the set of prices produced by *laissez faire* has no claim to be considered optimal, but in many cases it is clear that actual prices diverge markedly from social opportunity costs and hence that price corrections could in principle be beneficial.

All economists, whatever their persuasion, have a bias in favour of competition and against monopoly. By extension, most economists are biased in favour of international competition and oppose restrictions on world trade: a liberal import policy often is the best way to prevent monopolistic exploitation. There is in fact much common ground among economists. What distinguishes the monetarists from everyone else is that they are at the extreme end of the spectrum of opinion. Where most economists qualify their support of private enterprise, competition, free trade and reliance on the market mechanism, the monetarists go the whole way and in practice admit few if any qualifications (although they usually accept some qualifications in theory). One qualification, however, that everyone accepts is that some prices are more important than others; some prices are key prices. The price of marmalade, for example, is less important than the price of electricity; the price of hammers is less important than the price of food grains. One cannot list a hierarchy of prices – a key price in one country may be less important in another – but there would be general agreement that the exchange rate, the price of finance capital (or interest rates) and the wage rate in the organised urban sector belong on any list of key prices.

Unfortunately, not only prices in general but many key prices often are distorted in the Third World and public policy, far from correcting market distortions, commonly is the cause of them. Exchange rates may be overvalued for years at a time with a consequent misalignment of domestic and foreign prices of tradable commodities. Producers are discouraged from selling in both the international and domestic markets – in the former because the overvalued exchange rate makes the price of exports relatively high and in the latter because the exchange rate makes the price of competing imports relatively low. The response then is usually to erect a host of barriers to imports to stem the outflow of foreign exchange and thereby to provide strong incentives to replace imports with domestic production. If done indiscriminately, import substitution can lead and in a number of cases has led to poor economic performance, regardless of the indicators used to measure performance [13]. But if it is done selectively as part of a coherent strategy of development, import substitution can provide a strong stimulus to industrialisation [14].

Similar problems arise in the capital market. In a number of countries, particularly in those experiencing a rapid rate of inflation, the real rate of interest in the organised credit market is negative, i.e., the nominal rate of interest is less than the expected rate of price increase. Even when the real rate of interest is not negative, it often is very low and savers therefore obtain a negligible return on their deposits. As a result there is a tendency for savers to transfer their funds from the formal credit market to the informal or curb market where they can obtain a higher rate of return. The credit market thus is bifurcated into two segments, in one of which real rates of interest may be negative and in the other very high.

Borrowers, of course, attempt to raise funds in the formal credit market and take advantage of the low rates of interest. Excess demand for credit occurs in this market and consequently the financial institutions are forced to introduce severe rationing. Those who manage to obtain funds at low rates of interest (and assuming they are prevented from re-lending in the curb market) have an incentive to adopt excessively capital intensive tehniques of production and this in turn has adverse implications for the efficiency of resource allocation, the level of employment in the formal sector of the economy and the distribution of income. Those who do not manage to borrow from the banking system are forced to rely on the curb market and their own savings. In practice it is small and new businesses that are discriminated against and large and well-established businesses that are favoured by credit rationing.

These segmented capital markets have been described as "repressed" by Ronald McKinnon and as "shallow" by Edward Shaw, two monetarist writers whose analysis has been influential [15]. McKinnon and Shaw advocate the removal of the ceiling on the nominal rate of interest in the formal credit market and the general liberalisation of all financial markets. The purpose is to allow the demand and supply of loanable funds to interact freely so that the market will clear in the usual way. The essence of their analysis is depicted in Figure 3.1 below.

Figure 3.1. **THE MARKET FOR LOANABLE FUNDS**

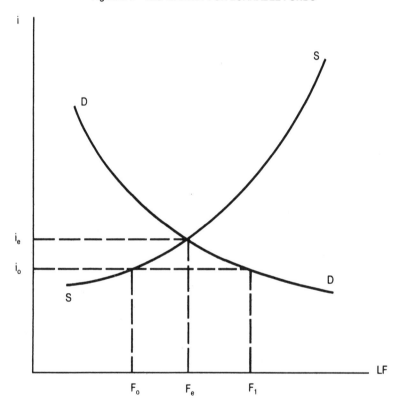

The diagram describes the market for loanable funds in the formal sector. Both the supply (SS) and the demand (DD) for loanable funds (LF) are assumed to be elastic with respect to changes in the rate of interest (i). Initially the rate of interest is suppressed to a level i_0 and this results in a supply of loanable funds from savers of F_0 and a demand from borrowers of F_1. Excess demand of $F_1 - F_0$ is created which is suppressed by rationing the F_0 amount of savings among the F_1 would be borrowers. The market fails to clear.

Financial liberalisation, in contrast, would result in a rise in the rate of interest to its equilibrium level (i_e). This would induce a flow of funds into the market of F_e, partly by encouraging additional saving and partly by encouraging lenders to transfer their funds from the curb market to the formal credit market. At the same time, the higher interest rate would reduce the quantity of credit demanded from F_i to F_e and the market would therefore clear. Interest rates would then reflect the opportunity cost of capital, credit would be channelled to the most profitable investment projects, optimal capital-labour ratios would be adopted on new investment projects and this would create additional employment opportunities and help to improve the distribution of income. Total savings would rise and this would permit a higher level of investment and a faster rate of growth.

The monetarist analysis is therefore attractive. One problem with the analysis is that it assumes that after liberalisation the credit market would clear and rationing would disappear. It is now widely agreed, however, that no matter how liberal is the financial system, the loanable funds market never will clear; banks always will be forced to ration credit [16]. That is, no customer would be allowed to borrow an unlimited amount at the going rate of interest; banks could not afford to allocate credit among customers exclusively by price, by interest rates; quantitative restrictions also are necessary. The reasons for this are, first, that no financial institution (or individual moneylender) can evaluate for certain a borrower's promise to repay; second, in the event of non-repayment or threatened non-repayment, the banks will incur high costs in liquidating assets held as security for the loan or in enforcing the loan contract; and third, even if collateral assets are sold when loans are not repaid, there is no certainty that the full value of the loan will be recovered. Thus even in the best of circumstances credit will be rationed.

An additional problem is that the monetarist analysis assumes the interest elasticity of savings is high. One of the benefits of financial liberalisation is that higher interest rates will lead to more funds being channelled through the formal sector and this will improve the efficiency of the capital market. A second benefit, and one that is crucial in accelerating the growth rate, is that higher interest rates are expected to lead to a higher aggregate rate of savings and this in turn will lead to a faster rate of capital accumulation, more rapid technical change and an acceleration in the rate of growth of output and productivity.

Optimism about the responsiveness of savings to changes in the real rate of interest is based in large part on early interpretations of the effects of the 1966 financial reforms in South Korea [17]. In the two years following the reforms there was a rapid expansion of the formal capital market and this was thought to be due to a surge in savings. More recent work on the South Korean reforms suggests that most of the expansion can be attributed to a switch in savings from the curb market to the formal market and not to a change in aggregate savings behaviour. Research in other countries as well has cast doubt on the assumption that total savings are highly responsive to changes in interest rates [18]. Thus one should be cautious and not expect that financial reforms alone will suffice to promote growth.

Not only is the capital market distorted but it is widely believed that the labour market is highly distorted as well. Wages in the formal sector may exceed the opportunity cost of labour for a number of reasons. First, the public sector may try to behave like a "good employer" and pay its employees relatively high wages. Given the large size of the public sector in many Third World countries this in itself can have a large impact. Second, the high wages in the public sector may spill over into the private sector. The government may act as a "wage leader" and, perhaps unintentionally, set an example that is followed by the large private sector enterprises. Third, foreign companies in particular, perhaps in an attempt to buy a little goodwill in a nationalist and possibly hostile environment, may pay wages above the going rate. That is, foreign owned corporations may wish to be seen to be good employers too. Fourth, the government may introduce minimum wage legislation in the formal sector. Provided the minimum wage is above the market wage and provided it is enforced, this may have the effect of discouraging labour-intensive methods of production throughout a large part of the economy. The possible consequences (depending in part on the wage elasticity of employment) would then be some combination of an increase in open unemployment, an expansion of low-wage employment in the informal sector and a fall in real incomes in that sector, and a general rise in poverty. Finally, wages may be pushed up by trade union activity. This is most likely to happen in those few sectors where labour is strongly organised and where, because of the capital intensity of the process of production, the wage bill is a relatively small portion of total costs. Mining is the most obvious example.

Certainly distortions of the type enumerated can occur, but once again, it is important not to exaggerate. Trade unions typically are weak in the Third World and the proportion of the labour force belonging to a union is small. Minimum wage legislation, although common, often is ignored by employers. Wages in the public sector for unskilled labour commonly are low. The private sector may pay wages that appear to be rather high, but the wage rate may contain a premium for scarce skills or an element intended to reduce labour turnover and hence reduce long-run costs. Thus not every "high" wage represents a "distortion". Still, distortions do exist and it would be wrong to pretend otherwise.

Quite apart from wage rates, interest rates and exchange rates a number of other important prices may fail to reflect social opportunity costs. Typical examples found in the literature include prices of urban sector public enterprises, some of which run at a loss and therefore make a negative contribution to domestic savings. The remedy proposed by monetarists is to raise the price of goods and services supplied by public sector enterprises. Another common example is relatively low prices for food and other agricultural products – or unfavourable terms of trade for the rural sector – with consequent food shortages combined with disincentives to export. Once again, the proposed remedy is to raise prices and improve agriculture's terms of trade.

The harm done by an irrational set of prices is obvious. Indeed there is much truth to Peter Timmer's remark that "getting prices right is not the end of development, but getting prices wrong frequently is" [19]. Except in socialist economies where resources are allocated in physical terms by central planners, a seriously defective price system is likely to result both in a low level of income and a slow rate of growth of income. But if the harm is obvious and the remedy simple, one must ask why so many governments have refrained from doing what is necessary. One possibility is that governments are stupid and ignorant. However given the amount of good advice that is readily available, this is not a plausible explanation. We must look deeper.

A second possibility is that governments have multiple objectives and too few policy instruments with which to achieve their objectives. Governments in effect are trying to kill seven birds with four stones. The demands upon government to achieve rapid growth, to stop inflation, to improve social conditions in urban areas, to help the peasantry, to strengthen the domestic manufacturing sector, to improve the equipment of the armed forces, to repay foreign loans, and so on probably exceeds the resources of the country and certainly exceeds the managerial capacity of the state. Some instruments may not be available to the government for political reasons, e.g., asset redistribution, while others are subject to constraints on their use, e.g., the level of corporate and personal taxation. The government thus is forced to compromise, to use the same instrument to achieve more than one objective and continuously to switch back and forth from one objective to another. At one time the government may use an overvalued exchange rate to moderate inflation and hope that exports will not suffer too much; when the hopes are dashed and exports stagnate, the government may change its exchange rate policy and hope the higher prices of, say, imported food will not provoke riots in the cities. Similarly, at one time the government may have a policy of low interest rates in order to stimulate industrial expansion, but when the liquidity of the financial system becomes intolerable it may have to change course and operate a restrictive monetary policy in order to control inflation. Or again, the prices of public sector enterprises may be set rather high in order to generate profits which can be reinvested for growth or they may be set rather low in order, say, to provide cheap electricity to industry and the urban population.

A third possibility is that government policy has a class bias. That is, it is often argued that governments are not responsive to the needs and wishes of the people as a whole but to the demands of their supporters and the needs of their constituency. Governments are not primarily concerned with the general interest but with particular interests. Viewed in this light, policies which appear to be irrational or misguided may be perfectly intelligible: there is no point in criticising a policy for leading to a misallocation of resources if the purpose of the policy is to allocate resources to specific groups who happen to be in favour with the government. In other words, government policy may be quite efficient in achieving the government's objectives while appearing to be quite inefficient to an outside observer who does not share those objectives. For example, one person's price distortion is another person's device for changing the distribution of income in his favour.

The monetarist avoids these difficult issues in three ways. First, classes and interest groups are ignored. Monetarist theory is based on the assumption that the economy consists of only two groups: (i) atomistic individuals who are independent of and essentially indistinguishable from one another and (ii) an infinity of small firms that operate under conditions of perfect competition. The question of class interests and organised groups simply does not arise. Second, the objectives of government in monetarist theory are exceedingly modest, namely, to provide the legal, institutional and financial framework necessary for a capitalist system to operate. That is all; the market will do the rest, including determining the rate of growth consistent with the savings preferences of households and the investment demands of business. The job of government is merely to provide a monetary system to facilitate exchange and a framework in which contracts can be enforced. If the government interferes with the market by imposing objectives of its own, it will merely introduce distortions and reduce efficiency.

Finally, there is the issue of the distribution of income. Most monetarists close their eyes and hope the issue will go away. Like classes, they would prefer to ignore the subject. If this is not possible, they claim there is no ethical basis for choosing between one distribution of income and another. The philosophers can't agree on what constitutes an optimal distribution of income, so there is nothing the economist can do. It is better to leave things as they are. If, however, a government insists on altering the distribution of income, there is only one proper way to do it, namely, by introducing lump-sum taxes and subsidies. Any other method creates distortions which affect incentives and reduce efficiency and output. The poor might actually lose from a redistribution of income if the fall in total income more than offsets their rise in the share of income. Moreover, since no one has yet figured out a practical way of introducing lump-sum taxes and subsidies, it is better to do nothing.

The trouble for the monetarists is that life is not so simple and these issues will not go away. This will become clearer when we examine the monetarist strategy in practice.

The country which has come closest to following a monetarist strategy of development for an extended period of time is Chile during the ten years 1973-1983 and we shall examine this case in some detail. Chile is unique in that it has followed three quite different development strategies in the last 48 years and each was chosen consciously, not accidentally, by the government of the day. In 1939 the government established a Development Corporation (CORFO) charged with the responsibility for promoting growth, partly by providing long term finance to private sector enterprises and partly by itself establishing public sector industries. Thus began a long period of state intervention in economic affairs and the pursuit of a classic import-substitution industrialisation strategy. This strategy came to an end in 1970 with the election as President of a socialist, Salvador Allende. By that time there were approximately 48 enterprises in the public sector and manufacturing accounted for about a quarter of total output [20]. The new government intended to build on that base and implement what it called a socialist strategy of development.

The socialist strategy however was short lived, coming to an abrupt end in September 1973 with the murder of President Allende, the overthrow of his government and the establishment of an authoritarian right wing military dictatorship. One cannot of course assess what the long-run consequences of a socialist strategy in Chile would have been, but there is no doubt that the transition from an import substituting to a socialist strategy of development was far from smooth. Well over two hundred enterprises were nationalised, the agrarian reform (begun under the previous Christian Democratic government) was sharply accelerated and its emphasis changed to encourage co-operative farming, detailed microeconomic interventions proliferated and, at the macroeconomic level, there was an enormous expansion of public expenditure with no offsetting increase in government revenue. Between 1970 and 1973 government expenditure rose 62.7 per cent in real terms while revenue fell over 18 per cent; as a result, the government's deficit soared from 2.9 per cent of GDP in 1970 to 24.6 per cent in 1973. The strategy certainly wasn't socialist; if anything it was an extreme form of Keynesianism.

Whatever label one puts upon it, the macroeconomic policy was so irresponsible it bordered on madness. At first, however, the gigantic injection of aggregate demand appeared to work. Real GDP increased 9 per cent in 1971, but output fell at an increasing rate in the subsequent two years and by the end of 1973 income per head was lower than in 1970. The state enterprises were operating at a loss and public sector savings were negative. The private sector, frightened by the nationalisation programme, ceased to save and invest. In 1972 net domestic savings were negative and in 1973 both net domestic savings and net domestic investment were heavily negative (–5.2 and –2.5 per cent of GDP, respectively). Capital accumulation, the engine of long-run growth, had come to a halt. Indeed, even worse, the country was consuming its capital. Meanwhile, prices exploded: the annual rate of inflation rose from 22.1 per cent in 1971 to 605.9 per cent in 1973. Clearly, things could not go on like that indefinitely. There was an urgent need for stabilisation.

General Pinochet's new government made four decisions: (*i*) the control of inflation would be its top priority, (*ii*) monetarist policies would be used to stabilise the economy, (*iii*) the stabilisation programme would be merely the initial phase of a long-run development strategy based on monetarist principles and (*iv*) the full power of the military dictatorship would be used to suppress all opposition to the monetarist reforms. Political parties were outlawed, the trade unions were smashed, oppositon leaders and critical intellectuals were tortured, killed, chased into exile or terrified into silence. Few of the checks and balances that restrain governments in democratic countries, and that temper policies and encourage compromise, were present in Chile and hence the monetarist experiment there comes as close to a pure case as one is ever likely to see.

The intellectual foundations for a monetarist strategy had been present in Chile for many years. The economics department of the Universidad Catolica was strongly influenced by monetarist doctrines. Indeed the department had a long-standing agreement with the economics department of the University of Chicago (the seedbed of monetarism in the United States) whereby Chicago regularly sent members of its faculty to teach at the Catolica as Visiting Professors and the Catolica in turn sent all its students destined for graduate training in economics to Chicago. In other words, Chicago had a monopoly both of visiting professorships and of economics research students from the Universidad Catolica. These Chicago-trained economists, known as the Chicago boys, designed and implemented the government's development strategy. They were assisted by a number of overseas advisers who were sympathetic to the regime and its policies, including a very senior economist from the economics department of the University of Chicago who made frequent trips to Chile. In addition, as we have seen, there was a substantial body of professional opinion in academic and international agency circles that the regime could call upon for support [21]. Thus the economic policies adopted by the government were not eccentric. On the contrary, they were widely welcomed and endorsed.

The reforms were introduced swiftly soon after the regime came to power [22]. (See Table 3.1 for a calendar of the major reforms.) Beginning in 1974 a massive privatisation programme was launched. All the banks except the Banco del Estado were returned to private ownership. The state enterprises were sold by auction to the private sector so that between 1973 and the early 1980s the number of companies under CORFO fell from approximately 300 to approximately twelve. There was thus a decisive transfer of wealth, ownership and control from the public to the private sector. The land reform, too, was reversed. About 30 per cent of the land expropriated under the Frei and Allende governments was returned to the former owners. Another 20 per cent was sold by auction to non-rural inhabitants. Many of the remaining peasant farmers were forced either to sell privately or rent out their land to larger landowners because the privatisation of the banking system meant that agricultural credit was no longer available on terms small farmers could afford [23].

Having disposed of the state enterprises, the majority of which were operating at a loss, the government acted to reduce the fiscal deficit. A tax reform was introduced in 1974 under which taxes on wealth and capital gains were abolished and taxes on profits were reduced. Revenues from these taxes were replaced by a value added tax, the coverage of which was widened to include basic consumer goods and the rate of which was increased to a uniform 20 per cent. The following year, when the stabilisation phase of the monetarist strategy was at its peak, public expenditure was sharply reduced. Social expenditure was cut heavily but state investment was cut even more severely, so that the proportion of social expenditure in total government expenditure actually rose. The government cited this fact as evidence of its compassion for the poor! The result of the cutbacks was a fall of 47.4 per cent in real government expenditure between 1973 and 1976 and a decline in the fiscal deficit from 24.6 to 2.3 per cent of GDP [24]. By this time, according to monetarist doctrine, the main source of inflation in the economy – the expansion of the money supply generated by public sector deficits – should have been removed.

Table 3.1 A CALENDAR OF MONETARIST REFORMS IN CHILE

Year	(1) Taxation and public spending	(2) Finance and banking	(3) Foreign trade and capital movements	(4) Exchange rate	(5) Ownership
1974	Taxes on wealth and capital gains eliminated; profits tax reduced; VAT raised to 20% and coverage increased	Interest rates freed; banking regulations relaxed; restrictions on foreign banks removed		-	Banks returned to private ownership; state enterprises auctioned to private sector; land reform reversed
1975	Sharp reduction in public spending	Tight monetary policy	Tariffs reduced; quantitative restrictions removed	-	-
1976	-	-	Withdrawal from Andean Pact	Peso revalued 10%	-
1977	-	-	Tariffs to be reduced to uniform 10% by 1979	Peso again revalued by 10%	-
1978	-	-			-
1979	-	-	Removal of most controls on international capital movements	Fixed exchange rate introduced	-
1980	Private pensions encouraged to replace state pensions	-	-		-
1981	-	-	-		-
1982	-	-	-	Fixed exchange rate abandoned; peso devalued 18%	-
1983	-	-	Tariffs increased to uniform 20%; exchange controls reimposed	Peso devalued and declared inconvertible; dual exchange rate introduced	Government resumes control of 70% of banking sector; assumes responsibility for repayment of private foreign debt.

Financial and banking reforms accompanied the tax and expenditure reforms. Interest rates were freed, banking regulations (including reserve requirements) were relaxed (indeed, the so-called *financieras* initially were allowed to operate with no supervision or regulation), restrictions on foreign banks were removed, and multi-purpose banking was permitted. Finally, the government made it clear that (*i*) it would not guarantee deposits, (*ii*) it would not guarantee the loans of overseas commercial banks and (*iii*) it would not rescue the banks and the *financieras* if they got into trouble, i.e., in effect there would be no lender of last resort. The banks, depositors and creditors were on their own. *Laissez faire* would prevail and financial repression would end [25]. These reforms of 1974 were linked, in 1975, to a tightening of monetary policy.

Also in 1975 a third set of monetarist reforms was introduced, those concerned with foreign trade and international capital movements. In that year quantitative restrictions on trade were removed and a number of Chile's very high tariffs were reduced. The following year Chile withdrew from the Andean Pact and thereby ceased to give trade preferences to the other five Latin American countries who were members of the Pact. In 1977 it was announced that tariffs would be reduced further until they reached a uniform rate of 10 per cent in 1979. Thus in the space of six years Chile moved from a position where tariffs were a simple average of 94 per cent to virtually free trade [26]. The process of creating an open economy was completed in 1979 when most controls on international capital movements were abolished.

Was the monetarist strategy a success? Let us begin by considering the effects of the reforms on the rate of inflation, real interest rates, domestic savings and gross investment. Most of the data to which we shall refer are contained in Table 3.2.

Table 3.2 **INFLATION, INTEREST RATES, SAVING AND INVESTMENT IN CHILE, 1970-1985**

Year	Inflation (% p.a.)	Real interest rate (%)	Net domestic saving (% of GDP)	Foreign savings (% of GDP)	Gross fixed investment (% of GDP)
1970	34.9	n.a.	7.5	1.2	15.0
1971	22.1	n.a.	4.2	2.0	14.6
1972	487.5	n.a.	–0.1	3.9	13.1
1973	605.9	n.a.	–5.2	2.6	12.6
1974	369.2	n.a.	9.4	0.5	17.0
1975	343.2	n.a.	–6.8	5.2	17.7
1976	197.9	n.a.	1.3	–1.7	13.3
1977	84.2	30.0	–1.0	3.7	13.3
1978	37.2	32.5	1.2	5.2	14.7
1979	38.0	5.5	2.5	5.4	14.9
1980	31.2	6.4	4.3	7.1	16.6
1981	9.5	51.9	–2.8	14.1	18.5
1982	20.7	43.4	–10.5	9.9	13.8
1983	27.0	3.9	n.a.	3.8	8.4
1984	19.4	41.4	n.a.	n.a.	12.3
1985	30.7	2.6	n.a.	n.a.	14.2

Sources: Col. (1): For 1970-82: Sebastian Edwards, *op. cit.*, Table 2, p. 227; for 1983-85: IMF, *International Financial Statistics.*

Col. (2): For 1977-80: Sebastian Edwards, *op. cit.*, Table 7, p. 237; for 1981-85, Morgan Guaranty Trust Co., *World Financial Markets*, December 1984 and August 1986.

Cols. (3)-(5): For 1970-82: Banco Central de Chile, *Cuentas Nacionales de Chile 1960-1982*, Santiago, Table 5, pp. 49-50; for 1983: OECD Development Centre data files; for 1984 and 1985: IMF, *International Financial Statistics*.

In September 1973 inflation was running at an annual rate of about 400 per cent. The government deficit, as we have seen, was huge, there were numerous price controls and the black market was flourishing. The initial effect of price liberalisation in October was not to reduce inflation but to produce a great upsurge in prices, so that for the year as a whole the rate of inflation was in excess of 600 per cent. However measures to achieve a balanced budget and reduce the rate of increase in the supply of money soon began to come into effect and by 1974 the deficit had been reduced to 10.5 per cent of GDP and then further to 2.6 per cent in 1975 [27]. Unfortunately, despite this large contraction of aggregate demand the rate of inflation remained exceptionally high, namely, 369 per cent in 1974 and 343 per cent in 1975. The fall in demand led not to a fall in prices but to a fall in output, to a fall in the volume of production, particularly in the industrial sector. (See Table 3.3 for data on growth rates and the level of output per head.) The economy was not responding as monetarist theory predicted. Indeed, in 1975 real output per head fell more than 14 per cent, but prices continued to rise several hundred per cent per annum. Chile behaved as if it were in a fix-price not a flex-price world.

At that point the government altered its tactics and decided to use the exchange rate not to ensure equilibrium in the balance of payments but to combat inflation. Recall that in 1975 trade restrictions were removed and tariffs reduced. Under normal circumstances this would have required a compensating devaluation of the peso in order to prevent the emergence of a large balance of payments deficit. Instead the government *revalued* the peso in 1976 and again in 1977, each time by 10 per cent, and thereby sacrificed the balance of trade to its first priority of reducing inflation. It is hardly surprising that during the period 1976-79 Chile's trade balance swung from surplus to deficit, the dollar value of exports rising 86.9 per cent while the value of imports rose 156.7 per cent. In its own terms, however, the policy worked and inflation fell steadily, reaching 38 per cent in 1979. In that year the government decided to fix the rate of exchange to 39 pesos to the U.S. dollar.

The justification for freezing the exchange rate, and implicitly for ignoring the balance-of-payments crisis, was that from the time tariffs were reduced to a nominal 10 per cent, Chile had become a fully open economy. In such an economy, it was argued, inflation was determined not by changes in the domestic money supply but by changes in the level of world prices plus changes in the nominal exchange rate. We were now back in a fix-price world with a vengeance, back to the theory of the price-specie-flow mechanism of the gold standard of the early decades of the century. The theory meanwhile had been dressed up and renamed the monetary theory of the balance of payments, but the assumed mechanism of adjustment was much the same: an outflow of foreign exchange reserves would lead to a contraction of banking liquidity and credit and this in turn would lead to a reduction in prices.

In a sense the theory worked. The rate of inflation continued slowly to fall, but after 1979 so too did the rate of growth of output per head. Indeed in 1982 Chile plunged into a deep depression and per capita production fell by nearly 16 per cent. Business had been squeezed almost to death by high interest rates, high indebtedness and falling sales, output and employment. The economy was on the verge of disaster.

The ending of financial repression and the encouragement of *laissez faire* in banking led as expected to a rise in interest rates. But no one, least of all the monetarists, could have expected that interest rates would rise so high or remain so high for so long. Real rates of interest (in this case, the current rate of interest minus the current rate of inflation) fluctuated wildly and in some years were 40 or 50 per cent a year. Only in 1979 and 1980, when foreign lending began to increase after the removal of controls on international capital movements, and again in 1983 and 1985 did real interest rates fall to reasonable levels. In other years, however, real rates of interest were 30 per cent or more. The real return on capital was not of course as high as this and consequently investment suffered. Speculators were active in the market, but no investor interested in long-term fixed capital formation could afford to borrow on such terms.

As can be seen in the last column of Table 3.2 gross investment remained very low, never rising even as high as 20 per cent of GDP. More alarming, as we shall see below, the whole of the net addition to the stock of fixed capital was financed with foreign savings. Chile was entirely dependent on overseas borrowing for its capital accumulation. Furthermore, the amount of accumulation that occurred was exceedingly modest: from 1974 to 1982 average net investment was only 5.5 per cent of gross domestic product. This clearly was far too low to sustain an acceptable rate of growth of income per head over the long run.

Monetarist theory would lead one to hope that the very high real rates of interest in Chile would stimulate savings and thereby permit a high rate of investment. Alas, aggregate net savings in the country were extraordinarily low and there is no evidence at all that the elasticity of savings with respect to changes in real interest rates is positive, let alone that savings are highly responsive to real rates of return in the organised financial market. In fact, during the nine year period from 1974 to 1982 net savings on average were minus 0.3 per cent of GDP! Numerous explanations have been put forward for the failure of the savings rate to rise. Sebastian Edwards argues that aggregate savings were low because revenues from the sale of state enterprises were used by the government to finance current government expenditure [28]. That is, private savings were offset by negative public savings. Arnold Harberger believes that the sale of public assets to the private sector increased the wealth of the rich to such an extent that they no longer had any reason or desire to save [29]. Presumably those who did not benefit from the transfer of assets or the appreciation of their wealth were too poor to save. Others have argued [30] that the availability of large scale foreign borrowing, particularly in 1981, enabled foreign savings to be substituted for domestic saving. Whatever the explanation, it is evident that the monetarist strategy of development failed to raise the savings rate.

Let us next consider the effects of the development strategy on the rate of growth, the level of per capita output and the well being of the working population. As can been seen in the first column of Table 3.3, real output per head in 1985, after twelve years of monetarist policies, was lower than in 1970 and it was only fractionally higher than in the final year of the Allende administration. In only three years, namely 1979 to 1981, did real output per head exceed that of 1970; in the other nine years of the Pinochet administration for which we have data per capita output and income were lower than in our base year. Moreover the rate of growth under the monetarist strategy was highly unstable. Indeed in four years per capita output actually fell, in two years severely. Rapid growth occurred in only one period, from 1977 to 1980, and this represented a cyclical upswing from a very depressed level. Over the period as a whole the trend rate of growth of output per head was zero.

The poor growth performance cannot be blamed on external factors. It is true that the price of copper, Chile's major export, fluctuated quite a bit and fell fairly steadily after reaching a high point in 1980, but the lowest points were in 1971 and 1972, i.e., during the time of the Allende administration. The monetarist experiment began during a period of high prices for copper. This can readily be seen in Figure 3.2. More important, the monetarist strategy was strongly supported by external resources. In 1981 and 1982 foreign capital equivalent to 14.1 and 9.9 per cent of GDP, respectively, flowed into the country. And over the period 1974-1982 the average annual inflow of foreign resources was 5.45 per cent of GDP. This more than compensated for a deterioration in the terms of trade. The truth of the matter is that on balance the external environment was favourable for the monetarist experiment.

Table 3.3 **INDICATORS OF POVERTY AND PROSPERITY IN CHILE, 1970-1985**

Year	Real GDP per capita (Index: 1970 = 100)	Rate of growth of GDP per capita (%)	Unemployment rate (%)	Real wage rate (Index: 1970 = 100)
1970	100.0	0.2	3.4	100.0
1971	107.1	7.1	3.8	129:0
1972	104.0	–2.9	3.1	114.5
1973	96.6	–7.1	4.8	64.4
1974	95.9	–0.7	8.3	60.0
1975	82.1	–14.4	15.0	63.9
1976	83.6	1.8	17.1	76.5
1977	90.2	8.0	13.9	81.3
1978	96.0	6.4	13.7	82.9
1979	102.2	6.5	13.4	83.7
1980	108.3	6.0	12.0	96.2
1981	112.6	3.9	9.0	109.5
1982	94.8	–15.8	20.0	107.9
1983	92.6	–2.3	19.0	98.2
1984	96.9	4.6	18.4	n.a.
1985	97.7	0.8	17.0	n.a.

Sources: Cols. (1) and (2): For 1970-82: Banco Central de Chile, *Cuentas Nacionales de Chile 1960-1982,* Santiago, Table 2, p. 40; for 1983-85: OECD Development Centre data file.
Col. (3): ILO, *Yearbook of Labour Statistics.*
Col. (4): Sebastian Edwards, *op. cit.,* Table 3, p. 229; for 1983: Banco Central de Chile, *Economic Report of Chile 1983,* Santiago, 1984.

Unfortunately the burden of stagnation of per capita income was not spread evenly throughout the country. The rate of unemployment soared from 4.8 per cent of the labour force in 1973 to 17.1 per cent in 1976. It then fell to a low of 9.0 per cent in 1981 before more than doubling in the following year. In 1985 it still was as high as 17 per cent, three and a half times higher than in the worst year of the Allende period. The average rate of unemployment during 1974-1985 was 14.7 per cent. These figures, bad as they are, obscure the true position.

In 1975 the government felt it had no alternative but to intervene in the labour market in an attempt to reduce unemployment, then running at 15 per cent. Contrary to all monetarist principles, the government didn't allow the market to work freely but instead created a "minimum employment programme" (PEM). In its first year the PEM employed 3.8 per cent of the labour force; in 1982, the last year for which we have data, it employed 9.2 per cent of the labour force. Over the entire eight years, 1975-1982, about 5.4 per cent of the labour force worked for low wages on public works projects for the PEM [31]. If the PEM workers are added to the unemployed one gets a better idea of the extent to which the economy was failing to use productively its available labour power. One also gets a clearer idea of the suffering ordinary men and women had to bear.

Figure 3.2. **THE PRICE OF COPPER**

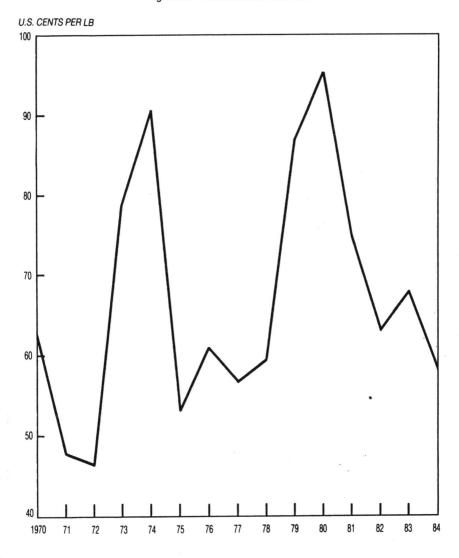

U.S. CENTS PER LB

Even those with a job suffered a great deal. Real wages in 1974 were 40 per cent below the level of 1970. They then rose steadily although they have never regained the peak achieved in 1971. Even so, they did rise. The main reason for this is that in 1979 the government intervened in the labour market in a major way again. The labour law of that year required employers in future to adjust nominal wages to at least cover the rise in inflation that had occurred since the last wage agreement was reached. Given that the rate of inflation fell in 1980 and 1981, this implied that real wages would rise in those two years. The labour law was adjusted in 1982, but in the eyes of monetarists the damage had been

57

done: a key price had been converted into a fix-price. Indeed, one author blames the 1982-83 depression on the fact that the government had interfered with the market mechanism and converted the labour market and the market for foreign exchange into fix-price markets [32]. If things go wrong, it seems the monetarists always have an explanation: prices weren't right!

Given the high unemployment, the large numbers working for very low pay on the PEM and the decline in real wage rates compared to 1970-72, it seems obvious that the distribution of income must have become far more unequal. Sebastian Edwards, however, is prepared to concede only that there was a "small deterioration" between 1970 and 1979 [33]. Others will perhaps take a less optimistic view. Be that as it may, even Edwards agrees that "there is little doubt that the distribution of wealth worsened during the period: the privatization of the banking sector and public enterprises resulted in the creation of a small number of conglomerates that controlled a large number of assets" [34]. The inescapable conclusion is that as regards growth and distribution the monetarist strategy of development has been a disaster for the ordinary people of Chile.

It has also been a failure in its own terms. The signs of failure first appeared in 1977 when a major bank, the Banco Osorno, came close to bankruptcy. Despite its doctrine of non-intervention, of allowing market forces to operate freely and of encouraging *laissez faire* in banking the government intervened. It rescued all depositors and, despite all previous pronouncements to the contrary, it also in effect guaranteed the private foreign debts of the Banco Osorno. Henceforth foreign lenders could reasonably assume they were insured against default. There was no risk in lending to Chile and consequently the discipline of the market vanished.

Foreign lending, as we have seen, rose rapidly and over 90 per cent of the lending was channelled to the private sector. By the early 1980s domestic savings had become negative, investment had remained low, the balance of payments position had become unsustainable and the economy was heading for a depression. It was inconceivable that the private sector would be able to service its overseas debts. Indeed by late 1981 the financial system was in serious trouble and again, monetarist theory notwithstanding, the Central Bank acted as lender of last resort and provided massive amounts of credit to the private banking system. By then, however, the entire development strategy was doomed and economic policy was thrown into reverse.

In 1982 the fixed exchange rate was abandoned and with it the "monetary theory of the balance of payments". The peso was devalued 88 per cent with inevitable implications of faster inflation. The devaluation, however, was insufficient and led merely to intense speculation against the currency. Once again the government had to abandon its previous policy and intervene in the market. In 1983 tariffs were doubled (to a uniform 20 per cent), the peso was devalued a second time and declared inconvertible, exchange controls were imposed and even a dual exchange rate was introduced. The main exchange rate was altered yet again in 1984, bringing the total depreciation since 1981 to 229 per cent. Perhaps the most bitter pill of all for the theorists, in 1983 in order to avert a collapse of the system the government stepped in and took control of 70 per cent of the domestic banking sector. That is, in effect the government re-nationalised the banking and financial system. The wheel had turned almost a full circle back to Allende and a state-run financial sector.

There was one major difference this time round, however. The Pinochet government not only nationalised the financial sector, it also nationalised private debts, both domestic and foreign. As in the case of the Banco Osorno, the government guaranteed repayment of overseas loans. Doubtless this decision came as a great relief to the foreign commercial banks that had provided the money and to the Chilean business class who borrowed it, but it represented a flagrant violation of the government's own rules and it imposed an immense burden on the general public. Of course it took an immense burden off the shoulders of the rich. And that indeed is the explanation. As Carlos Diaz-Alejandro observed, "when most everyone (who counts) is bankrupt, nobody is!" [35].

The government's development strategy had a pronounced class bias from the very beginning and despite the failure of the strategy as a whole, the property-owning classes on whom the regime relied for support gained significantly. The government began by selling state enterprises to the rich. The buyers paid for the assets by borrowing abroad through the commercial banking system. There never was a realistic prospect of repaying the debt, given that the funds were not used to increase the productive potential of the economy and given that in fact the long-run rate of growth of output per head was zero. Never mind. When the inevitable occurred and the financial system disintegrated, the government bailed out the rich and relieved them of their debts. The foreign creditors were more than happy since they escaped the consequences of wholesale default, a default which they had every reason in law and justice to expect. Instead of placing the cost of adjustment where it belonged – on the Chilean conglomerates who freely entered into debt and on the foreign bankers who happily loaned the vast sums of money – the burden was thrust onto the backs of the working class.

The people as a whole were left in 1984 with the obligation to service a foreign debt of $17,266 million, thanks to the government agreeing to guarantee repayment in their name. The servicing of this debt was equivalent to 15.2 per cent of the country's gross national product and 54.6 per cent of its exports of goods and services! Yet only 8.8 per cent of the debt was the result of borrowing by government; 91.2 per cent was private debt. The private debtors, however, were given relief. Astonishingly, the rich were left with the former state enterprises, which in effect they had received as a virtual gift. No doubt the new owners laughed all the way to the (state run) bank.

Monetarism in Argentina

There are a number of similarities between the monetarist experiments in Argentina and Chile. In both countries monetarism was introduced by a military dictatorship. In both countries the armed forces seized power after overthrowing a left wing or populist government that had seriously mismanaged the economy. In both, monetarism was associated with the suppression of civil liberties and state violence on a massive scale and in both countries monetarism failed as a strategy of economic development.

The background to the story of monetarism in Argentina begins with the rule of Juan and Isabel Peron from 1973 to 1976. In the early years of the 1970s real output per head in Argentina grew between 0.8 and 1.8 per cent a year (see Table 3.4). This was not a spectacular performance but it did represent genuine progress. The Peronist regime, however, attempted simultaneously to accelerate the pace of expansion and to distribute a higher share of the national income to the working class. The main instrument used by the government to achieve these objectives was public sector expenditure. This can be seen from the fact that the public deficit rose sharply from 4.4 per cent of GDP in 1973 to 10.3 per cent in 1975, the last full year of the Peron administration.

At first the policy seemed to work: growth of per capita GDP did accelerate briefly, reaching 3.7 per cent a year in 1974, and the share of wages rose dramatically. In 1972 the share of wages was only 81.9 per cent as high as it had been in 1970, but by 1975 the wage share had recovered to 95.8 per cent of the 1970 level. That is, the share of wages rose by 17 per cent in just three years. The situation quickly proved to be unsustainable, however.

Table 3.4 OUTPUT, PRICES AND THE SHARE OF WAGES IN ARGENTINA, 1970-1985

Year	Real GDP per capita (1970=100)	Growth of GDP per capita (per cent per annum)	Rate of inflation (per cent per annum)	Real deposit rate of interest (per cent per annum)	Share of wages in GDP (1970=100)
1970	100.0	1.37	n.a.	n.a.	100.0
1971	101.4	1.76	n.a.	n.a.	98.8
1972	103.2	0.83	58.9	n.a.	81.9
1973	104.0	1.62	61.2	n.a.	86.4
1974	105.7	3.70	20.2	n.a.	94.5
1975	109.6	-3.29	189.9	n.a.	95.8
1976	106.0	-1.65	443.0	n.a.	64.3
1977	104.3	4.19	176.2	66.2	60.8
1978	108.6	-5.30	171.4	-46.2	63.5
1979	102.9	5.23	163.2	-64.2	69.1
1980	108.2	-0.91	100.0	-12.0	77.5
1981	107.2	-7.95	104.0	18.7	73.2
1982	98.7	-6.17	165.2	1.0	69.8
1983	92.6	1.16	344.2	63.6	n.a.
1984	93.7	1.49	826.7	-268.7	n.a.
1985	95.1	-6.38	672.2	n.a.	n.a.

Source: Cols. (1) - (4): International Monetary Fund, *International Financial Statistics Yearbook*, various years.
Col. (5): Joseph Ramos, "Stabilization and Adjustment Policies in the Southern Cone, 1974-1983", *Cepal Review*, No. 25, April 1985, Table 3, p. 93.

First, prices exploded. In 1974 consumer prices increased (by the standards of Argentina) at the modest rate of 20.2 per cent a year. The following year the rate of inflation was 189.9 per cent and in 1976 it was 443 per cent. Second, per capita GDP far from rising, fell steeply by 3.3 per cent in 1975 and by another 1.7 per cent in 1976. Third, the share of wages collapsed in 1976 to only 64.3 per cent of what it had been six years earlier. And finally, the polity began to tear itself apart. There was unprecedented disorder and terrorist groups of both the extreme right and extreme left perpetrated numerous acts of violence, killing and wounding many innocent persons and destroying property. Something was bound to give way and it was no surprise when in March 1976 the military under General Videla took power.

The new government acted quickly to discard the economic policies of the Peronist regime in order to implement a radically new monetarist strategy of economic development. A large number of trade and financial reforms were introduced in 1976 and 1977. The very heavy taxes on exports were reduced, quantitative restrictions on imports were removed and tariffs were cut in a series of steps in 1976, 1977 and 1978. All of these measures were intended to open up the economy, to alter the set of relative prices facing buyers and sellers so that they would conform more closely to world prices and to move quite sharply in the general direction of free trade. The exchange rate, however, was used not to stimulate exports or control the balance of payments but to dampen the rate of inflation. That is, adjustments to the rate of exchange were allowed to lag behind domestic price increases and as a result the exchange rate soon became seriously overvalued.

Government tax and expenditure policies were tightened up in order to bring the public sector deficit under control. At the same time steps were taken to eliminate financial repression by encouraging greater competition among financial institutions and by freeing interest rates so that they could reflect the forces of supply and demand [36]. Multiple branch banking was permitted, free entry into the banking sector was allowed and, as in Chile, supervision of the banks by the authorities practically disappeared. Interest rates, having been controlled by the Central Bank for more than three decades and having been fixed at negative real rates, rose sharply and consequently loanable funds were attracted from the informal or parallel credit market (the *mercado de aceptaciones*); indeed, real deposits in the financial system rose by 20 per cent in just two years.

Foreign borrowing was the fuel that fed the expansion of the financial system. Between 1976 and 1982 the external public debt rose from 4.6 to 32.1 per cent of GNP and at the end of the period Argentina's debt was $24 593 million. None of this foreign capital was used to finance investment. Indeed, gross investment declined precipitously from 22 per cent of GDP in 1976 to 13 per cent in 1983. The World Bank estimates that over the period 1979-82 capital flight accounted for 65.1 per cent of gross capital inflows [37], and most of the rest probably was used to increase military expenditure and supplement private consumption. Undoubtedly the overvalued exchange rate contributed to the outflow of capital but the generally depressed economic conditions provided few incentives for domestic investment. Speculation was more attractive than productive activity. Moreover, the supply of credit in the economy increasingly was based on foreign monetary assets: between 1972 and 1981 foreign credit rose from 32.6 to 51.7 per cent of the total credit in the country [38] and foreign credit increased from 10.7 to 27.4 per cent of GDP.

Even so, the initial impact of the reforms appeared at the time to be favourable. Per capita output rose by more than 4 per cent in 1977, but the rise was short-lived and the trend immediately turned downwards so that by the end of 1983, when the military regime fell, per capita GDP was 13.7 per cent lower than it had been at the beginning of 1978. More success was achieved by the monetarist policies in reducing the rate of inflation. In 1976, as we have seen, prices rose 443 per cent. The rate of increase declined sharply in 1977 (to 176.2 per cent a year) and continued to decline although at a more moderate rate for the next three years. In 1980, the best year, prices rose by exactly 100 per cent. Thereafter the rate of inflation began to accelerate again and by 1984 prices were spiralling out of control. In that year consumer prices rose by 826.7 per cent.

The early years of the monetarist strategy also saw an improvement in the accounts of the public sector. The government's deficit was sharply reduced and in the four-year period from 1977 to 1980 the deficit averaged just under 3.1 per cent of Argentina's GDP. In 1981, however, the deficit rose three-fold to 11.3 per cent of GDP and remained very high at 7.5 per cent of GDP in 1982 [39]. Changes in the relative size of the deficit were matched by changes in the rate of inflation: when the deficit contracted so did the rate of price increase and when the deficit expanded, inflation accelerated. There is little doubt that in Argentina during this period variations in public expenditure led to variations in aggregate demand and these, in turn, were responsible for variations in the rate of inflation.

The financial reforms did have their intended effect of raising interest rates. The real deposit rate of interest became less negative during the course of the reforms and achieved positive levels during 1981 to 1983. Real lending rates were, of course, substantially higher than the deposit rate of interest. It is evident from the data in Table 3.4, however, that real rates of interest fluctuated wildly and hence the financial environment faced by investors was unstable and unpredictable. The ending of "financial repression" seems to have produced financial chaos. The real rate of interest paid by borrowers was about 35 per cent on average and obviously bore no relationship to the real rate of return on physical investment in plant and machinery. Far from contributing to greater economic efficiency, the monetarist reforms led to greater inefficiency and eventually to a collapse of the system.

Signs of failure of the strategy first appeared in 1979, three years after the reform programme started, when the economy slipped into a recession. There were numerous factors contributing to the downturn in economic activity but four elements stand out as particularly important [40]. First, there were the very high real rates of interest which discouraged capital formation. Second, there was the overvalued exchange rate which resulted in a deterioration in the current account of the balance of payments, rising imports and greater competitive pressure on domestic producers. Third, there was a large increase in real wages and in unit labour costs. As can be seen in the last column of Table 3.4, the share of wages in GDP rose by 27.5 per cent between 1977 and 1980 after having fallen sharply between 1975 and 1977. Finally, the combination of cheap imports, high interest rates and rising labour costs squeezed profits, made it more difficult for companies to repay their loans to the banking system and pushed some enterprises into bankruptcy. This in turn precipitated a crisis in the financial sector.

As early as 1978 it was obvious that the financial system was in trouble and that the reforms were not working as anticipated. In that year there were fourteen bank failures, compared to only two the previous year (see Table 3.5). In 1979 the number of bank failures rose again, to 20. Then in 1980 a major crisis erupted. On March 28th of that year the most important private bank in Argentina, the Banco de Intercambio, was forced to close. This led to a collapse of confidence in the banking system as a whole and the greatest "run" on the banks in the history of Argentina. The Central Bank tried to stop the runs by providing advances to financial institutions in difficulty, but even so, by the end of the year 28 banks had gone into liquidation. In 1981 the number of bank failures fell by half, to 14, but then more than doubled again in 1982 to 29. That was the end of the monetarist experiment. In

1982 the monetary authorities took control of a large part of the financial system, effectively nationalising it, and reimposed controls over interest rates.

Table 3.5 **INDICATORS OF FINANCIAL COLLAPSE IN ARGENTINA, 1977-1983**

Year	Real deposits with the financial system (Index: 1977 = 100)	Bank failures (number)
1977	100.0	2
1978	102.7	14
1979	120.5	20
1980	118.5	28
1981	113.1	14
1982	82.3	29
1983	78.5	n.a.

Source: Ernesto V. Feldman, "La Crisis Financiera Argentina: 1980-1982. Algunos Comentarios", *Desarrollo Economico,* Vol. 23, No. 91, October-December 1983, Table 1, p. 454 and Table 2, p. 455.

The ultimate effect of monetarism was not to liberalise the banking system and open it up to private competition but to force the state to exercise even more control than previously. Equally paradoxical, the effect of monetarism was not to "monetise" the economy and channel more loanable funds through the formal credit market but to demonetise the economy. There was a massive flight of depositors from the financial system such that between 1979 (the peak year) and April 1983 the volume of real deposits with the financial system declined by nearly 35 per cent (see Table 3.5). Seldom can a strategy of development have been so poorly conceived or produced such terrible results. At the end of the experiment the economy was in ruins, state terrorism was rampant (far worse than the terrorism that preceded the military takeover) [41] and the country was at war.

The days of the military regime were numbered although in fact the government held on until December 1983. Ironically, it was not the destruction of the economy that caused the junta to lose public support, nor was it the horrendous abuse of human rights. The military regime lost power because it lost the Falklands war. The government abandoned monetarism a year before the public abandoned the government, but it is clear that during the six years of the monetarist strategy of development economic performance was remarkably bad and as a result most people were substantially worse off than they had been in 1975.

Conclusions

The experiences of Argentina and Chile have taught us a number of things about a monetarist strategy of economic development. First, getting prices right isn't enough. *Laissez faire* by itself is likely to damage economic performance – efficiency as well as growth – unless it is accompanied by sensible macroeconomic policies. The fundamental lesson of Keynes remains valid: if left to its own devices a capitalist economy is likely to perform far below its potential. Governments must therefore assume responsibility for the overall management of the economy, not only through monetary policy but also through tax and expenditure policy and the control of the government deficit. One can't leave everything to the market. This point is now recognised by Ronald McKinnon, one of the most distinguished monetarist economists, who writes that "maintaining macroeconomic control in the transition is more difficult than I initially imagined" [42].

Second, it is now known that getting prices right isn't as easy as perhaps was once thought. There are limits to what is possible even in totalitarian states and military dictatorships. Governments, all governments, regardless of their ideological colouration face constraints. The Chilean government found it impossible to abstain from interfering in the labour market – to temper unemployment, to create a minimum number of jobs, to put a floor on real wages – and both the Chilean and Argentinian governments felt compelled to intervene in the financial market and bail out the banks. *Laissez faire* is not a practical political proposition.

One of the reasons for this, third, is that prices are not politically neutral. They affect the distribution of income. That is, a change in relative prices inevitably implies a transfer of real incomes and those who lose by such a transfer can be expected to resist if they can. Speaking of price distortions and attempts at liberalisation in Africa, Brian Van Arkadie rightly points out that "typically, the disequilibrium arose because the national authorities could not meet all the competing needs placed on the system" [43]. The "inefficient" prices the monetarists deplore often arise not from stupidity on the part of the government but from a vain attempt to satisfy incompatible and excessive demands for higher incomes. It is not very helpful in such circumstances to say that an attempt to distribute more income than the economy is capable of producing is bound to be self-defeating; presumably the government knows this but is unable to find an economic solution to what is essentially a political problem. Thus in the absence of either a tight monetary policy or an incomes policy, both of which require either a political consensus or a powerful government, a devaluation of the exchange rate, for example, is likely to lead to higher nominal wages and accelerated inflation rather than to a change in the relative price of tradables.

Fourth, it isn't always obvious what is the "right" price. For example, if the state is responsible for a high proportion of total investment, liberalisation of the capital market might have very little effect on investment allocation. Similarly, if the state is deeply involved in marketing agricultural commodities, as in many African countries, a change in the internal terms of trade may have little effect on agricultural production, unless specific measures are taken to ensure that prices at the farm gate rise. Of course a monetarist would say that these are not arguments against relying on the price mechanism, they are arguments in favour of privatisation. Fair enough, but then one must make it clear that a monetarist strategy presupposes particular institutional arrangements.

In any case, fifth, experience has shown that free markets will not necessarily produce the "right" prices. That is, the prices generated by the market mechanism may be "distorted" and fail to reflect social costs and benefits. The extraordinarily high real rates of interest in Chile and Argentina are a case in point. They couldn't possibly have reflected the social opportunity cost of capital; indeed real interest rates in those two countries were highly distorted by intense and long-sustained speculative activity. Related to this, sixth, is the fact that the prices produced in liberalised markets, whether "right" or not, may not produce the desired or expected effects.

Laissez faire in the financial markets was carried to such an extreme in Chile and Argentina that the authorities ceased to supervise the banking system. Far from producing a set of price signals leading to an efficient allocation of resources, *laissez faire* led to the collapse of many of the most important financial institutions in the two countries. Curiously, the governments of both countries failed in their first duty to a monetarist strategy, namely, to maintain a viable currency system and exchange economy. In Argentina the economy actually became partially demonetised when real deposits in the banking system declined by more than a fifth between 1977 and April 1983. More generally, in none of the southern cone countries of South America did freeing interest rates and the relaxation of controls lead to financial "deepening" and a rise in the private savings ratio. Long-term bank lending did not occur, the stock exchanges failed to develop as institutions channelling savings into productive investment, and a long-term bond market failed to emerge. Instead, all that happened was that government owned development corporations and other public institutions that did provide long-term finance were destroyed. Carlos Diaz-Alejandro puts it succinctly when he comments that policies intended to free domestic capital markets resulted in "widespread bankruptcies, massive government interventions or nationalisations of private institutions, and low domestic savings" [44]. This was precisely the opposite of what was expected.

Seventh, it is now clear that flexibility of prices is a mixed blessing. In principle it is desirable that prices should be free to adjust to changes in supply and demand, but if freedom of adjustment is in practice associated with rapid oscillations of real prices, this can be harmful, particularly if a number of key prices are affected. Unpredictable exchange rates and interest rates, for example, increase uncertainty, raise costs, make it difficult for enterprises to plan investment and production and consequently lower efficiency and growth. A fix-price element in the economy would in fact contribute to stability. It is the "real" price, however, that should be fixed, not the nominal one. Most observers agree, for instance, that it was a mistake in Chile in 1979 to fix the nominal exchange rate and allow the real exchange rate to vary unpredictably [45]. It would have been far more sensible to concentrate on stabilizing the real exchange rate so that clear signals were sent to those engaged in international commerce. Others have argued that in a highly inflationary environment savers should be offered an asset with a guaranteed zero real rate of interest (such as indexed savings accounts) alongside currency (with its zero nominal rate of interest) [46]. Something similar in spirit already exists in several advanced capitalist economies such as the United Kingdom where indexed bonds are readily available. The effect of these bonds is to set a floor to the real rate of interest in the financial markets.

On top of this, eighth, experience has shown that controls on international capital movements should be retained. This is especially important when economic policy is going through a transition to a more liberal regime, for it is during the transition that risks and uncertainty are high and the temptation for savers to move their capital abroad is great. Even in "normal" periods, however, when the economy is relatively stable, there may well be a need to prevent domestic savings leaking abroad. This became evident in the first half of the 1980s when high real interest rates in the United States acted as a magnet attracting funds from all over the world, from poor countries as well as from other rich ones.

Lastly, we have learned that monetarist theory, despite the intellectual appeal of its powerful simplicities, is deeply flawed. Its simplifying assumptions are so unrealistic that the edifice of theory constructed upon them cannot safely be used as a guide to policy. In fact in those few countries which have attempted to follow a monetarist strategy of development the results have been disastrous and many millions of people have been forced to endure much hardship.

NOTES AND REFERENCES

1. We shall return to the subject of Latin America's departure from orthodox doctrines during the 1930s in Chapter 5.

2. See Alejandro Foxley, *Latin American Experiments in Neo-Conservative Economics*, Berkeley, University of California Press, 1983.

3. Milton Friedman, *Capitalism and Freedom*, Chicago, University of Chicago Press, 1952; F.A. Hayek, *The Road to Serfdom*, London, Routledge and Sons, 7th ed., 1946; M. Friedman and R. Friedman, *Free to Choose*, Penguin, 1980.

4. See for example John Rawls, *A Theory of Justice*, Oxford, Clarendon Press, 1971.

5. For a polemical statement of the monetarist position see Deepak Lal, *The Poverty of Development Economics*, Institute of Economic Affairs, Hobart Paper No. 16, London, 1983.

6. M. Friedman and R. Friedman, *op. cit.*, p. 13.

7. See B. Greenwald and J.E. Stiglitz, "Externalities in Economies with Imperfect Information and Incomplete Markets", *Quarterly Journal of Economics*, Vol. CI, No. 2, May 1986; J.E. Stiglitz and A. Weiss, "Credit Rationing in Markets with Imperfect Information", *American Economic Review*, Vol. 71, No. 3, June 1981.

8. J.E. Stiglitz, "The New Development Economics", *World Development*, Vol. 14, No. 2, February 1986.

9. Kenneth Arrow and Gerard Debreu, "Existence of an Equilibrium for a Competitive Economy", *Econometrica*, Vol. 22, No. 3, July 1954.

10. Kaushik Basu, "One Kind of Power", *Oxford Economic Papers*, Vol. 38, No. 2, July 1986.

11. J.R. Hicks, *Capital and Growth*, Oxford, Clarendon Press, 1965, Chapter VII.

12. Nicholas Kaldor, "Limits On Growth", *Oxford Economic Papers*, Vol. 38, No. 2, July 1986, p. 194.

13. See Chapter 4.

14. See Chapter 5.

15. Ronald I. McKinnon, *Money and Capital in Economic Development*, Washington, D.C., Brookings Institution, 1973 and Edward S. Shaw, *Financial Deepening in Economic Development*, New York, Oxford University Press, 1973.

16. J.E. Stiglitz and A. Weiss, *op. cit.*

17. Ronald I. McKinnon, *op. cit.*

18. See, for example, Alberto Giovannini, "Saving and the Real Interest Rate in LDCs", *Journal of Development Economics*, Vol. 18, Nos. 2-3, August 1985.

19. Peter Timmer, "Choice of Techniques in Rice Milling in Java", *Bulletin of Indonesian Economic Studies*, Vol. 9, July 1973, p. 76.

20. CORFO owned 46 enterprises and there were about a dozen more responsible to other government agencies, including the state copper corporation (CODELCO) and the national petroleum enterprise (ENAP).

21. There is a large literature on applied monetarist economics. Two prominent studies are Anne O. Krueger, *Liberalization Attempts and Consequences*, Cambridge, Mass., Ballinger Publishing Co., 1978 and Bela Balassa, ed., *Development Strategies in Semi-industrial Economies*, Oxford, Oxford University Press, 1982. Anne Krueger was until recently a high official at the World Bank; Bela Balassa combines an academic position with being a senior consultant to the World Bank. The World Bank has many employees and its staff encompasses a range of views, but there is no doubt that the official view of the Bank has shifted far to the right since Robert McNamara ceased to be President.

22. For two contrasting reviews of the Chilean reforms see Ricardo Ffrench-Davis, "The Monetarist Experiment in Chile: A Critical Survey", *World Development*, Vol. 11, No. 11, November 1983 and Sebastian Edwards, "Stabilization with Liberalization: An Evaluation of Ten Years of Chile's Experiment with Free-Market Policies, 1973-1983", *Economic Development and Cultural Change*, Vol. 33, No. 2, January 1985. Both articles contain numerous references to the literature.

23. In addition, many *campesinos* were expelled from the land after farms were returned to the former owners or sold to new owners. Hardship among the rural poor during this period was severe.

24. Sebastian Edwards, *op. cit.*, Table 2, p. 227.

25. For a brilliant analysis of the financial reforms in Chile see Carlos Diaz-Alejandro, "Good-Bye Financial Repression, Hello Financial Crash", *Journal of Development Economics*, Vol. 19, No. 1/2, September-October 1985.

26. Ricardo Ffrench-Davis, *op. cit.*

27. Sebastian Edwards, *op. cit.*

28. *Ibid.*, p. 238.

29. Arnold C. Harberger, "Observations on the Chilean Economy, 1973-1983", *Economic Development and Cultural Change,* Vol. 33, No. 3, April 1985, pp. 451-2. Speaking of the period 1976-81, he says private savings were low "because of the tremendous appreciation ... in the real value of private wealth (shares, real estate, etc.)."

30. See, for example, Ricardo Ffrench-Davis, *op. cit.*

31. The percentage of the labour force employed each year on the PEM was as follows:
    1975 3.8   1979 4.4
    1976 6.6   1980 5.7
    1977 5.6   1981 4.6
    1978 3.6   1982 9.2
    Source: Sebastian Edwards, *op. cit.,* Table 3, p. 229.

32. Sebastian Edwards, *op. cit.* Also see Arnold Harberger, *op. cit.*

33. *Ibid.,* p. 230.

34. *Ibid.*

35. Carlos Diaz-Alejandro, *op. cit.,* p. 18.

36. See Roque B. Fernandez, "La Crisis Financiera Argentina: 1980-1982", *Desarrollo Economico,* Vol. 23, No. 89, April-June 1983.

37. IBRD, *World Development Report 1985,* Oxford University Press, 1985, p. 205.

38. *Ibid,* p. 60.

39. Joseph Ramos, "Stabilization and Adjustment Policies in the Southern Cone, 1974-1983", *Cepal Review,* No. 25, April 1985, Table 2, p. 90.

40. See Ernesto V. Feldman, "La Crisis Financiera Argentina: 1980-1982. Algunos Comentarios", *Desarrollo Economico,* Vol. 23, No. 91, October-December 1983.

41. See Ernesto Sabato, ed. *Nunca Mas,* the report of the National Commission on the Disappeared, Buenos Aires, 1984.

42. Ronald I. McKinnon, "The Order of Liberalization: Lessons from Chile and Argentina", in Karl Brunner and Allan H. Meltzer, eds., *Economic Policy in a Changing World,* Amsterdam, North Holland, 1982.

43. Brian Van Arkadie, "Some Realities of Ajdustment: An Introduction", *Development and Change,* Vol. 17, No. 3, July 1986, pp. 379-80.

44. Carlos Diaz-Alejandro, *op. cit.,* p. 1.

45. Arnold Harberger, however, is an exception. He believes that fixing the nominal exchange rate was not a major policy mistake. See his "Observations on the Chilean Economy, 1973-1983", *loc. cit.*

46. Carlos Diaz-Alejandro, *op. cit.*

Chapter 4

THE OPEN ECONOMY

One of the oldest propositions in economics is that unrestricted international trade is beneficial to all participating countries [1]. Indeed, it has been argued in the Heckscher-Ohlin theory that trade is a partial substitute for international mobility of labour and capital and under very restrictive assumptions it has been shown that factor prices (wage rates and the rate of profit) will become equal in all countries under a free trade regime [2]. International trade in such conditions acts as a powerful engine of growth, raising real incomes everywhere and narrowing the difference in incomes between rich countries and poor. Trade alone cannot eliminate inter-country differentials in per capita income – that would require a fully open world economy in which labour and capital were free to move without restrictions – but it could go a long way towards reducing world poverty and international inequality. Even under seemingly unrestrictive assumptions it can readily be demonstrated that a country is better off when participating in world trade than under a closed economy.

This attractive outcome is in principle possible whenever cost (or price) ratios in a country differ from those in the world at large. These ratios may differ for many reasons: because the labour force is unevenly distributed among countries, because of differences in human capacities, skills and capabilities, because natural resource endowments vary, because specific factors are unequally spread throughout the world, because historical accidents, government policy or individual initiative have influenced the volume and composition of the existing stock of capital, or because consumption preferences or tastes differ. In other words, differences in either supply or demand conditions can lead to profitable trade.

In a closed economy the pattern of consumption is necessarily identical to the pattern of production, but once a country is open to international trade the composition of output can diverge markedly from the composition of final and intermediate demand. This gives rise to two sources of gains from trade. First, there are the gains to consumers that arise from opportunities to exchange goods and services at price ratios different from those prevailing under autarky. Second, there are the gains that arise from opportunities to specialise in the production of those goods and services in which a country has a comparative advantage. These gains however will not be realised unless an economy is flexible, i.e., unless factors of production are mobile and move quickly and at little cost from one sector to another and unless factor prices are responsive (upwards and downwards) to shifts in supply and demand [3]. Not all Third World countries can meet these conditions.

Resources often are specific to a particular industry and cannot quickly and costlessly be transferred to another. Zambia cannot convert her copper mines into fields of maize. Mexico cannot convert her petroleum deposits into manufactured goods. Côte d'Ivoire, Sri Lanka and Ghana cannot easily and quickly expand their palm oil, tea and cocoa plantation sectors or convert them to other crops without undertaking large investments which, in some cases, have long gestation periods. In situations such as these, not uncommon in small countries, factors of production are rather immobile because of the specificity of the natural resource endowment. This immobility is reinforced when, as can occur, expenditure on the training and education of the labour force and on investment in physical capital are low.

In countries where the rate of capital accumulation in the broadest sense is low, it is difficult to alter the composition of output and hence to take advantage of the potential gains from international trade. Once a particular structure of production has become established, labour and capital tend to become immobile because they become incorporated into the productive process in the form of durable and specific skills and equipment. This stock of labour skills and capital equipment cannot readily be transferred from one industry to another. This is why in practice economies seldom are able to change the composition of output by shifting the stock of capital and human resources from contracting to expanding activities, and when they attempt to do so it invariably is costly and painful. Instead structural change usually is more successful when it occurs simultaneously with growth by channelling new investment and the new entrants to the labour force into the expanding activities. It is increments to the stock of capital and human resources that give an economy flexibility, not the size of the stock itself and it is for this reason that the ability to exploit opportunities created by international trade is integrally related to a country's rate of growth and above all to its rate of investment. Thus in this view it is growth which enables a country to harvest the "static" or allocative gains from trade.

This view is now widely accepted and provides the theoretical justification, for instance, for structural adjustment loans to Third World countries attempting to open their economies or to respond to changes in their international terms of trade. In the absence of growth, adjustment requires not only that resources be sectorally mobile but also that factor prices be flexible. If in addition to factor immobility, real factor prices are "sticky", changes in relative international commodity prices may result in a lower level of output (and income) rather than in a change in the composition of output. It is easy to see how this could happen.

An exogenous change in a country's terms of trade implies that the price of at least one commodity has fallen relative to all other prices. The industry in which this occurs is now less competitive, less profitable than before. The marginal revenue product of factors used in that industry, and hence the demand for factors of production in that industry, will decline and if the industry is to remain commercially viable the prices of factors used in that industry also must decline. If they are inflexible downwards and resist market pressures, the output of the industry will contract and the least profitable enterprises will go out of business. The extent to which production falls will of course depend on cost conditions in the industry. For example, if production takes place under conditions of rising marginal cost, then as output contracts, costs will fall and a point may eventually be reached at which the industry is once again competitive albeit at a reduced size.

It is not difficult to imagine that the losses incurred from a fall in output and a rise in unemployment in the contracting industry could outweigh the gains from trade arising from the possibility of exchanging commodities at different price ratios. In such circumstances the overall gains from trade would be negative, i.e., the country would suffer a net loss of real income. Paradoxically, given relative commodity and factor prices and the level of output and employment in the country, it pays to trade although under the assumptions postulated trade lowers welfare. This is not of course an argument for autarky but it does qualify in a major way the classic case for free trade. The classical view, based on full employment, given resources and zero cost of adjustment, can be misleading. Structural change typically occurs not by reallocating a given stock of factors of production and sliding along a given "production possibilities curve" but by directing investment into the relatively more profitable activities and gradually withdrawing or failing to renew resources in the less profitable ones. Structural transformation thus is largely a function of the rate of investment and the cost of adjusting to changes in relative prices is inversely related to the rate of growth.

Government intervention and endogenous distortions

While it may be true that free trade almost always is better than no trade, it does not follow that more trade is better than less trade. Indeed numerous arguments have been put forward in favour of tariffs and more generally in favour of protecting domestic industry from foreign competition. Many of the most important arguments centre on the presence of what Jagdish Bhagwati has called endogenous distortions, i.e., defective price signals originating from market imperfections [4].

The price distortions can originate from a variety of sources. For example, the private rate of time discount may be higher than the social rate of discount. Private entrepreneurs may have too short a time horizon and require too high a rate of profit with the result that many socially profitable investments are not undertaken. Or the domestic capital market may be poorly developed and fail to perform efficiently its roles of providing an attractive outlet for savings and a source of finance for investment. As a result, the overall level of savings may be depressed and the composition of investment may be sub-optimal. Alternatively, there may be imperfections in the labour market. The social return on skilled labour, for instance, may be high yet private businessmen may be unwilling to invest in training facilities out of fear that their trained labour then would be bid away by competitors. Individual workers might be unable to pay for their own training (because of their low income) and unable to finance it by borrowing (because of an inability to provide security for the loan to the banks). Lastly, for a variety of reasons, the real cost of labour to industry may exceed its opportunity cost in agriculture and consequently there may be a pervasive obstacle to industrialisation.

Considerations such as these have long led economists to advocate tariff protection for infant industries in economically underdeveloped regions of the world [5]. The infant industry argument for protection however is not as straightforward as it seems. First, protection raises prices to consumers and this imposes a real cost, a real loss of welfare on the economy. Of course, it is expected that eventually the infants will grow up and become competitive and prices will fall, after which point the economy will reap substantial benefits. These eventual benefits, however, may be long delayed and hence, second, both costs and benefits should be discounted and compared with the help of a social discount rate. Protection cannot be justified by an expectation that sometime in the indefinite future the protected activity will become internationally competitive and consumers will be able to purchase the commodity at world prices. Indeed, only if the present value of expected future benefits exceeds the present value of the costs of protection is a tariff justified, and no industry is likely to pass this test (given a sensible discount rate) unless it can become profitable in, say, twenty years or less. That is, the infant industry argument for protection is really an argument for temporary, short-term assistance and not an argument for high tariffs maintained over a long period of time.

Third, it is not clear that the infant industry argument is about tariffs at all. There may be good reasons for governments to intervene and assist industrial development in the early stages, but it is not obvious that tariff protection is the best form of assistance. Tariffs may help to compensate for the original market imperfections which created the price distortion and discouraged industrialisation, but at the same time they introduce a distortion of their own, namely a bias in favour of sales in the domestic market and against sales in export markets. This bias in general is undesirable [6] in that assistance is provided only to that portion of a firm's output that is sold domestically rather than to the whole of the firm's output.

The optimal policy in the presence of endogenous distortions is to intervene directly at the point of distortion [7]. Thus if the distortion arises from underinvestment in training, the optimal solution is not a tariff but either government provision of training facilities or a direct subsidy to privately organised training schemes. If the market imperfection takes the form of an industrial wage rate that is greater than the opportunity cost of labour, the best policy is a general subsidy to the wages of unskilled labour. This subsidy should be financed out of tax revenue, ideally raised in a non-distorting way, such as through a lump-sum tax. Again, if the price distortion originates in an imperfection in the capital market, the optimal policy is to tackle the distortion at its source through taxes and subsidies as appropriate.

In general, tariffs will seldom be the best policy to cope with endogenous distortions. Other forms of subsidies and taxes are likely in principle to be preferable. In practice however the ideal may be unattainable either because the taxes needed to finance the subsidies introduce distortions of their own, or because institutional factors which inhibit industrialisation also inhibit the implementation of theoretically optimal government policies or because the balance of political forces in the country is such that it is impossible to obtain consent for optimal tax-cum-subsidy policies whereas a programme of industrial protection by tariffs is acceptable. When optimal policies genuinely are not feasible for any of these reasons, then tariffs make sense. But it must be recognised that in such cases they are only a second-best policy.

Policy-imposed distortions

Many of the price distortions one encounters in Third World countries (and in the industrialised countries too) are not "endogenous" but are policy-imposed. That is they are a consequence of government action rather than "natural" phenomena demanding corrective action by government. It is not difficult to compile long lists of policy-induced distortions in commodity markets (e.g., tariffs), in capital markets (e.g., credit rationing) and in the labour market (e.g., minimum wage laws) [8]. Some analysts perhaps inadvertently give the impression that almost all government policies introduce distortions which reduce efficiency, the level of real incomes and the rate of growth of output. Progressive income taxes allegedly reduce the incentive to work, social security programmes increase the cost of labour and discourage employment, low interest rates reduce the efficiency of investment, the level of savings and the rate of growth, etc. The implication seems to be that governments should do nothing or at least as little as possible, that markets should be allowed to work their magic without interference, that *laissez faire* should prevail. Above all, governments should adopt a policy of free trade.

Quite apart from the fact that governments may have different objectives from those of the free traders – for instance, distributional objectives – there is a question of the empirical significance of policy-imposed distortions and in particular the welfare costs of tariff protection. A number of studies have been made of tariffs in the industrialised countries and even the most ardent free traders recognise that "estimates of the cost of protection in developed countries are generally low, hardly reaching one per cent of the gross domestic product" [9]. That is, the static or once-for-all loss of income arising from tariffs is equivalent to a few months' growth.

The first study of the costs of protection in a Third World country was conducted by Arnold Harberger. He estimated that in Chile in the mid-1950s the welfare costs of external distortions of various sorts (tariffs and quantitative restrictions) were "less than 2.5 per cent of national income" [10]. Joel Bergsman estimated that in Brazil in 1967 the misallocation of resources attributable to tariff protection was "less than 1 per cent of G.N.P." [11]. Other studies indicate that in Third World countries with high rates of protection, the welfare costs range between 3.7 per cent in the Philippines in 1965 to 9.5 per cent in Brazil in 1966 (prior to the subsequent reduction in tariffs) [12].

These orders of magnitude – even the very high estimate for Brazil in 1966 – do not suggest that the static costs of resource misallocation are serious when seen from the perspective of a country's long-term economic development. If the case for an open economy depended on demonstrating that tariffs impose a heavy but once-for-all loss of real income, the case would not be very persuasive. Fortunately, the case for export-oriented development does not rest on such slender grounds but instead is based on the view that the more open is an economy the faster is its rate of growth likely to be.

The evidence for this proposition will be considered below, but before doing so it is important to note that there are specific difficulties that are likely to arise during the transition from protection to an export-oriented development strategy. First, the short-run demand for foreign exchange after liberalisation almost certainly will be considerable. One effect of a lengthy period of import and foreign exchange controls is to create an enormous pent up demand for foreign exchange which if suddenly released can cause severe balance-of-payments difficulties. Second, there is a problem of how to induce confidence that the decontrolled system will last. If confidence is lacking there will be intense short-run speculative demand for foreign exchange that will aggravate the problems created by the long-run pent up demand. Thus unless exceptionally large amounts of foreign exchange are made available, e.g., from foreign loans, liberalisation should occur gradually on a step by step basis.

Exports and growth

It is important to avoid confusion about the meaning of such phrases as an open economy, an export-promoting strategy of development and export-oriented growth. Our concept of an open economy is one which permits the free flow of factors of production internationally as well as the free flow of goods and services. At this stage of the argument however we shall concentrate on freedom of trade. The degree of openness has little to do with the contribution of exports to aggregate demand and cannot properly be measured by, say, the share of exports in gross domestic product. Both India and the United States, for example, have a low ratio of trade to GDP, but India is a semi-closed economy whereas the United States is an open economy. Similarly, both Jamaica and Côte d'Ivoire have a high trade ratio, but only Côte d'Ivoire has adopted an export-promoting strategy of development. In general, large countries will tend to have low trade ratios and small countries will tend to have high ones, so the share of exports in GDP tells one very little about the type of development strategy that has been followed. Changes in the trade ratio over time may indicate whether an economy has become less or more influenced by international economic forces, but even here one must be careful not to infer changes in economic policy from changes in trade ratios.

The trading side of an open economy, then, refers to a country's policy or development strategy and not to the composition of demand. That is, it refers to the structure of incentives people face, not to the structure of output. A few writers characterise the open economy as one in which incentives are biased in favour of exports. Anne Krueger speaks of "a general bias toward exports" and says that export promotion "has consisted of encouragement to exports, usually beyond the extent that would conform" to the marginalist rules for an efficient allocation of resources [13]. Again, she claims that "export-oriented regimes have fairly realistic exchange rates and provide at least as much, if not more, incentive to sell abroad as to sell domestically" [14].

Anne Krueger's definition of an export-oriented development strategy has the advantage of being symmetrical to a protectionist strategy of development, in that the set of incentives is biased towards import substitution in the latter and towards export promotion in the former. It is however an extreme position and the majority of economists who advocate export-oriented growth are concerned that incentives should not be biased against exports rather than that they should positively favour them [15]. Jagdish Bhagwati, for example, makes it clear that by an export-promoting strategy he means one in which the effective exchange rate for exports is not significantly different from the effective exchange rate for imports. The intention is to eliminate bias against exporting, "thereby restoring the incentive to export as much as to produce for the home market" [16]. This seems to be the most widely accepted view and is the one we shall adopt. That is, by an open economy we mean one where the effective exchange rate is neutral as between selling abroad or at home and hence does not contain an implicit subsidy to exports.

The question then becomes what are the effects of international trade upon the rate of growth in such an economy. This is the reverse of the issue discussed at the beginning of the chapter, where it was argued that a rapidly growing economy with a high rate of accumulation is better able to take advantage of whatever opportunities exist from trading abroad. Of course trade and growth may interact: a high rate of growth of national output may help to stimulate trade and a high rate of growth of world trade may encourage more rapid expansion of national production. Both sides of the equation are therefore interesting.

Max Corden has lucidly analysed the effects of trade on growth and we shall follow him quite closely [17]. First, assuming resource mobility and factor price flexibility, there are the static gains from trade identified by Ricardo. These raise the level of per capita income and this rise in per capita income then is compounded by any given rate of growth. The static allocative gains from trade may be substantial, particularly if exporting permits Third World countries to exploit economies of scale in situations where because of low income per head the domestic market is small [18]. A mass of consumers, as someone once said, is not the same thing as a mass market, and even in populous Third World countries the demand from the domestic market may be insufficient to enable economies of large scale production to be exploited in many manufacturing processes. In such circumstances, exporting enables a country to enjoy the benefits of increasing returns.

Second, assuming the marginal propensity to consume is not unity, the rise in the level of income will be accompanied by an increase in investment. This higher investment, in turn, will raise the rate of growth of output indefinitely, so long as the economy does not run into diminishing returns to capital. Third, trade lowers the relative price of imports and of domestically produced substitutes for imports. If capital goods happen to be relatively import-intensive, as is likely in many Third World countries, foreign trade will reduce the cost of investment relative to consumption. Assuming there is some price substitution effect, this will push up the level of investment and rate of growth further.

Fourth, an open economy is likely to have a lower incremental capital-output ratio. That is, the productivity of investment is likely to be higher in an open economy than in a protected one. The improved allocation of resources that accompanies an export-promoting strategy of development will almost certainly raise investment efficiency. In addition, an open economy is likely to be in a better position to import improved technology from abroad, and this too will help to lower the incremental capital-output ratio. To the extent that growth depends primarily on the rate of accumulation of capital and on the productivity of investment, a lower incremental capital-output ratio will lead to an acceleration in the rate of aggregate economic growth.

Lastly, international trade affects the distribution of income. In general an export-promoting strategy of development will shift the distribution of income in favour of the factors of production employed in the export sector. If the savings propensities out of factor incomes differ, and if factor proportions differ among sectors, this will have repercussions on investment and growth. It is usually assumed that exports use intensively the relatively abundant factor of production. This implies that in labour abundant Third World countries, an export-oriented strategy would result in a higher share of wages in national income and presumably in a more equal distribution of income. If the propensity to save of workers is less than that of property owners, the rate of savings, investment and growth could decline.

One of the great advantages of an export-oriented strategy in a labour-abundant economy is that it enables a country to concentrate growth in employment-intensive activities [19]. This can have a major impact on raising real wages and improving the distribution of income. If for example the capital-labour ratio in the import substituting industry M is x times larger than in the export industry Y, a switch of a given amount of investment from M to Y will enable the economy to create (x-1) times as many jobs. In some semi-closed countries x is a very large number whereas in open economies it tends to be small. Let us consider the range in two extreme cases. Thus in Taiwan, an open economy, the capital-labour ratio in transport equipment is only 2.6 times that in the processed foods industry [20]. But in Bangladesh, where the range of intra-industry factor proportions is much greater, the capital-labour ratio in the government-owned engines and turbines sub-sector is 45.4 times as large as that in textiles [21].

Not all Third World countries export labour-intensive products. Some countries, notably in Latin America and Africa, export land intensive or natural resource intensive products. If land owernship is concentrated, as in the latifundia dominated parts of Latin America, an export-oriented strategy of development will raise land rents and increase inequality in the distribution of income. That is, it will be biased in favour of the rich. A similar thing will occur in the mineral exporting countries if the mining sector is controlled by transnational corporations [22]. Most of the mineral rents will accrue as profits to foreign-owned companies and be repatriated abroad. The country may benefit rather little from the expansion of its export sector: gross domestic product may rise rapidly while gross national product rises slowly.

In some countries, e.g., Peru, Chile and Argentina, populist governments have reacted against the income distributional implications of an export-oriented strategy by penalising the export sector and protecting national industry. In cases such as these the bias of government policy against exports did not always, or did not just reflect "export pessimism"

– a fear that world market conditions would be unfavourable for the country's exports, it also reflected a bias against the class of large landowners and against foreign corporate investors in mining [23]. This indirect political attack on privileged groups was, however, a decidedly second-best policy since it did little to improve the well-being of the poor or change the overall distribution of income while it inflicted much damage on the most productive sectors of the economy. First-best policies would have included a land reform (as in Taiwan), intelligent and strong bargaining with transnational corporations over the distribution of mineral rents (as in Botswana) or nationalisation of natural resources (as in Algeria).

Nationalisation of the mining and petroleum sector or skilful bargaining with transnational corporations over the level of corporate profits tax, royalty payments and the exchange rate applied to mineral exports do not directly improve the distribution of income among citizens of the country. These measures shift the distribution of rents from foreign companies to the government of the host country. What then happens to the distribution of income depends on what the government does with the revenue. Often in fact the main beneficiaries are civil servants, the armed forces, the small labour aristocracy employed in the minerals sector and the urban middle class; the rural poor in particular often receive few benefits [24]. Nonetheless, even in the worst case of some mineral-rich economies, it is better to tackle distributional problems directly rather than to attempt to resolve them indirectly by biasing the entire development strategy against the high productivity sector.

Arithmetical implications of an open economy

It may be useful to quantify some of the assumptions that have been made in order to obtain an impression of the possible numerical significance of an open economy strategy. Let us assume the rate of growth depends only on the investment ratio and the incremental output-capital ratio. The rate of growth of the population is constant at 2.0 per cent a year.

Initially the economy is protected. Investment accounts for 15 per cent of domestic product and the incremental output-capital ratio is 0.33. The rate of growth of total product is therefore 4.95 per cent a year and average incomes per head rise 2.95 per cent a year. After five years average income per capita will have increased 15.7 per cent (see the first column of Table 4.1).

The improvement in resource allocation following the adoption of an open economy is assumed, perhaps a little optimistically, to raise domestic product by 5 per cent. The "initial" level of per capita income in the open economy should therefore be raised correspondingly. Let us assume the marginal propensity to save is 20 per cent. As a result the investment ratio rises by one percentage point, to 16 per cent of domestic product. Assume further – because of improved resource allocation, greater competition and imports of foreign technology – the incremental output-capital ratio rises by 12 per cent, i.e., from 0.33 to 0.37. As a result of all these changes the rate of growth of total product accelerates to 5.92 per cent a year and the annual growth of income per head rises to 3.92 per cent. After five years per capita income will be 27.3 per cent higher than it was in the year before the new strategy was introduced.

The cumulative effect of relatively modest changes in assumptions is substantial. In the arithmetic model in Table 4.1, the adoption of an open economy strategy of development increases the aggregate rate of growth by nearly 20 per cent and the rate of growth of income per head increases by nearly 33 per cent. After only five years the level of per capita income is 10 per cent higher than it otherwise would have been. If in addition to these effects on growth the open economy helps to improve the distribution of income – by increasing competition and reducing monopoly rents, by increasing the employment-intensity of development, and by raising the share of wages in national income – the impact on the incidence of poverty could be considerable.

Table 4.1 **THE ARITHMETIC OF EXPORT-LED GROWTH**

	A protected economy	An open economy
1. Initial level of per capita income	100.00	105.00
2. Investment ratio	0.15	0.16
3. Incremental output-capital ratio	0.33	0.37
4. Rate of growth of dometic product (= 2 x 3) (per cent per annum)	4.95	5.92
5. Population growth rate (per cent per annum)	2.00	2.00
6. Growth of per capita income (per cent per annum)	2.95	3.92
7. Level of per capita income after five years	115.65	127.26

The empirical evidence, however, does not provide much support for the expanded neo-classical model presented in Table 4.1. In an early study Alfred Maizels claimed to find an association between the growth of exports and the growth of per capita income in developing countries [25], but subsequent research has cast doubt on some of his findings. If the export sector were merely an enclave, one would expect export growth to have no effect on the growth of the rest of the economy and its effect on the growth of GDP as a whole would simply reflect changes in the ratio of exports to GDP. On the other hand, a dynamic export sector could attract resources from the rest of the economy (savings, skilled labour) and possibly retard its growth and even reduce the standard of living of those left behind. The correlation between export growth and the growth of non-export GDP would in this case be negative. Only if there were well-developed linkages between the export sector and the non-export sectors would one expect the growth of exports to provide a stimulus to overall development. Thus in theory the association between the expansion of exports and the rest of the economy could be negligible, negative or positive depending on circumstances.

Even if rapid growth of exports does lead to a rapid growth of GDP, it does not follow that GNP also will grow rapidly. Much depends on the "returned value" in the export sector. If a high proportion of export proceeds remains in the domestic economy as wage payments, profits of domestically-owned enterprises, taxes and royalties, and as payments to domestic suppliers of material inputs and services, then there is likely to be a positive correlation between the expansion of exports and of the economy as a whole. Gross national product will expand in parallel with gross domestic product. But if "returned value" is low, the expansion of GDP may not be mirrored in an expansion of GNP and the correlation between export growth and overall development may be weak.

In effect, this is what the empirical research has shown. Using rank correlation analysis on cross-section data, Michael Michaely found a positive association between the change in the ratio of exports to GNP and the growth of per capita GNP for 41 countries in the period 1950-73, but the correlation was found "not to exist at all" for the poorest 18 countries in his sample [26]. Similar mixed results have been found in other cross-section studies [27]. Helleiner's study of poor countries in Africa shows that the relationship between export orientation and the rate of growth of output in the poorest countries is extraordinarily weak and there is a strong suggestion from his work that the positive effect of exports on overall

76

growth does not begin until a minimum level of development has been achieved and strong intersectoral linkages have been established [28].

The hypothetical results in Table 4.1 are based entirely on manipulating assumptions and the actual consequences of an open economy strategy in the real world are much more complex than is suggested by a simple model. In any case, as was stressed earlier, by an open economy we mean policy neutrality as regards exports, and this does not necessarily imply rising export ratios or even a rapid growth of exports. Hence the results of empirical studies of the type referred to above must be interpreted cautiously. They may tell us little about the virtues of an open economy strategy. Our own statistical findings will be mentioned later, but first let us consider how the world economy has performed in the last 25-35 years.

Growth and change in the world economy

The international economy after 1950 experienced a remarkable transformation. Tariff barriers were reduced (particularly in the industrialised countries), quota restrictions on trade were virtually eliminated in all but a few countries, barter trade was abandoned (except for some trade with the socialist countries) and restrictions on the international movement of capital were gradually reduced (again, particularly in the industrialised countries). World trade consequently surged ahead, assisted by the rapid growth of total output in Europe and Japan.

Europe and Japan were not exceptional, however. On the contrary, per capita income rose almost everywhere, often quite swiftly, with the important exception of parts of sub-Saharan Africa, where living standards declined after 1973. World trade grew even faster than total world output and consequently in most countries the ratio of exports to gross domestic product increased, sometimes dramatically [29]. Over the entire period from 1950 to 1985 the quantum of world exports grew nearly 6.5 per cent a year (see Table 4.2). This thirty-five year period however should be divided in two because in 1974, following the steep rise in oil prices during the previous year, there was a sharp break in the trend rate of growth.

Table 4.2 **GROWTH IN THE VOLUME OF WORLD TRADE, 1950-1985**
Per cent per annum

Simple exponential trend estimates	
1950-85	6.45
1950-74	7.07
1974-85	3.12
Kinked exponential trend estimates	
1950-74	7.23
1975-85	4.04
Log quadratic estimate of trend	
1950-85	6.45
acceleration coefficient a	−0.04

a) This is the c in the equation $\ln Q_t = a + bt + ct^2 + u_t$.
Source: Calculations based on IMF data.

There are several ways of describing the change in the trend rate of growth of world exports that occurred in 1974 and these are presented in Table 4.2. The least satisfactory way of describing the data is with a log quadratic equation. This has the disadvantage from our point of view of implying a constant rate of change (acceleration or deceleration) of the rate of growth itself whereas we know that the change occurred abruptly after the first sharp rise in oil prices. The log quadratic equation does however show that when looked at as a whole, there was a tendency for the rate of growth of the volume of world trade to decline.

The usual way to describe a change in trend is to divide the full period into sub-periods and estimate separate exponential trend rates of growth for each sub-period. Applying this method it is estimated that world trade grew nearly 7.1 per cent a year until 1974 and then began to grow only 3.1 per cent. That is, the rate of growth fell by much more than half. There is however a disadvantage in comparing sub-periods in this way in that the estimated trend lines are likely to be discontinuous and this can lead to anomalies. Kinked exponential models, in contrast, impose linear restrictions so as to eliminate the discontinuity between sub-periods and usually provide the best basis for comparing one sub-period with another [30]. Applying this method, with a kink in 1974, it is estimated that the trend rate of growth of exports from 1950 to 1974 was over 7.2 per cent a year and then fell to 4.0 per cent a year during the following decade.

The share of the Third World in total trade fell markedly (see Table 4.3). Between 1950 and 1970, according to the IMF, the share declined from 37.9 to 22.7 per cent, i.e., by 40 per cent! The initial decline was due to the collapse of commodity prices at the end of the Korean War, but the share of the Third World also fell substantially between 1960 and 1970. Thereafter the share rose, but in 1985 the Third World still accounted for only 27.7 per cent of total world exports, using the IMF's definition. This was well below the share they enjoyed thirty-five years earlier. These figures illustrate the fact that the developing countries as a group failed to participate fully in the expansion of international commerce during the period when commerce was expanding most rapidly. Some Third World countries did of course participate fully – indeed their trade grew faster than the world average and consequently their individual shares of world trade actually increased – but in the majority of poor countries exports grew much less rapidly than the world average. This relatively poor performance was due in part to bad luck, and in particular to a concentration of exports on primary products for which demand increased slowly, but equally important was government policy that was biased against exporting. In addition, in the case of textiles and some agricultural products there were important barriers to trade imposed by the industrialised countries.

Table 4.3 **SHARE OF DEVELOPING COUNTRIES IN WORLD EXPORTS, 1950-1985**
Per cent

	IMF	UNCTAD
1950	37.9	n.a.
1955	27.2	25.9
1960	28.9	22.0
1965	25.9	20.1
1970	22.7	18.5
1975	29.2	24.7
1980	32.8	28.8
1985	27.7	24.0

Sources: Col. (1): Calculations based on IMF data. Col. (2): UNCTAD, *Handbook of International Trade and Development Statistics,* Supplement 1986. The IMF data exclude the Soviet Union and Eastern European countries and this has the effect of raising the share of the Third World in "world" trade.

Ironically, it was only when the rate of growth of world trade began to decline that the Third World as a whole was able to improve its relative performance and halt the fall in its share of exports. Liberalisation came too late to do much good. This does not imply that it did no good – for the situation today might have been even worse had policies of indiscriminate protection continued – but the fact remains that many Third World countries jumped on the trade bandwagon about the time the band stopped playing and the wagon slowed down. Indeed a number of countries – the oil exporters, some mineral exporters and many countries in sub-Saharan Africa – have experienced negative growth of exports since 1973 or 1974.

The bias against exports of many Third World countries cannot in general be explained by adverse movements in the terms of trade (see Figure 4.1). Indeed the terms of trade of non-oil producing Third World countries were fairly constant between 1960 and 1974, the year in which there was a break in the trend rate of growth of world exports [31]. From 1974 onwards, however, the terms of trade began to decline and between the peak in 1974 and the trough in 1981 the fall was just over a third. The main problem was of course the rise in oil prices in 1973 and 1979. But there was more to it than that. The deceleration in international trade had a greater effect on the prices of goods exported by Third World countries – particularly on primary commodities – than on the prices of goods exported by the industrialised countries and this further contributed to the deterioration of the terms of trade of non-oil producing developing countries. The result was that much of the Third World suffered not only from a slowly growing volume of trade but also from falling relative prices.

In 1986, however, oil prices collapsed and as a result the terms of trade of many non-oil producing Third World countries improved. Energy exporting countries, in contrast, experienced a substantial loss of national income per head. Indeed average living standards fell between 10 and 20 per cent in a number of countries including Algeria, Malaysia and Venezuela. Thus energy exporters suffered a large fall in real income while energy importers continued to suffer from historically poor, even if slightly improved, terms of trade.

Many countries reacted to the slowing down of world trade and to the deterioration in their terms of trade by borrowing in the world capital markets. That is, they attempted to compensate for the growing shortage of foreign exchange by increasing their foreign indebtedness with the commercial banking system. At the time this was a sensible decision from both a national and international point of view [32]. It enabled the Third World to continue its economic expansion, albeit at a slower rate, and it helped to counteract deflationary pressures in the international economy arising from restrictive demand management policies in the United States, Western Europe and Japan. Had the Third World been unwilling to borrow world trade would have grown even less rapidly than it did and the world recession would have been even worse.

Borrowing by the Third World was facilitated by two factors. First, funds for lending by the commercial banks were readily available because of the large balance of payments surpluses of the petroleum exporting countries. The oil price increases of 1973 and 1979 created huge savings which the OPEC countries were unable to invest productively in their own economies and which therefore had to be recycled and invested abroad. Second, real rates of interest were very low and often negative. They were much lower than the rate of growth of export earnings and hence it could reasonably be assumed that debt servicing would present no problem. In the event, alas, this reasonable assumption proved to be wildly optimistic.

The first column of Table 4.4 contains data on nominal world interest rates as measured by the London interbank offer rate (LIBOR) on three month United States dollar deposits. The actual rate paid by Third World borrowers was of course much higher than this, but movements in LIBOR rates are likely to have been similar to movements in commercial bank lending rates. It can be seen from the Table that nominal interest rates tended to rise until 1974, fell sharply in the mid-1970s, rose steeply after the second oil shock in 1979 and gradually declined after 1981. By 1986 nominal interest rates had returned to about the same level as 1977. This was made possible because the pronounced disinflationary policies pursued by the advanced industrial economies after 1979 achieved their intended effect of reducing the rate of inflation; this then allowed the central banks to lower nominal interest rates.

Figure 4.1. **TERMS OF TRADE OF NON-OIL PRODUCING DEVELOPING COUNTRIES**

INDEX 1980 = 100

Real interest rates, however, followed a very different path from nominal rates. As far as a Third World debtor is concerned, what matters is the nominal rate of interest that must be paid on the foreign debt after adjusting for changes in export prices. In the second column of Table 4.4 we include annual percentage changes in the US dollar price of exports from developing countries. Prices rose moderately until world inflation accelerated and petroleum prices exploded in the 1970s. Then, when the world recession struck in the 1980s, the dollar prices of developing country exports fell. As a consequence real interest rates rose to unprecedented heights.

80

If one considers the period from 1963 onwards, it can be seen that real international interest rates fall into three sub-periods (see Figure 4.2). During the 1960s real rates of interest were modest and compatible with the real rate of growth of world trade. That is, interest rates were never higher and usually much lower than the underlying trend in the rate of growth of export earnings. This was followed by the decade of the 1970s in which real interest rates varied enormously from one year to another and the average real rate was negative. Between 1974 and 1975 the real LIBOR swung from minus 94.5 per cent to plus 4.8 per cent, a change of 99.3 percentage points! The average real LIBOR during 1970-80 was minus 14.1 per cent. It is hardly surprising that developing countries borrowed heavily during those years. During the 1980s, however, real interest rates rose dramatically and in the period 1981-85 the average real LIBOR was 14.5 per cent, i.e., 28.6 percentage points higher than in the previous period. Not surprisingly, one Third World country after another encountered serious debt servicing problems. Indeed unless real interest rates fall substantially or the growth of world trade accelerates markedly, or both, some combination of default, debt forgiveness and a moratorium on repayments is inevitable [33].

Table 4.4   **NOMINAL AND REAL RATES OF INTEREST, 1963-1986**
Per cent per annum

	LIBOR	Export prices of developing countries	Real rate of interest
1963	3.9	0.8	3.1
1964	4.3	3.2	1.1
1965	4.8	1.5	3.3
1966	6.1	1.5	4.6
1967	5.5	-1.5	7.0
1968	6.4	0.0	6.4
1969	9.8	3.0	6.8
1970	8.5	3.7	4.8
1971	6.6	7.1	-0.5
1972	5.5	7.3	-1.8
1973	9.2	35.2	-26.0
1974	11.0	105.5	-94.5
1975	7.0	2.2	4.8
1976	5.6	6.1	-0.5
1977	6.0	11.7	-5.7
1978	8.7	1.8	6.9
1979	12.0	28.3	-16.3
1980	14.1	40.4	-26.4
1981	16.9	6.1	10.8
1982	13.3	-3.9	17.2
1983	9.7	-10.1	19.8
1984	10.9	-1.0	11.9
1985	8.4	-4.5	12.9
1986	6.9	n.a.	n.a.

Note: The real rate of interest is calculated as the LIBOR rate on three month deposits minus the annual percentage change in the price index of exports from developing countries.

Source.   IMF, *International Financial Statistics,* various issues, and IMF, *International Financial Statistics Yearbook 1985,* Washington, 1985.

Figure 4.2. **THE REAL RATE OF INTEREST PAID BY DEVELOPING COUNTRIES**

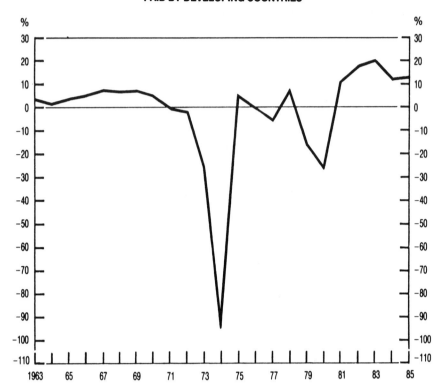

International capital movements

The open economy strategy of development implies that an economy is open not only to international commerce but also to international capital movements. Standard theory in fact would lead one to expect capital to flow strongly from countries where it is relatively abundant and hence where returns are relatively low to countries where capital is scarce and returns are high. The Third World, where capital is assumed to be scarce, should therefore be a major recipient of private foreign direct investment and of portfolio investment (including foreign bank loans). Foreign aid, according to this view, would merely supplement flows that should occur naturally in response to differences in international rates of return on capital.

The inflow of foreign capital into the Third World should have multiple benefits. First, it should raise the rate of investment. Second, it should be a vehicle for transferring technology. Third, it should be a way to introduce improved management techniques. All of this should help to raise the rate of growth of average incomes and increase employment. Fourth, by increasing the supply of capital, it should drive down the rate of profit. This should result in a more equal distribution of income and ensure that the incomes of wage earners (and the poor in general) rise more rapidly than the incomes of capitalists (and the rich in general). Thus international capital movements should reinforce or multiply the benefits derived from free trade.

In practice however international capital flows to developing countries have been of little quantitative significance. This is evident from the data in Table 4.5. In the quarter century between 1960 and 1985 foreign direct investment never amounted to more than 0.9 per cent of the gross domestic product of developing countries and in most years it was considerably less than this. On average during the period direct investment was equivalent to only 0.5 per cent of GDP. Portfolio investment, of which loans by international banks are by far the most important, was even less significant: on average during the period portfolio investment was equivalent to only 0.45 per cent of GDP. That is, market-oriented flows of foreign capital have averaged just under one per cent of GDP and the range has been between 1.8 per cent in 1978 and 0.1 per cent in 1985.

Foreign aid has been more significant than private capital flows, although it is important not to exaggerate the role it has played. At its peak in 1961 and 1962 official development assistance was equivalent to 1.9 per cent of the gross domestic product of developing countries. However it fell steadily thereafter and in 1985 foreign aid represented only 0.8 per cent of the GDP of the Third World. On average aid accounted for under 1.4 per cent of the Third World's GDP.

Table 4.5 **INTERNATIONAL CAPITAL FLOWS TO DEVELOPING COUNTRIES, 1960-1985**
Per cent of total GDP of developing countries

	Foreign direct investment	Portfolio investment	Official development assistance	Total
1960	0.7	0.2	1.8	2.7
1961	0.7	0.2	1.9	2.8
1962	0.5	0.1	1.9	2.5
1963	0.5	0.1	1.8	2.4
1964	0.4	0.2	1.7	2.3
1965	0.7	0.2	1.7	2.6
1966	0.6	0.1	1.7	2.4
1967	0.5	0.2	1.6	2.3
1968	0.7	0.2	1.6	2.5
1969	0.6	0.2	1.4	2.2
1970	0.7	0.1	1.4	2.2
1971	0.6	0.1	1.3	2.0
1972	0.6	0.3	1.4	2.3
1973	0.6	0.4	1.2	2.2
1974	0.1	0.3	1.1	1.5
1975	0.9	0.8	1.2	2.9
1976	0.6	0.8	1.1	2.5
1977	0.6	0.7	1.1	2.4
1978	0.6	1.2	1.2	3.0
1979	0.6	1.1	1.1	2.8
1980	0.4	0.7	1.1	2.2
1981	0.6	1.0	1.0	2.6
1982	0.4	0.9	1.1	2.4
1983	0.3	0.7	1.1	2.1
1984	0.4	1.0	1.2	2.6
1985	0.2	–0.1	0.8	0.9

Sources: Data bases of the OECD Development Assistance Committee and the OECD Development Centre.

Combining the three flows – foreign direct investment, portfolio investment and foreign aid – gives an indication of the total flow of capital to the Third World. During the period we are considering foreign capital imports represented approximately 2.3 per cent of the gross domestic product of developing countries on average, with a low of 0.9 per cent in 1985 and a high of 3.0 per cent in 1978 when bank lending was near its peak. These figures can be compared with investment rates in the Third World of 20-25 per cent. That is, on average foreign capital has financed about 10 per cent of total investment.

Such a flow of investment finance is unlikely to be decisive in determining whether a country's development strategy succeeds or fails. Many economists believe that on balance foreign aid and other forms of foreign capital have made a positive contribution to economic development; others in contrast are more sceptical [34]. But whether negative or positive, the effect of capital imports in most Third World countries is likely to be marginal. Moreover, the long-term trends do not appear to be favourable to large flows of foreign capital. In Figure 4.3 we plot the total flow of foreign capital to the Third World expressed as a percentage of the Third World's GDP. It can be seen that between 1960 and 1974 international capital flows declined fairly steadily, falling from 2.7 per cent in 1960-62 to 1.5 per cent in 1974. The recycling of petro-dollars between 1975 and 1979 reversed the trend and raised capital imports to 2.7 per cent of GDP during that five year period. In 1980, however, the downward trend reasserted itself and in 1985, as we have seen, total capital imports were the lowest they had been in the preceeding quarter century.

Figure 4.3. **CAPITAL FLOWS TO DEVELOPING COUNTRIES**
(per cent of Third World GDP)

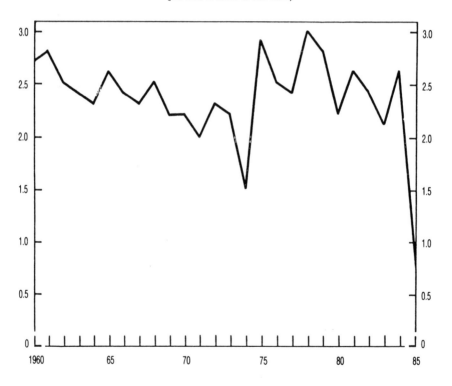

Much more serious than the downward trend is the fact that capital flows declined abruptly in 1985 at precisely the time when many of the major debtor countries in the Third World were attempting to restructure their economies. Having experienced a decline in the rate of growth of the volume of exports, a fall in the terms of trade and a sharp rise in real interest rates, much of the Third World was forced to make painful adjustments to the composition of output and the level of real income. Ideally, what was required was a switch of expenditure to exports from domestic absorption, but as explained at the beginning of the chapter, changes in the pattern of production can most easily be achieved when the rate of investment is high and rising. Unfortunately, by 1985 investment ratios in Latin America and Africa – the two regions with the most serious debt problems – were low and falling. Thus in Africa in 1978 investment was 27.9 per cent of GDP; in 1985 it had fallen to only 19.5 per cent. In Latin America in 1978 investment was 25 per cent of GDP; in 1985 it was only 17.2 per cent [35]. Given that output could not be restructured merely by switching expenditure, the Third World had no alternative but to reduce expenditure, i.e., to cut domestic consumption and investment. This inevitably reduced the rate of growth, lowered living standards, increased unemployment and raised the incidence of poverty. Indeed, per capita GDP in Africa fell every year between 1981 and 1985 by an average of 2.2 per cent and income per head continued to fall in 1986 and 1987. In Latin America per capita GDP fell in three out of the five years between 1981 and 1985 and for the period as a whole real incomes declined on average by 1.5 per cent a year [36].

Some of this hardship could have been avoided had foreign capital been available to sustain investment. But in fact portfolio investment was actually negative in 1985 as debt service on old loans by the Third World exceeded new loans by foreign commercial banks. Foreign direct investment in 1985 was only half as large a percentage of Third World GDP as it had been a year earlier and official development assistance was only two-thirds as large. In other words, the relative and absolute reduction in foreign lending, direct investment and aid aggravated the structural adjustment problems of the Third World. Capital flows in an open world economy made matters worse rather than better.

The international migration of labour

An open world economy would permit not only a free flow of capital but also a free flow of labour. In such a world labour, both skilled and unskilled, could be expected to move from the developing countries where wages and income from self-employment are low to the advanced economies where the returns to labour are high. This international migration would reduce the supply of labour in poor countries and increase it in rich. In the process, unemployment in the Third World would decline, real wages would rise, the share of wages in the national income almost certainly would increase and consequently the distribution of income would become more equal. In addition, migration would help to reduce international differences in real standards of living.

In reality, of course, this process is not allowed to occur on a large scale. The rich countries impose tight immigration controls in order to restrict the inflow of foreign workers and protect the real wages of their own working class. Those migrants allowed past the immigration barriers usually end up working either in relatively poorly paid and often unskilled occupations or else are highly qualified people such as doctors who are in short supply in the rich countries. That is, the labour market for immigrants tends to be segmented. In addition, demand in the lower half of this segmented labour market tends to fluctuate violently, rising rapidly when growth in the OECD countries is swift and falling off quickly when the pace of expansion slackens. Immigrant labour in effect often is used as a regulatory valve in the advanced economies: the inflow of labour is increased and the rate of repatriation reduced when the economy expands and vice versa when the economy goes into recession [37].

Circular migration of this type has the great advantage from the point of view of the recipient country that in periods of high unemployment many of those who lose their jobs can be forced to return to their country of origin. In this way part of the cost of unemployment is shifted from the rich countries to the poor [38]. Conversely, during periods of rapid growth and low unemployment circular migration of labour has an advantage over permanent immigration in that part of the long-term overhead costs of labour is borne by the sending country, namely, the cost of maintaining children until they reach working age and the cost of retirement [39]. Thus circular migration helps to keep wage costs down in periods of rapid growth in the demand for labour. The offer price of labour is lower than it otherwise would be and the elasticity of supply is higher.

In some cases migration plays an important role in the development of the sending countries. This is true, for instance, of emigration from the islands of the South Pacific to New Zealand and Australia, of migrant labour from North Africa (Algeria, Morocco and Tunisia) to France, of circular migration from Egypt to the oil-producing countries of the Middle East, of migrant labour from Turkey to West Germany, of illegal migration of Mexican workers to the United States and of circular migration from Botswana and Lesotho (and from several other southern African countries) to South Africa. In extreme cases a country can become totally dependent on exporting labour. In Lesotho, for example, between 50 and 60 per cent of the male labour force is employed in South Africa, mostly in the mining sector. Remittances from this migrant labour force increased 13 per cent a year in real terms during the 1970s and by 1981-2 accounted for more than 68 per cent of Lesotho's GNP [40].

Although there is much debate about the economic consequences of the migration of labour, and whether there are positive net benefits to the sending country, it is clear that the migrants themselves benefit through higher wages, the relatives and kinsmen left behind benefit from remittances and – if the volume of migration is large enough – the social class from which the migrants come benefits from a combination of reduced unemployment and higher real earnings. Insofar as the migrants come from the poorer sections of the community, large-scale emigration of labour will improve the distribution of income among households [41].

Unfortunately, data on international migration of labour – whether permanent emigration, circular migration or movements of refugees – are scarce and unreliable. Scattered evidence does suggest, however, that many and perhaps most migrants come from rural areas and have below average incomes at the time of migration. Half the migrants from Turkey are from rural areas [42], the traditional source of migrants in Bangladesh is the relatively poor agricultural district of Sylhet, and in the Philippines many of the migrants come from the backward region of Ilocos. The traditional supplier of migrant labour in Jordan is the Al-Kura sub-district, a very poor region in the northwestern part of the country. In Thailand and Pakistan migrant workers are drawn primarily from the rural areas, from all parts of the country, but northeast Thailand and the North West Frontier Province of Pakistan – two poor regions – are heavily represented. It seems thus that the poor are major beneficiaries of whatever opportunities for international migration exist.

Seldom, however, is international migration a genuine option for most workers in Third World countries. Table 4.6 contains data from seven Asian countries which shed some light on the role of migration in development. The figures for the stock of migrants working abroad almost certainly are underestimates since some migration is unrecorded. Moreover, in four cases – India, the Philippines, Sri Lanka and Thailand – the data refer only to migrants working in the Middle East. It is generally believed that about 80 per cent of migrants from Asia work in the Middle East and hence a mental upward revision of the figures on the stock of migrants from these four countries certainly is appropriate. On the other hand, the number of migrants to the Middle East has fallen sharply in recent years, particularly after the decline in oil prices accelerated in 1986, and many workers have been repatriated. It is probable therefore that the stock of migrants today is considerably smaller than the figures recorded in the Table for the first half of the 1980s.

Be that as it may, the data in the fourth column of the Table suggest that in India, Bangladesh and Thailand less than one per cent of the economically active population is employed abroad. In South Korea migrants account for 1.3 per cent of the labour force and in the Philippines probably about 2.5 per cent. In Sri Lanka and Pakistan, the two countries with the highest proportions of migrant workers, between three and four persons out of every hundred are employed abroad. In terms of employment, therefore, migration is marginal in all seven countries.

The picture changes however when one looks at remittances. The figures recorded in the Table probably reflect remittances at or near their peak. The downturn of economic activity in the Middle East will lead inevitably not only to a reduction in immigration but also to a decline in the amount of money sent home by migrant workers. In the early 1980s however remittances accounted for a high proportion of total foreign exchange receipts in many Asian countries. Only in South Korea could one regard workers' remittances as marginal, since they were equivalent to 5.1 per cent of total export earnings in 1984. In Thailand they were twice as large as this and in the Philippines and India remittances were equivalent to 19 and 27 per cent of export earnings, respectively.

Bangladesh and Pakistan are heavily dependent on remittances as a source of foreign exchange. Indeed in 1981, remittances were four-fifths as large as exports in Bangladesh and they were considerably larger than exports in Pakistan. Free international labour markets were as important for them as free international commodity markets. It is rarely recognised that the poor of the world would gain more potentially from unrestricted mobility of labour than from free trade in goods and services. As it is, even with tight controls on immigration in the rich countries, remitted earnings from labour often are more important to the developing countries than inflows of foreign capital.

We saw in the previous section that between 1960 and 1985 foreign capital in the form of direct investment, loans from commercial banks and official aid accounted on average for 2.3 per cent of the GDP of the Third World, with a low of 0.9 per cent in 1985. These numbers can be compared with the relative importance of remittances in GDP in the seven Asian countries in Table 4.6. As can be seen in the last column of the Table, in each case remittances were much larger than 0.9 per cent of GDP in the country concerned and in four of the seven countries – India, South Korea and Thailand being the exceptions – remittances were much larger than 2.3 per cent of GDP. In other words, despite obstacles to migration, remittances played a bigger role in the economies of these countries than foreign capital played in the economy of the average Third World country.

If the Third World were forced to choose between an international economy with relatively free capital movements but restricted labour migration, as at present, and free mobility of labour but restricted capital movements, it is certain that the second combination would contribute more to the alleviation of global poverty than the first. Indeed foreign aid,

Table 4.6 **MIGRANT LABOUR FROM SEVEN ASIAN COUNTRIES**

Country	Year	Stock of foreign labour migrants	Migrants as per cent of country's economically active population	Remittances (millions of U.S. dollars)	Remittances as per cent of total exports	Remittances as per cent of GDP
Bangladesh	1981	178 500	0.58	629 b	79.7 b	6.4 b
India	1983	930 000 a	0.38	2 617	27.0	1.6
Pakistan	1981	800 200	3.60	2 760 c	106.5 c	11.7 c
Philippines	1983	500 000 a	2.44	944	19.0	3.8
South Korea	1984	196 100	1.31	1 490	5.1	1.9
Sri Lanka	1983	185-215 000 a	3.24-3.75	272 d	25.5	6.3
Thailand	1983	230 000 a	0.89	650	10.2	2.2

a) Labour migrants in the Middle East only.
b) 1983.
c) 1984.
d) All private transfers.

Sources: J.W. Huguet, "International Labour Migration from the ESCAP Region", mimeo., OECD Development Centre, January 1987, Table 1, p. 6 and Table 2, p. 19; ILO, *Yearbook of Labour Statistics*, Geneva, various years; IBRD, *World Development Report*, Oxford, Oxford University Press, various years.

in this context, can be seen as small and inadequate compensation for the effects of illiberal labour market policies practiced by regimes which usually support liberal capital market and trade policies.

Evidence from some countries

Let us turn now to consider the relative importance of foreign trade in the 19 countries listed in Chapter 2 that are of particular interest to us. As explained earlier, the ratio of trade to gross domestic product does not indicate the extent to which an economy has followed an export-oriented strategy of development. That depends solely on whether government policies are neutral as between exporting and import substitution, and both a high and a low ratio of exports to GDP are consistent with policy neutrality. The export ratio does however provide an indication of the degree to which an economy is exposed to the influences of international trade and is likely to be stimulated or retarded by impulses originating outside its borders.

Table 4.7 contains data on merchandise exports expressed as a percentage of GDP. Note that exports of services such as tourism are not included in the calculations. The period covered is 1960 to 1985. Data for the beginning and terminal years are included as well as 1974, the year when there was a sharp break in the trend rate of growth of world exports.

Consider first the sub-period 1960-1974 when world trade was expanding rapidly and export opportunities for the developing countries presumably were at their greatest. During this period world trade grew faster than world output, but in Malaysia, Sri Lanka, Pakistan (1960-72), Ghana, Tanzania, Mexico and Peru the opposite occurred: exports increased less rapidly than GDP and the export ratio consequently fell. In another seven countries – China, India, Egypt, Argentina, Brazil, Chile (1960-73) and Colombia – the export ratio remained roughly constant. In only four of the eighteen countries [43] did the export ratio rise, namely, in the Philippines, Botswana, Côte d'Ivoire and Kenya. That is, only in these four countries did the evolution of the national economy mirror that of the world economy. All of the other economies failed to participate fully in the boom in international trade.

Next consider the sub-period 1974-1985 when the growth of world trade slowed down markedly. In six countries exports grew more slowly than gross domestic product and hence the trade ratio declined. These were Tanzania and Ghana (where the trend from the earlier period continued), Egypt (where previously the trade ratio had been roughly constant) and the Philippines, Côte d'Ivoire (1974-83) and Kenya (where the trade ratio previously had been rising). In India and Colombia the export ratio continued to remain roughly constant, in Chile it remained constant around the new high level attained in 1974 and in Pakistan the trade ratio remained constant after its recovery in 1973 and 1974. The remarkable thing about this sub-period however is that nine of the countries – almost half the sample – managed to increase their export ratios despite the slow-down in the volume of world trade, the general decline in the terms of trade and the high real interest rates on commercial debts.

Indeed four of the nine countries are in Latin America and have been struggling to service their international debts. These are Argentina, Brazil, Mexico and Peru. In a sense they were forced to swim against the world tide and expand their exports in order to avoid default. The export ratio also rose in Sri Lanka, Bangladesh and China, which in very different ways adopted more liberal trading policies, and in Malaysia, which has followed liberal trade policies for much of the period since independence and has a very high trade ratio.

Table 4.7 **EXPORT RATIOS IN NINETEEN COUNTRIES, 1960-1985**
Merchandise exports as a percentage of GDP

	1960	1974	1985
Asia:			
China	5.0	5.2	10.1
India	4.2	4.5	4.4
Pakistan	8.8	9.9	8.3
Bangladesh	–	2.2	5.6 *a*
Malaysia	59.3	44.6	49.2
Philippines	9.0	18.6	14.1
Sri Lanka	24.7	18.3	23.0
Africa:			
Botswana	23.1	43.7	67.6 *a*
Côte d'Ivoire	27.5	39.5	47.1
Egypt	13.5	13.3	6.5
Ghana	26.7	18.0	9.7
Kenya	13.2	22.3	16.9
Tanzania	28.3	19.6	4.6
Latin America:			
Argentina	8.6	9.3	12.1
Brazil	7.8	7.6	10.9
Chile	12.2	22.4	23.9
Colombia	11.3	11.5	10.2
Mexico	6.0	4.1	11.9
Peru	18.0	11.8	18.9

a) 1984.
Sources: OECD Development Centre data base and IMF, *International Financial Statistics,* Washington, various issues.

Quite apart from changes in trade ratios, we are interested in the rate of growth of export earnings. It is often argued that a shortage of foreign exchange can act as a constraint on the rate of growth and insofar as this is true, presumably it is the availability of foreign exchange per head that is relevant if one is interested in per capita growth rates. Accordingly in Table 4.8 we include estimates of the trend rate of growth of per capita exports measured in current US dollars. The period covered is 1950 to 1985 and this is broken into two sub-periods with the break-point in 1974. The choice of sub-periods reflects of course the change in the trend rate of growth of the volume of world trade as described in Table 4.2 and it must be accepted that these sub-periods are not necessarily the best ones for each country seen individually. Still, it facilitates comparison if the same periods are used for all countries. Once again we give simple exponential trend estimates for the sub-periods and kinked exponential estimates. Our comments will be based on the kinked estimates [44].

Considering the period as a whole, the best performance by far was by Botswana where exports per head grew 16.6 per cent a year. Next best was China where the economic reforms in the late 1970s led to a very rapid rate of growth of exports. Other good performers were Mexico (an oil exporter), Côte d'Ivoire, Bangladesh (1972-84) and Brazil, in each of which exports grew 7-8 per cent a year on average over a long period. At the other extreme are five countries where exports per head increased 4 per cent or less a year: Ghana (1.2 per cent), Sri Lanka (1.6), Tanzania (2.6), Pakistan (3.3) and Colombia (4.0). The eight countries in the middle enjoyed rates of growth of dollar earnings per head between 4.2 (Egypt) and 6.6 per cent a year (Kenya). In no country was the trend in export earnings per head negative.

Table 4.8   TREND RATES OF GROWTH OF EXPORT EARNINGS PER CAPITA IN NINETEEN COUNTRIES, 1950-1985

Per cent per annum

	Simple exponential trends			Kinked exponential trends	
	1950-85	1950-74	1975-85	1950-74	1975-85
Asia:					
China	8.1	5.2	15.5	5.0	11.6
India	4.9	1.7	4.7	1.9	8.5
Pakistan	3.3	-0.8	7.9	-0.8	8.1
Bangladesh	7.8 a	-	8.4 b	-	-
Malaysia	6.5	1.5	11.6	1.6	12.4
Philippines	6.2	3.7	5.5	3.8	8.9
Sri Lanka	1.6	-2.0	7.2	-2.1	5.9
Africa:					
Botswana	16.6 c	11.2 d	15.1 e	11.6 d	22.3 e
Côte d'Ivoire	7.9	6.2	2.2	6.4	9.7
Egypt	4.2	1.2	7.9	1.2	7.6
Ghana	1.2	0.1	-7.9	0.5	2.1
Kenya	6.6	6.3	-1.9	6.7	6.5
Tanzania	2.6	3.7	-5.9	4.0	1.1
Latin America:					
Argentina	6.0	2.8	7.4	2.9	9.6
Brazil	7.3	2.0	9.4	2.1	13.2
Chile	6.1	4.0	6.9	4.0	8.5
Colombia	4.0	-0.2	5.1	-0.1	8.9
Mexico	7.9	2.2	23.3	1.9	15.0
Peru	6.1	5.5	6.9	5.5	6.8

a) 1972-84.
b) 1974-84.
c) 1955-84.
d) 1955-74.
e) 1975-84.

Sources: OECD Development Centre data base and IMF, *International Financial Statistics*, Washington D.C., various issues.

Alas, that was not true in the first sub-period (1950-74). Exports per head actually declined 2.1 per cent a year in Sri Lanka, 0.8 per cent in Pakistan and 0.1 per cent in Colombia, and in Ghana they increased only very slowly, viz., 0.5 per cent a year. Only five countries experienced a rate of growth of exports of 5 per cent or more. Three of these were in Africa (Botswana, Kenya and Côte d'Ivoire), one was in Asia (China) and the other in Latin America (Peru).

Changes in the trends in export growth between 1950-74 and 1975-85 reflect changes in the volume of exports and in the dollar price of exports. In only two cases (Kenya and Tanzania) did exports increase more slowly after 1974 than they did before; in all other cases there was an acceleration in growth and often a very sharp one. The switch in Latin America from an import substituting to a more export-oriented pattern of growth comes out very clearly in the Table. The effects of the adoption of more export-oriented policies in Asia also are apparent. And lastly, there is the mixed and confusing picture in Africa that is highlighted by comparing the simple exponential trend estimates with the kinked exponential estimates. One can only hope that in Côte d'Ivoire, Ghana, Kenya and Tanzania the kinked estimates turn out to be the better descriptions of the underlying trends in exports.

It is not obvious that they will. The world recession of the 1980s, the continued slow growth in the volume of world exports, the deterioration of the terms of trade of the developing countries (including in the 1980s the oil exporting countries) and the extraordinarily high real rates of interest have squeezed many developing countries very hard and forced them to make major adjustments in an environment that is unfavourable to investment, trade and growth. Trends based on a period starting in 1975 may be a poor guide to the future, for it was only in 1980 and onwards that the growth of per capita income came under sustained pressure and in many years was negative in Latin America, Africa and the Middle East.

Table 4.9 contains data on the balance of trade in 15 of our sample countries for which information is available for the crucial period 1980-85. During that period the value of merchandise exports fell in seven out of the 15 countries, i.e., in nearly half the sample, and in most cases the fall was by 20 per cent or more. The main reason for the collapse of export earnings was of course a fall in world prices of primary commodities. Despite this, however, eight countries increased their exports and, again, usually by a substantial amount. Total export earnings for the 15 countries increased by 13 per cent between 1980 and 1985, largely because of the surge in exports from Brazil, Mexico and Malaysia.

The brunt of the adjustment to the adverse international environment was borne by imports. In 11 of the 15 countries there was an absolute decline in the value of merchandise imports and only in Malaysia and Pakistan was there a significant increase, of 10.5 and 8.8 per cent, respectively. In the sample as a whole imports fell by over a quarter in just five years and this evidently contributed to the slowing down in the growth of world trade as a whole.

These were two consequences of the sharp reduction in imports combined with a modest expansion of exports. First, as can be seen in the third column of Table 4.9, there were large swings in the balance of trade. Indeed there was a positive swing in the balance of trade in every country except Pakistan and Ghana. That is, in the other 13 countries, balance of trade surpluses became larger (as in Malaysia, Côte d'Ivoire and Peru) or countries moved from deficit to surplus (Chile, Mexico, Argentina and Brazil) or the trade deficits diminished (India, Bangladesh, the Philippines, Sri Lanka, Kenya and Colombia). Taken as a whole, the balance of trade for the 15 countries improved by the huge sum of $40 657 million.

92

Table 4.9   **CHANGE IN THE BALANCE OF TRADE, 1980-1985**

	Merchandise exports	Merchandise imports	Change in trade balance	Trade balance
	(Percentage change)		($ million)	
Asia:				
India a	22.8	1.9	1 619	–4 025
Pakistan	3.1	8.8	–401	–3 277
Bangladesh	26.0	–2.8	273	–1 287
Malaysia	17.6	10.5	1 169	3 575
Philippines	–20.0	–33.9	1 457	–482
Sri Lanka	22.7	6.2	126	–657
Africa:				
Côte d'Ivoire	–4.3	–46.4	1 083	1 482
Ghana	–42.7	–26.4	–232	–36
Kenya	–25.3	–45.0	737	–347
Latin America:				
Argentina	4.7	–62.5	6 250	4 877
Brazil	27.3	–42.6	15 289	12 466
Chile	–20.4	–46.0	1 513	749
Colombia	–6.8	–12.8	276	–21
Mexico	36.1	–28.8	11 237	8 407
Peru	–23.9	–29.0	261	1 098
Total	13.0	–25.6	40 657	22 522

a)   1980-84.
Source: IMF, *International Financial Statistics,* Washington, February 1987.

Second, in 1985, as can be seen in the last column of Table 4.9, seven out of the 15 countries had a balance of trade surplus. Five of these were Latin American countries attempting against great odds to service massive foreign debts. Another two countries, Colombia and Ghana, were running small trade deficits. The others had rather larger deficits but none of them posed a threat to the countries concerned, i.e., they were readily covered by capital imports, workers remittances and exports of services. Again, taken as a whole, the 15 countries had a large balance of trade surplus of $22 522 million, with the six Latin American countries running a surplus of $27 576 million partially offset by deficits in Asia. In other words, the group of developing countries represented in the Table moved in five years from a position in which they were net recipients of real resources from the rest of the world to a position in which they were transferring real resources abroad equivalent to more than 21 per cent of their export earnings. Resources, far from flowing to the poor countries from the rich, were flowing in the opposite direction.

Conclusions

The open economy as a strategy of development for Third World countries is more difficult to apply today than it was thirty or thirty-five years ago and less likely to meet with success. Nonetheless, it remains an important alternative and some of the features of the strategy are likely to form part of most successful policy packages introduced by developing countries. This is the most important conclusion to emerge from the survey of historical experience, but a number of more specific points also have emerged.

93

First, countries which have persistently and comprehensively discriminated against exporting by heavy protection against imports and grossly overvalued exchange rates have missed many opportunities to accelerate their development. The case for policy neutrality as between producing for the home and foreign markets is strong. Second, there are indeed endogenous distortions which can be reduced or eliminated by government interventions, but policy should attack these distortions at their source. Tariff protection almost always will be a second-best policy and can in principle make matters worse rather than better. Third, arguments for promoting an economic activity because of the existence of economies of scale, increasing returns and learning-by-doing effects are if anything grounds for an undervalued exchange rate, not tariff protection and an overvalued exchange rate. If intervention is justified, an optimal policy would be a direct subsidy to output. The case for policy neutrality as between exports and import substitution thus is not a case for *laissez faire*, but neither is it a case for undiscriminating interventions.

It is of course true that tariffs raise revenue whereas subsidies to output represent a charge on the budget. But if the promotion of industry really is a high priority of government it should be possible to find other sources of revenue. Obvious candidates include a profits tax, a land tax, an income tax, a general sales tax or a tax on value added. There is no need in principle for fiscal considerations to determine the nature of public intervention.

Fourth, the benefits to development of an open trading economy have relatively little to do with an improved composition of output and a more preferred pattern of consumption. Indeed the static or once-for-all gains from freer trade are unlikely to be very great in most countries. In any case, fifth, an improved allocation of resources is inseparable from economic growth and both require sustained high rates of investment. The effects of trade upon the level of capital formation and the efficiency of new investment are more important than its effect on static allocative efficiency. Going further, sixth, the ability of a country to exploit the opportunities existing in an open economy or that may arise therein from time to time depends upon its rate of investment. Adjustment, restructuring, expansion are extremely difficult and sometimes impossible in the absence of investment. It is for this reason that policies to stimulate investment take priority over policies to stimulate trade. High rates of net investment give an economy flexibility and highly flexible economies are best able to take advantage of their potential comparative advantages and to withstand the inevitable and unavoidable shocks to which the world economy is prone.

Seventh, those Third World countries which have a comparative advantage in the export of crops produced on small peasant farms, e.g., Thailand, or in exporting labour-intensive manufactured goods, e.g., Taiwan, will find that an open economy strategy of development is compatible with and even encourages a more equal distribution of income. However the distribution of income in those countries that export minerals (Zambia), petroleum and gas (Angola), crops grown on large commercial plantations (Malaysia) or agricultural commodities produced under a system of concentrated land ownershp (Argentina, Guatemala) is certain to become worse under an open economy strategy. This is definitely not an argument in favour of discouraging exports, but it does underline the need to pay careful attention to the distributive implications of the strategy of development. In some countries a land reform may be desirable (as occurred in Taiwan); in others it will be necessary to come to an agreement with transnational corporations over the division of mineral rents (as in Botswana); and in still others it may be thought that nationalisation of the petroleum sector is desirable (as happened in Algeria and Venezuela). Of course when rents from natural resources are transferred from private ownership, domestic or foreign, to the state, the effect on the distribution of income will depend on how the government chooses to spend its revenues.

94

The defenders of *laissez faire* sometimes argue that an open economy requires and encourages a liberal polity. Opponents counter by arguing that export-oriented regimes more often than not are authoritarian. However our own conclusion, eighth, is that there is no direct connection between an open economy strategy of development and the extent of democracy or authoritarianism. As we saw in the previous chapter, governments pursuing extreme policies are likely to require extreme measures to implement them and this can easily lead to authoritarianism. Even in less extreme situations, if the benefits of economic growth are captured by a minority of relatively well-off members of the population, those left behind are likely eventually to become discontented. Social tension and political violence are likely to increase and this will force the government either to introduce redistributive measures or to become repressive. Such a process of growing discontent and repression can occur as readily in a country following an import-substituting industrialisation policy as in a country with an open economy. Authoritarianism, then, is not peculiar to the open economy. Nor is it a condition for its success, as Botswana and Côte d'Ivoire demonstrate in their different ways. Neither country is authoritarian – far from it – and both have followed an open economy strategy of development for many years.

Jagdish Bhagwati has ventured the "modest hypothesis" that democratic countries may find it harder than authoritarian ones to shift from protectionist policies to an open economy [45]. While this may be true, it is apparent that any development strategy creates vested interests and political groupings which favour its perpetuation. Equally, any change in policy will benefit some and impose costs on others in the form of an absolute fall in their standard of living, a relative decline in income or a loss of political influence, power, status or prestige. The problem thus may be a general one: the difficulty of effecting a transition from one strategy to another, regardless of the strategy or the nature of the political regime. The problems China is experiencing in its attempts to introduce major economic reforms suggest that non-democratic countries may not possess special advantages.

Given that the political and economic costs of the transition may be high, one must ask whether these are more than compensated by the longer run benefits of an export-oriented strategy. The evidence, alas, as we saw earlier, is inconclusive. Our own investigations confirm this inconclusiveness. A cross-section multiple regression analysis of 16 countries, i.e., the 19 countries in our sample excluding China, Argentina and Chile, failed to detect any relationship between the growth of exports (or changes over time in the share of exports in GDP) and the rate of growth of either GDP or the non-export components of GDP. The investment ratio was found to be significant in explaining aggregate growth but the growth of exports was not.

Time series analysis was no more encouraging. Botswana (a minerals-dependent exporter) and Côte d'Ivoire (a successful agricultural exporter) were singled out as the two best examples in our sample of open economies. When the rate of growth of GDP from 1960 to 1981/2 was regressed on the investment ratio, the rate of growth of population (as a proxy for the growth of the labour force) and the rate of growth of exports, the coefficient on exports was positive in both cases. This is hardly surprising given the large share of exports in total output. However, the export coefficient in the case of Côte d'Ivoire was statistically insignificant. When the growth of GDP minus exports was substituted for GDP as the dependent variable in the equation, the coefficient on exports became negative (and statistically significant) in both Botswana and Côte d'Ivoire. Our ninth conclusion therefore is that the relationship between exports and economic growth is at best very weak.

Until 1980 the volume of world trade grew much faster than world output and it was reasonable to hope that countries with open economies would be able to use international commerce as an engine of growth. In the period from 1980 to 1986, however, the volume of world trade grew only slightly faster than world output, viz. 2.6 as compared to 2.4 per cent a year, and in addition the dollar prices of non-oil primary commodities fell over the period by about 21 per cent [46]. It is obvious that in such conditions it is difficult for foreign trade to be the leading sector. Of course, an individual country's exports may grow much faster than the world average and to the extent that they do, the foreign trade sector could play a leading role. Moreover, it is not inevitable that the growth of world trade in, say, the 1990s will be as slow as in the 1980s; it is conceivable that it could return to the trend rate of growth of 1950 to 1974. This however seems unlikely. Indeed there is a danger that continued slow growth and increased protectionism in the industrialised countries will depress world trade and make it increasingly difficult for the developing countries to earn through exports the foreign exchange needed to sustain their own development and service their foreign debts [47]. Even if increased protectionism ultimately is avoided, the threat of protectionism combined with general uncertainty about the terms of trade, rates of interest and the rules of the trading game are likely to affect action and outcomes in the present, and in particular to dampen investment in the developing countries in the export sector.

None of this implies that Third World countries should add to their already severe problems by adopting policies which make exporting even more difficult than in any event is likely to be the case. Neutrality as between producing for the home and foreign markets still is likely to be the most sensible policy. But external circumstances probably will be such that if neutral policies are followed, investment and growth in the coming decade will be more inward oriented than would have been the case under similar policies 15 or 20 years ago. That is, whatever may have been its role in the past, foreign trade in future is unlikely to be the mainspring of development. The same is true of foreign capital and the international migration of labour. The open economy will have its place but its place will not be in the centre of the stage. As Arthur Lewis said so well,

> "... international trade became an engine of growth in the nineteenth century, but this is not its proper role. The engine of growth should be technological change, with international trade serving as lubricating oil and not as fuel" [48].

NOTES AND REFERENCES

1. David Ricardo, *Principles of Political Economy and Taxation*, 1817, Ch. 7.

2. Paul Samuelson, "International Trade and the Equalization of Factor Prices", *Economic Journal*, Vol. 58, No. 2, June 1948 and Paul Samuelson, "International Factor Price Equalization Once Again", *Economic Journal*, Vol. 59, No. 2, June 1949. Samuelson's argument is a specific application of the Heckscher-Ohlin theory of international trade.

3. See G. Haberler, "Some Problems in the Pure Theory of International Trade", *Economic Journal*, Vol. 60, No. 2, June 1950; S.B. Linder, *An Essay on Trade and Transformation*, Stockholm, Almqvist and Wiksell, 1961, pp 24-8; Keith Griffin, *Underdevelopment in Spanish America*, London, Allen and Unwin, 1969, pp 93-97.

4. J.N. Bhagwati, "The Generalized Theory of Distortions and Welfare", in J.N. Bhagwati, R.W. Jones, R.A. Mundell and J. Vanek, eds., *Trade, Balance of Payments and Growth: Essays in Honour of Charles P. Kindleberger*, Amsterdam, North Holland, 1971.

5. See for example the Romanian economist, M. Manoilescu, *The Theory of Protection*, London, King, 1931 and the German economist, Friedrich List, *Das Nationale System der Politischen Okonomie*, Tübingen, Mohr-Siebeck Verlag, 1959 (1st ed., 1841). For a neo-Listian perspective on the European periphery and the contemporary Third World see Dieter Senghaas, *The European Experience: A Historical Critique of Development Theory*, Leamington Spa, Berg, 1985.

6. Under exceptional circumstances a country's share of the world export market for a particular commodity may be so great that its sales affect the world price. An optimal export tax could then be imposed to restrict sales abroad and thereby increase the world price of the commodity and improve the country's terms of trade. In the unlikely event that a country has monopsonistic power in its import markets it can improve its terms of trade by imposing an optimal tariff.

7. See J.N. Bhagwati, *op. cit.*

8. See for example Bela Balassa, *Change and Challenge in the World Economy*, London, Macmillan, 1985, Essay 2 and S.P. Magee, "Factor Market Distortions, Production and Trade: A Survey", *Oxford Economic Papers*, Vol. 25, No. 1, March 1973.

9. Bela Balassa, *op. cit.*, p. 6.

10. A.C. Harberger, "Using the Resources at Hand More Effectively", *American Economic Review*, Vol. XLIX, May 1959, p. 140.

11. Joel Bergsman, *Brazil: Industrialization and Trade Policies*, London, Oxford University Press, 1970, pp 178-9. Also see Chapter 5 below.

12. See Bela Balassa *et al.*, *The Structure of Protection in Developing Countries*, Baltimore, Johns Hopkins University Press, 1971, p. 82. Also see W.M. Corden, "The Costs and Consequences of Protection: A Survey of Empirical Work", in Peter B. Kenen, ed., *International Trade and Finance: Frontiers for Research*, Cambridge, Cambridge University Press, 1975.

13. Anne O. Krueger, "Trade Policy as an Input to Development", *American Economic Review*, Vol. 70, No. 2, May 1980, p. 288. Hla Myint argues that the exploitation of "economies of scale and increasing returns from specializing for a wider export market ... may require a pro-export policy instead of a strict neutrality between exports and domestic production implied by the static comparative costs theory". See his "Exports and Economic Development of Less Developed Countries", in Carl K. Eicher and John M. Staatz, eds., *Agricultural Development in the Third World*, Baltimore, Johns Hopkins University Press, 1984, p. 238.

14. Anne O. Krueger, "Comparative Advantage and Development Policy 20 Years Later", in Moshe Syrquin, Lance Taylor and Larry Westphal, eds., *Economic Structure and Performance: Essays in Honor of Hollis B. Chenery*, Orlando, Academic Press, 1984, p. 141.

15. This is the position, for example, of Ian Little, Tibor Scitovsky and Maurice Scott, *Industry and Trade in Some Developing Countries*, London, Oxford University Press, 1970.

16. J.N. Bhagwati, "Rethinking Trade Strategy", in John P. Lewis and Valeriana Kallab, eds., *Development Strategies Reconsidered*, New Brunswick, N.J., Transaction Books for the Overseas Development Council, 1986, p. 93.

17. W.M. Corden, "The Effects of Trade on the Rate of Growth", in J.N. Bhagwati, R.W. Jones, R.A. Mundell and J. Vanek, eds., *op. cit.*

18. This point is emphasized by Anne Krueger in her "Comparative Advantage and Development Policy 20 Years Later", in Moshe Syrquin, Lance Taylor and Larry Westphal, eds., *op. cit.*

19. This is stressed by Anne Krueger in her "Trade Policy as an Input to Development", *op. cit.*

20. Bela Balassa and associates, *Development Strategies in Semi-industrial Economies*, Baltimore, Johns Hopkins University Press, 1982, Table 10.19, p. 342.

21. *Bangladesh: Country Study and Norwegian Aid Review*, Bergen, Christian Michelsen Institute, 1986, Table C.1, p. 271.

22. See Stephen R. Lewis, Jr., "Development Problems of the Mineral-Rich Countries", in Moshe Syrquin, Lance Taylor and Larry Westphal, eds. *op. cit.*

23. Raul Prebisch was the most influential "export pessimist" in Latin America but Ragnar Nurkse was perhaps the most widely read theorist of this school of thought. See Ragnar Nurkse, *Problems of Capital Formation in Underdeveloped Countries*, New York, Oxford University Press, 1953 and Ragnar Nurkse, *Patterns of Trade and Development*, Stockholm, Almqvist and Wiksell, 1959. Also see Raul Prebisch, "Commercial Policy in Underdeveloped Countries", *American Economic Review*, Vol. XLIX, May 1959.

24. See Stephen R. Lewis, Jr., *op. cit.*

25. Alfred Maizels, *Exports and Economic Growth of Developing Countries*, London, Cambridge University Press, 1968.

26. Michael Michaely, "Exports and Growth: An Empirical Investigation", *Journal of Development Economics*,

Vol. 4, No. 1, March 1977, p. 52. Also see P.S. Heller and R.C. Porter, "Exports and Growth: An Empirical Reinvestigation", *Journal of Development Economics*, Vol. 5, No. 2, June 1978. Balassa found a positive association between export growth and GDP growth net of exports for eleven developing countries. See B. Balassa, "Exports and Economic Growth: Further Evidence", *Journal of Development Economics*, Vol. 5, No. 2, June 1978.

27. A summary of the results of several studies is included in Hollis Chenery, Sherman Robinson and Moshe Syrquin, *Industrialization and Growth: A Comparative Study*, Oxford, Oxford University Press, 1986, Table 2-4, p. 29. Also see Rati Ram, "Exports and Economic Growth: Some Additional Evidence", *Economic Development and Cultural Change*, Vol. 33, No. 2, January 1985.

28. G.K. Helleiner, "Outward Orientation, Import Instability and African Economic Growth: An Empirical Investigation", in S. Lall and F. Stewart, eds., *Theory and Reality in Economic Development*, London, Macmillan, 1986.

29. Between 1965 and 1984 the share of exports in GDP rose in Indonesia from 5 per cent to 23 per cent, in Turkey from 6 to 12 per cent, in Greece from 9 to 19 per cent, in Spain from 11 to 24 per cent.

30. Kinked exponential models are carefully explained in James Boyce, "Kinked Exponential Models for Growth Rate Estimation", *Oxford Bulletin of Economics and Statistics*, Vol. 48, No. 4, November 1986.

31. Data on the terms of trade can be obtained from UNCTAD, *Handbook of International Trade and Development Statistics*, New York, 1985.

32. See Keith Griffin, *World Hunger and the World Economy*, London, Macmillan, 1987, Ch. 10.

33. One should remember that default on overseas debt and debt forgiveness are not uncommon and certainly are not confined to developing countries. For example, the Soviet Union in 1918 repudiated all foreign debt incurred during the Czarist period. Germany owes huge sums arising from reparations at the end of the First World War. Under the 1953 London Agreement on German external debts all claims against Germany were deferred indefinitely. The United Kingdom, France, Italy and other European countries owed the United States in 1984 some $27.7 billion from First World War debts. These European debtor countries, however, have linked repayment of their debt to repayment by Germany of its debts, which have conveniently been deferred indefinitely. In effect, all First World War debts have been forgiven. (See US National Advisory Council on International Monetary and Financial Policies, *Annual Report 1984*, Washington, D.C., 1984, p. 42.)

34. For a good defence of foreign aid see Robert Cassen, *Does Aid Work?*, Oxford, Oxford University Press, 1986; and for a sceptical view see Keith Griffin, *op. cit.*, Ch. 9.

35. IMF, *World Economic Outlook*, Washington, D.C., October 1986, Table A7, p. 44.

36. *Ibid.*, Table A6, p. 43.

37. See for example J.A. Bustamante, "Mexican Migration: The Political Dynamic of Perception", in C.W. Reynolds and C. Tello, eds., *U.S.-Mexican Relations: Economic and Social Aspects*, Stanford, Stanford University Press, 1983.

38. This has been important, for example, in Switzerland and West Germany.

39. The classic example is of course South Africa where apartheid is used among other things to minimize immigration while ensuring an elastic supply of foreign labour. The phenomenon of "illegal" immigration of Mexican workers to Texas and California in the United States is structurally similar. (See M. Burawoy, "The Functions and Reproduction of Migrant Labor: Comparative Material From Southern Africa and the United States", *American Journal of Sociology*, Vol. 81, 1976.)

40. Dharam Ghai, "Successes and Failures in Growth in Sub-Saharan Africa: 1960-82", in Louis Emmerij, ed., *Development Policies and the Crisis of the 1980s*, Paris, OECD Development Centre, 1987.

41. See Keith Griffin, "On the Emigration of the Peasantry", *World Development*, Vol. 4, May 1976. For a survey of the anthropological literature see Michael Kearney, "From the Invisible Hand to Visible Feet: Anthropological Studies of Migration and Development", *Annual Review of Anthropology*, 1986. If migrants come from the professional classes, i.e., there is "brain drain", income inequality will increase and in extreme cases the rate of growth of the economy could be adversely affected. See Keith Griffin, *International Inequality and National Poverty*, London, Macmillan, 1978, Ch. 1.

42. Suzanne Paine, *Exporting Workers: The Turkish Case*, University of Cambridge, Department of Applied Economics, Occasional Paper 41: University of Cambridge Press, 1974, Table 8, p. 89 and Table 12b, p. 187.

43. Bangladesh during most of this period was the province of East Pakistan and is therefore excluded from the analysis.

44. Note that in six cases simple exponential trend calculations produced lower estimates in both sub-periods than in the period as a whole. The six cases are India, the Philippines, Botswana, Côte d'Ivoire, Ghana and Kenya.

45. J.N. Bhagwati, "Rethinking Trade Strategy", in John P. Lewis and Valeriana Kallab, eds. *op. cit.,* p. 101.

46. IMF, *World Economic Outlook,* Washington, D.C., October 1986, Table A1, p. 37 and Table A20, p. 58.

47. A recent study of non-tariff barriers to trade in the industrialised countries shows that they "are significantly more prevalent on imports from developing economies than from industrial ones" and that between 1981 and 1983 they increased at a significant pace. (See Julio J. Nogués, Andrzej Olechowski and L. Alan Winters, "The Extent of Nontariff Barriers to Industrial Countries' Imports", *World Bank Economic Review,* Vol. 1, No. 1, September 1986.)

48. W. Arthur Lewis, *The Evolution of the International Economic Order,* Princeton, Princeton University Press, 1978, p. 74.

Chapter 5

INDUSTRIALISATION

It is a common observation that rich countries tend to be industrialised. Colin Clark noted nearly half a century ago that as aggregate growth proceeds the share of output and employment in agriculture falls while the share of output and employment in industry (and in services) rises [1]. A quarter of a century later Simon Kuznets refined this observation by detecting broad regularities in the sectoral composition of output and employment and the level of per capita income [2]. Using data from the developed countries Kuznets claimed that as income per head rose, the contribution of agriculture to total output declined in a predictable way, while the contribution of services remained roughly constant and the contribution of manufacturing rose. Looked at in terms of employment, Kuznets' data indicated that as per capita income rose, the proportion of the labour force engaged in agriculture fell while the proportions engaged in services and manufacturing increased, although the rise in manufacturing was not as pronounced as in services.

These generalisations about patterns of development in rich countries stimulated a great deal of research to see if similar patterns were evident in poor countries. Using the national income data that gradually were becoming available in the Third World, Hollis Chenery and his associates conducted numerous cross-country studies which did indeed appear to indicate that the size and composition of the industrial sector was related to the level of per capita income [3]. That being so [4], discussion then concentrated on the explanation for the apparent uniformity in the pattern of growth.

An obvious explanation is that changes in the composition of output reflect changes in the composition of demand. As average incomes rise, the demand for some goods will increase more rapidly than others, and in the case of "inferior" goods, demand may contract absolutely. It is well established that the income elasticity of demand for food is less than one and it is highly plausible that the income elasticity of demand for manufactured consumer goods is greater than one. It thus follows that when average incomes rise, the demand for food (and by extension, the demand for agricultural products as a whole) will grow less than proportionately while the demand for the products of industry will grow more than proportionately. In a closed economy these changes in the composition of demand normally would lead to corresponding changes in the composition of production and if demand elasticities are broadly similar in all countries, the regularities noted by Clark, Kuznets and Chenery would readily be explained. Of course the correspondence between demand and output would be weakened in an open economy, particularly in small countries where foreign trade accounts for a high proportion of national income, but even so, the effects on the composition of domestic output of a gradual evolution in the pattern of demand could be expected to be considerable.

An implication of this view is that industrialisation occurs more or less automatically as average incomes rise. That is, industrialisation is a consequence of growth rather than a cause of it. Manufacturing simply responds passively to incremental demand.

A second explanation puts the emphasis on supply-side factors. Industry tends to be more capital intensive than agriculture. Thus high savings and investment rates, by reducing the relative scarcity of capital, will favour the expansion of the manufacturing sector and associated industrial activities. Similarly, industry has a greater need for skilled labour than agriculture. If public policy or private initiative results in an expansion of training and educational facilities, the increased supply of skilled labour will help to promote industry. Again, some industrial processes, e.g., chemicals, steel, cement, power generation, are characterised by economies of scale. An increase in output in these activities could result in lower costs, lower prices and a larger quantity demanded. More generally, quite often in industry, because of complementarities and externalities, the whole is larger than the sum of its parts. For example, it may not pay to invest in the manufacture of consumer durables because cheap electric power is not available to households, and it may not pay to invest in a large electric generating plant producing cheap power because of a lack of demand. Both projects viewed in isolation appear to be unprofitable. Viewed together, however, they may be highly profitable because of the close complementarity between them. Particularly in countries with small domestic markets, investment projects frequently will be "lumpy" and a combination of economies of scale and ignorance of investment plans in other industries may inhibit enterpreneurs from undertaking projects with high social rates of return [5].

Implicit in this second explanation of the observed patterns of growth is the presumption that government policy – by accelerating investment, increasing the supply of skilled labour, exploiting economies of scale where they exist and by designing investment programmes that take complementarities between projects into account – can increase the speed of industrialisation, systematically raise the productivity of labour and thereby raise the rates of growth of aggregate output and income. In other words, a coherent policy for industrialisation could constitute a strategy of overall economic development. Governments acting directly and indirectly by creating favourable conditions for the private sector can promote industrial expansion. Industry, far from merely responding passively to the evolution of demand, could be used by government as the leading sector in sustained, rapid growth.

Support for this approach can be found in the historical experience of the now industrialised countries. Alexander Gerschenkron, in his studies of nineteenth century European industrialisation, stressed the role of the banks and the state and argued that the greater the relative economic backwardness of a country, the more centralised was the development effort [6]. The agents of industrialisation shifted from private entrepreneurs during the first industrial revolution in England, to investment banks in Germany and then to the state in Tsarist Russia. The later the date at which a country began to industrialise, the more modern and large-scale was the technology employed. Gerschenkron's analysis was greatly enriched by a detailed study of the continental European experience by Dieter Senghaas [7]. He shows that all the European countries, except of course Great Britain, developed behind protective barriers of one sort or another. Indeed, the European countries went beyond mere tariff protection and selectively delinked from the international economy. During a period of "dissociation" the internal economy was restructured: the production of primary commodities was integrated into processing industries, a capital goods industry was started and mass production of basic consumer goods was developed. Only after major institutional and structural changes were well underway did the countries allow themselves to become reintegrated into the competitive world economy. Free trade was not followed until after the domestic market was developed and conquered.

Warwick Armstrong, summarising the findings of a study of Germany, Japan, Sweden and the United States, comes to "one inescapable conclusion": successful implementation in those four countries of a national strategy of industrialisation depended upon "the ability of the sovereign state, in collaboration with a powerful industrial class, to control and promote the conditions of growth. Institutional support provided by investment banks, a directed technical education system, labour control, selective protection policies, and the borrowing and adaptation of new technology for further domestic innovation, were all part of the larger project to achieve national industrial development" [8]. If this is the way development was brought about in the past, it is reasonable for the Third World to enquire whether a similar approach might not be successful in future.

Industry in the Third World

Let us first consider, however, the place industry now occupies in the Third World (see Table 5.1). Perhaps surprisingly, the average share of industry in gross domestic product is about the same in the Third World as it is in the advanced capitalist economies, namely 35 per cent. But this is a coincidence that tells us little about the structural changes that are occurring in the two groups of countries. First, the share of industry has been falling secularly in the rich countries to make way for a rising share of services (which now accounts for more than 60 per cent of total output). Second, superimposed on this trend, there has been a cyclical contraction of industry in the United States and Western Europe as a result of the world recession of the 1980s. Third, the share of industry has been rising secularly in the Third World (largely at the expense of the share of agriculture) and this rise has not been seriously interrupted by the recession thanks to the continued expansion of output in several of the largest Third World countries including China and India.

Moreover, it is important to bear in mind that industrial production is not synonymous with the manufacturing sector. Industry includes not only manufacturing but also mining, construction, electricity, gas and water. If one looks just at the manufacturing sector the Third World still lags behind the advanced capitalist economies. In 1981, for example, manufacturing value added accounted for 19 per cent of gross domestic product in the Third World (excluding China) and 27.6 per cent in the developed market economy countries [9]. But here too the share was tending to rise in the Third World and fall in the advanced economies.

The first column of Table 5.1 shows that the share of industry varies quite considerably among our 19 countries. The lowest shares are in Ghana and Bangladesh (9 and 12 per cent respectively) and the highest in Botswana and China (45 and 44 per cent respectively). Several qualifications, however, are necessary. First, the figure in the Table for Tanzania is for 1965 whereas the data for all the other countries refer to 1984. Tanzania almost certainly had a lower share of industry in 1984 than it did in 1965 and it probably would come at the bottom of the league with Ghana. The manufacturing sector in Tanzania collapsed after the first sharp rise in oil prices, its share of GDP falling from 11.1 to 5.8 per cent [10], and this evidently would have pulled down the share of industry as a whole. Second, the high proportion of output attributed to industry in Botswana is of course due to its large mining sector. If the 19 countries were to be ranked by the share of manufacturing in total output, Botswana would be third from the bottom after Tanzania and Bangladesh. Thus the high degree of industrialisation in Botswana is a bit of an illusion. Third, China is of course a socialist country and pursued a very different strategy of development from the non-socialist Third World countries. This does not mean that China's industrialisation is illusory, but only that discussion of its strategy for economic development must wait until Chapter 8.

Table 5.1 **SIZE AND RATE OF GROWTH OF THE INDUSTRIAL SECTOR**

	(1) Industrial production, 1984 (% of GDP)	(2) Industrial labour force, 1980 (% of total)	(3) Growth of manufacturing output per head, 1960-83 (% per annum)
Asia:			
China	44	19	7.6
India	27	13	2.2
Pakistan	29	16	3.9
Bangladesh	12	6	1.9
Malaysia	35	19	7.8 b
Philippines	34	16	2.2
Sri Lanka	26	14	2.1
Africa:			
Botswana	45	13	n.a.
Côte d'Ivoire	26	8	3.9 c
Egypt	33	20	4.8
Ghana	9	18	0.3 c
Kenya	21	7	4.7
Tanzania	14 a	5	n.a.
Latin America:			
Argentina	39	34	1.6
Brazil	35	27	4.7
Chile	39	25	-2.5
Colombia	30	24	2.7
Mexico	40	29	3.5
Peru	40	18	0.9

a) 1965.
b) 1965-83.
c) 1960-82.

Sources: IBRD, *World Development Report 1986*, Oxford University Press, 1986; IBRD and OECD Development Centre data tapes.

In regional terms, Latin America clearly is the most industrialised, followed by Asia and then Africa. Similar conclusions arise from considering the share of employment in industry (see column (2) of the Table). In Latin America about a quarter of the labour force earns its living in industry, in Asia about 15 per cent (with only Bangladesh being well below average) and in Africa about 12 per cent (with wide variation around the average). The productivity of labour in industry is much higher than that in the economy as a whole and it appears that the smaller the proportion of the labour force employed in industry, the larger is the productivity differential. A rough calculation suggests, for example, that in Africa the average productivity of labour in industry is approximately 2.5 times the national average; in Asia it is about twice as high and in Latin America 1.5 times as high. Although one would not expect the average productivity of labour to be the same in all sectors of the economy – efficient resource allocation requires only that the marginal productivity of labour be the same – differentials as large as these are indicative of severe structural distortion [11].

Next let us consider trends in the long-run rate of growth of manufacturing production per head. In column (3) of the Table it can be seen that in general the per capita output of manufactured goods has increased rapidly over more than two decades. Only in Chile has there been a fall and that was caused by the sharp depression that began in 1972 and was accentuated by monetarist policies in subsequent years, as discussed in Chapter 3. In Ghana and Peru, growth has been very slow, namely, less than 1 per cent per head per annum, and in Argentina and Bangladesh it has been less than 2 per cent a year. But in the remaining dozen countries for which data are available growth rates have been high, with a range of 2.1 per cent in Sri Lanka to a remarkable 7.8 per cent in Malaysia. An unweighted average of the rates of growth of manufacturing output per head in the 17 countries for which we have data is 3.1 per cent a year. A weighted average would of course be much higher because of the exceptionally fast growth in China of 7.6 per cent a year. But even if China is excluded from consideration, manufacturing output per head in the Third World has increased quite rapidly.

Third World manufacturing in a global context

It is widely believed that the growth achieved in the manufacturing sector in the Third World is due to its being highly protected and consequently that it is incapable of competing in world markets. Because of this, it is thought that exports of manufactured goods account for only a small proportion of total exports in most Third World countries. A few exceptions are recognised – particularly Hong Kong, Singapore, South Korea and Taiwan – but the general impression commonly conveyed is that most Third World countries rely almost entirely on exports of raw materials, unprocessed primary commodities, petroleum and mineral ores in order to earn foreign exchange. The truth, however, is quite different: the majority of Third World countries do export manufactured goods and in many cases these exports account for a substantial part of total foreign exchange earnings.

Of course most manufacturing in the Third World is for the domestic market, not for export. And many of the manufactured goods that are exported are technically unsophisticated or are raw materials that have gone through only the first few stages of processing. Nevertheless, large numbers of manufactured goods are being exported and they are increasing rapidly. In 1982, for instance, manufactures accounted for 22.9 per cent of all exports from the developing countries, and 53.3 per cent of total exports excluding mineral fuels and related materials [12]. More detailed information on 14 countries is included in Table 5.2. As can be seen in the first column of the Table, in eight of the 14 countries manufactured exports account for more than half of the total and in Pakistan and Brazil they account for 90.3 and 70.9 per cent respectively. Even in such an unindustrialised country as Ghana one-fifth of the exports are manufactured goods.

Moreover, during the period 1973-81, the export of manufactured goods grew as fast as or faster than total exports in exactly half the countries represented in the Table. This includes Pakistan, Malaysia and the Philippines in Asia, Côte d'Ivoire and Kenya in Africa and Brazil and Colombia in Latin America. The boom in oil prices during this period helped earnings from petroleum exports in Mexico and Peru and it is hardly surprising that in those two countries the export of manufactured goods increased less rapidly than the total.

Table 5.2 **EXPORTS OF MANUFACTURED PRODUCTS**

	Manufactured exports as percentage of total exports, 1979-81	Average annual percentage rate of growth, 1973-81 *a*	
		Manufactured exports	Total exports
Asia:			
India	65.3	13.8	14.2
Pakistan	90.3	14.3	14.3
Malaysia	47.4	20.0	18.4
Philippines	55.0	18.8	15.6
Africa:			
Côte d'Ivoire	33.6	19.6	14.5
Egypt	44.1	4.4	14.2
Ghana	20.8	5.3	9.2
Kenya	60.8	26.9	20.8
Latin America:			
Argentina	57.8	11.1	13.7
Brazil	70.9	22.7	18.0
Chile	78.8	19.4	20.4
Colombia	32.3	13.9	12.2
Mexico	32.2	7.4	22.3
Peru	57.8	8.5	10.5

a) Current prices.
Source: UNIDO, *Handbook of Industrial Statistics 1984*, New York, 1985.

The Third World still accounts for only a small proportion of world value added in manufacturing. In 1982 this was 14.7 per cent, of which 3.9 per cent came from China; 61 per cent of manufacturing output originated in the developed market economies and the remaining 24.3 per cent in the Soviet Union and Eastern Europe [13]. The share of the developing countries in world manufacturing production is rising rapidly. For example, between 1963 and 1980 the proportion of world manufacturing output originating in the developing countries (excluding China) rose from 8.1 to 11.0 per cent[14]. These general trends also occurred in the individual countries represented in the Table. For instance, during the period 1973 to 1981, manufacturing output grew faster than the world average in ten countries, at the same rate in Peru, and more slowly than the world average in Ghana, Argentina and Chile [15].

Within the Third World, again excluding China, manufacturing output is slightly concentrated. Two countries – Brazil and Mexico – accounted in 1981 for 36.6 per cent of all the manufacturing in the 97 developing countries for which data are available. Another eight countries – India, South Korea, Argentina, Turkey, Indonesia, the Philippines, Venezuela and Hong Kong in descending order – accounted for a further 32.1 per cent. Thus the top ten countries, representing 51.5 per cent of the Third World's population, accounted for 68.7 per cent of the Third World's manufacturing production [16]. The degree of concentration, however, seems to be falling since in 1963 the top ten countries accounted for

70.2 per cent of manufacturing production in the Third World. Moreover, the composition of the top ten has changed, Peru, Chile and Egypt having been replaced by Indonesia, Venezuela and Hong Kong.

The Third World also is beginning to make an impact on the world market for manufactured goods. During the first five years of this decade the share of the developing market economy countries in total world exports declined from 27.9 per cent in 1980 to 24.6 per cent in 1984 (see Table 5.3). The fall is due entirely, however, to the decline in oil prices which sharply reduced the share in world trade of the OPEC countries. As can be seen in the Table, the share of OPEC fell by nearly 42 per cent, i.e., from over 15 per cent of world exports to less than 9 per cent. The non-OPEC Third World countries, in contrast, raised their share of world exports nearly 25 per cent in just five years, i.e., from 12.6 per cent in 1980 to 15.7 per cent in 1984.

Table 5.3 **SHARE OF DEVELOPING MARKET ECONOMY COUNTRIES IN WORLD TRADE, 1980-1984**

Percentages

	1980	1981	1982	1983	1984
Total exports	27.9	27.6	26.2	24.9	24.6
OPEC countries	15.3	14.1	12.0	9.9	8.9
Non-OPEC countries	12.6	13.5	14.2	15.0	15.7
Total exports of manufactures	9.1	10.5	10.7	10.9	n.a.
Chemicals	6.3	6.8	6.9	7.2	7.7
Machinery and transport equipment	5.4	6.1	6.4	7.7	8.7
Other manufactured goods	15.2	17.3	17.8	19.2	20.7

Sources: United Nations *Statistical Yearbook 1983/84*, New York, 1986; UNIDO, *Industry in the 1980s: Structural Change and Interdependence*, New York, 1985.

Manufactured exports from the developing countries have been rising steadily for the last quarter century. In 1960 the developing countries accounted for only 3.9 per cent of world trade in manufactures [17]. By 1970 their share had risen to 5.0 per cent and by 1980 to 9.1 per cent. In 1983, the last year for which data are available, the share was 10.9 per cent. It is safe to say therefore that the Third World has made a breakthrough in selling industrial products in the highly competitive international market.

The remarkable thing is that the final, decisive phase of this breakthrough occurred at a time when world trade was declining. Far from being an engine of growth, international commerce in recent years has put a brake on global expansion. During the period on which we are concentrating, 1980 to 1984, world trade fell 1.2 per cent a year, yet exports from the developing countries actually rose 4.3 per cent a year. The same pattern is evident in the major export categories of manufactured goods. Thus during 1980-84, exports of chemicals from the advanced economies increased precisely zero, whereas exports from the developing countries increased 6.1 per cent per annum. As a result, the share of the Third World in the international chemicals market increased 22.2 per cent (from 6.3 to 7.7 per cent of the market). Similarly, exports of machinery and transport equipment increased 1.5 per cent a year from the advanced economies, but this was greatly exceeded by an annual growth rate of 15.8 per cent from the developing economies. As a result, their share of the world machinery and transport market rose 61.1 per cent in just five years (from 5.4 to 8.7 per cent). Finally, exports of "other manufactured goods" actually fell 3.4 per cent a year from the advanced economies, whereas in the developing economies they rose 6.6 per cent a year. This enabled the developing countries to increase their share in this market to 20.7 per cent.

Thus the Third World swam successfully against the tide; it was not carried along by a swiftly moving current of international trade. Of course if world trade continues to be sluggish there is no guarantee that the Third World will be able to increase its share of manufactured exports further. Moreover, even if it does, a rising share of a sluggish total may not provide a strong stimulus to growth. As it is, exports of manufactured goods are increasingly concentrated in a relatively small number of Third World countries. In 1985, just five countries (Taiwan, South Korea, Hong Kong, Brazil and Singapore) accounted for 74 per cent of all manufactured exports from the Third World; the next five countries (India, Malaysia, Thailand, Argentina and the Philippines) accounted for an additional 9 per cent. Thus ten countries representing less than 45 per cent of the Third World's population (excluding China) accounted for 83 per cent of the Third World's exports of industrial products [18].

The rise in oil prices in 1973 and again in 1979 led to a steep decline in the rate of industrial growth throughout the world. Comparing the period 1965-73 with 1973-84 the average annual percentage rates of growth of industrial output were as follows [19]:

	1965-73	1973-84
Industrial market economies	5.1	1.8
Middle-income economies	9.1	4.4
Low-income economies	8.9	7.4

That is, the rate of growth fell most in the rich countries and least in the poor countries (including China) so that there emerged a strong inverse relationship between the level of per capita income and the rate of growth of industrial output.

This recent history poses a number of questions for the future. First, was the period from, say, 1950 to 1973 a golden age of world growth that is unlikely to be repeated? Will normal growth rates in future in the advanced economies return to the much slower rates that characterised their expansion in the nineteenth and first half of the twentieth centuries? Second, if so, is it realistic to assume that world trade in a slow growth environment will continue to grow much faster than aggregate world output? Third, if the growth of international trade slows down significantly will the Third World nonetheless be able to continue to increase its share of world manufacturing exports? And assuming it is able to do this, fourth, will exports of manufactured goods enable the Third World (or at least a significant part of it) to achieve a rapid rate of growth of per capita income? Finally, if not, could the Third World develop more rapidly by following a more inward-oriented strategy of industrialisation?

The answers to these questions are not obvious, but there seems little immediate prospect in the OECD countries of a return to the rapid growth enjoyed in the 1950s and 1960s. Equally, the era of trade liberalisation may have come to an end, at least temporarily, and the immediate danger is that there may be greater protection of manufacturing in the industrialised countries and continued slower growth of international trade. In such an environment it is likely to be difficult for the Third World as a whole to base its industrialisation on production for export. Some of the smaller countries may be able to do so, and in principle it may be desirable for them to do so, particularly if their resource endowment is limited, but among the giants of the Third World (which of course account for a large majority of the people) internal growth, domestically generated technical change and import substitution are likely to be of increasing importance [20].

If changes in the world economy force the developing countries to pursue a more inward-looking policy for industrialisation, they should be able to do so with much less difficulty than in the 1950s and 1960s. There are two reason for this. First, as we have seen, the industrial sector is much larger than it was then and a policy of relatively greater self-reliance is more feasible. Second, and more important, the Third World now has a sizeable capital goods industry (see Table 5.4). In 1963 capital goods represented only one-fifth of manufacturing output in the developing countries whereas today it is between a quarter and a third. This means that if necessary the Third World can produce its own investment goods; it need not import them from the rest of the world. If international commerce expands more slowly in future, and if consequently the growth of exports from the Third World slows down, this need not produce a foreign exchange constraint on investment and economic growth as in the past. That is, because of its fairly large capital goods sector, the Third World is able to transform a higher proportion of its domestic savings directly into investment without having to use foreign trade as an indirect means of transformation. If machines can be produced at home rather than imported, the rate of growth is no longer constrained by the availability of foreign exchange but only by the rate of savings. This is an enormous advantage to a country that wishes to grow rapidly in a world economy in which exports are growing slowly.

This does not imply of course that the developing countries should ignore whatever opportunities for profitable trade exist. But if trading opportunities diminish a more inward looking strategy is feasible, particularly in those countries which have a substantial capital goods sector. Indeed, in most of the large Third World countries it may not be possible to increase exports rapidly without disturbing international markets to such an extent that protectionist reactions are provoked. In such cases the only long run alternative to greater import substitution may be slower growth.

In the short run, however, a slowing down of world trade may lead not to greater import substitution in the Third World but to deindustrialisation, i.e., to a relative contraction of the industrial sector. This is what happened in a number of countries after the shock of the steep rise in oil prices in 1973. For example, of the 19 countries represented in Table 5.1, the share of manufacturing in gross domestic product continued to rise steadily during 1973-81 in nine; in three countries (the Philippines, Mexico and Peru) it remained roughly constant; in another three (Egypt, Brazil and Colombia) it fell between 0.5 and 1.0 percentage points; and in the remaining four countries (Sri Lanka, Tanzania, Chile and Argentina) the share of

Table 5.4 **COMPOSITION OF MANUFACTURING OUTPUT IN DEVELOPING COUNTRIES**

Percentages

	1963	1973	1979
Consumer non-durables	51.9	40.1	37.6
Industrial intermediates	27.3	31.5	31.2
Capital goods (including consumer durables)	20.8	28.4	31.2

Source: UNIDO, *Industry in a Changing World,* New York, 1983, Table III.2, p. 63.

108

manufacturing in GDP fell between 2.9 and 6.8 percentage points. In other words, in seven out of the 19 countries the output of manufactured goods during that eight-year period increased less rapidly than output in the other sectors of the economy. Import substitution did not occur, the dynamism of the industrial sector diminished and the overall rate of growth of the economy declined.

Three approaches to industrialisation

One can distinguish three approaches to industrialisation in the Third World. The first and most commonly adopted approach is to concentrate on replacing imports of manufactured consumer goods by domestic manufactures. This is the well-known strategy of import-substituting industrialisation. The strategy has been implemented within the context of a mixed economy and although direct state investment in industrial enterprises is not uncommon, most investment in manufacturing has been undertaken by the private sector. The role of the state has been to create a set of incentives that guides private initiative in the desired direction. In practice governments have tended to provide indiscriminate protection to manufacturing rather than to attempt to be selective or to identify individual "infant industries" for specific encouragement. Governments have often behaved as if they regarded the entire manufacturing sector as an "infant" deserving of protection and hence there was no need to be discriminating. The lack of discrimination in providing support does not imply, however, that the policies have been unbiased. Indeed, as we shall see, the incentives created by policies designed to promote import-substituting industrialisation have introduced many biases into the economy, some of them unintended and unanticipated.

The most frequently adopted measures have centred on trade policy. High tariffs, sometimes supplemented by quotas and other non-tariff barriers to trade, have been universal. In addition, multiple exchange rates have been used both to encourage "non-traditional" exports (usually manufactured goods) and to discourage imports of consumer goods. Occasionally, above all in Africa, export taxes and the pricing policies of monopoly state marketing boards have been used to generate government revenues, which in turn have been used among other things to cover the losses of state industrial enterprises.

Protection against imports usually has been accompanied by preferential access of industrialists to finance capital. In some countries monetary policy has been used to keep interest rates low, sometimes negative in real terms. In other countries special development banks or development corporations have been established for the specific purpose of providing capital to new industries. And in yet other countries a large part and perhaps all of the commercial banking system has been brought into public ownership and the government has been able to channel funds directly to those firms it wished to help. Whatever the mechanism, the provision of relatively inexpensive credit has been a conspicuous feature of import-substituting industrialisation.

These trade and credit policies have altered the structure of the economy in a number of ways. First and most obviously, they have encouraged the growth of manufacturing industry and by implication have introduced disincentives to the expansion of other sectors, notably agriculture. The bias against agriculture takes several forms: a redirecting of public investment away from activities which support agriculture (irrigation, rural electrification, farm-to-market roads) in favour of activities which support industry; a rise in the price of manufactured consumer goods purchased by the farming population relative to the price of agricultural goods; and a rise in the price of material inputs used in agriculture, e.g., fertilizers and mechanical equipment, relative to the price of agricultural products. Thus from the point of view of production, the profitability of farming is reduced and from the point of view of consumption, the incentive to farmers to increase output in exchange for manufactured consumer goods also is diminished.

Second, import-substituting industrialisation has altered (deliberately) not only the intersectoral composition of output but also (usually unintentionally) the intra-industry composition of output. One reason for this is that nominal tariff rates seldom are uniform and hence some industries receive a much higher nominal or apparent degree of protection than others. Tariff rates proliferate through historical time in response to particular political pressures or economic circumstances, but when one examines the structure of protection at any given moment it often appears to be arbitrary and irrational without rhyme or reason. A further complication arises from the fact that many manufactured goods are used as inputs in the production of other manufactured goods. Steel is used in the production of consumer durables, cloth is used in the production of clothing, etc. If both steel and consumer durables are given protection from imports, say, with an identical nominal tariff rate, the real or effective rate of protection to value added in the consumer durables industry will be much less than that in the steel industry – because the former will have to purchase high cost inputs from the latter [21]. Indeed in extreme cases some industries have negative effective protection, presumably contrary to what the policymakers intended when the tariffs were imposed.

Third, tariff protection provides only partial assistance to an industry. It protects local industry from foreign competition in the domestic market but provides no assistance in foreign markets. Unlike a general subsidy to production, tariffs introduce a strong bias in the manufacturing sector in favour of sales in the domestic market and against sales in the international market [22]. In other words, import-substituting industrialisation is biased not only in favour of the manufacturing sector but also against exports, including exports from the manufacturing sector. While one can adduce good arguments for wishing to promote industrial output and to encourage industrial expansion, it is not easy to think of good reasons why one should wish to discourage industrial output from being sold abroad and encourage it instead to be sold at home. Yet that is what tariffs do.

Fourth, the strategy has also affected factor proportions in manufacturing and indeed throughout the economy. By lowering the relative cost of finance capital, incentives have been created in industry to use more mechanised techniques of production than would otherwise be profitable, to invest in plant with a larger capacity than the domestic economy can support and to economise on the employment of labour. These tendencies toward high capital-labour ratios, low capacity utilisation and low employment creation are reinforced if an overvalued exchange rate also is present, as is often the case. That is, if there is an excess demand for foreign exchange at the ruling exchange rate, import licenses or permits will have to be used to allocate foreign exchange among the competing users. Unless the licenses are sold by auction, those who obtain the right to purchase foreign exchange at the official rate will be able to import capital goods relatively cheaply and this will give them an incentive not only to adopt capital-intensive methods of production but also foreign exchange-intensive methods of production.

Fifth, import-substituting industrialisation has altered the distribution of income among the various factors of production. It has increased the share of industrial profits in national income, lowered rents in export-oriented agriculture and in mining and reduced the share of wages. Often in fact protection has been excessive (or partially redundant) in the sense that it has been higher than necessary to encourage an industry to become established.

Particularly in countries where the domestic market is small and the number of firms needed to satisfy demand for a particular commodity consequently is few, competition has been absent and monopoly profits have been high. This has accentuated the tendency for import-substituting industrialisation to shift the distribution of income towards profits. This change in factor shares sometimes is welcomed on the grounds that the propensity to save out of profits is higher than the savings propensity out of rent and wages. Thus there is thought to be an added bonus to the strategy in the form of higher savings, investment and aggregate growth [23].

A sixth effect of the strategy has been to increase inequality in the distribution of income and wealth among households. The poor in the rural areas and in the informal urban sector have lost ground relative to the upper income groups in the cities. Moreover, where the initial distribution of income was unequal, the process of import-substituting consumer goods has led to a composition of manufacturing output which tends to strengthen the initial inequalities. The concentration of income at the top end of the distribution results in a relatively large demand for luxury goods, i.e., for goods with high income elasticities of demand. These goods originally were imported but thanks to tariff protection are replaced by domestic production and in consequence the capital structure of industry and the composition of manufacturing output come increasingly to rely on income inequality as the source of effective demand. Any reduction in inequality threatens the commercial viability of large parts of the manufacturing consumer goods sector and consequently is resisted. That is, import-substituting industrialisation creates vested interests among producers in favour of income inequality among consumers.

Lastly, the trade and credit policies have affected settlement patterns and the spacial distribution of the population. They have encouraged rural to urban migration and in some cases an explosive expansion of large metropolitan agglomerations. Rapid urbanisation, in turn, has imposed heavy costs and forced some diversion of scarce investment funds toward social infrastructure – urban housing, urban water and sewage works, roads, street lighting, etc. Inevitably, however, the provision of social overhead capital has lagged behind demand and as a result slum conditions have proliferated and many millions of people have been forced to live in urban squalor [24].

Not all of these effects or biases have been present in all countries pursuing import-substituting strategies of industrialisation and of course the strength of the various biases has not been the same everywhere even when they are present. Nonetheless, they have been sufficiently common and sufficiently strong to create disenchantment among supporters and strong criticism from the champions of an open economy [25]. There is no doubt that cases can be found of a gross misallocation of resources in particular industries, as in the notorious Chilean automobile industry [26], and in some instances inefficiency has been so great that when inputs and outputs are valued at world prices, the value of material inputs has exceeded that of outputs, i.e., the industry has been characterised by negative value added [27]. These are exceptional cases, however, not typical ones.

As we have seen, investment in industry has been quite high and the growth of manufacturing output per head has been rapid. It certainly is not correct to imagine that average income per head would increase if manufacturing plants in the Third World were closed down – as the findings of negative value added imply! A more serious criticism is that import-substituting industrialisation far from easing balance-of-payments problems actually makes them worse. Once luxury or non-essential consumer goods have been eliminated from the import bill and replaced by domestic production, only essential consumer goods and capital and intermediate goods are imported. Imports of essential consumer goods cannot be reduced almost by definition and imports of capital and intermediate goods are likely also to be essential to maintain production and investment. In such circumstances, the argument goes, the balance-of-payments constraint on growth is likely to be very tight and the country in effect will be more dependent on external trade than before import-substituting industrialisation began.

The force of the argument depends however on an assumption that once a country has embarked on import substitution it is unable subsequently to switch to exporting manufactured goods. This assumption, at least for some countries, has proved to be false. Indeed the natural sequence for most capitalist economies is to start the process of industrialisation by substituting imports and later, when costs have fallen as a result of learning by doing, to produce for foreign markets. As Arthur Lewis has said " ... it is hard to begin industrialisation by exporting manufactures. Usually one begins by selling in a familiar and protected home market and moves on to exporting only after one has learnt to make one's costs competitive" [28].

There is however a second approach to industrialisation in the Third World that merits mention. This approach was devised to enable a country to industrialise under conditions of stagnant or slowly growing exports. Under such conditions the foreign exchange needed to import capital goods to sustain a high rate of investment is not available and consequently the country must either reduce its growth ambitions to the rate permitted by export earnings or it must develop its own capital goods sector. The Indian statistician and planner, P.C. Mahalanobis, clearly influenced by the Soviet experience [29], designed a development strategy for India that was spearheaded by the development and expansion of the capital goods industries [30].

Unlike import-substituting industrialisation which proceeds by supplying already established markets for consumer goods, a strategy based on promoting the capital goods sector does not enjoy the advantage of a domestic market ready to absorb the output of the new industries. Consequently capacity has to be built ahead of demand in the expectation or hope that demand will materialise as growth occurs. In a large country such an expectation is perhaps reasonable, but in a small country there will be a danger of widespread excess capacity in the capital goods sector. This in turn will make it impossible to exploit economies of scale; average costs will tend to be high and firms might be forced to operate at a loss for long periods of time.

Private industrialists are unlikely to be willing to bear the risks of building far in advance of demand or of carrying large losses for long periods. The strategy therefore implies that the state will have to play a leading role in establishing and running the capital goods enterprises. Small scale, light manufacturing of consumer goods can be left to the private sector, which can be granted protection as under an import substituting strategy, but the main thrust of industrialisation under this strategy would come from publicly financed investment in state enterprises. The country would of course still have a mixed economy, but compared to a pure import substituting strategy, the mix would be tilted toward the public sector.

The losses of state enterprises would have to be covered out of general government revenue. If tax receipts were insufficient to do this, the public sector as a whole would be in deficit. That is, the public sector's contribution to national savings would be negative. The danger would then arise that unless private sector savings were buoyant or taxes could readily be raised, an industrialisation strategy designed to increase the supply of investment goods would falter because of an inadequate supply of savings. In a centrally planned economy where all resources are allocated in physical terms, this problem in principle should not occur since material balances would ensure that consumption does not absorb resources

112

needed for planned investment. But in a mixed economy the policymakers have to ensure not only that the physical resources necessary for investment are in principle available (either from domestic production or imports) but also that consumption does not reduce savings below the level needed to finance the desired investment. Unless policy is skilfully implemented there is a danger that a strategy designed to alleviate a foreign exchange constraint on development will end up by creating a savings constraint.

The most direct way to alleviate a foreign exchange constraint is of course by increasing exports. The third approach to industrialisation in the Third World attempts to do precisely that, namely, to design the strategy of development around exports of manufactured goods. This is undoubtedly the hard way to industrialise, but in some cases, e.g., Hong Kong and Singapore, there was little choice. In other cases, e.g., South Korea and Taiwan, the import-substituting phase of industrialisation was relatively short and policy soon switched to an emphasis on exporting. The results were spectacularly successful. It has been argued that the import-substituting phases were vital for the success of the subsequent exporting phases, but this is difficult to demonstrate conclusively.

Many of the biases inherent in a strategy of import substitution are absent or at least less strong in a strategy of industrial export promotion. The greater openness of the economy means that comparative advantages can more readily be exploited. This in turn will help to increase overall efficiency in the use of resources and to raise average incomes. Manufacturing production in an export-oriented strategy is likely to be labour intensive because only in that way will costs be low enough to be internationally competitive. As a result the growth of employment in manufacturing is likely to be higher than in an import substitution strategy.

Wage costs typically are kept low by restrictions on trade union activity or by their outright prohibition. Hours of work (including overtime) and the intensity of work are great. Two and three shifts are usual. Considerable reliance in some industries is put on female labour. Some analysts regard these practices as evidence of "wage repression" and believe them to be an integral part of the strategy. It is of course true that wages are repressed in the sense that organised labour is not free to push earnings much above the opportunity cost of labour. It is also true that in labour disputes the government, if it intervenes, usually does so on the side of management rather than in support of the workers. On the other hand, average wages in countries pursuing export-led industrialisation tend to be relatively high and to increase much more rapidly than countries otherwise comparable. And of course the employment of labour in manufacturing tends to rise much more quickly.

Relatively low capital-labour ratios and high rates of growth of employment are likely to be associated with a higher wage share in value added and a more equal distribution of income among households. Moreover, if factor price distortions can be kept to a minimum and if monopolistic concentrations of industry can be avoided, the personal distribution of income could remain relatively equal in the course of development and inequality could possibly even decline. If for example the growth of manufacturing is associated with constant real wages and diminishing unemployment in the early stages and rising real wages and full employment in the later stages, the degree of inequality probably would fall, except in the unlikely event that the elasticity of substitution between labour and capital is greater than unity. Thus for all these reasons the hard way to industrialise, if it is feasible, is in principle the best way.

Actual practice, however, seldom conforms fully to theory and it is instructive to examine the experience of countries that have followed the three different approaches that have been identified. In the sections that follow we shall consider Brazil as a case of successful import-substituting industrialisation, India as an example of a country which has consciously developed a domestic capital goods sector and South Korea as a country which has concentrated on exporting manufactured goods to the rest of the world.

Brazil: from import substitution to exports of manufactures

Brazil is by far the largest country in Latin America and its history of import-substituting industrialisation contains many features to be found in other Latin American countries. In Brazil as elsewhere import substitution did not begin as a deliberate strategy of economic development, rather it was a more or less spontaneous reaction to a series of external shocks that began with the disappearance of the market for Brazilian rubber in the late nineteenth century and was followed in rapid succession by the disruption of international trade in the First World War, the collapse of the country's terms of trade during the Great Depression of the 1930s and the disruption of international commerce yet again during the Second World War. Each of these shocks provoked a wave of import-substituting industrialisation which led to a step-by-step rise in the share of manufacturing in gross domestic product.

The Great Depression probably was the point of no return for Brazil. In just two years, between 1929 and 1931, the country's terms of trade declined by 46.4 per cent and then fell again sharply in 1938, so that the terms of trade in 1938 were 57 per cent lower than they had been at the time of the stock market crash on Wall Street [31]. The volume of imports fell precipitously. Indeed at the low point in 1932 they were 63.8 per cent below the 1929 level [32]. It is hardly surprising that Brazilians (and other Latin Americans) began to doubt the advantages of an open economy.

In fact there was a sharp break from the liberal international economic order and the gold standard rules. Brazil devalued the currency, imposed exchange controls, increased tariff protection, suspended payments of interest and capital on the foreign debt in 1931 and then again in 1937 suspended all public debt payments for three years. "In the end, the foreign debts were written down to less than a quarter of their nominal value" [33]. The measures evidently worked. The fall in GDP between 1929 and 1931 was limited to 5.3 per cent; thereafter output began to increase at a rapid rate and between 1931 and 1938 real GDP rose by 56.4 per cent [34].

The decline in world coffee prices was partially offset by internal price supports and this helped to maintain high incomes for the wealthy plantation owners in the state of Sao Paulo. The plantation owners, then and later when coffee prices recovered, reinvested their capital in manufacturing industries. As a result, to this day over half of Brazil's manufacturing output originates in Sao Paulo. In the 1930s the role of the central government under Getulio Vargas was greatly strengthened relative to local power holders and the traditional large landowners linked to the export sector. In some cases (as in coffee) part of the landowning class was converted into an industrial class and in other cases new industrial groups allied with the state emerged. In either event the final outcome was impressive. Industrial output over the entire period 1929-1938 increased 6.1 per cent a year. Import-substituting industrialisation had demonstrated what it could do.

The Second World War gave a further stimulus to industry, as in many other parts of Latin America. In Brazil, by 1945, industrial production probably accounted for 20 per cent of gross domestic product [35]. In response to greater international competition after the war, Brazil in 1947 reintroduced exchange controls, imposed a system of multiple exchange rates and increased tariff protection, particularly favouring the domestic production of consumer goods.

Again, in 1956-61, this time under Juscelino Kubitschek, there was a new surge of industrialisation [36]. There was massive state investment in electric power and transport and in the capital and intermediate goods industries. The private sector was given high protection in the consumer goods industries but low or negative effective protection in capital goods (which was partly compensated by direct government subsidies). Multiple exchange rates were also used. Liberal policies toward foreign capital were adopted and in response direct foreign investment in manufacturing rose very rapidly. Motor vehicles, shipbuilding, steel, engineering and heavy electrical equipment were especially favoured by foreign investors.

In 1969 the most recent surge of industrial expansion began. This period, which ended effectively in 1976, was marked by extraordinarily rapid growth and in fact is known as the Brazilian miracle. The "miracle", however, is part of the Brazilian pattern of boom and bust, as can clearly be seen in Figure 5.1. The long-term trend rate of growth of industrial output over nearly three and a half decades (1950-1984) was 7.7 per cent per annum. In contrast the average of the annual rates of growth in the major sub-periods was as follows:

Kubitschek expansion (1955-61)	10.9
Crisis of the 1960s (1962-68)	3.5
Economic miracle (1969-76)	12.7
Debt crisis (1977-84)	0.7

Superimposed on the cyclical pattern of expansion was a long-run change in the structure of manufacturing output. Although the origin of the industrialisation strategy was in import substitution of consumer goods, the development of intermediate and capital goods was not neglected. In fact by 1967 intermediate and capital goods accounted for nearly 56 per cent of value added in manufacturing and basic consumption goods for less than a third. Sixteen years later the structure had evolved further: in 1983 the share in manufacturing value added of capital and intermediate goods was 62 per cent and the share of basic consumer goods was just under a quarter (see Table 5.5). Brazil thus has created a balanced and well-integrated industrial sector and in principle the country should be capable of self-reliant growth. It has completed the transition from specialisation on consumer goods to a diversified composition of manufacturing output.

The level of protection in Brazil was very high by Asian standards and higher than in Colombia and Mexico, although not as high as in Argentina. In 1967, for example, nominal protection of the manufacturing sector (including not only tariffs but also exchange premia and port charges) was 48 per cent and effective protection was 73 per cent [37]. This was excessive even from a protectionist point of view in that Brazilian costs under competitive conditions were not 48-73 per cent higher than cif prices of imported manufactured goods. The high tariffs, exchange premia and port charges enabled Brazilian industrialists to establish uncompetitive enterprises and to reap large monopoly rents – partly in the form of high incomes and partly in the form of an "easy life" and avoidable high costs.

Joel Bergsman estimates that in 1967 the total cost of protection to Brazil was "perhaps 8-10 per cent of GNP" [38]. But he goes on to say,

> "Only a small part of this – less than 1 per cent of GNP – was the result of misallocation. The rest consists of monopoly profits plus avoidable higher costs. This implies that moving to free trade in 1967 would have resulted in a saving amounting to only something less than 1 per cent of GNP,

Figure 5.1. **BRAZIL: ANNUAL CHANGE IN INDUSTRIAL OUTPUT**

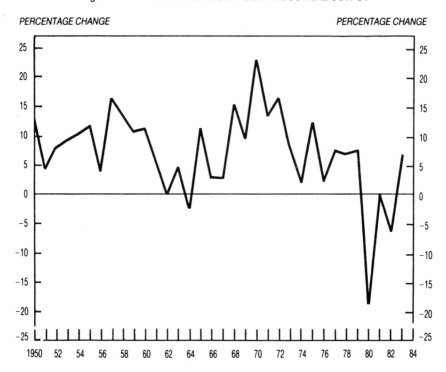

PERCENTAGE CHANGE   *PERCENTAGE CHANGE*

Table 5.5 **THE COMPOSITION OF MANUFACTURING OUTPUT IN BRAZIL, 1967-1983**

Percentage of value added

	1967	1975	1983
Basic consumer goods *a*	32.3	25.9	24.7
Intermediate and capital goods *b*	55.7	60.9	62.0
Other manufactured goods *c*	12.0	13.2	13.3

a) ISIC 31 (food and tobacco), 32 (textiles and clothing).
b) ISIC 35 (chemicals and plastics), 36 (non-metallic minerals), 37 (basic metals), 38 (machinery and equipment).
c) ISIC 33 (wood and wood products), 34 (paper and printing), 39 (other).
Sources: UNIDO, *Industry and Development Global Report 1986,* Vienna, 1986; IBRD, *World Tables,* Baltimore, Johns Hopkins University Press, 1983.

through substitution of more profitable export activities for less profitable import substituting activities" [39].

Protection, then, did not lead so much to a misalloation of resources and inefficiency as to a concentration of income. Moreover the degree of inequality appears to have increased over time. Regis de Castro Andrade reports that the percentage share in the personal

116

distribution of income among the economically active population aged 10 to 65 evolved as follows [40]:

	1960	1970	1976
Lowest 50 per cent	17.7	14.9	11.8
Highest 5 per cent	27.7	34.9	39.0
Gini coefficient	0.50	0.56	0.60

The overall distribution of income as measured by the Gini coefficient was very unequal in 1960 and became steadily worse over the next sixteen years. Indeed Brazil must have about the most unequal distribution of income of any country in the world [41].

The general deterioration occurred in both the lower half of the distribution and at the very top. The share of the richest 5 per cent of income earners rose dramatically from 27.7 per cent in 1960 to 39 per cent in 1976 while the share of the poorest 50 per cent fell sharply from 17.7 to 11.8 per cent. That is, in 1976, an average person in the upper 5 per cent of the income earning population received 33 times as much as an average person in the bottom half of the population.

The state is of course in alliance with the industrial and property owning classes. It is responsible for more than 40 per cent of total fixed investment. It has a controlling interest (but seldom complete ownership) in mining, steel, chemicals, oil and petrochemicals, the railroads, electric and nuclear power. And during the time of the "economic miracle" the private sector received massive subsidies and tax exemptions to encourage the export of manufactured goods. "As a result, exporters of manufactured goods enjoyed gross subsidies allowing them to place their products abroad at fob prices from 40 to 60 per cent lower than the domestic prices of the same goods" [42].

It is hardly surprising therefore that exports of manufactures rose rapidly in the late 1960s. Moreover, as we saw in Table 5.2, exports of manufactured goods continued to rise rapidly throughout the 1970s, so that by the end of the decade they accounted for more than 70 per cent of total exports. This occurred, furthermore, in a context in which the Brazilian economy gradually became more open to the world at large. Thus in 1970 exports accounted for 6.5 per cent of GDP; in 1975, for 7.1 per cent; in 1980, for 8.5 per cent; and in 1984, when the country ran a huge balance of trade surplus in a struggle to service its foreign debt [43], 14.4 per cent. Thus Brazil successfully completed the transition from import-substituting industrialisation to export promotion of manufactured goods.

The transition was the outcome of a partnership between the indigenous industrial class, the state and foreign investors. The contribution of direct foreign investment to Brazil's industrialisation has been enormous, perhaps larger than that of any other country which has made a sucessful transition from import substitution to export promotion. As early as 1978, for instance, foreign enterprises accounted for 44 per cent of Brazil's manufacturing output and were responsible for 50 per cent of the country's exports of manufactured goods [44]. Foreign influence is therefore considerable. Indeed, of the three members of the partnership, the Brazilian industrial class is undoubtedly the most junior.

India: the State, capital goods and self-reliance

The Indian experience of industrialisation differs from the Brazilian in a number of ways. First, after Independence in 1947 the government took responsibility for the country's economic development. Policy was formulated within the framework of a series of five-year plans in which the public sector was expected to play the leading role and the private sector was to be guided in the desired direction by government controls and incentives. Second, beginning with the Second Five-Year Plan (1955-60) particular emphasis was placed upon the growth of the capital goods sector. One reason for this emphasis was "export pessimism", a belief that the world market would grow relatively slowly, that the terms of trade were likely to move against India's primary export commodities and that India could not become internationally competitive in manufactured products without an initial and probably rather long period of domestic protection. In addition, third, the country wished to be independent not only in a formal political sense but also economically. It did not want to be dependent on foreign sources for its basic capital goods nor was it willing to accept foreign direct investment (except as a means of obtaining foreign technology); it was, however, prepared to accept foreign aid, although in practice external assistance seldom was more than 3.5 per cent of GNP and usually was much less. Basically, India wished to be and was self-reliant.

While it would be misleading to claim that India's policies for industrial development have remained unchanged since Independence, and even more misleading to claim that agricultural policy has remained unchanged, the general thrust of industrial policies was remarkably consistent for thirty years, namely from 1955 to 1985. The Mahalanobis legacy was indeed an enduring one and India remained faithful to his vision of capital goods as the leading sector and the state as the leading actor. Public investment has consistently accounted for 40-55 per cent of the total. Private investment in industry has been regulated (some would say restrained) by a series of measures, of which industrial licenses and import licenses have been the most important. That is, until recently imports were restricted by quotas (supplemented by tariffs) and allocated in physical terms by type of product and by type of user [45]. To prevent the degree of monopoly in the private sector from being excessive, price controls also have been imposed on products regarded as essential: fertilizer, cement, aluminium, sugar, pharmaceutical products, etc.

If one assumes that the primary objective of economic policy was to develop a capital goods sector so that India's rate of accumulation could be independent of the growth of export earnings, then industrialisation must be judged a success (see Table 5.6). The share of the capital goods sector rose steadily from less than 5 per cent of industrial output at the beginning of the Second Five-Year Plan to nearly 18 per cent in 1979/80. The share of the so-called basic goods (fertilizer, cement, electric power, etc.) also increased substantially over the twenty-three year period. Basic and capital goods combined accounted for 48.5 per cent of total industrial output by the beginning of the present decade.

The same picture emerges if one compares relative rates of growth. During the two decades from 1959/60 to 1979/80 net value added in the capital goods industries grew much faster than in any other sub-sector, namely, 8.1 per cent a year as compared to 6.2 in basic goods, 4.9 in consumer goods and only 4.2 in the intermediate goods sub-sector. Thus in relative terms the priority given to capital goods by the policymakers was achieved.

Also achieved in practice was the priority accorded to public sector investment as compared to private. The problem, however, is that the dynamism of public sector investment declined markedly after the mid-1960s. This can clearly be seen by examining the data on annual rates of growth of total fixed investment [46]. During roughly the Second and Third Five-Year Plans, i.e., from 1956/7 to 1965/6, public sector fixed investment increased 10 per cent a year and private sector fixed investment 3.2 per cent a year. The average for the two sectors was a respectable 6.1 per cent annual rate of growth. In the following period 1966/7 to 1979/80 the rate of growth of fixed investment in the public sector fell by nearly a

Table 5.6 INDIA: CHANGES IN INDUSTRIAL STRUCTURE, 1956-1979/80

| | 1956 | Percentage share of industrial output | | | | | Rate of growth, 1959/60–1979/80 c (Per cent per annum) |
		1960/1	1965/6	1970/1	1975/6	1979/80	
Basic goods a	22.1	27.5	30.6	30.7	31.9	30.8	6.2
Intermediate goods	24.6	21.0	19.1	19.0	17.5	16.3	4.2
Capital goods	4.7	10.7	15.0	15.2	16.3	17.7	8.1
Consumer goods b	48.4	40.8	35.4	35.1	34.3	35.3	4.9

a) Basic goods comprise salt, fertilizers, cement, basic metals, electricity and mining.
b) Consumer goods include both durables and non-durables.
c) Net value added.

Sources: Isher Judge Ahluwalia, *Industrial Growth in India: Stagnation Since the Mid-Sixties*, Delhi, Oxford University Press, 1985, Table 2.1, p. 9 and Table 2.5, p. 19; Isher Judge Ahluwalia, "The Role of Policy in Industrial Development", paper presented to a conference on Economie industrielle et stratégies d'industrialisation dans le Tiers-Monde, ORSTOM, Paris, 26-27 February 1987, Table 1, p. 31.

half (to 5.2 per cent) while growth in the private sector remained virtually unchanged (at 3.1 per cent). As a result the overall rate of growth of fixed investment fell by a third to 4.1 per cent a year. The public sector locomotive had run out of steam.

Long-term rates of growth of output and productivity in India's manufacturing sector have been a little disappointing. In the three decades 1950-80 production increased on average 5.1 per cent a year (see Table 5.7). Isher Ahluwalia has shown, however, that there was a sharp slowing down of growth after 1965 and that the momentum achieved in the period 1955-65 has never been regained [47], although it is hoped that the policy reforms that began in 1985 will lead to a revival. She has also shown that for twenty years, namely from 1955 to 1975, total factor productivity in manufacturing actually declined; it has however begun to rise since about 1975.

The sluggish growth of industry has meant that gross domestic product also has grown rather slowly. Indeed from 1950 to 1980 GDP grew only 3.6 per cent a year and GDP per capita only about 1.3 per cent. Given the slow growth of average incomes one would not expect major changes in the distribution of income and our expectations are supported by the data. The degree of inequality in India is moderate and certainly not as great as in Brazil, but between 1964 and 1967 the distribution of household income in India as a whole apparently became much more unequal, the Gini coefficient rising from 0.35 to 0.46. But then it fell to 0.42 in 1975 and hence one can infer no trend in inequality in either direction from this fragmentary evidence [48].

Table 5.7 **INDIA: GROWTH OF OUTPUT AND PRODUCTIVITY IN MANUFACTURING, 1950-1983**
Per cent per annum

	Manufacturing value added	Total factor productivity in manufacturing
1950-80	5.1	n.a.
1955-65	6.2	-0.1
1965-75	3.3	-1.5
1975-80	4.5	0.5
1980-83	5.8	n.a.

Sources: UNIDO, *Industrial Development Review Series: India,* Vienna, 5 July 1985, Table 1, p. 4; Isher Judge Ahluwalia, "The Role of Policy in Industrial Development", *op. cit.,* Table 3, p. 33 and Table 5, p. 36.

The industrial reform programme that started in 1985 has three broad objectives: (*i*) to reduce the emphasis on public sector investment and increase that of the private sector, (*ii*) to switch policy instruments from a reliance on physical controls to financial incentives and (*iii*) to shift from import-substituting industrialisation towards a more open economy. Measures have been taken to release the energies of private entrepreneurship and to promote more competition. The investment licensing system has been simplified and 25 industries have been delicensed altogether. Corporate and personal income taxes have been reduced as have the excise taxes on many manufactured products. Some fiscal incentives have been introduced to encourage investment by small and medium-sized enterprises. These incentives presumably were introduced to help correct the imbalance created by the investment licensing system which favoured exceptionally large establishments. Indeed disregarding household manufacturing and workshop enterprises, India is said to be "the country where very large enterprises (over 1 000 workers) dominate manufacturing factory

120

employment to a greater extent than any other country in the world – including the United States" [49].

The government has reduced subsidies to manufacturing enterprises and has also reduced a number of price controls. Some export incentives have been introduced and export duties have been abolished on three-quarters of the items previously liable to duty. Most important, the import licensing system has been simplified and the number of quantitative trade restrictions has been greatly reduced. Lastly, policy has become slightly more encouraging to direct foreign investment.

India's policies have been out of synchronisation with the world economy. When international trade was expanding swiftly, India's policies were very inward-oriented. Now that international trade has slowed down, India has decided to liberalise her trade regime and become more export-oriented. India's ratio of exports to GDP is about the lowest in the world and although manufactures account for about 70 per cent of exports, it should be possible to increase very substantially the country's share of the world market for selected manufactured goods. The change in trade policy is therefore to be welcomed as better late than never. There certainly is no reason actively to discriminate against exports. At the same time one must recognise that in current trading conditions a strategy of export-led growth is unlikely to be as successful as it would have been for India twenty years ago or even as it could be today for a smaller country. Hence expansion of domestic demand probably will continue to be important for the growth of India's industrial sector.

South Korea: planned exports of manufactures

South Korea's experience is in marked contrast with that of India. At the end of the Korean War (1950-53) the economy was in ruins. Fixed investment was less than 6 per cent of gross national product, manufacturing output was less than 9 per cent of GNP and exports accounted for only 2 per cent of GNP. Imports were 2.3 times as large as exports. There was of course a recovery when hostilities ceased and the mining and manufacturing sectors quickly regained momentum. Growth as a whole, however, was relatively slow and at the beginning of the 1960s the economy clearly was in crisis. In 1960, national savings financed only 7.5 per cent of gross investment, the rest coming from abroad as foreign aid. GNP grew only 1.1 per cent and income per head fell. In 1961, mining and manufacturing output increased only 4.4 per cent and in that same year a new military government took power.

The new government introduced a new economic strategy of export-oriented industrialisation. This was not a strategy of *laissez faire*, quite the reverse as we shall see. An important component of the strategy however was to align South Korean prices with international prices in order to exploit the country's comparative advantage and maintain the competitiveness of its exports. The won was devalued early in 1961 and at fairly frequent intervals thereafter; in between devaluations export subsidies were used to make certain that the real exchange rate for exporters remained competitive. On the whole the policy worked reasonably well, although towards the end of the period 1974-80 (during which the nominal exchange rate was held constant) South Korea's exports began to suffer. There is little doubt that the 1980 devaluation should have occurred at least twelve months earlier [50].

The financial regime was changed at the same time as the exchange rate regime. In 1961 the government took control of the five major banks and used this control to implement its investment and output plans. Capital was supplied to private entrepreneurs at subsidised rates and other government policies (tariffs, price controls, profits tax, depreciation allowances, control of entry into an industry) were used to discriminate between firms, favouring those which complied with the planners' wishes and penalising those who refused to conform [51]. In 1965 nominal interest rates were more than doubled and this had two beneficial effects [52]. First, by increasing the cost of borrowed capital it encouraged firms to adopt more labour-intensive methods of production and thus to increase employment. Second, it encouraged savers to switch their placements from the curb market to the formal capital market, and this in turn made it easier for the government-controlled banks to implement central plans.

Government intervention in the capital market helped to create an oligopolistic structure of industry. The firms that benefitted from the differential access to credit and from concessionary loans at low real rates of interest grew very rapidly while those firms that were unable to obtain loans or have their loans renewed remained small and often went bankrupt. As a result, the average size of enterprise in South Korea is large and the twenty largest firms account for half of manufacturing output [53]. This high concentration of industry has of course made it easier for the government to become involved in the detailed implementation of its plans.

The Economic Planning Board was established in 1961 and included both planning and budget functions. At the same time a Ministry of Commerce and Industry, based on MITI in Japan, was created to promote industrial exports. Indeed the Ministry maintained constant pressure on industry "through monthly export promotion meetings monitored directly by the President" [54]. Planning in South Korea, as John Enos explains, is remarkable for

> " ... its omnipresence on the economic scene. Through the agency of its ministers and civil servants, employed in the Economic Planning Board, the various departments and ancillary bodies, the government has populated the industrial environment. Having participated in planning, in negotiations with foreign suppliers, in establishing or directing firms to employ the imported technology; and in procurement of finance, equipment and personnel; having been present during the construction of plant, during the start-up of equipment, and during its subsequent operation and improvement; the functionaries of government have become quickly aware of departures from schedules and deficiencies in material and manpower. It has been easier to impose controls, and those controls have been more effective, when the controllers have been always on the spot" [55].

This system of detailed intervention and of close supervision in furtherance of carefully planned exports of manufactures was very successful. As can be seen in Table 5.8, the share of manufacturing in GNP nearly doubled between 1960 and 1975 and by 1984 had risen further to just over 29 per cent of gross national product. During the same period, exports rose from 3.4 per cent of GNP in 1960 to 28.1 per cent in 1975 and then to 41.5 per cent in 1984. In three decades South Korea was transformed from virtually a closed economy to a very open one.

Foreign capital has been an important source of investment finance throughout the industrialisation drive. Three points however should be noticed. First, the dependence on foreign capital did fall somewhat until about 1970, after which it remained stable. The third column in Table 5.8 shows that in 1955 national savings financed only 42.4 per cent of total

	Exports	Manufacturing	National Savings
	(Per cent of GNP)		(per cent of gross domestic capital formation)
1953	2.0	8.9	57.3
1955	1.7	11.4	42.4
1960	3.4	13.7	7.5
1965	8.5	17.9	49.1
1970	14.2	20.8	64.7
1975	28.1	26.5	63.3
1980	37.7	28.8	63.2
1984	41.5	29.3	n.a.

Source: Bank of Korea, *National Income in Korea 1982*, Seoul, 1982; Economic Planning Board, *Major Statistics of Korean Economy 1985*, Seoul, 1985.

gross investment and foreign savings the rest. By 1970 however national savings were able to finance 64.7 per cent of investment, reducing the share of foreign savings to a little more than a third. Second, direct foreign investment has never played a significant role in the country's development. Most foreign capital imports have been either public or commerical loans and in the period 1975 to 1984, for instance, foreign investment accounted for only 4.6 per cent of the total of foreign loans and investments [56]. Third, when foreign direct investment was allowed into the country it was tightly controlled. Usually joint ventures were established (with Koreans having a controlling interest) rather than wholly-owned foreign subsidiaries and occasionally the joint venture subsequently became wholly Korean-owned. Moreover, "foreign engineers, technicians and managers have been replaced with Koreans, always deliberately and systematically" [57]. Foreign owned industry, in short, has been domesticated.

The performance in terms of rates of growth has been impressive. This is shown in Table 5.9. The rate of growth of gross domestic product accelerated sharply after the new strategy came into effect. During the period 1953-62, GDP in real terms grew about 4.7 per cent per annum whereas in the subsequent period 1962-85 the rate of growth was 8.7 per cent a year. The growth of value added in manufacturing also accelerated but the rate of acceleration was not as dramatic as in the case of GDP because the trend rate of growth in the manufacturing sector already was high prior to the change of government, although as previously noted manufacturing grew very slowly in 1961. Total exports and especially exports of manufactured goods increased very rapidly. There was an initial leap in the level of exports when the new strategy was introduced and then an acceleration in their rate of growth. Over the entire period 1953-85 total exports (in constant won) grew 23 per cent a year; manufactured exports over the slightly shorter period from 1957 to 1985 grew 32.3 per cent a year. By the beginning of the 1980s manufactured goods accounted for well over 90 per cent of total exports.

It is sometimes imagined that because of the export orientation of South Korea's manufacturing industries, output must be concentrated on light industry and manufactured consumer goods. This is not correct, however. The share of basic consumer goods in manufacturing value added has fallen steadily and by 1983 accounted for only 36.1 per cent of the total (see Table 5.10). Conversely, the share of intermediate and capital goods has

Table 5.9 **RATES OF GROWTH IN SOUTH KOREA, 1953-1985**
Per cent per annum

	1953-62	1962-85	1953-85
Gross domestic product	4.7	8.7	8.0
Value added in manufacturing	11.7	16.0	15.5
Total exports c	15.0	22.8	23.0
Exports of manufactured goods c	23.7 a	27.3	32.3 b

a) 1957-62.

b) 1957-85.

c) The estimates for the rates of growth in the two sub-periods are not consistent with the rate of growth for the period as a whole. Kinked exponential trend rates were then calculated in an attempt to correct for this, but in fact the results were even less satisfactory because the estimated growth rates in the earlier period turned out to be higher than in the later period.

Sources: Bank of Korea, *National Income in Korea 1982*, Seoul, 1982; Economic Planning Board, *Stastical Yearbook 1986*, Seoul, 1986; OECD Development Centre data tapes.

risen steadily from 42 per cent of manufacturing value added in 1967 to nearly 56 per cent in 1983. The structure of the manufacturing sector in South Korea thus is not fundamentally different from that in Brazil or India, two countries with a much larger domestic market [58]. It certainly is not the case that South Korea's strategy of planned exports of manufactures has implied neglect of capital and intermediate goods. It should be added, however, that some of the capital goods industries are not competitive, or not yet competitive, on world markets and have required substantial protection to be commercially viable.

Table 5.10 **COMPOSITION OF MANUFACTURING OUTPUT IN SOUTH KOREA, 1967-1983**
Percentage of value added

	1967	1975	1983
Basic consumer goods a	47.3	40.3	36.1
Intermediate and capital goods b	42.0	51.1	55.9
Other manufactured goods c	10.7	8.6	8.0

a) ISIC 31 (food and tobacco), 32 (textiles and clothing).

b) ISIC 35 (chemicals and plastics), 36 (non-metallic minerals), 37 (basic metals), 38 (machinery and equipment).

c) ISIC 33 (wood and wood products), 34 (paper and printing), 39 (other).

Sources: UNIDO, *Industry and Development Global Report 1986*, Vienna, 1986, IBRD, *World Tables*, Baltimore, Johns Hopkins University Press, 1983.

Another misconception about South Korea's development strategy is that it has been based on sweated labour, low wages and government regulation of the labour market. The truth of the matter is that during the drive for industrialisation the labour market was broadly competitive and restrictive practices and monopolistic pricing of labour were avoided. Moreover, the supply price of labour in urban areas was relatively high, not low. The main reason for this is that South Korea had two radical land reforms, the first in 1947 which reduced full-time tenancy from 70 to 33 per cent and the second in 1950 which virtually eliminated the remaining tenancy arrangements and created a small peasant farming system based on owner-operated holdings. The land reforms created a very equal distribution of income in the rural areas and raised the opportunity cost of peasant labour. As a result the manufacturing sector had no alternative to paying higher real wages than would have been necessary in the absence of redistributive reforms in the countryside.

In 1963 employment in the manufacturing sector accounted for only 8 per cent of total employment. Unemployment among non-farm households at that time was 16.4 per cent. During the following years however manufacturing employment rose rapidly and unemployment declined as follows [59]:

	Manufacturing employment (Per cent of total)	Unemployment of non-farm households (Per cent)
1963	8.0	16.4
1968	12.8	8.9
1973	15.9	6.8
1978	22.4	4.7
1983	22.6	5.4

The high unemployment kept wages low during the early period of export-oriented industrialisation and real wages in manufacturing actually declined 0.5 per cent a year during 1960-65. However real wages rose very quickly thereafter in response to lower unemployment and increased pressure of demand in the labour market. In 1965-70 real wages increased 7.4 per cent a year and in 1970-83 they increased by 7.7 per cent a year [60]. These are much faster rates of increase than can be observed in most other Third World countries.

The degree of inequality in the distribution of income in South Korea is low. The land reforms created favourable initial conditions and the competitive labour market in a context of rapid growth helped to ensure that industrialisation would be accompanied by an expansion of employment and a rise in the share of wages in national income. The oligopolistic structure of industry has of course pushed up the share of non-wage income in manufacturing value added and it is this probably that accounts for the fact that the distribution of income in South Korea is not as equal as in, say, Taiwan [61].

The official data suggest there is no clear trend in the distribution of household income in either direction (see Table 5.11). The Gini coefficient increased significantly between 1965 and 1976 but then fell between 1980 and 1982, so that at the end of the period it was only a little higher than at the beginning. A similar pattern occurred in the share in total income of the richest quintile. The share of the top 20 per cent of households rose from 41.8 per cent of total income in 1965 to 45.4 per cent in 1980 and then declined to 43 per cent in 1982. The share of the poorest 40 per cent of households was nearly the mirror image of this, falling from a peak of 19.6 per cent in 1970 to a trough of 16.1 per cent in 1980 but then rising sharply to 18.8 per cent in 1982.

The worst year from the point of view of the distribution of income evidently was 1980 and one might be tempted to argue that this points in the direction of things to come. Such an argument however is premature and possibly wrong. The reason is that 1980 was the only year since the new development strategy was introduced in 1961 in which GNP failed to rise substantially. In that year in fact real GNP fell sharply by 5.2 per cent and per capita GNP by 6.8 per cent. The increase in inequality in 1980 probably therefore reflects a cyclical downturn in the economy rather than a secular trend. If so, it means that South Korea is one of the very few Third World countries which has managed to combine rapid

Table 5.11 **THE DISTRIBUTION OF HOUSEHOLD INCOME IN SOUTH KOREA, 1965–1982**

	Gini coefficient	Richest 20 per cent	Poorest 40 per cent
1965	0.34	41.8	19.3
1970	0.33	41.6	19.6
1976	0.39	45.3	18.9
1980	0.39	45.4	16.1
1982	0.36	43.0	18.8

Source: Jang-Ho Kim, *Wages, Employment and Income Distribution in South Korea: 1960-83,* New Delhi, ILO-ARTEP, March 1986, Table 21, p. 75.

industrialisation, profound structural change and a relatively egalitarian distribution of income.

Conclusions

We have seen that industrialisation can be a successful strategy of economic development in the Third World. Three distinct approaches have been identified which have different characteristics and consequences. One approach is based on import-substituting consumer goods, although there is no reason in principle or in historical experience why a country that embarks upon such an approach cannot in a later phase develop a substantial capital goods industry and also begin to export manufactured goods. Let us call this approach the Brazilian model. A second approach starts by concentrating on establishing capital and intermediate goods industries within a semi-closed economy. Again, there is nothing in principle to prevent such a country in a later stage from becoming more open and producing manufactured goods for export. This we shall call the Indian model. The third approach – the South Korean model – is based on planned exports of consumer goods within a policy environment that ensures that domestic and international prices remain broadly aligned.

Each model has its strengths and weaknesses and one's overall assessment inevitably depends on the relative weight given to each. In what follows we shall use eight criteria of evaluation and subjectively rank the three models by the eight criteria. The first criterion is the long-run rate of growth of industrial output. By this criterion the South Korean model seems to be best and the Indian model the least successful. One's judgement might have been different however if world trade had expanded less rapidly than it did in the 1950s and 1960s. Second, there is the question of the stability of growth. Here the Indian model can claim to be the most successful and the Brazilian model the least. The South Korean model, vulnerable to perturbations in international commerce, occupies an intermediate position. When it comes, third, to the growth of industrial exports, the South Korean model as one would expect is far superior to the others while the Indian model appears to be the least successful.

It sometimes is claimed that large countries such as India and Pakistan do not have the option of basing their industrialisation on the export of manufactured goods, or more generally of following an export-oriented strategy of development. This is a path, it is claimed, that only small countries such as South Korea and Singapore can follow. This view, however, clearly is mistaken. The striking fact is that South Korea and Singapore export several times as much as India and Pakistan. The two small countries have of course a higher ratio of exports to GNP and a higher value of exports per capita, but they also have a much higher value of total exports. In 1985, for example, merchandise exports from South Korea

Table 5.12   AN EVALUATION OF THREE APPROACHES TO INDUSTRIALISATION

	South Korean model	Brazilian model	Indian model
1. Growth of industrial output	1	2	3
2. Stability of growth	2	3	1
3. Growth of industrial exports	1	2	3
4. Development of the capital goods industries	3	=1	=1
5. Efficiency of industrial production	1	2	3
6. Creation of employment	1	2	3
7. Degree of equality	1	3	2
8. Growth of per capita income	1	2	3

were $26 442 million and from Singapore, $21 500 million. Pakistan in that year exported only $2 648 million worth of goods and India (in 1983) only $9 770 million. That is, Singapore exported more than twice as much as India and South Korea exported nearly ten times more than Pakistan.

Returning to the evaluation of the three models, the Indian and Brazilian models appear to be more or less equally good in promoting the development of the capital goods industries, and by this fourth criterion the South Korean model ranks last, although it is not far behind the other two. However, fifth, the rankings are different when one considers efficiency in the allocation of resources. Here the South Korean model is superior with the Brazilian and Indian models following some distance behind. The same ranking holds when the sixth criterion is considered, the growth of employment. This is hardly surprising since an efficient allocation of resources implies utilising all factors of production fully and in the case of Third World countries, adopting relatively labour-intensive methods of production.

Seventh, there is the question of the degree of equality. Much depends upon the distribution of income and wealth before a particular approach to industrialisation is adopted. In Third World countries where a majority of the population lives in rural areas and a large part obtains a livelihood from agriculture, land reform obviously is the key issue. However given the "initial conditions" for good or ill, it does seem that the South Korean model of industrialisation, because of its employment intensity, is likely to be associated with a relatively more equal distribution of income. At the other extreme, the Brazilian model, because of the large subsidies it implies for private entrepreneurs, is likely to lead to a high degree of inequality. The Indian model probably falls somewhere in between.

Lastly, there is the growth of per capita income. This depends not only on the rate of growth of manufacturing output but also on such things as the rate of capital formation, the efficiency of investment and the linkages between the industrial sector and the rest of the economy. Taking everything into consideration it seems probable that by this criterion the South Korean model ranks first and the Indian third. What, then, of an overall ranking?

The South Korean model ranks first on six out of the eight criteria; it ranks second in terms of stability of growth and third in terms of the capital goods sector. Unless one gives extraordinarily high weight to the development of the capital goods sector and to the avoidance of fluctuations in output and income, the South Korean model of industrialisation clearly deserves to be placed first. At the other extreme is the Indian model. It ranks third on five out of the eight criteria, including the growth of per capita income, industrial output, manufactured exports and employment. It also ranks third in terms of industrial efficiency. It is hard to avoid the conclusion therefore that the Indian model of industrialisation is the least successful of the three. We thus end with the models ranked in the following order: South Korea as the most successful, followed by Brazil with the Indian model as the least successful.

This ranking raises questions about possible connections between the political regime and the strategy of development. It is sometimes claimed, for example, that the success of export-led industrialisation in some of the newly industrialising countries of Asia (the so-called NICs) has depended upon the repression of labour in order to keep wage costs low and prices internationally competitive [62]. In Latin America it has been argued that import-substituting industrialisation has required an authoritarian political system, i.e., a regime capable both of maintaining order and a very unequal distribution of income [63]. The findings in this chapter could be said to lend superficial support to these notions. Moving away from the stylised models to the country experiences that lie behind the models, it is undeniable that India is a democratic country, that Brazil has had extended periods of dictatorship punctuated by short periods of qualified democracy and that South Korean politics are highly authoritarian and undemocratic. There is thus a temptation to suggest that there may be a trade-off between democratic politics and efficient industrial development. It would be hasty however to draw such a conclusion since so many other interpretations are consistent with the facts.

Authoritarianism in South Korea, for instance, probably has little to do with the approach to industrialisation that was adopted and a great deal more to do with the political tensions created by the decision of external powers to divide the country in two [64]. Similarly, repression in Brazil almost certainly has more to do with the very unequal distribution of income and wealth in that country than with import-substituting industrialisation. Conversely, it is unlikely that if India were to change its pattern of industrialisation – as indeed it appears to be doing – it would for that reason run a risk of becoming less democratic. Certainly politics and economics ultimately are inseparable, and there may be a link of the type postulated between the degree of democracy and the strategy of industrialisation, but until more evidence is available the Scottish verdict of not proven appears to be justified.

NOTES AND REFERENCES

1. Colin Clark, *The Conditions of Economic Progress*, London, MacMillan, 1940.

2. Simon Kuznets, *Economic Growth and Structure: Selected Essays*, New York, W. W. Norton, 1965 and Simon Kuznets, *Modern Economic Growth: Rate, Structure and Spread*, New Haven, Yale University Press, 1966.

3. Hollis Chenery, "Patterns of Industrial Growth", *American Economic Review*, Vol. 50, No. 4, September 1960; Hollis Chenery and Lance Taylor, "Development Patterns: Among Countries and Over Time", *Review of Economics and Statistics*, Vol. 50, No. 4, November 1968; Hollis Chenery and Moshe Syrquin, *Patterns of Development 1950-1970*, Oxford, Oxford University Press, 1975; Hollis Chenery, Sherman Robinson and Moshe Syrquin, *Industrialisation and Growth: A Comparative Study*, New York, Oxford University Press, 1986.

4. Some authors did challenge the proposition that there are uniform patterns of industrialisation. See for example Robert Sutcliffe, *Industry and Underdevelopment*, London, Addison-Wesley, 1971, Ch. 2. Also see C.H. Kirkpatrick, N. Lee and F.I. Nixson, *Industrial Structure and Policy in Less Developed Countries*, London, Allen and Unwin, 1984.

5. See George Richardson, *Information and Investment*, London, Oxford University Press, 1960; Robert Sutcliffe, *op. cit.*, Ch. 6.

6. Alexander Gerschenkron, *Economic Backwardness in Historical Perspective*, Cambridge, Harvard University Press, 1962.

7. Dieter Senghaas, *The European Experience: A Historical Critique of Development Theory*, Leamington Spa, Berg, 1985.

8. Warwick Armstrong, "Imperial Incubus: The Diminished Industrial Ambitions of Canada, Australia and Argentina, 1870-1930", paper presented to a conference on Economie industrielle et stratégies d'industrialisation dans le Tiers-Monde, ORSTOM, Paris, 26-27 February 1987, p. 12.

9. UNIDO, *Handbook of Industrial Statistics 1984*, New York, 1985.

10. *Ibid.*

11. This point is discussed again in Chapter 6 in the context of the relatively low average productivity of labour in agriculture.

12. UNIDO, *Industry in the 1980s: Structural Change and Interdependence*, New York, 1985, Table III.1, p. 38.

13. *Ibid.*, p. 35.

14. UNIDO, *Industry in a Changing World*, New York, 1983, Table II.1, p. 23.

15. UNIDO, *Handbook of Industrial Statistics 1984*, New York, 1985.

16. UNIDO, *Industry in the 1980s, loc. cit.*, Table II.3, p. 21.

17. UNIDO, *Industry in a Changing World, loc. cit.*, Table VII.1, p. 190.

18. Michel Fouquin, "L'inégalité des pays en développement face au commerce internationale", paper presented to a conference on Economie industrielle et stratégies d'industrialisation dans le Tiers-Monde, ORSTOM, Paris, 26-27 February 1987, Table 2, p. 11.

19. IBRD, *World Development Report 1986*, Oxford University Press, 1986.

20. A similar conclusion is reached by Ajit Singh in his "The Interrupted Industrial Revolution of the Third World: Prospects and Policies for Resumption", paper presented to a conference on Economie industrielle et stratégies d'industrialisation dans le Tiers-Monde, ORSTOM, Paris, 26-27 February 1987.

21. See W.M. Corden, "The Structure of a Tariff System and the Effective Protective Rate", *Journal of Political Economy*, Vol. LXXIV, No. 3, June 1966.

22. This is a major theme of Ian Little, Tibor Scitovsky and Maurice Scott, *Industry and Trade in Some Developing Countries*, London, Oxford University Press, 1970.

23. See Mahbub ul Haq, *The Strategy of Economic Planning: A Case Study of Pakistan*, Karachi, Oxford University Press, 1963. Also relevant is Amartya Sen, *Choice of Technique*, Oxford, Blackwell, 3rd edition, 1968.

24. For a humane and moving picture of life in an urban slum in Calcutta see Dominique Lapierre, *The City of Joy*, Bungay, Suffolk, Richard Clay (The Chaucer Press), 1985.

25. See Ian Little, Tibor Scitovsky and Maurice Scott, *op. cit.*; Albert Hirschman, "The Political Economy of Import-Substituting Industrialisation in Latin America", *Quarterly Journal of Economics*, Vol. LXXXII, No. 1, February 1968; John Power, "The Role of Protection with Particular Reference to Kenya", *Eastern Africa Economic Review*, Vol. 4, No. 1, June 1972; John Power, "Import Substitution as an Industrialization Strategy", *Philippine Economic Journal*, Spring 1966.

26. L.L. Johnson, "The Problems of Import Substitution: The Chilean Automobile Industry", *Economic Development and Cultural Change*, Vol. 15, No. 2, Pt. 1, January 1967.

27. See for example R. Soligo and J.J. Stern, "Tariff Protection, Import Substitution and Investment Efficiency", *Pakistan Development Review*, Vol. 5, No. 2, Summer 1965.

28. W. Arthur Lewis, *The Evolution of the International Economic Order*, Princeton, Princeton University Press, 1978, p. 10.

29. For a discussion of the Soviet strategy of industrialisation see Chapter 8.

30. See P.C. Mahalanobis, *The Approach of Operational Research to Planning in India*, London, Asia Publishing House, 1963. Also see K.N. Raj and A.K. Sen, "Alternative Patterns of Growth Under Conditions of Stagnant Export Earnings", *Oxford Economic Papers*, Vol. 13, No. 1, February 1961.

31. Angus Maddison, *Two Crises: Latin America and Asia 1929-38 and 1973-83*, Paris, OECD Development Centre, 1985, Table A-7, p. 87.

32. *Ibid.*, Table A-6, p. 87.

33. *Ibid.*, p. 27.

34. *Ibid.*, Table A-1, p. 84.

35. Joel Bergsman, *Brazil: Industrialization and Trade Policies*, London, Oxford University Press, 1970.

36. See Regis de Castro Andrade, "Brazil: The Economics of Savage Capitalism", in Manfred Bienefeld and Martin Godfrey, eds., *The Struggle for Development: National Strategies in an International Context*, Chichester, John Wiley, 1982. Also see Joel Bergsman, *op. cit.*

37. Joel Bergsman, *Ibid.*, Table 3.3, p. 42. The estimate for the average rate of effective protection excludes perfumes and soaps where the rate was 3 670 per cent!

38. *Ibid.*, p. 178.

39. *Ibid.*, p. 178-9.

40. Regis de Castro Andrade, *op. cit.*, Table 2, p. 172.

41. Compare the data in Table 24, pp. 226-7 of the IBRD, *World Development Report 1986*, Oxford University Press, 1986. The distribution of land in Brazil probably is also the most unequal in the world. At one extreme 342 big landowners own 47.5 million hectares, an area considerably larger than Japan. Their average holding is 138 889 ha. At the other extreme 2.5 million peasant farmers have an average of two ha. each. (See "The Peasants' Revolt", *The Economist Development Report*, November 1985, pp. 1-2.)

42. Regis de Castro Andrade, *op. cit.*, p. 180.

43. In 1984, Brazil's surplus on the trade balance was US$ 13.1 billion, equivalent to 48.5 per cent of its merchandise exports. In 1985, the trade balance surplus was $12.5 billion.

44. Rhys Jenkins, "Latin American Industrialization and the New International Division of Labour", paper presented to a conference on Economie industrielle et stratégies d'industrialisation dans le Tiers-Monde, ORSTOM, Paris, 26-27 February 1987, Table 7, p. 31. Also see Peter Evans, *Dependent Development: The Alliance of Multinational, State and Local Capital in Brazil*, Princeton, Princeton University Press, 1979.

45. The best study of industrial policy in India from Independence to the late 1960s is Jagdish Bhagwati and Padma Desai, *India: Planning for Industrialization*, London, Oxford University Press, 1970. Also see Jagdish Bhagwati and T.N. Srinivasan, *Foreign Trade Regimes and Economic Development: India*, New York, Columbia University Press for the National Bureau of Economic Research, 1975.

46. Isher Judge Ahluwalia, *Industrial Growth in India: Stagnation Since the Mid-Sixties*, Delhi, Oxford University Press, 1985, Table 5.1, p. 75.

47. *Ibid.*

48. *Ibid.*, Table 4.1, p. 58.

49. I.M.D. Little, "Small Manufacturing Enterprises in Developing Countries", *World Bank Economic Review*, Vol. 1, No. 2, January 1987, p. 225.

50. Y.C. Park, "Foreign Debt, Balance of Payments and Growth Prospects: The Case of the Republic of Korea, 1965-88", *World Development*, Vol. 14, No. 8, August 1986.

51. See John Enos, "Korean Industrial Policy", *Prometheus*, Vol. 4, No. 2, December 1986.

52. Tony Michell, "South Korea: Vision of the Future for Labour Surplus Economies?", in Manfred Bienefeld and Martin Godfrey, eds., *op. cit.*

53. Tibor Scitovsky, "Economic Development in Taiwan and South Korea, 1965-81", in L.J. Lau, ed., *Models of Development: A Comparative Study of Economic Growth in South Korea and Taiwan*, San Francisco, ICS Press, 1986.

54. Tony Michell, *op. cit.*, p. 196.

55. John Enos, *op. cit.*, p. 245.

56. Economic Planning Board, *Major Statistics of Korean Economy 1985*, Seoul, 1985, Table 10-21, p. 246.

57. John Enos, *op. cit.*, p. 251.

58. South Korea's population in 1984 was 40.1 million or 30.2 per cent of the size of Brazil (132.8 million) and 5.4 per cent of the size of India (742.6 million).

59. Jang-Ho Kim, *Wages, Employment and Income Distribution in South Korea: 1960-83*, New Delhi, ILO-ARTEP, March 1986, Table 2, p. 56 and Table 4, p. 58.

60. *Ibid.,* Table 10, p. 64.

61. See Tibor Scitovsky, *op. cit.,* p. 139. Scitovsky stresses the fact that firms on average are much smaller in Taiwan than South Korea and also that Taiwan followed a high interest rate policy compared to South Korea.

62. See C.H. Kirkpatrick, "Export Led Development, Labour Market Regulation and the Distribution of Income in Asian NICs: The Case of Singapore", paper presented to a conference on Economie industrielle et strategies d'industrialisation dans le Tiers-Monde, ORSTOM, Paris, 26-27 February 1987. More orthodox views can be found in G.S. Fields, "Employment, Income Distribution and Economic Growth in Seven Small Open Economies", *Economic Journal,* Vol. 94, No. 373, March 1984 and I.M.D. Little, "The Experience and Causes of Rapid Labour-Intensive Development in Korea, Taiwan Province, Hong Kong and Singapore; and the Possibilities of Emulation", in E.L.H. Lee, ed., *Export-Led Industrialisation and Development,* Bangkok, ILO-ARTEP, 1981.

63. Albert Hirschman, "The Turn to Authoritarianism in Latin America and the Search for its Economic Determinants", in D. Collier, ed., *The New Authoritarianism in Latin America,* Princeton, Princeton University Press, 1979; A. Stepan, ed., *Authoritarian Brazil,* New Haven, Yale University Press, 1973; G. O'Donnell, *Modernization and Bureaucratic Authoritarianism,* Institute of International Studies, University of California, Berkeley, 1973; Alejandro Foxley, *Latin American Experiments in Neo-Conservative Economics,* Berkeley, University of California Press, 1983, Ch. 2; F.H. Cardoso and E. Faletto, *Dependency and Development in Latin America,* Berkeley, University of California Press, 1979, Ch. 5; John Sheahan, "Market-Oriented Policies and Political Repression in Latin America", *Economic Development and Cultural Change,* Vol. 28, No. 2, January 1980.

64. An analogous explanation could apply to Taiwan.

Chapter 6

THE GREEN REVOLUTION STRATEGY

Most of the people in Third World countries live in rural areas, most of them are engaged in agriculture and the majority are poor. Hence giving agriculture high priority in development has an intuitive appeal. Indeed it can be argued that in terms of population, employment and production agriculture is the most important sector of the economy (see Table 6.1).

In the Third World as a whole, 70.8 per cent of the population reside in the countryside and less than 30 per cent in the cities. In Africa and Asia the rural population accounts for an even higher proportion of the total, namely, 73 and 71.9 per cent respectively, whereas in Latin America internal migration has reduced the rural population to only 34.7 per cent of the total [1]. If one compares individual countries the range is, of course, even wider. For example, in the 19 countries included in Table 6.1, the range extends from Bangladesh (where nearly nine out of ten of the people live in rural areas) to Argentina (where fewer than two out of ten do so).

Not everyone of working age who lives in the countryside is employed in agriculture. Some are artisans, shopkeepers and traders, others are fishermen or herdsmen, while still others work in small-scale rural industries. In parts of Africa most of the farming is done by women, their menfolk (who may or may not reside in the countryside) having gone to the cities in search of more remunerative employment. Many people have multiple sources of income and hence cannot be classified neatly under one employment category. It is quite common, for example, for a small landowning peasant to supplement his income with wage labour on a neighbour's farm and to engage in part-time petty trading. Other members of the household may have equally varied occupations and thus the family's total income may be derived from many sources. Hence data on the composition of the labour force should be treated with caution.

It is evident, however, that the agricultural labour force will be relatively smaller than the rural population [2]. Even so, the data in the second column of Table 6.1 indicate that in 1980 more than 50 per cent of the labour force was engaged in agriculture in 11 out of the 19 countries. Indeed, in parts of Africa, notably Tanzania and Kenya, the agricultural labour force accounted for more than 80 per cent of the total and in the three large Asian countries of China, India and Bangladesh the proportion was about 70 per cent. Latin America again stands apart. In none of the six countries in the Table does the proportion of the labour force in agriculture exceed 40 per cent and in the highly urbanised countries of Argentina and Chile the proportion is 13 and 16 per cent, respectively. Thus, in terms of employment, agriculture is dominant in Africa and Asia but not in Latin America.

Table 6.1 **RELATIVE SIZE OF THE AGRICULTURAL SECTOR**

	(1) Rural population, 1985 (Per cent of total)	(2) Agricultural labour force, 1980 (Per cent of total)	(3) Agricultural production, 1984 (Per cent of GDP)
Asia:			
China	79.4	69	36
India	74.5	70	35
Pakistan	70.2	55	24
Bangladesh	89.6	75	48
Malaysia	65.8	42	21
Philippines	62.6	52	25
Sri Lanka	78.4	53	28
Africa:			
Botswana	84.7	70	6
Côte d'Ivoire	62.9	65	28
Egypt	55.3	46	20
Ghana	69.3	56	52
Kenya	83.9	81	31
Tanzania	83.5	86	46 a
Latin America:			
Argentina	17.3	13	12
Brazil	32.5	31	13
Chile	18.9	16	6
Colombia	35.8	34	20
Mexico	33.6	37	9
Peru	35.5	40	8

a) 1965.
Sources: Column (1): United Nations, *World Population Prospects,* New York, 1986. Columns (2) and (3): IBRD, *World Development Report 1986,* Oxford University Press, 1986.

When it comes to production, however, agriculture rarely accounts for as much as half of gross domestic product. In Ghana the proportion is slightly above this and in Bangladesh slightly below, but in most other Third World countries value added generated in agriculture, forestry, hunting and fishing, i.e., in the agricultural sector as a whole, is small, particularly when compared with the number of people employed in the sector. In Botswana, a mineral economy, only 6 per cent of total income originates in agriculture despite the fact that 70 per cent of the labour force is employed there. In Peru, another mineral economy, agriculture accounts for 8 per cent of GDP and 40 per cent of employment. Botswana and Peru are extreme cases, but only in Ghana and Argentina among our 19 countries is there a close correspondence between agricultural output and employment. In all the other countries the divergence is great.

This divergence between employment and output in agriculture is evidence of structural distortion, of a misallocation of resources as reflected in enormous differences between the average productivity of labour in agriculture compared to the non-agricultural sectors. Using the data in the second and third columns of Table 6.1 it is possible to make rough calculations of the ratio of output per worker in non-agriculture to agriculture. Thus in Colombia, the productivity of labour in the rest of the economy is about twice as high as in agriculture; in Brazil, the Philippines, Bangladesh, Pakistan and China, the ratio is between three and four; in India and Côte d'Ivoire, between four and five; in Mexico, nearly six and in Kenya the productivity of labour in the non-agricultural sectors is nearly ten times higher than in agriculture.

These high ratios suggest that relative prices have been turned against agriculture or that the sector has been starved of resources, or both. They also suggest that income differentials between agriculture and the rest of the economy must be very wide and, indeed, that poverty must be concentrated in the countryside. There is not a perfect correspondence between the productivity of labour in agriculture and average incomes in rural areas, since some rural households may receive remittances from urban areas or be engaged in non-agricultural rural activities or, as we have seen, have multiple sources of income, but even after taking these qualifications into account it is very likely that low productivity in agriculture will be associated with low rural incomes and a high incidence of poverty.

Low incomes, of course, do not imply stagnation of production. Indeed in the Third World as a whole agricultural output since 1960 has increased nearly 2.8 per cent per annum. Given that the population of the Third World grew about 2.3 per cent a year during this period, agricultural output per head probably rose about 0.5 per cent a year. Moreover, the pace of change appears to have accelerated so that by the middle of the 1980s per capita agricultural production was rising about 1 per cent a year. There are two reasons for this acceleration. First, the rate of growth of output increased 25 per cent between the decade of the 1960s and the period 1970-85, namely, from 2.4 to 3.0 per cent a year. Second, population expansion slowed down from its peak in 1970 of 2.6 per cent a year to about 2.0 per cent in 1985, a decline of 23 per cent. These long-run favourable trends indicate that fears of a Malthusian crisis are unfounded and place the African famines of the 1970s and 1980s in their proper global and temporal perspective.

Africa, however, acts as a powerful reminder that agricultural growth in the Third World has been uneven. Some countries have been far more successful than others, and some in fact have failed miserably. The situation for the period 1965 to 1985 for the 19 countries that interest us most is depicted in Table 6.2. It can be seen at a glance that Asia as a whole has performed better than Latin America and Africa. Among our six Asian countries only Bangladesh experienced a fall in per capita agricultural output. All of the others have done at least moderately well and Malaysia and China rather better than any other country in our sample of 19. Indeed, because of the combination of China's large agricultural sector and the rapid growth that sector has enjoyed, China exerts a large upward influence on the average per capita rate of growth of agriculture in the Third World. If China were removed from the calculation, performance in the rest of the Third World would be much less impressive.

Consider our 19 countries as an example. The average rate of growth of agricultural output per head of the entire sample over the 20-year period included in Table 6.2, weighted by size of population, was 1.08 per cent. Excluding China, the average rate of growth, again weighted by population, falls to 0.49 per cent a year, i.e., to less than half. China, clearly, exerts an enormous influence on the overall picture.

Turning to Africa, the Table illustrates what is well known: many countries in the region have experienced agricultural decline over a long period, in fact virtually since independence. Ghana, Tanzania and Kenya are unfortunately typical of a distressingly large number of countries. Botswana, as we have seen, is something of an exception since the agricultural sector is in any case tiny. Côte d'Ivoire is the encouraging counter-example and suggests that the obstacles to agricultural expansion in Africa can be overcome even within the existing state of technology. It may not be necessary to wait for a technological breakthrough or green revolution before initiating sustained rural development.

134

Table 6.2 **AVERAGE ANNUAL PERCENTAGE RATE OF GROWTH**
OF AGRICULTURAL OUTPUT PER HEAD, 1965-1984

Asia:

China	1.9
India	0.8
Pakistan	0.4
Bangladesh	0.7
Malaysia	2.1
Philippines	1.3
Sri Lanka	0.4

Africa:

Botswana	-2.5
Côte d'Ivoire	1.7
Egypt	0.4
Ghana	-2.9
Kenya	-1.0
Tanzania	-0.4

Latin America:

Argentina	0.2
Brazil	0.8
Chile	0.0
Colombia	0.8
Mexico	-0.6
Peru	-1.7

Source: FAO, *Production Yearbook*, Rome, 1975 and 1985.

The long-run performance of the agricultural sector in much of Latin America has been poor. Indeed, in two of our countries – Peru and Mexico – per capita growth has been negative and in Chile it has been zero. In Brazil, Colombia and Argentina, in contrast, average rates of growth of agricultural output per head have been positive. The problem, not evident from the Table, is that in Mexico and Colombia the rate of growth has been slowing down and in recent years has been negative. Mexico in particular has lost momentum. Growth was satisfactory until the early 1970s, largely because of massive state investment in irrigation in the northern part of the country and the swift adoption there of higher-yielding varieties of wheat. Those sources of growth, however, have now become exhausted and the country has not succeeded in extending the technological transformation of agriculture to other regions and other crops. The green revolution in Mexico has fizzled out.

So far the discussion has been concerned essentially with the agricultural sector as a whole. We have seen already, however, that change in the rural areas of the Third World cannot adequately be described by simple averages. The countryside is a mosaic and the varied configurations within each country need to be taken into account. The institutional structure in particular can greatly affect both the pace of growth and the distribution of the benefits from growth. In some countries land is unevenly divided between a small group of large landowners who possess most of the land and a large group of small peasants who occupy only a small fraction of it. The so-called latifundia-minifundia complex in parts of Central and South America is an example of this. In other areas, as in Côte d'Ivoire, Sri Lanka and Malaysia, large, commercially-oriented plantations exist to produce primary commodities for export, e.g., palm oil, tea and rubber. These plantations may be owned and operated by the state, by large local landowners or by foreign companies. In still other areas

135

much of the land may be farmed by small tenants, on either a sharecropping or fixed rental basis. Both cash crops and food for local consumption are produced this way. Tenant farming often is accompanied by a high incidence of landlessness and in some cases about half of the agricultural labour force is landless or nearly so. South Asia contains many examples. In a few instances, notably in South Korea and Taiwan, the land is evenly distributed among small peasant farmers who then are supported, in the successful cases, by peasant associations, service co-operatives and other local rural institutions. Finally, there are socialist agricultural organisations – state farms, collectives, producer co-operatives and communal tenure arrangements – which can be found in pockets in many Third World countries but which are dominant in such socialist countries as China, North Korea and Vietnam.

Within most Third World countries several of these forms of land tenure coexist. Superimposed on the land tenure systems are regional variations in topography (the highlands v. the lowlands, hill farming v. the fertile valleys), climate (arid v. humid climate, high and low rainfall areas), water control (rainfed v. irrigated agriculture), cropping patterns (cash crops v. food grains, farming v. ranching) and ease of access to markets (transport, power, proximity to urban areas). These variables produce a complex mosaic in rural areas which is obscured by national aggregates and statistical averages.

Above all the mosaic ensures that the rural poor are not a homogeneous class, a uniform group of people in similar circumstances facing similar problems. On the contrary, the poor are highly heterogeneous; they consist of many different groups of people who differ from one another by region, major sources of income, asset endowment and in some cases even by sex. Those classified as poor may include casual agricultural wage workers, unionised plantation workers, deficit food farmers who supplement self-provisioning with food purchased in the market from wages earned as part-time labourers, small peasants producing cash crops and other workers such as fishermen, herdsmen and artisans. These diverse groups of people will be affected differently and will respond differently to such economic phenomena as the introduction of a new technology, a change in money wages or a rise in food prices. Some groups in particular will be harmed by, say, a rise in food prices whereas others will be helped, and in assessing policies for rural (and overall) development it is important to consider the losers as well as the gainers.

Poverty and prices

There is no doubt that in recent years many poor people in rural areas have become further impoverished. This is hardly surprising in countries where per capita national income has fallen, as in Ghana and many other parts of sub-Saharan Africa. Nor is it surprising that the rural poor have become worse off in countries where agricultural output per head has declined, even though GDP per capita has continued to increase, as in Kenya since the mid-1970s. More remarkable is the fact that some sections of the rural poor have experienced declining incomes even in countries where both GDP and agricultural output per head have risen or at worse remained stationary. Yet this is precisely what has happened in several countries, including the Philippines and India [3]. The reasons for this paradox will become clear as the chapter proceeds but one point should be made straight away.

The problem of impoverishment has been especially serious among those dependent on wages as their major source of income, i.e., among landless agricultural workers. Fragmentary or incomplete evidence suggests that the incidence of landlessness has been rising, particularly in South and Southeast Asia but also in parts of Africa. Furthermore, the average number of days worked per year per labourer appears to have fallen slightly as has the security of employment. That is, a growing proportion of the rural population has been reduced to workers dependent on insecure, part-time, casual agricultural employment. This growing labour force, unfortunately, often has encountered a falling real wage rate. The combination of a shift in occupation towards wage labourers, a falling number of days of employment and a declining real wage has meant that many rural households have suffered a substantial reduction in their real income per head. This cannot be proved beyond a shadow of doubt because of lack of data, but the data that exist point to a serious problem in a number of countries. This obviously is a topic that merits further research.

In Table 6.3 some data have been assembled on trends in real wages in agriculture for the recent period, 1975-84. Nine countries accounting for 1 130 million people are represented. Only in Pakistan has there been an obvious and dramatic rise in real earnings. This was due not to an excess demand for labour at the initial wage rates but to large-scale emigration of labour from the rural areas of Pakistan to Saudi.Arabia and the Gulf States combined with massive workers' remittances from abroad [4]. In Sri Lanka, despite rising GDP and agricultural output per head, the real earnings of tea plantation workers rose only to 1979 and thereafter fell fairly steadily. Nonetheless, in 1984 real earnings were 31 per cent higher than in 1975. In Chile, the minimum real wage for agricultural workers recovered from 1975, the low point for the economy [5], to reach a peak in 1982, after which it again fell sharply to (nearly) the level of 1976.

In Maharashtra (and several other states of India) wage rates today for male agricultural workers (deflated by the price index for agricultural workers) are lower than they were in the mid-1970s. This is despite the fact that national income per head in India has increased substantially and agricultural output per head of the rural population has increased slightly. In Bangladesh, real wages in agriculture continue their long-run decline despite much improved national and agricultural growth rates. In the Philippines, too, real wage rates in agriculture continue to fall despite relatively rapid per capita growth of national income and of agricultural output. In Ghana the earnings of agricultural workers collapsed in parallel with the collapse in production, although it is hard to believe the fall was as great as the figures suggest. In Kenya real earnings were stagnant between 1976 and 1979 and then began to fall rapidly, so that by 1983 they were 12 per cent below the level of 1975. Finally, in Mexico, the real minimum wage for agricultural workers, having been roughly constant between 1977 and 1983, fell sharply in 1984 and finished 14 per cent below its initial level in 1975.

Rural wage earners have been particularly vulnerable for several reasons. First, on the supply side of the labour market, the size of the total labour force has continued to increase at a rapid rate. Fertility rates and with them, overall population growth rates, have begun to fall in many Third World countries, but this has had relatively little effect so far on the growth of the labour force, and consequently there has been downward pressure on wage rates in both urban and rural areas. Second, rural to urban migration, although often rapid, has not been sufficiently great to absorb the entire increase in the rural labour force. Particularly in countries where the rural labour force remains a very high proportion of the total, the absolute increase in the number of those seeking employment in agriculture has been large and this inevitably has tended to depress wage rates. Third, as already mentioned, in many countries there has been a structural change in the occupational distribution of the rural working population away from peasant holdings and tenant farming towards wage labour. This structural change is at least in part independent of population growth and has exerted further downward pressure on wage rates. Fourth, on the demand side of the labour

137

Table 6.3 **REAL WAGES IN AGRICULTURE, 1975–1984**
(Index based on the initial year)

	India a	Pakistan b	Bangladesh c	Philippines d	Sri Lanka e	Ghana f	Kenya g	Chile h	Mexico h
1975	-	100	-	-	100	100	100	100	100
1976	100	91	100	100	109	68	123	131	-
1977	83	97	85	106	119	67	116	159	111
1978	94	101	87	101	124	43	121	165	109
1979	98	106	75	90	162	29	123	164	112
1980	96	113	97	77	151	32	117	164	111
1981	88	145	86	77	133	23	114	197	116
1982	92	135	89	71	136	21	94	199	127
1983	95	159	-	-	123	15	88	161	111
1984	-	252	-	-	131	-	-	137	86

a) Daily wage rate of males in Maharashtra.
b) Daily earnings.
c) Nominal wage rate deflated by the retail price of rice.
d) Daily wage rate.
e) Male workers on tea plantations; daily earnings deflated by the Colombo cost of living index.
f) Average monthly earnings deflated by the consumer price index for rural areas.
g) Agricultural earnings per month.
h) Minimum wage for male agricultural workers.

Sources: ILO, *Yearbook of Labour Statistics 1985*, Geneva, 1985; S.R. Osmani, "The Food Problem of Bangladesh", mimeographed paper presented to the Food Strategies Research Conference, World Institute of Development Economics Research, Helsinki, Finland, 21-25 July 1986, Table 8, p. 24; Hamid Tabatabai, "Economic Decline, Access to Food and Structural Adjustment in Ghana", ILO, World Employment Programme Working Paper WEP 10-6/WP80, July 1986, Table 12, pp. 30-1; Ehtisham Ahmad and Nicholas Stern, "Employment and Wages in Pakistan", Development Economics Research Centre, University of Warwick, Discussion Paper No. 62, June 1985, Table 3.2, p. 25

market, it is evident that in many countries the growth in the demand for agricultural labour has been sluggish. This, in turn, may be due to relatively slow growth of agricultural output (upon which the demand for rural labour primarily depends) or to a low output elasticity of demand for labour (the value of which depends in part on the type of technology used to increase output). These forces operating on the labour market are well understood and do not require further discussion.

Less well understood perhaps is the link between the market for food, which largely determines the price of the most important wage good, and real wage rates. The very poor, who tend to be concentrated in the rural areas, often spend between 70 and 80 per cent of their total income on food. Hence if the relative price of food rises, the real incomes of those poor persons who buy food in the market will fall, *ceteris paribus*. In fact the real price of food appears to have increased in many countries, as the data in Table 6.4 show. That is, in 11 out of the 18 countries included in the Table, the average increase in the price of food (as shown in the first column of the Table) exceeded the increase in consumer prices as a whole (as shown in the second column). The average increase in the relative price of food, i.e., the difference between the two price indexes, is shown in the last column. Particularly in Asia and Africa [6], where nine out of the twelve countries in the Table from those two regions experienced a long-run increase in the relative price of food, upward pressure in the food market may have exerted downward pressure on real wages of agricultural labour. This, then, is a fifth reason why wage workers in the rural areas of the Third World may have become impoverished: the rise in nominal agricultural wages may have lagged behind rising food prices [7].

It is important to notice that a rise in the real price of food does not necessarily imply a fall in food output. All that is necessary is that the growth in demand for food should exceed the growth in supply. This can occur even when food production per head has been rising steadily, as in the Philippines. If the growth of food output is not "fast enough", i.e., if there is an imbalance in sectoral growth rates, the real price of food will increase, and this will tend to depress the real incomes of wage workers and others who buy food unless nominal wages (and other sources of income) rise in line with food prices. As we have seen, in not a few countries representing hundreds of millions of people, wages have tended to lag behind changes in the price of food and this has further impoverished large numbers of already poor people.

Of course it could be argued that poverty eventually depends on what happens in the "real" economy and not on changes in relative prices. According to this view it is only unanticipated price changes that matter and since they are unanticipated, presumably they matter only in the short run. To those on the receiving end of price changes, however, they are just as real as the quantity changes that preoccupy economists who focus exclusively on the "real" economy and it is no consolation to the poor to be told that "eventually" relative prices don't matter. Eventually can be a long time.

Not all the poor, as has been emphasized, work for wages. Some are peasant farmers who produce food for the market. They obviously will benefit from higher relative food prices, and the larger their marketable surplus, the larger the gains. Other peasants produce cash crops for the market and their fate depends in large part on movements in commodity prices, although if they hire workers and buy food, movements in those prices also are relevant.

If the real price of a cash crop drifts downwards one would expect farmers to change their cropping patterns in order partially to offset the negative impact on their standard of living. For example, if cotton prices fall, producers can be expected to reduce the area

	Food	All items	Change in relative price of food: Col. (1) minus Col. (2)
Asia:			
India *a*	7.8	7.3	0.5
Pakistan	8.6	8.3	0.3
Bangladesh *b*	13.8	14.0	–0.2
Malaysia *c*	4.5	3.8	0.7
Philippines *d*	12.9	12.0	0.9
Sri Lanka	7.9	7.4	0.5
Africa:			
Botswana *e*	13.9	13.5	0.4
Côte d'Ivoire	8.9	8.2	0.7
Egypt *f*	10.3	7.9	2.4
Ghana	28.3	36.1	–7.8
Kenya *g*	7.2	7.6	–0.4
Tanzania	12.3	11.7	0.6
Latin America:			
Argentina *h*	92.2	99.8	–7.6
Brazil *i*	56.5	57.8	–1.3
Chile	80.1	75.8	4.3
Colombia	18.5	17.3	1.2
Mexico	18.3	18.6	–0.3
Peru *j*	28.7	29.8	–1.1

a) Data for the years 1969 and 1970 are missing.
b) The period covered is 1967-84 excluding 1970-72 for which the data are missing.
c) Data for the years 1965 and 1966 are missing.
d) Data for the years 1970 and 1982 are missing.
e) The period covered is 1975-84.
f) Data for 1970 are missing.
g) Data for the years 1970-72 are missing.
h) Data for the years 1975-80 are missing.
i) Data for the years 1970-71 are missing.
j) Data for 1966 are missing.
Source: ILO, *Bulletin of Labour Statistics,* Geneva, various issues.

devoted to cotton and to increase the amount of land allocated, say, to wheat. In the case of tree crops, however, land reallocation is less easy since farmers cannot switch back and forth between crops (uprooting trees when prices fall, replanting when prices rise) without incurring very high costs. Moreover, there is normally a lag of several years between planting and the first harvest, after which the trees continue to bear fruit for a great many years. Thus fixed costs represent a high proportion of total costs of production and marginal costs, once the trees have reached maturity, usually are very low. As a result, short-run supply curves tend to be inelastic and when prices fall, farmers cannot readily avoid the impact.

The impoverishment of the cocoa farmers of Ghana is a good if extreme illustration of what can happen [8]. Over the 35 year period beginning in 1950 the government, through its marketing board, systematically reduced the real price of cocoa. Indeed the real producer price of cocoa, i.e., the nominal price deflated by the rural consumer price index, fell 82.4 per cent over the period. Production was at first unaffected – in fact it rose until 1965 – but by 1985 output had fallen to only 69.5 per cent of the initial level. As a result of the lower prices and output, real income from cocoa farming in Ghana in 1985 was only 12.2 per cent of what it had been in 1950. The country's most important export industry was in ruins and those attempting to earn a livelihood in the industry were suffering acute poverty [9].

Productivity and the size of farm

Output and living standards depend not only upon prices but also upon the distribution of productive assets and rural institutions. In the rural areas the most important productive asset is land. Unfortunately, in many Third World countries the ownership of land is highly unequal and this inevitably results in an unequal distribution of income among the rural population. Operational holdings, however, usually are distributed less unequally than titles to land because many large landowners prefer to hire out all or part of their land to tenants (on either a fixed rental or sharecropping basis) rather than cultivate it themselves with hired labour. Even so, the distribution of operational holdings often is unequal and hence the question arises as to the relationship between farm size and factor productivity.

There is abundant evidence from all over the Third World that factor productivity tends to vary systematically with farm size. Three findings in particular seem well established [10]. First, output per worker tends to increase with farm size. Second, gross output per hectare (or yield) tends to fall as the size of farm increases. Third, value added (or net income) per hectare also tends to fall as the size of farm rises. There are exceptions to these tendencies but they are relatively few. Moreover, the tendencies remain even when one adjusts for differences in soil quality as between large and small farmers. In general, small farmers produce more output per unit of land than large farmers.

The agronomic reasons for this are by now pretty clear. First, small farmers use more labour-intensive methods of cultivation for any given crop. They devote more time and are more careful in land preparation, weeding and harvesting. Large farmers, in contrast, use more capital-intensive methods of cultivation, substituting agricultural chemicals and machinery for labour. A partial exception is fertilizer. In many countries, particularly in Asia, the intensity of fertilizer use is invariant with respect to size of landholding and some cases have been found in which small farmers actually apply more fertilizer per hectare than large. In parts of Africa, however, fertilizer applications are much larger on the larger farms and this leads to considerably higher labour productivity and to a widening of income disparities. Second, the cropping pattern differs between small and large farms. Small peasants tend to choose relatively more labour-intensive crops such as vegetables whereas large farmers devote a higher proportion of their land to activities which require relatively less labour such as grazing livestock. Third, small farmers cultivate a higher proportion of their land whereas one finds that on large farms a higher proportion is left idle, or is fallow, or is used for pasture or is forest. Finally, the cropping ratio tends to be higher on small farms. That is, because of greater use of multiple cropping techniques, small farmers obtain more harvests per year than large farmers.

The explanation for these differences in behaviour has nothing to do with motivation: all farmers, large and small, are doing the best they can (viz., "maximizing profits") given the circumstances they face. Nor has the explanation much to do with risk or differences in attitudes towards uncertainty. True, the implications of a crop failure for a small peasant on the margin of subsistence are more serious than those for a large farmer, but even small peasants can share risks (e.g., by sharecropping), or spread the effects out over time (e.g., by

141

borrowing from moneylenders) or share the burdens of catastrophe with others (e.g., through the institution of the extended family). The essence of the difference between small and large farmers is in the market opportunities they confront [11].

Small farmers often find it more dificult to market their output. Because their marketable surplus is low, they are more likely to have to use middlemen to transport, process and sell their produce. Their costs of marketing therefore tend to be higher and the prices they receive at the farm gate lower. Of course where they are able to sell their produce directly to the final consumer, small farmers may receive a higher price than the larger farmers. Similarly, except where small and marginal farmer programmes have been well established, small farmers have more restricted ease of access to government-supplied services (notably extension services and technical advice), to subsidised production inputs (e.g., fertilizer) and to the formal credit system. But above all, small and large farmers face a very different set of relative factor prices and consequently a different set of production incentives. In broad terms, the relative effective (and often implicit) price of land and finance capital are high for small farmers, while the price of labour is relatively low, especially when labour of low opportunity cost comes from within the peasant farming household itself.

Small farmers thus have an incentive to economise on land and capital, whereas large farmers have an incentive to economise on labour. Small peasants respond to these incentives by farming their land very intensively with labour-using methods of cultivation. The capital-labour ratio thus tends to be low, although capital per unit of land sometimes is higher on the small farms than it is on the large. In contrast, large farms have relatively high capital-labour ratios and low labour-land ratios. The result is that output per man rises with farm size while output per hectare falls. Resources are allocated inefficiently, total output is lower than it need be, and the distribution of income is unequal.

The policy implications are twofold. First, one can try to improve transport and marketing facilities, ensure more equitable access to government services and institutions, and eliminate "imperfections" in factor markets. India has adopted this approach and has had some success. Second, one can redistribute land from large landowners to small peasants. The two approaches are best seen as complementary to one another, not as alternatives. Land reform helps to shift factor proportions closer to the optimum and thereby increases efficiency in the allocation of resources and consequently raises the level of output. More important, redistributive land reforms result in a much more equal distribution of income and wealth in rural areas; they change the "initial conditions" such that the benefits of subsequent growth tend to be evenly spread. In this way land reform results not only in a once-for-all reduction in poverty and inequality, it also helps to create an institutional environment which prevents poverty and inequality from reappearing in the course of growth. Lastly, a political point, in capitalist countries, land reforms can help to legitimise private property and the liberal political institutions on which democratic systems rest [12].

The East Asian experience is instructive because in that region more than in any other land reform was combined with other policies designed to improve efficiency, equity and growth. The reforms in South Korea and Taiwan are well known and their success is largely unquestioned, but the reforms are sometimes thought to be irrelevant to the rest of the world because of the political circumstances under which they were introduced. There is no doubt that the communist threat from the mainland concentrated the mind of the Nationalist government on Taiwan; it is equally clear that the Nationalist government found it easy to introduce a series of land reforms because it was not dependent upon the political support of the Taiwanese landowners. Similarly, in South Korea, land reform was facilitated and became more urgent because of the social upheaval brought about by the Korean War. Moreover it was convenient for the government that land reform could be presented as part of a process of removing the vestiges of Japanese colonialism. Finally, in both countries, the distribution of operational holdings as distinct from ownership holdings was very even and this made it easy to transfer land titles without disrupting production. The historical, institutional and political contexts evidently were decisive in both cases, but what is important for the argument here is that land reforms were in fact introduced, they were seen by the government as being of strategic importance for the development effort, and they worked in the sense that economic efficiency increased, agricultural growth accelerated, an equitable distribution of income and wealth were created and social conflict in the countryside was eliminated.

In Japan, too, land reform played a significant role in creating an efficient and prosperous peasantry. In 1940 only 31.1 per cent of the cultivators owned their land; 42.1 per cent were part owners and 26.8 per cent were pure tenants. In 1946, however, under the occupying forces, virtually all tenants were transformed into owners and many part owners also received title to all the land they farmed. By 1950, in fact, only 5.1 per cent of the cultivators were pure tenants. The proportion of part owners had fallen to 32.4 per cent while the proportion of full owners had nearly doubled to 61.9 per cent [13]. The land reform was complemented by farmers' associations, co-operatives and irrigation associations which helped to ensure that technical efficiency was maintained (notably in the irrigation and input supply systems), marketing services were well organised and the viability of a small peasant farming system remained unimpaired.

Finally, land reform also played a key role in China. The political context was entirely different from that in South Korea, Taiwan and Japan since land reform in China was a product of a communist revolution and was intended as part of a socialist strategy of development, but some of the objectives in China were similar to those in the other three cases. Land reform in China was intended to reduce poverty and raise the standard of living of poor peasants, to destroy the economic and political power of the landlord class, to create a more egalitarian society, to organise the peasantry and increase output and efficiency and to provide an institutional framework for accelerated investment and growth. Institutional transformation occurred in a series of phases beginning with a redistributive land reform and the formation of mutual aid teams. This was followed by the creation of small and then large producer co-operatives and, later still, by the introduction of the multi-tiered commune system. After 1978 the commune system was radically altered and under the "production responsibility system" China reverted to a small peasant farming system. In most regions, however, communal institutions remain and still play a role, the importance of which varies from one locality to another. In general, though, they continue to be vitally significant in the management of irrigation systems.

This is of considerable importance not only for the rest of Asia but in Africa and Latin America as well. In almost all agricultural economies water control is the key to high yields and the key to water control, in turn, is irrigation. Consider, for example, the relationship between irrigation and rice yields in South, Southeast and East Asia [14]. In the six countries where the net irrigated area is 45 per cent or more of the net sown area, the unweighted average yield of rice is 37.2 quintals per hectare. These six countries [15] are Japan, Taiwan, South Korea, Sri Lanka, North Korea and China (in order of proportion of area irrigated) and yields range from a high of 50.7 quintals per hectare in North Korea to a low of 15.9 quintals in Sri Lanka. Note that in five of the six countries there has been a major land reform; the exception is Sri Lanka, which happens to have the lowest yields.

At the opposite extreme are six countries where 20 per cent or less of the land is irrigated and where the average yield is only 13.5 quintals per hectare, i.e., little more than a third as high as the yields in the first group of countries. This second group includes Thailand, the Philippines, Laos, Burma, Nepal and Kampuchea. In between is an intermediate group of five countries, viz., Indonesia, Malaysia, Vietnam, India and Bangladesh, where between 20.7 and 36.1 per cent of the land is irrigated and average rice yields are about 17.9 quintals per hectare. Looked at this way, the role of irrigation as a leading input in raising rice output in Asia becomes evident [16]. And rice is of course the most important food crop in Asia which, in turn, is the most populous region of the Third World.

The question arises whether there are connections between the degree of equality, rural institutions and investment in irrigation [17]. We have seen that countries which have had successful land reforms have achieved a high degree of equality in the rural areas. They have also managed to build strong rural institutions (farmers' associations, co-operatives, communes) capable of initiating collective action for, among other things, irrigation development. Egalitarian peasant farming systems, because of the small average size of holding, undoubtedly require collective action for successful development. At the same time, egalitarian farming systems seem to facilitate collective action. There are two main reasons for this. First, a high degree of equality makes it difficult for a minority of influential and wealthy farmers to pursue their self-interest at the expense of the rest of the community, e.g., by appropriating a disproportionate share of the irrigation water for their own use. Second, a high degree of equality reduces social conflict and creates an environment in which people are more likely to work together for the common good. That is, collaboration among members of a community is easier when everyone is confident they will receive a fair share of the benefits. Thus land reform tends to be associated with a strategy of development that produces multiple benefits: a more equal distribution of income and wealth, a high degree of local participation in economic affairs, a more efficient utilisation of existing resources of land, labour and water and an institutional framework conducive to more rapid technical change, investment and growth. The difficulty is that land reform implies profound social and political changes and these seldom are welcomed by those who control the state.

The early green revolution

It is natural therefore to seek an alternative strategy which makes land reform unnecessary. In the early 1960s it was thought that such a strategy had been discovered. It was called the green revolution.

The green revolution represents an attempt to substitute technical change for institutional change, to use scientific progress as an alternative to social progress. Instead of land reform the Third World was encouraged to concentrate on the introduction and rapid diffusion of high-yielding varieties of food grains, notably wheat and rice. At first glance such an approach has many attractions. First, because the green revolution is concerned with increasing food production, it was thought that the strategy would make a direct impact on problems of famine, malnutrition, hunger and poverty in rural and urban areas alike. Subsequent research has shown, however, that the connection between the supply of food and the incidence of hunger often is rather weak [18]. The poor go hungry because they do not have the purchasing power with which to acquire food, not necessarily because food is unavailable. This is true even during famines. Still, everything else being equal, it is hard to deny that more food should in principle make it easier to reduce the incidence of hunger if a government were determined to do so.

144

A second attraction of the green revolution strategy is that it is scale neutral. The higher-yielding seeds could be used equally successfully on small and large farms and hence both small peasant farmers and large landlords would be in a position to innovate. The new technology would spread rapidly and the benefits would be widely shared. Thirdly, the new technology would increase the demand for labour, for example in weeding and harvesting, and this would result in a combination of more days of employment and higher wage rates. The benefits of technical change would trickle down from landowners to landless agricultural workers. Moreover, fourth, the benefits would multiply if the shorter growing season of some of the new varieties permitted multiple cropping to spread. In these ways the green revolution also would contribute indirectly, through generally higher living standards, to the alleviation of hunger and poverty.

Fifth, increased food output was expected to lead to lower food prices and this would be of particular benefit to those in poverty. Indeed, because the proportion of income devoted to food consumption is higher the lower is a household's per capita income, falling food prices would ensure that the benefits of the green revolution accrued disproportionately to the poor. The distribution of income among households would therefore become more equal. We shall comment on this argument in a moment, but for the time being one should recall the point made earlier that in many countries the long-run relative price of food has risen, not fallen.

In practice, however, many of the advantages of the green revolution that were foreseen when the strategy was first formulated have in fact materialised, but a great many qualifications must be made. First, the green revolution has not led to an acceleration in the rate of growth of agricultural output as a whole. Agricultural growth rates remain modest and the most that can be said is that without the green revolution the rate of growth of agricultural production might have been even slower. It is of course impossible to know what would have happened if the new varieties of wheat and rice had not been developed, just as one will never know what would have happened in Europe if the potato had not been discovered in the New World, but a calculation based on an assumption that everything else would have remained unchanged is rather implausible. Second, the impact of the green revolution has tended to be concentrated in specific regions of a country, namely those which enjoyed good irrigation facilities. Since such regions also tend to enjoy higher than average rural incomes per head, the new technology has tended to accentuate regional rural inequalities. However, insofar as the green revolution has raised average incomes in rural areas, it has helped to reduce rural-urban inequalities. The problem about this third point, unfortunately, is that there is little evidence that the new technology has in practice raised rural incomes. Indeed, in those cases where increased food output has resulted in lower food prices, the major beneficiaries of growth may have been the urban population.

Fourth, while the new technology has been scale neutral, rural institutions, relative prices and government policies often have not been. As a result, large farmers typically were the first to innovate and reaped large initial gains in income. Small farmers followed behind, sometimes quite quickly, but by then grain prices may have fallen and consequently the income gains per hectare of the lagging small farmers were less than those of the leading large farmers. Both large and small farmers were able to introduce the new technology, but they did so at different rates and hence obtained different incomes, despite the fact that the increase in physical output per hectare may have been comparable on both types of farm.

Fifth, the green revolution has increased the demand for labour but this has not been fully reflected in better employment conditions for landless labourers. In the case of small farmers, some of the additional demand for labour has been supplied by members of the household working longer hours and more days per year. In the case of large farmers, some of the additional potential demand has been offset by labour-saving mechanisation, particularly by investment in tractors. The net increase in the demand for wage labourers sometimes has failed to match the increase in the growth of the labour force and hence in some cases, as we have seen, the landless have actually experienced a decline in their standard of living. Seldom did income trickle down to the very poor, and where it did, the magnitude of the flow was small. It is probable therefore that within the rural areas the distribution of income has become more unequal in the period since the green revolution began.

Sixth, where the green revolution resulted in a fall in the real price of food, this undoubtedly helped the urban population, and within the urban areas, the poor probably benefitted disproportionately. In the rural areas, however, the picture is more complex. Those small farmers who innovated only after a lag (often poor peasants) may have seen the fall in price erode the value of the rise in output so that their real income remained roughly unchanged. Those small farmers for whom the technology was unsuitable, e.g., because they grew rice in upland, rainfed conditions, would have experienced no rise in output but a fall in income because of the decline in grain prices. They were clearly worse off. Those farmers who were net buyers of food in the market, e.g., farmers growing cash crops, and both the agricultural and non-agricultural labour force were clear gainers. But among the gainers the benefits in some cases may have been distributed unevenly. The reason for this is that the distribution of the benefits from, say, lower wheat prices depends upon the amount consumed by the different social classes. In some countries wheat is a "superior" good at the prevailing low levels of income. The very poor consequently spend relatively as well as absolutely less on wheat than other groups and hence their proportionate gains in real income compared to the not quite so poor are small. The overall effect from the price change on the national distribution of income thus is indeterminate. All one can say with certainty is that some people enjoyed substantial gains while others suffered substantial losses. There can be no general presumption that the overall distribution of income improved as a result of the new technology.

These mixed and inconclusive findings can be compared with the claim that the green revolution "has had a dramatic impact on incomes and food supplies in many developing countries" [19]. We shall want to consider this claim more carefully when we examine the cases of India and the Philippines, countries which have been very successful in introducing high-yielding varieties of wheat and rice, respectively. For the moment, however, it is worth noting that whatever may have happened to the trend rate of growth of production, the introduction of the new technology seems to have increased the instability of production, that is, the amplitude of fluctuations in output. There are several reasons for this.

The high-yielding varieties of food grains are more sensitive than traditional varieties to pests, disease and fluctuations in the weather. These are genetic characteristics of the plants which have persisted for about two decades despite increasing efforts of plant breeders to develop greater tolerance to pests, disease and drought. The problem is compounded by the fact that farmers tend to grow the high-yielding varieties in "pure" stands rather than intermix them with traditional varieties. As a result, when a pest or disease does strike the effect on output can be serious. It is for these reasons that the high-yielding varieties tend to be associated with a higher risk of crop failure, although when planted in an optimal physical environment average yields also are higher.

In addition to natural hazards the high-yielding varieties of wheat and rice are more susceptible to adverse economic influences. The varieties were bred to be highly responsive to nitrogenous fertilizer and because of their sensitivity to pests and disease, they do best when protected by modern chemical inputs such as pesticides. Dependence on modern purchased inputs, however, means that farmers are subjected to greater uncertainty about the market price of inputs, especially the price of fertilizer. Variations in input prices lead to variations in input use, physical output and farm income. The same is true when inputs are allocated not by price but by administrative means. Variations in government supplies of fertilizer and other modern inputs will lead to sharp movements in output and incomes.

Fluctuations in output, in turn, will lead to even greater fluctuations in the marketable surplus. The reason for this is that marketed supplies of grain are a residual, the amount left over after the requirements of the farm household have been met. This residual supply will vary from year to year much more sharply than total supplies. Indeed the smaller the proportion of total output that is sold on the market – the "thinner" is the market – the more likely it is that the amplitude of fluctuation of the marketable surplus will be a multiple of that of total production. Sharp variations in the marketable surplus will then lead to sharp variations in the opposite direction in market prices, unless the government is able to counteract this tendency either through a domestic food stocks policy or through a contra-cyclical food import policy. Note, however, that if the government does stabilize grain prices for the consumer when marketable surpluses fluctuate, this will destabilize incomes of the producers.

This merely shows that the greater risk and uncertainly that have accompanied the green revolution have imposed real costs. Of course the costs may have been exceeded by the benefits, but someone had to bear the costs, the producers, the consumers or the government. This argument can be put in more general terms. It is now recognised by even the strongest supporters of the green revolution that "where existing institutions favour very unequal asset and income distributions, technological change has tended to amplify the inequality" [20]. The main beneficiaries in the rural areas have been producers who control optimal production environments, i.e., farms on good soils in well-irrigated regions, and in some countries "optimal production environments are frequently controlled by the larger and better-off farmers" [21]. The costs of technical change have tended to fall on the landless and on farmers occupying marginal land in unirrigated regions.

Defenders of the green revolution, however, accuse their critics of confusing the impact of the green revolution with "the impact of institutional arrangements, agricultural policies, and labor-saving mechanization" [22]. Moreover, they argue that it is wrong to blame the green revolution as a strategy of development "for undesirable developments occurring as a consequence of inappropriate institutions and policies" [23]. This argument is a bit disingenuous, however, since the purpose of the green revolution strategy was precisely to circumvent the need for institutional change. Technical progress was regarded as an alternative to land reforms and institutional transformation – the "green" revolution was to be a substitute for the "red" – and it is misleading twenty years later to claim that there was nothing wrong with the original strategy and that the fault lies entirely with "inappropriate institutions and policies".

Agricultural growth and rural poverty in India

India is an important laboratory for those wishing to study the effects of a development strategy based on technical change in agriculture because the green revolution was adopted by the Indian government as conscious policy during the Third Five-Year Plan period (1961-66) and the policy has continued to this day. The experience of the Second Plan (1956-61), in which primacy was given to large-scale heavy industry over agriculture, and the severe droughts of 1965 and 1966, during which the country had to import food on a massive scale in order to prevent widespread starvation, led to a reappraisal of development policy and a decision to follow a modified strategy based on industrialisation combined with the rapid introduction of high-yielding varieties of wheat and rice.

In many respects the new strategy as regards agriculture has been a success. First, the area devoted to high-yielding varieties increased rapidly. In the case of rice, the area sown to high-yielding varieties rose from 880 000 hectares in 1966 to 15.6 million in 1977, an increase of 1 673 per cent in just over a decade! The new wheat seeds spread even more swiftly, from 540 000 hectares in 1966 to 15.5 million in 1977, or nearly a 29-fold increase [24]. Second, production during the same period also increased substantially, namely, by 62 per cent in the case of rice and by an extraordinary 179 per cent in the case of wheat. Indeed the green revolution in India has more aptly been called the wheat revolution. Third, the country has been able to reduce its dependency on imported food and achieve self-sufficiency in grains, one of the objectives behind the strategy. Fourth, above all, the country has been able to accumulate a substantial stockpile of grain and thereby banish the threat of famine. Indeed, by the end of the 1970s India had nearly 15 million tons of grain in stocks.

The disappointing side of the picture is that the green revolution failed to alter the performance of the agricultural sector as a whole. One gets a very different impression of performance if one includes all crops, not just wheat and rice, and in addition takes into consideration demographic expansion. Growth of agricultural output per head in the nine years before the beginning of the green revolution, 1955 to 1964, was 0.4 per cent a year. In the fifteen years after the revolution, 1967 to 1982, and excluding the drought years in the middle of the 1960s, the rate of growth was only marginally higher, namely, 0.5 per cent a year. Considering the entire 27 year period, 1955-82, and including the drought years, the trend rate of growth of output per head was almost stagnant at 0.2 per cent a year. Moreover, this trend is not statistically different from zero! Thus however one looks at the data the growth rate has been low.

A second disappointment is that despite having switched from a development strategy that gave priority to heavy industry to one that gives some priority to technical change in agriculture, the incidence of rural poverty, i.e., the proportion of the rural population below the official poverty line, has remained stubbornly high and has evinced no long run tendency to decline (see Table 6.5). Moreover, there is little noticeable difference between the incidence of rural poverty in the pre-green revolution years and the post-green revolution years. This can be seen, rather crudely but simply, by comparing the average incidence of poverty in the eight years for which we have observations in the period 1956-64 with the average incidence in the eight years for which we have observations in the period 1967-77. In the former period poverty afflicted 45.6 per cent of the rural population on average whereas in the latter period it afflicted 41.1 per cent of the population, a difference of only 4.5 percentage points.

If one plots the data from Table 6.5 on the incidence of poverty alongside the data on per capita agricultural output, one can see that both series fluctuate and that the fluctuations tend to be approximate mirror images of one another. When good harvests result in a short-term rise in agricultural output per head this tends to produce a fall in the incidence of rural poverty and conversely for a decline in output (see Figure 6.1). If anything, the production series shows greater cyclical instability in the post-green revolution period than in the decade beginning in 1955, illustrating a point made earlier.

The longer-term movements in the time series, however, underline what we already know, namely, that despite the change in development strategy the green revolution did not

Table 6.5   **AGRICULTURAL GROWTH AND RURAL POVERTY IN INDIA, 1955-1982**

	(1) Agricultural production per head (1974-76 = 100)	(2) Incidence of rural poverty (percentage)	(3) Wheat output (million metric tons)	(4) Rice output (million metric tons)
1955	99.6		9.0	41.1
1956	100.5	54.1	8.8	43.1
1957	98.6	50.2	9.4	38.2
1958	99.6	46.5	8.0	46.2
1959	101.6	44.4	9.9	47.1
1960	103.5	38.9	10.2	51.3
1961	104.5	39.4	11.0	53.4
1962	102.5		12.1	47.8
1963	102.5	44.5	10.8	55.3
1964	101.6	46.8	9.9	58.5
1965	92.5	53.9	12.2	45.9
1966	90.5	56.6	10.4	45.6
1967	96.5	56.5	11.4	56.4
1968	97.6	51.0	16.5	59.6
1969	99.6		18.6	60.6
1970	103.6	47.5	20.1	62.5
1971	102.6	41.2	23.8	64.6
1972	95.2	43.1	26.4	57.9
1973	102.4	46.1	24.7	66.1
1974	94.4	50.0	21.8	66.3
1975	104.9		24.2	70.5
1976	100.7		28.8	64.3
1977	108.6	39.1	29.0	74.0
1978	110.1		31.7	80.7
1979	100.6		35.5	63.6
1980	103.6		31.8	80.3
1981	107.4		36.3	80.4
1982	101.6		37.8	68.0

Note: It may help to put the figures in columns (3) and (4) in perspective by recalling that between 1955 and 1982 the population increased by 87.7 per cent.

Sources: Cols. (1), (3) and (4):   FAO, *Production Yearbook,* Rome, various years.
Col. (2):   Montek S. Ahluwalia, "Rural Poverty, Agricultural Production, and Prices: A Re-examination", in John W. Mellor and Gunvant M. Desai, eds., *Agricultural Change and Rural Poverty: Variations on a Theme by Dharm Narain,* Delhi, Oxford University Press, 1986, Table 7.1, p. 60 and for 1974/5, John. W. Mellor and Gunvant M. Desai, "Agricultural Change and Rural Poverty: A Synthesis", in *ibid.,* p. 195.

lead to a breakthrough in overall agricultural production. Many people, including the distinguished Indian economist Montek Ahluwalia, have held out "the hope that strategies for raising agricultural production would tend to reduce poverty even if they were not accompanied by radical institutional changes such as land reforms ..." [25]. As each year passes, however, the rational basis for hoping that technical change alone will suffice becomes weaker. Indeed, the failure of poverty in India to take a decisive turn for the better merely reinforces Ahluwalia's conclusion that "trickle-down processes alone would probably take an inordinately long time" [26] to reduce poverty significantly. Something more is needed. In the end, in fact, Ahluwalia admits that "it must be conceded that even on

Figure 6.1. **AGRICULTURAL OUTPUT AND RURAL POVERTY IN INDIA**

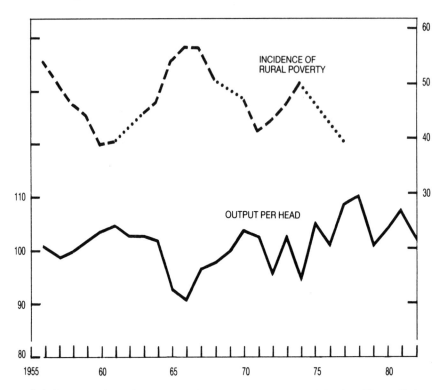

optimistic assumptions, the process [of reducing poverty] would be slow if we relied on growth alone" [27].

Just how slow is demonstrated by Jaime Quizon and Hans Binswanger in a study which uses a general equilibrium model to investigate the effects of the green revolution on the distribution of income in India [28]. They show that in the early period, until about 1972/3, the gains from introducing high-yielding varieties accrued to the wealthier rural groups. Grain prices remained high because the government used the increased domestic output to reduce food imports and consequently the early innovators enjoyed a sharp rise in farm profits. The rural poor gained very little. After 1972, however, higher grain output was reflected in a lower price of food and the chief beneficiaries then became urban residents. Those "farmers who had not adopted the Green Revolution technology – and whose yields had not increased – were harmed" [29]. Looking at the rural population as a whole, "real aggregate per capita income among rural people grew by only 8 per cent during the early Green Revolution, after which it declined and stagnated" [30]. As a result, average incomes in the rural areas in 1980/1 were only about 2 per cent higher than they were twenty years earlier, in 1960/1.

That of course is only an average and some groups must have done less well than the average. An obvious group to have suffered is the class of landless agricultural workers. Quizon and Binswanger suggest their real wages may have fallen 4 per cent between 1960 and 1980 [31], and this is consistent with other findings. Moreover, regional variations in India are considerable and there is no doubt that the position of the landless would have been far

150

worse in some regions than others. Research on the role of women in agriculture also is instructive. In particular, the possibility of a sustained downward pressure on the living standards of wage labourers is suggested by the fact that while female participation rates in rural India are low and falling, female participation rates among agricultural wage labourers are higher than average and rising [32]. Similarly, the proportion of *harijans* (i.e., untouchables) and tribal minorities among the landless labour force also has been rising [33]. The signs of distress, although far from conclusive, are there for those who look for them. It is premature therefore to say that "there is no basis whatsoever for asserting that the incidence of rural poverty in India has been rising from the sixties onwards" [34]. Such a claim could be made with confidence only if the aggregate data were disaggregated by region and socio-economic group. Until this is done, when it comes to formulating policies for rural poverty it would be wise in India to hope for the best but to assume the worst.

A complete strategy of agriculture-led development

Much has been learned since the early days of the green revolution about the essential components of a successful strategy of agriculture-led development. John Mellor and his associates at the International Food Policy Research Institute have played a prominent role in revising and extending the strategy and their ideas have been influential in both national and international circles [35]. The revised strategy, while selective in terms of priorities for policy, is comprehensive in terms of its implications for development as a whole.

As in the original strategy, "the key is improved, land-augmenting, and cost-reducing technology for agricultural production" [36]. The types of technologies envisaged, however, are much broader than the original emphasis on high-yielding, fertilizer-responsive food grains. Improved seeds remain important, but the focus is expanded to include not only food crops but also cash crops. Moreover, the revised strategy looks not only for varieties that are responsive to nitrogenous fertilizer but also for varieties that have a genetic resistance to pests and disease, that have a greater tolerance for drought and, particularly in the case of Africa, for varieties that will do well in poor soils and in regions of low and uncertain rainfall. Beyond plant breeding, emphasis is placed on irrigation as a "leading input" and, as before on greater use of fertilizer. All of this can be regarded as a logical extension of the early green revolution strategy, but the extension is important not least because it represents a shift in emphasis from "landlord biased" to "peasant biased" technology [37].

Next, the revised strategy assigns a much more important role to government. The plant breeders no longer are expected to bear almost all the responsibility for accelerating agricultural growth. Indeed, "substantial public-sector investment" is needed; "infrastructure requirements are massive"; and "the needs for rural electrification and communications are critical" [38]. Thus in addition to financing agricultural research, the government now is required to invest heavily in transportation, power, communications, input supply systems and rural education. If once it was thought that development could be achieved by spending a few million dollars on discovering a "miracle seed" – it was "all in a grain of rice" [39] – today it is known that there are no short cuts and no miracles. All strategies of development require a major investment effort, much of which, particularly in the rural areas, must come from government.

Unlike the early experience in India (where food prices rose), and contrary to much contemporary advice (such as that given by the World Bank), the new agriculture-led development strategy does not advocate raising farm prices and turning the terms of trade

151

in favour of agriculture. Indeed, "incentives provided by higher price alone" are regarded as "essentially antidevelopmental" [40]. It is acknowledged, of course, that farmers are responsive to price signals and that if relative crop prices change they will alter their cropping pattern. It does not follow from this, however, that total agricultural output will respond rapidly to an improvement in the sector's terms of trade. In fact it is likely that aggregate supply "is only slightly responsive to price" [41]. If the supply of land is fixed, or if the cost of bringing marginal land under cultivation is high, the sown area is unlikely to expand very much in response to higher prices and profits. Similarly, if the use of traditional inputs with existing technology has reached a point of diminishing returns, greater price incentives will not lead to substantially higher output even if there is a substantial increase in input use. What is needed in these circumstances is not higher prices but improved technologies which cut costs and raise the profitability of farming.

Moreover, higher agricultural prices tend to retard the development of other sectors of the economy. Industries which rely on agriculture for their raw materials, e.g., the cotton textile industry, will experience higher costs and lower profits and this will threaten employment, output, investment and growth in those industries. Higher food prices will threaten all industries, not just those that purchase inputs from agriculture, since higher food prices will lead to generally higher wage costs (even if wages do not rise as much as food prices). Thus improvements in agriculture's terms of trade inevitably come at the expense of growth in the rest of the economy. Incomes in agriculture as a whole certainly will increase, but output may not. In which case growth in the economy as a whole will suffer.

Equally serious, higher food prices will reduce the real incomes of some of the poorest sections of society, e.g., the landless labourers, and thereby frustrate attempts to alleviate mass poverty. Pinstrup-Andersen reports estimates from a variety of sources showing that a 10 per cent increase in the price of food will reduce the real income of the poorest decile of the population by 8.5 per cent in Sri Lanka, 7.7-9.0 per cent in Nigeria, 7.3 per cent in India, 6.0 per cent in Thailand and 5.6 per cent in Egypt [42]. Considerations such as these have led many analysts to conclude that an agriculture-led development strategy should aim not for higher farm prices but for lower ones (preferably brought about by cost-reducing technological innovations) and if necessary, food prices for poor consumers should be kept low through food rationing schemes and price subsidies.

The combination of improved technology, state investment and low food prices should ensure that unlike the original green revolution strategy, the revised strategy results in a rapid rate of growth in the demand for labour. It is unrealistic to assume, even in the most favourable cases, that the growth of agricultural output will generate enough demand to employ fully all the additions to the rural labour force. Thus agriculture's share of total employment can be expected to fall. However, an agriculture-led strategy of development should lead indirectly to rapid growth of employment in other activities. This will occur for several reasons.

First, the growth of agricultural output and the resulting increase in incomes will have multiplier effects. The demand for goods and services with high income elasticities will expand as the direct beneficiaries of agricultural growth begin to spend their new incomes and alter their pattern of expenditure. This growth of demand, it is thought, is likely to be concentrated on locally produced goods and services and thus agricultural growth will lead to the rapid development of rural off-farm activities. Moreover it is also thought that the production of these goods and services will be highly labour intensive and hence rapid growth in non-farm rural output will be accompanied by rapid growth of non-farm rural employment.

Second, some of the additional farm income will not be devoted to current consumption but will be saved and used to finance durable assets [43]. In practice much of this saving may be channelled into house building. This will provide a stimulus to the building materials and construction industries, both of which tend to be labour intensive. Some savings may be devoted to directly productive investment and at least part of this additional expenditure will circulate within the rural areas and create additional demand for labour. And of course the large state investment programme that is envisaged will be a major source of employment for those living in the countryside.

Third, the low and possibly falling price of food will help to keep wage costs low and this will encourage expansion in the urban areas too and of industry in general. Indeed industrialisation plays a central role in the revised green revolution strategy: it has responsibility for providing employment for the growing labour force and thereby for helping to reduce poverty. The difference with other strategies is that industry is neither export-oriented (as in the more outward-looking strategies) nor it is shielded from foreign competition (as in the import-substituting strategies): it emerges organically out of agricultural growth and the patterns of demand that accompany that growth. In this sense it is reminiscent of the first industrial revolution as described by Arthur Lewis:

> "The distinguishing feature of the industrial revolution at the end of the eighteenth century is that it began in the country with the highest agricultural productivity – Great Britain – which therefore already had a large industrial sector. The industrial revolution did not create an industrial sector where none had been before. It transformed an industrial sector that already existed by introducing new ways of making the same old things" [44].

It is known, however, that in the early stages of development in Great Britain few of the benefits of growth reached the poor. The revised green revolution strategy hopes to prevent this problem from reappearing today, two centuries later, by a series of supplementary measures intended to reduce the supply of labour, increase its mobility and create jobs in pockets of high unemployment. Policies to reduce the rate of growth of the population and hence, with a lag, the growth of the labour force are "seen as vital" [45]. Improved transport and communications, a consequence of state investment, will facilitate rural-rural and rural-urban migration, and this will help to even out the regional disparities which a green revolution strategy inevitably creates. Lastly, large-scale rural public works are advocated during the transitional period when the strategy is getting underway.

Miracle rice in the Philippines

The Philippines is the home of the green revolution in rice and has been by far the most successful country in adopting the new technology. The first of the so-called miracle rice varieties (IR-8) was developed in the mid-1960s at the International Rice Research Institute in the Philippines and the spread of IR-8 and later generations of high-yielding rice seeds was swift. In 1965 there were no high-yielding varieties of rice planted in the Philippines, but by 1968 high-yielding rice accounted for 21 per cent of the total rice area. The percentage doubled by 1970 (to 43 per cent) and nearly doubled again (to 78 per cent) by 1980. Only Sri Lanka, where 71 per cent of the rice area is sown with high-yielding varieties can compare with the Philippines.

Thus in terms of the spread of innovation, the rice revolution in the Philippines has been a success. It has also been a success in terms of the rate of growth of production. Indeed, comparing 1955-66 with 1966-82, the rate of growth virtually doubled, from a trend rate of growth of rice output of 2.2 per cent a year in the pre-green revolution period to 4.3 per cent in the post-green revolution period. This undoubtedly is an impressive acceleration in growth, and given that the population has been increasing about 2.8 per cent a year since the mid-1960s, per capita production of rice must have been rising about 1.5 per cent a year.

In contrast with India, the green revolution strategy in the Philippines was associated with a sharp rise in the rate of growth of agriculture as a whole. Whereas in the period 1955-66 the trend rate of growth of per capita agricultural output was actually slightly negative, namely, –0.1 per cent a year, per capita output grew rapidly during the following period, particularly after 1974. Indeed, curiously, almost all of the growth in output per head seems to have occurred in just three years, 1974 to 1976 (see Table 6.6). Considering the entire 16-year period, 1966-82, and taking at face value the jump in 1974-76, the rate of growth per head was a remarkable 1.6 per cent a year. If one accepts as a rough rule of thumb that for biological reasons the maximum long-run rate of growth of any agricultural system is unlikely to exceed 5 per cent, then performance in the Philippines during the early green revolution must have been about as good as one can reasonably expect of a country with an underdeveloped agrarian economy.

Table 6.6 **AGRICULTURAL PRODUCTION IN THE PHILIPPINES, 1955-1982**

	Rice (Million metric tons)	Total agricultural output per head (Index: 1974-76 = 100)
1955	3.3	87.8
1956	3.3	92.3
1957	3.2	93.2
1958	3.7	90.5
1959	3.7	88.7
1960	3.7	91.4
1961	3.9	90.6
1962	4.0	92.4
1963	3.8	90.6
1964	4.0	89.7
1965	4.1	88.8
1966	4.1	90.6
1967	4.6	89.7
1968	4.4	86.9
1969	5.2	89.7
1970	5.6	90.6
1971	5.1	88.8
1972	4.9	90.1
1973	5.5	91.6
1974	5.7	88.7
1975	6.2	101.7
1976	6.4	109.6
1977	6.9	106.5
1978	7.3	110.2
1979	7.0	104.8
1980	7.8	106.4
1981	8.2	108.7
1982	8.3	108.3

Source: FAO, *Production Yearbook*, Rome, various years.

Exclusive reliance was not placed on plant breeding to sustain development in the country. In fact, the Philippines tried a little bit of everything to support a strategy of agriculture-led development. Major investments were made in roads and these must have increased the speed of communications and cut marketing costs. The irrigation system also was expanded and some effort was made to supply electric power to rural areas. Agricultural credit programmes were introduced. Even land reform was discussed and laws passed, although in practice almost nothing was achieved. Land producing export crops was excluded from the programme, the landless were not entitled to participate, landlords owning less than seven hectares were unaffected by the law, and tenants were required to pay full compensation for the land they received within 15 years. Corruption and evasion were widespread; expectations were raised but results were minimal.

The distribution of land in the Philippines is extraordinarily unequal. Recent figures do not exist, but in 1953 it was estimated that 0.36 per cent of families owned 42 per cent of the land [46]. Nothing has happened in the last 35 years to alter fundamentally the picture represented by that statistic. Inequality in the Philippines today is qualitatively as great as ever. Indeed, if anything, the distribution of income has become worse and the share of the poor has fallen. Estimates of the percentage of total income received by families in the bottom 40 per cent of the distribution are as follows [47]:

1956	12.6
1961	12.1
1965	11.5
1971	12.0
1980	9.9
1981	9.9
1982	9.4
1983	9.8

In the rural areas average incomes per head have increased, but as in India, there are indications that certain occupational groups have suffered a decline in their standard of living or have had to make strenuous efforts to maintain levels of consumption. There are unmistakable signs of an increase in underemployment and a reduction in the average number of days worked per year. At the same time, there has been a rise in female participation rates in the rural labour force. There has also been an increase in unpaid family labour. Finally, there has been a decline in the real wage rate in most sectors of the agricultural economy. The demand for labour evidently has not kept pace with supply, the employment situation has deteriorated and earnings of some groups of workers have fallen. It has not been possible to translate the technological breakthrough in plant breeding into a rapid growth of jobs and consequently the livelihoods of some sections of the rural population have suffered.

The data in Table 6.7 refer to wage rates in rice and maize (the two staple food crops) and coconuts and sugar (two export crops). Between them these four crops account for more than 85 per cent of the cultivated area, with rice and maize accounting for nearly 60 per cent of the land. Thus the data cover almost all agricultural workers during the period 1970-82 when the green revolution was at its height. It can readily be seen from the Table that real wages of workers in the rice sector fell in the first half of the 1970s, rose briefly to a peak in 1977 and then began to fall again. By 1982 real wages were 15 per cent below what they were in 1970. The green revolution in rice, despite the rapid growth in production, was unable to prevent a deterioration of real incomes of rice workers.

Table 6.7 **REAL DAILY WAGE RATES IN THE PHILIPPINES, 1970-1982**
(Index: 1970 = 100)

	Rice	Maize	Coconut	Sugar
1970	100	100	100	100
1971	97	98	108	91
1972	100	97	103	91
1973	90	94	97	111
1974	84	95	98	96
1975	92	101	104	117
1976	118	130	117	103
1977	120	131	114	144
1978	118	125	117	122
1979	102	117	103	113
1980	86	97	88	96
1981	85	87	97	91
1982	85	81	101	89

Source: Bureau of Agricultural Economics, Government of the Philippines.

A very similar pattern was followed in the maize sector. Wages fell, rose and fell again such that by 1982 they were 19 per cent below the level of 1970. Given that wages in maize normally are lower than those in rice, the maize workers must have been among the poorest in the country. The situation was not quite so bad for coconut plantation workers. For the period as a whole there was a zero trend in real wages and compared to other crops, relatively little fluctuation in wages. Sugarcane workers, in contrast, suffered violent fluctuations in real wages from year to year and, after 1977, a steady decline of 38 per cent. Comparing 1982 with 1970, however, the decline, at 11 per cent, was somewhat less horrific. The situation for all four categories of workers deteriorated further after 1982 and there is little room for doubt that landless agricultural labourers in, say, 1985 were much worse off than they had been a decade and a half earlier.

Looking back over the last two decades or so it is clear that technological change has not been a substitute for institutional change in the Philippines. Public investment programmes in transport, irrigation and power have supplemented the efforts of the plant breeders, but even so, social conditions have deteriorated. Unrest in the countryside has grown by leaps and bounds. The incomes of some groups have fallen. Organised rural violence by Muslim insurgents in Mindanao and by the New People's Army in other parts of the country has received increasing moral and material support from poor tenants and landless workers. Pressure for a radical redistribution of land continues to mount. Indeed land reform remains very much on the political agenda and the future of the green revolution as a strategy of development is uncertain.

Recent policy reforms in Bangladesh

In Bangladesh, however, the green revolution strategy is just beginning. In late 1979 the government introduced a number of reforms that were designed to accelerate agricultural development and improve the well being of the population. One thrust of the reforms has entailed a sharp rise in the proportion of development expenditure allocated to the agricultural sector. In 1973 this was as high as 34 per cent, but by 1977 agriculture's share of development expenditure had fallen to only 19 per cent. The proportion was raised to 28 per cent in 1985, still low given the relative size of the rural population but an improvement

156

none the less. Emphasis is being placed on investment in irrigation and in recent years the amount of land irrigated has doubled. Even so, roughly three-quarters of all cultivated land cannot be reached by the existing irrigation facilities and about half the land that is potentially irrigable with existing facilities remains unirrigated. Water management – drainage as well as irrigation – still is a serious problem in Bangladesh and it remains an open question whether the problem can be solved within the existing institutional framework.

A second thrust of the reform programme has been a shift in favour of reliance on market forces. Government controls and subsidies have been reduced and increasingly the free market has been used to determine input prices and the price of food paid by consumers. On the input side, the most important change has been in the market for fertilizers. The government distribution system has been dismantled and fertilizer now flows through the private distribution network. At the same time, the state subsidy to the price of fertilizer paid by farmers has been reduced. As a result, fertilizer subsidies fell from 10 per cent of development expenditure in 1978 to 2.4 per cent in 1984. The funds thereby released are intended to be used for investment in major irrigation projects. Small-scale investments in tubewells and irrigation pumps will be left to the private sector.

A similar policy has been followed with respect to food price subsidies. The "statutory rationing" system which supplies subsidised food grains to the entire population of the major urban areas has declined and the "modified rationing" system which supplies grain in the rural areas to those classified as poor has virtually collapsed. In the 1960s, before independence, modified rationing accounted for about 55 per cent of all food grains channelled through the public foodgrain distribution system. By the mid-1980s, however, the proportion was down to 18 per cent [48]. An expanded food-for-work programme has partially compensated for the decline in rationed supplies in the rural areas, but it is clear that consumers, however poor or hungry they may be, are in future increasingly expected to obtain their food through purchases in the open market.

The economic reforms in Bangladesh have been widely applauded. *The Economist* has described them as "sensible policies" [49] and the World Bank has claimed that "Bangladesh shows how ... policy reforms ... can bear fruit on a large scale in even the poorest countries" [50]. Perhaps it is too early to judge the success of the particular reforms that have been introduced, but one cannot doubt that reforms of some sort were vitally necessary. Indeed between independence in 1971 and the beginning of the reforms in 1979, the country experienced two famines, in 1974 and 1979. Real agricultural wages in 1979 were lower than at the time of independence and agricultural output per head was only about 12 per cent above the pre-independence level. The period between 1970 and 1975 was particularly bad. Food production per capita remained stagnant; the distribution of income and of landed wealth in the rural areas became more unequal; and the living standard of the poorest people in the rural areas – landless agricultural workers, food deficit farmers and non-farm rural workers – declined.

Since 1979 there have been signs of improvement (see Table 6.8). Wheat output increased by two-thirds in just one year, 1980, and by another 71 per cent in the following five years. Bangladesh, like India, has had a wheat revolution. The significance of this is limited, however. Only a small proportion of the cultivated land is devoted to wheat and a small switch out of one of the major crops can have a dramatic effect on wheat area and output. Wheat is not an important source of calories, especially for the poor, and wheat production accounts for only about 6 per cent of the combined output of wheat and rice.

The main food crop by far is rice. Yet only about 22 per cent of the rice area is planted with high-yielding varieties, one of the lowest figures in Asia. Some of the land is subject to deep flooding and is not suitable for the new varieties, but of the land that is in fact suitable, only about a third is sown with high-yielding varieties. Similarly fertilizer, although its use is growing rapidly, normally is applied in very small doses. Indeed no fertilizer at all is applied to 40 per cent of the cereal land. There is thus plenty of room for technical improvement in rice cultivation in the use of modern seeds, chemical fertilizers and irrigation. And happily some improvement seems to have occurred. Indeed in the six years after 1979 rice output increased on average 3.1 per cent a year. Given that the population is growing about 2.5 per cent a year, this implies a growth of rice output per head of approximately 0.6 per cent a year, clearly an encouraging result. This may be very misleading, however, because 1979, the base year for our calculation, was an abnormally bad year for rice. If instead of 1979 the calculation is based on 1977, it turns out that rice output grew on average only 1.7 per cent a year, i.e., 0.8 per cent less rapidly than the population. Thus there is still some doubt whether the new policies in Bangladesh have succeeded in raising rice output per head.

Table 6.8 **AGRICULTURAL PRODUCTION IN BANGLADESH, 1970-1985**

	Rice	Wheat	Total agricultural output per head
	(Million metric tons)		(Index: 1979-81 = 100)
1970	16.7	0.10	87.6
1971	15.1	0.11	77.3
1972	14.9	0.11	79.0
1973	18.3	0.09	87.6
1974	18.5	0.11	82.4
1975	19.1	0.12	90.3
1976	17.6	0.21	87.0
1977	19.3	0.26	94.0
1978	19.6	0.35	99.0
1979	18.4	0.49	98.2
1980	21.0	0.82	101.0
1981	20.4	1.10	101.8
1982	21.3	0.96	104.4
1983	21.7	1.10	107.5
1984	21.9	1.20	107.8
1985	21.9	1.40	110.6

Source: FAO, *Production Yearbook*, Rome, various years.

There is no doubt, however, that since the reforms total agricultural output per head has increased. This is true whether one chooses 1977 or 1979 as the base year. Using the latter, it appears that per capita agricultural production increased 12.6 per cent up to 1985, or at an annual rate of just over 2 per cent a year. This, if sustained over a long period, would be a very good performance.

Even a sustained good growth performance, however, might not be sufficient to overcome the structural problems in the rural sector. The proportion of landless agricultural workers in the rural labour force continues to creep upwards and is now over 37 per cent. Small landowers slowly but surely have been forced to sell their land to middle-sized farmers and this has contributed not only to the growth of landlessness but to increased concentration of wealth. Rapid population growth has, of course, resulted in rapid growth of the labour force and this, in turn, has exerted strong pressure in the labour market. There has been a persistent tendency towards excess supply of rural labour as reflected in a combination of falling real wage rates and probably also in a reduction in the average number of days worked per person per year.

Non-farm rural employment has grown rapidly from 19 per cent of the labour force in 1974 to 39 per cent in 1981 [51]. This is the pattern one would expect in a successful agriculture-led development strategy. In Bangladesh, however, the change in the structure of rural employment towards non-farm activities may be a symptom not of dynamism in the countryside but of gradual further impoverishment. Workers are being pushed off the land, not attracted to more remunerative occupations in small-scale rural industry. Indeed it is reported that nearly one-third of the labour force in rural industries is engaged in activities where the return to labour is lower than the agricultural wage rate [52]. Similarly, another study found that in 10 out of 14 major cottage industries the wage rate for employees was less than the wage received by unskilled labour in agriculture [53]. These are signs of economic decline rather than of expansion. The gloomy picture is completed by the fall in the rice equivalent of nominal wages (see Table 6.3). Real wages have picked up from their extraordinarily low level of 1975, but in 1982 they still were below the levels that prevailed prior to independence [54] and were even 11 per cent less than real wages in 1976.

Meanwhile, even the production side of the new strategy may be running into difficulties. Corruption and political patronage have destroyed the country's system of rural credit [55]. Poor peasants are unable to borrow and the more prosperous farmers are unwilling to repay their loans. Yet the removal of fertilizer subsidies, far from diminishing the need for credit, has increased requirements for working capital on the part of small and large farmers alike [56]. If the small farmers in particular are unable to obtain credit, they will be forced to change their input mix and possibly their cropping pattern. Already there are reports of "small farmers who are going back to low-yielding varieties of crops" [57]. If this is true, and if production begins to falter, the government may be tempted to respond by raising agricultural prices. This would be a disaster for the economy for reasons explained earlier in the chapter.

Only 30 per cent of the farmers produce a marketable surplus and thus would be in a position to benefit from higher prices [58]. They represent only about 12 per cent of the rural population. The 70 per cent of farmers who either are self-sufficient or who are net purchasers of grain would be worse off, squeezed by higher food and fertilizer prices and by less (and probably more expensive) credit. This group represents 28 per cent of the rural population. The landless agricultural workers (26 per cent of the rural population) and the non-agricultural wage earners (9.3 per cent of the rural population) also would be severely affected by higher food prices. That is, 12 per cent of the rural population certainly would gain from higher prices and 63 per cent certainly would lose; what would happen on balance to the remaining 25 per cent is uncertain. The overall effect, however, is obvious: inequality and poverty would increase substantially and the political viability of the development strategy would be threatened. This outcome is not inevitable but nor is the success of the policy reforms guaranteed. The jury still is out and the verdict remains unknown.

Conclusions

A number of conclusions emerge from our analysis. First, it is possible through biological research to improve agricultural productivity in the Third World. Gains similar to those in rice and wheat can be expected to be achieved in other crops. In this sense the original conception of the green revolution has been shown to be valid. Second, it is unlikely, however, that technological breakthroughs in individual crops will be sufficient to improve dramatically the growth performance of the agricultural sector as a whole. Experience has shown that a strategy based on plant breeding alone is likely to fail.

Third, a more complete strategy of agriculture-led economic development is not possible unless investment in the rural areas is given high priority. Rural development requires a good transport and communications network, electric power and, above all, a good water management system. Fourth, the government inevitably must play a major role not only in financing research and the required high level of investment, but also in providing basic educational and family planning services. A green revolution strategy of development assigns a different role to government than some other strategies but not a smaller one.

Price policy under a revised green revolution strategy is more subtle than may at first appear. But the main conclusion, fifth, is that on the whole the government ought not to raise farm prices but on the contrary allow them to fall gradually as cost-reducing technological innovations come into effect. The advantage of this approach is that technical improvements in agriculture will be translated into lower wage costs in the rest of the economy and this will encourage a rapid growth of employment and of industrial output. A further advantage is that falling food prices are likely to have favourable consequences for the distribution of income. In fact, sixth, during the transition period food rationing and food-for-work programmes may be advisable.

The weakness of the original green revolution strategy, and even of the revised strategy, is that it tries to substitute technical change and agricultural expansion for institutional reform and direct measures to improve the distribution of income and productive assets in rural areas. But the evidence indicates, seventh, that a green revolution strategy has been most successful in those countries where the "initial conditions" have included a relatively high degree of equality. The land reforms and the strong co-operative and communal institutions that were built upon them in South Korea, Taiwan, Japan and China are cases in point. Conversely, eighth, in countries such as India, Bangladesh and the Philippines where land reform has not occurred and where rural institutions are relatively weak, implementation of a green revolution strategy of development has encountered serious difficulties. In particular, the increase in agricultural growth has been modest or the decline in rural poverty has been disappointing, or both.

Despite its problems, however, the green revolution strategy deserves much credit. It has helped to shift attention to food (the most important wage good) and to agriculture in general (the sector where most of the poor are to be found). While denying the need for institutional change, it has indirectly raised questions of land reform, local participation and the role of co-operative and communal organisation. Moreover, the revised green revolution strategy has helped to build a bridge between those who place their faith in technology and those who concentrate on the satisfaction of basic needs. It has done this by emphasizing employment creation and the close link between food prices and the incidence of poverty, by acknowledging the prominent part governments must play and finally by accepting that there are times when governments must interfere with market processes, as in food rationing schemes. The revised green revolution strategy remains distinctive, it is not a redistributive strategy of development, but as we shall see in the next chapter, the two have a number of features in common.

NOTES AND REFERENCES

1. The best reference book for demographic data is United Nations, *World Population Prospects,* New York, 1986. The United Nations, *Demographic Yearbook,* published annually in New York, also is of great value.

2. Table 6.2 seems to suggest the opposite in the cases of Côte d'Ivoire, Tanzania, Mexico and Peru but this is because the rural population estimates refer to 1985 whereas the agricultural labour force estimates refer to 1980, when the rural population was relatively larger.

3. One of the early studies where an attempt was made to measure changes in rural poverty over time was International Labour Organisation, *Poverty and Landlessness in Rural Asia*, Geneva, 1977. Also see Azizur Rahman Khan and Eddy Lee, eds., *Poverty in Rural Asia*, Bangkok, ILO-ARTEP, 1985 and Keith Griffin and A.K. Ghose, "Growth and Impoverishment in the Rural Areas of Asia", *World Development*, Vol. 7, No. 4/5, April/May 1979. Bangladesh is interesting because there the incomes of the rural rich rose despite falling per capita output.

4. Between 1970 and 1984 workers' remittances, not all of them destined for the rural areas of course, rose from $86 million a year to $2 567 million.

5. See Chapter 3, Table 3.3.

6. Rising food prices in Asia were underlined in Keith Griffin and Ajit Ghose, "Growth and Impoverishment in the Rural Areas in Asia", *World Development*, Vol. 7, Nos. 4/5, April-May 1979. Dharam Ghai and Lawrence Smith showed that "an increase in the real consumer food price in practically all African countries is perhaps the most significant agricultural price change in the seventies". ("Food Policy and Equity in Sub-Saharan Africa", ILO, World Employment Programme Working Paper WEP 10-6/WP55, August 1983, p. 29.) Also see Dharam Ghai and Lawrence D. Smith, *Agricultural Prices, Policy and Equity in Sub-Saharan Africa*, Boulder, Colorado, Lynne Rienner Publishers, 1987.

7. In countries where the real price of food is rising, the fall in real wages of agricultural workers may be understated by deflating nominal wages by a general consumer price index (as was done in several cases for the countries represented in Table 6.3). The reason for this is that the poor devote a higher than average proportion of their total expenditure to food and hence a "poor person's price index" would give a higher weight to food than a price index representative of the average buyer.

8. See Hamid Tabatabai, "Economic Decline, Access to Food and Structural Adjustment in Ghana", ILO World Employment Programme Working Paper WEP 10-6/WP80, July 1986, pp. 17-20.

9. In fact the share of exports in GDP in Ghana fell from 28 per cent in 1960 to 2 per cent in 1982. Performance of the economy improved after the reforms of 1983 and by 1984 the export share had recovered to 11 per cent.

10. See, for example, R.A. Berry and W.R. Cline, *Agrarian Structure and Productivity in Developing Countries*, Baltimore, Johns Hopkins University Press, 1979 and G.A. Cornia, "Farm Size, Land Yields and the Agricultural Production Function: An Analysis for Fifteen Developing Countries", *World Development*, Vol. 13, No. 4, April 1985.

11. Keith Griffin, *The Political Economy of Agrarian Change*, London, Macmillan, 1974.

12. This point is made by Miguel Urrutia in "Latin America and the Crisis of the 1980s", in Louis Emmerij, ed., *Development Policies and the Crisis of the 1980s*, Paris, OECD Development Centre, 1987.

13. S. Hirashima, "Poverty as a Generation's Problem: A Note on the Japanese Experience", in John. W. Mellor and Gunvant M. Desai, eds., *Agricultural Change and Rural Poverty: Variations on a Theme by Dharm Narain*, Delhi, Oxford University Press, 1986, Table 14.2, p. 152.

14. See James K. Boyce, "Irrigation Development in Asian Rice Agriculture: Technological and Institutional Alternatives", paper prepared for the World Institute for Development Economics Research, Helsinki, Finland, May 1986, Table 1, p. 8a.

15. Although Pakistan meets our criterion of irrigated area, it is excluded from the calculation because only 10 per cent of the sown area is devoted to rice.

16. See S. Ishikawa, *Economic Development in Asian Perspective*, Tokyo, Kinokuniya, 1967.

17. See James K. Boyce, *op. cit.*, pp. 37-46. Also see his *Agrarian Impasse in Bengal: Institutional Constraints to Technological Change*, Oxford, Oxford University Press, 1987.

18. Amartya Sen, *Poverty and Famines: An Essay on Entitlement and Deprivation*, Oxford, Oxford University Press, 1981.

19. Per Pinstrup-Andersen and Peter B.R. Hazell, "The Impact of the Green Revolution and Prospects for the Future", *Food Reviews International*, Vol. 1, No. 1, 1985, p. 1.

20. *Ibid.*, p. 20.

21. *Ibid.*, pp. 9-10.

161

22. *Ibid.*, p. 9. Prominent defenders of the green revolution include Yujiro Hayami and Vernon Ruttan, *Agricultural Development: An International Perspective*, Baltimore, Johns Hopkins University Press, rev. ed., 1985 and Randolph Barker and Robert Herdt with Beth Rose, *The Rice Economy of Asia*, Washington, Resources for the Future, 1985. One of the early writers to emphasize the role of technical change in agriculture was T.W. Schultz, *Transforming Traditional Agriculture*, New Haven, Yale University Press, 1964.

23. Per Pinstrup-Andersen and Peter B.R. Hazell, *op. cit.*, p.2.

24. J.S. Sharma, *Growth and Equity: Policies and Implementation in Indian Agriculture*, IFPRI Research Report 28, Washington, International Food Policy Research Institute, November 1981, Table 3, p. 21.

25. Montek S. Ahluwalia, "Rural Poverty, Agricultural Production, and Prices: A Re-examination", in John W. Mellor and Gunvant M. Desai, eds., *Agricultural Change and Rural Poverty: Variations on a Theme by Dharm Narain*, Delhi, Oxford University Press, 1986, p. 69.

26. *Ibid.*, p. 71.

27. *Ibid.*, p. 72.

28. Jaime Quizon and Hans Binswanger, "Modeling the Impact of Agricultural Growth and Government Policy on Income Distribution in India", *World Bank Economic Review*, Vol. 1, No. 1, September 1986.

29. *Ibid.*, p. 107.

30. *Ibid.*, p. 112.

31. *Ibid.*, Table 1, p. 109.

32. Kalpana Bardhan, "Economic Growth, Poverty and Rural Labour Markets in India: A Survey of Research", World Employment Programme Research Working Paper WEP 10-6/WP54, International Labour Office, Geneva, March 1983, p. 58.

33. *Ibid.*, p. 60.

34. Montek S. Ahluwalia, *op. cit.*, p. 62.

35. Among the many writings of John W. Mellor, see his *The New Economics of Growth: A Strategy for India and the Developing World*, Ithaca, Cornell University Press, 1976; "Agriculture on the Road to Industrialization", in John P. Lewis and Valeriana Kallab, eds., *Development Strategies Reconsidered*, New Brunswick, N.J., Transaction Books for the Overseas Development Council, 1986; "Agricultural Change and Rural Poverty", IFPRI Food Policy Statement No. 3, Washington, D.C., October 1985.

36. John W. Mellor, "Agricultural Change and Rural Poverty", *loc. cit.*

37. Keith Griffin, *The Political Economy of Agrarian Change, loc. cit.*

38. John W. Mellor, "Agriculture on the Road to Industrialization", *loc. cit.*, p. 84.

39. Gelia T. Castillo, *All in a Grain of Rice*, Laguna, Philippines, Southeast Asian Regional Centre for Graduate Study and Research in Agriculture, 1975.

40. John W. Mellor, "The Role of Government and New Agricultural Technologies", IFPRI Food Policy Statement No. 4, Washington, D.C., November 1985.

41. John W. Mellor, "Agriculture on the Road to Industrialization", *loc.cit.*, p. 78.

42. Per Pinstrup-Andersen, "Food Prices and the Poor in Developing Countries", *European Review of Agricultural Economics*, Vol. 12, Nos 1/2, 1985, Table 1, p. 71. Also see John W. Mellor, "Food Price Policy and Income Distribution in Low-Income Countries", *Economic Development and Cultural Change*, Vol. 27, No. 1, October 1978.

43. See, for example, Bruce F. Johnston and Peter Kilby, *Agriculture and Structural Transformation: Economic Strategies in Late-Developing Countries*, New York, Oxford University Press, 1975.

44. W. Arthur Lewis, *The Evolution of the International Economic Order*, Princeton, N.J., Princeton University Press, 1978, p. 10.

45. John W. Mellor, "Agricultural Change and Rural Poverty", *loc.cit.*

46. Peter Krinks, "Rectifying Inequality or Favouring the Few? Image and Reality in Philippine Development", in David A.M. Lea and D.P. Chaudhri, eds., *Rural Development and the State*, London, Methuen, 1983, Table 4.1, p. 103.

47. IBRD, *The Philippines: Recent Trends in Poverty, Employment and Wages*, Washington, D.C., June 1985, p. 16.

48. S.R. Osmani, "The Food Problems of Bangladesh", paper presented to the Food Strategies Research Conference, World Institute of Development Economics Research, Helsinki, Finland, 21-25 July 1986, p. 34.

49. "Bangladesh: Where the Right Policies Get No Credit", *The Economist,* 18th October 1986, p. 22.

50. IBRD, *World Development Report 1986,* Oxford University Press, 1986, p. 106.

51. S.R. Osmani, *op. cit.,* p. 24.

52. *Ibid.,* p. 25. Also see M. Hossain, "Employment and Labour in Bangladesh Rural Industries", *Bangladesh Development Studies,* Vol. XII, Nos. 1 and 2, 1984.

53. M. Hossain, *Employment Generation Through Cottage Industries: Potential and Constraints,* Bangkok, ILO Asian Regional Team for Employment Promotion, 1984.

54. For real agricultural wages in Bangladesh for the period 1949-75 see Azizur Rahman Khan, "Poverty and Inequality in Rural Bangladesh", in ILO, *Poverty and Landlessness in Rural Asia,* Geneva, 1977.

55. "Bangladesh: Where the Right Policies Get No Credit", *loc. cit.*

56. This point is emphasized in S.R. Osmani, *op. cit.*

57. "Bangladesh: Where Right Policies Get No Credit", *loc. cit.,* p. 24.

58. See R. Ahmed, *Agricultural Price Policies Under Complex Socioeconomic and Natural Constraints: The Case of Bangladesh,* IFPRI Research Report 27, Washington, International Food Policy Research Institute, 1981.

Chapter 7

REDISTRIBUTIVE STRATEGIES

For nearly four decades from 1914 to 1950 the world economy suffered from war, stagnation, a great depression, war again and finally post-war reconstruction. It was natural that after such a sequence of events governments in both the industrialised and in the newly independent Third World countries would make growth their first priority. Latin America, long independent but still a relatively poor part of the globe, had experienced rising incomes per head during the period 1914-50, but it had suffered a severe setback during the first half of the great depression and was anxious to maintain the growth momentum that was rekindled by the structural reforms of the early 1930s [1]. Thus in Latin America, too, growth was the top priority. Only in China, which had experienced a revolutionary change of regime in 1949, was the quest for growth subservient to the commitment to create a socialist society and even there the need to increase production was seen to be urgent. The big exception in the 1950s was of course Africa, which still was largely colonised and which did not therefore have control over its economic policies. Beginning with the 1960s, however, most of Africa achieved its independence and growth then became top priority there too. Thus virtually the entire world by 1960 wished to pursue growth-oriented strategies of development.

As we saw in Chapters 4-6, the strategies that were adopted after 1950 in the capitalist Third World countries differed markedly from one another, but more often than not they had at least one thing in common: they were designed to increase the rate of growth of output and thereby improve the material well being of the population. Growth was a means to an end, not an end in itself. The objectives were to eliminate poverty, illiteracy and disease, to increase the range of human choice, to give mankind greater control over the natural environment and thereby to increase freedom. It was a presupposition of those who advocated faster growth that all would benefit and the effects would be "greatly to increase both the material and the cultural standards of the people" [2].

The case for growth was eloquently put by Arthur Lewis more than three decades ago.

> "At primitive levels, man has to struggle for subsistence. With great drudgery he succeeds in wresting from the soil barely enough to keep himself alive. ... Regularly he is visited by famine, plague or pestilence. Half his children die before reaching the age of ten, and at forty his wife is wrinkled and old. Economic growth enables him to escape from this

164

servitude. ... Famine is banished, the infant mortality rate falls from 300 to 30 per thousand; the death rate from 40 to 10 per thousand. Cholera, smallpox, malaria, hookworm, yellow fever, plague, leprosy and tuberculosis disappear altogether. Thus life itself is freed from some of nature's menaces" [3].

Long before it became a topic of great interest, Arthur Lewis recognised the heavy cost to women of underdevelopment and the substantial benefits to them of economic development. As he said,

"Women benefit from [growth] even more than men. ... Woman gains freedom from drudgery, is emancipated from the seclusion of the household, and gains at last the chance to be a full human being, exercising her mind and her talents in the same way as men. It is open to men to debate whether economic progress is good for men or not, but for women to debate the desirability of economic growth is to debate whether women should have the chance to cease to be beasts of burden, and to join the human race" [4].

Finally, in an appeal to statesmen, Lewis observed that "in these democratic days, most countries of the world are passing through a phase where bitter civil strife is inevitable unless there is a rapid increase in production per head" [5]. Growth, hence, was in the interest of all, the elite and the masses, the rich and the poor. In the event, the rate of growth actually achieved in the Third World was much faster than even the optimists anticipated. Indeed, as documented in Chapter 1, the rate of growth of income per head in the developing countries since 1950 has been without precedent.

Despite this, signs that all was not well began to appear in the late 1960s, and during the 1970s an increasing number of analysts became convinced that the benefits of development often were not reaching the poor or at least not in full measure. An early study by David Turnham of the OECD assembled evidence of growing underemployment of labour, especially in agriculture [6]. This was followed a year later by a paper by Albert Fishlow on the distribution of income in Brazil, a country which accounts for more than a third of the population of Latin America. Fishlow showed that between 1960 and 1970, a period when per capita income in Brazil rose 22 per cent, inequality in the distribution of income became much worse, the Gini coefficient rising from 0.59 to 0.63 in only one decade [7]. Studies of other countries, from Pakistan to Peru, indicated that Brazil was not unique [8]. Indeed it soon became a commonplace to argue that throughout much of the Third World growth was accompanied by increased inequality.

Worse was to come. In a cross-section analysis of 74 countries, Irma Adelman and Cynthia Taft Morris argued that growth in the early stages is accompanied not just by widening inequality but also by a decline in the standard of living of well over half the population. Not just the poor but many of those in the middle of the income distribution were harmed by growth. In their words,

"The position of the poorest 60 percent typically worsens, both relatively and absolutely, when an initial spurt of narrowly based dualistic growth is imposed on an agrarian subsistence economy. Our study suggests that, in an average country going through the earliest phases of economic development, it takes at least a generation for the poorest 60 percent to recover the loss in absolute income associated with the typical spurt in growth" [9].

Research on individual countries failed to produce examples of growth accompanied by the impoverishment of the poorest 60 per cent of the population, but a number of cases were found where the standard of living of significant sections of the poor declined despite an increase in average per capita income. A study by the ILO of seven countries in Asia, which between them account for 70 per cent of the rural population of the Third World, indicated quite widespread falls in real income of the rural poor [10]. Typically, during the 1960s, the poorest 20-40 per cent of the rural population was found to be worse off than previously. And the decline in real income was found to be concentrated on particular classes or occupational groups, namely, landless farm workers, small peasant cultivators who supplemented farm income by off-farm employment and plantation workers.

Scattered evidence from Latin America and Africa suggested that the phenomenon of impoverishment of certain groups in poverty in a context of rising average incomes was not confined to South and Southeast Asia [11]. Alarm bells were ringing throughout much of the Third World. Growth was not eradicating poverty at the speed anticipated or desired and in some instances the incidence of poverty actually was rising. The Pakistani economist Mahbub ul Haq summarised the situation as follows:

> "In country after country, economic growth is being accompanied by rising disparities, in personal as well as in regional incomes. In country after country, the masses are complaining that development has not touched their ordinary lives. Very often, economic growth has meant very little social justice. It has been accompanied by rising unemployment, worsening social services and increasing absolute and relative poverty" [12].

The cry at that time was not that growth was slow but that the effects of rapid growth were disappointing. Today of course the situation is very different. Growth rates are much slower than they were in the 1960s and 1970s, many countries have experienced a fall in average real incomes and the incidence of poverty in those countries has undoubtedly increased. In this sense the problem of world poverty in the 1980s is larger and more intractable than it was earlier. Yet a far ranging reassessment of growth-oriented development strategies did not have to wait until the crisis of the 1980s; the case for putting the poor first began to be made a decade earlier.

The World Employment Programme of the ILO had a major impact. Through its research activities and its comprehensive employment missions to Colombia, Sri Lanka, the Philippines, Kenya, Tanzania and elsewhere perceptions were gradually changed and alternative policies discussed [13]. It soon was recognised, for example, that open unemployment was a serious issue only among certain age groups (the youth) and for certain social classes (those with a secondary and in a few cases a university education). Aggregate unemployment in the Third World usually was rather low. The poor often were not unemployed, they simply had low incomes. The solution to the employment problem for these "working poor" was not to create more jobs, more employment, but to create more productive employment.

In the urban areas the ILO discovered that many of the working poor were self-employed or wage earners in small workshops and factories which had little fixed capital and used very labour-intensive methods of production. Others provided a wide range of services (itinerant salesmen, street vendors, domestic servants) that, again, were very labour intensive. These activities were usually unregistered, often unrecognised officially and occasionally illegal or prohibited. The ILO deliberately called attention to these activities by putting a label on them, the "informal sector". The informal sector, the ILO believed, was able potentially to grow rapidly and to generate large numbers of more productive and remunerative jobs. Yet government regulations systematically discriminated against the poor of the informal sector (e.g., through licensing laws, zoning and building regulations, health and safety legislation), state investment programmes favoured large-scale, capital-intensive projects and factor prices (minimum wage legislation, subsidised credit, import licensing and overvalued exchange rates) encouraged the development of capital-intensive goods and services in the formal sector. In other words, development policy was biased against the informal sector and hence against the poor.

However in most Third World countries – the highly urbanised parts of Latin America are exceptions – the majority of the poor are in the countryside. Some are engaged in non-agricultural activities (fishermen, foresters, traders, artisans) but most are farmers of one sort or another (small peasant proprietors, tenant cultivators, landless agricultural workers). Some of the rural poor may be seasonally unemployed, notably in rainfall dependent areas which produce only one harvest a year, but the main problem, once again, was not lack of employment but very low incomes often after long days of backbreaking work.

The focus on rural employment inevitably raised many fundamental policy issues. First, there was the question of the relative neglect of the countryside and the concentration of resurces in the urban areas, and within the urban areas on the formal sector. "Urban bias", as it came to be called, was an early theme of the ILO [14]. Second, there was the question of the balance of government expenditure as between agriculture and industry. The ILO tended to take the view that a more employment-oriented pattern of development required faster agricultural growth. Third, there was the question of the terms of trade of the agricultural sector. Here the ILO recognised the dilemma discussed in the previous chapter: faster growth of agricultural output might in some circumstances be promoted by higher food prices, but given that the majority of the poor (in the urban areas certainly, but also in the countryside) were net buyers of food, improved terms of trade for agriculture would probably result in greater poverty, i.e., lower real incomes of the working poor.

The concern with employment naturally led the ILO to direct its attention to the position of specific occupational groups. This in turn encouraged it to look at poverty as a phenomenon afflicting households with specific demographic profiles (families with high dependency ratios, the elderly) or falling especially hard on particular classes and occupations living in specific localities. That is, poverty came to be analysed as social and economic phenomena and not as a homogeneous statistical category such as the bottom 40 per cent of the income distribution or persons with an income below some critical level. This recognition of the heterogeneity of poverty has an advantage from a policy-making point of view [15] because all policies affect particular groups, classes, regions, etc., in specific and often contradictory ways; policies never affect deciles directly but only as a by-product of their consequences for specific demographic groups, socio-economic classes or geographical regions. Thus if one is interested in designing policies to alleviate poverty, it is helpful if the poor are classified in such a way that the connection between policy action and the effect on poverty is logical and transparent.

Associated with this approach to the analysis of employment problems and poverty was an interest in economic institutions and the social relations of production. Organisational arrangements within the informal urban sector have already been mentioned. Within the rural sector attention tended to focus on land tenure arrangements, the role of co-operative institutions and the organisation of large scale, labour-intensive public works projects. Once these topics began to be probed, however, it became impossible to stop because the analysis inexorably raised questions about the equity of existing arrangements, the degree of inequality in the distribution of income and the extent of concentration in the ownership of productive assets.

The World Employment Programme evolved quite quickly from its initial preoccupation with increasing employment to, next, raising labour productivity, then to structural change and poverty alleviation and finally to redistribution of income in favour of the poor. What started out as *ad hoc* advice on how to create more jobs ended as a redistributive strategy of development. In retrospect the World Employment Programme can be regarded as a vast learning process for the international community, for rich and poor countries alike. It may not have affected policy dramatically, but it certainly increased our understanding of many important development issues.

Redistribution on the margin

The ILO was not alone in shifting the emphasis of development from growth of output to a redistribution of income. Indeed in academic circles the possibility had long been discussed of channelling to the poor the increments of output arising from growth [16]. The idea did not enter the public arena, however, until the Development Research Centre of the World Bank under Hollis Chenery gave strong support to a strategy of "redistribution of the benefits of growth" and attempted to quantify the implications of adopting such a strategy [17].

Five distinct strategies were in fact considered by the World Bank: (*i*) a *laissez faire* growth strategy, (*ii*) a strategy of wage restraint which deliberately shifted the distribution of income against the poor in an attempt to raise savings and accelerate the rate of growth, (*iii*) a consumption redistribution strategy in which 2 per cent of total income is redirected each year for 25 years to the poor, (*iv*) an investment redistribution strategy in which 2 per cent of total income is redirected each year for 25 years to investment projects which benefit the poor, and (*v*) a strategy of asset redistribution. In practice no attempt was made to simulate the fifth strategy and it was quietly forgotten.

The growth strategy was called the Basic Solution and the results of the remaining three strategies were compared over a 40-year period with the Basic Solution. The poor were defined as the bottom 40 per cent of the income distribution and thus no attempt was made (or in fact could be made) to trace the implications of particular redistributive policies for particular groups of people. Abstract "income" was distributed by unspecified "policies" to an abstract statistical category identified as the poor. In a real economy, of course, the level and composition of output and the distribution of income are jointly and simultaneously determined, but for the purposes of the model it was assumed that they were independent of one another. Hence, at least on the margin, how much was produced (of luxury automobiles, vintage wines and designer dresses?) was regarded as quite separate from the question of who received it. The sequence was produce first and redistribute later.

Simulation of the strategy of wage restraint shows that, while it was of benefit to the rich, i.e., the top 20 per cent of the population, wage restraint clearly harmed the poor and middle-income groups. Even after 40 years the per capita consumption of the poor was 17 per cent lower than it would have been under the Basic Solution [18]. Thus it was impossible to make a case for restraining the consumption of the poor in the short run on grounds that in the long run they would be better off. Growth maximisation increased poverty rather than reduced it.

The strategy of direct consumption transfers was in some respects even worse. The poor did indeed receive positive benefits during the 25 years when the redistribution of consumption was assumed to occur, but this was at the expense of a lower overall rate of investment and growth and of a lower per capita income for the population as a whole. Moreover, as soon as the consumption transfers ceased, the per capita consumption of the poor declined and at the end of the 40-year period the level of consumption of the poor was 19 per cent lower than it otherwise would have been [19]. In other words, in the long-run consumption transfers are even less beneficial to the poor than wage restraint!

This brings us to the strategy of investment transfers. It is assumed that 2 per cent of GNP is transferred each year to the poor for 25 years, not in the form of consumption but in the form of various capital assets that raise production and income of the poor directly. The investment transfers include "provision of credit and physical inputs, access to physical infrastructure, investment in human capital ... access roads, irrigation, drainage, and so forth ... " [20]. The effect of this at the end of the 40-year period is to raise the per capita consumption of the poor by 23 per cent above what it otherwise would have been [21]. This strategy, thus, unlike wage restraint and consumption transfers, does increase the well-being of the poor although it can be argued that the results are rather modest. The World Bank, however, is more positive and says that its "major conclusion as to the choice of strategy is that there is considerable potential for raising income in low-income groups through a policy of 'investment transfers'. Such a strategy, although operating at the margin, can achieve substantial improvements in patterns of asset concentration over time" [22].

There are however three reasons to doubt the efficacy of any strategy which envisages annual transfers to the poor over a long period of time, be they transfers of consumption or capital goods. First, the political conditions necessary for the success of the strategy are exceptional. Substantial resources must be redistributed to the poor each year for a quarter of a century and the pattern of output and income then created must be maintained for a further 15 years. That is, the general strategy must be sustained for four decades. That is asking a lot of the political system given that at the end of those four decades the per capita consumption of the majority of the population is significantly lower than it would have been in the absence of the transfer policy. Under the investment transfer strategy, for example, the consumption of the middle-income groups falls by 19 per cent and that of the upper-income groups by 17 per cent [23].

It is very doubtful that the upper 60 per cent of the income distribution would be prepared to sacrifice their own standard of consumption for the benefit of the lower 40 per cent over such a long period. It is even more doubtful that the middle class would be prepared to make a larger sacrifice than the richest 20 per cent of the population. Even if particular political circumstances prevailing at the time make it possible for the government of a particular country to initiate an investment transfer strategy, it is likely that after a few years a majority coalition of the less poor would force the government to stop the strategy and possibly reverse it. In other words, transfer strategies probably are not politically viable because they cannot be sustained long enough to be effective. Indeed they are likely in most countries to be short-lived.

Second, assuming transfer strategies are initiated and sustained, there is the problem of ensuring that the transfers reach the intended beneficiaries. It has been emphasized repeatedly that the poor are not a homogeneous category; they are a very mixed group.

Therefore policy packages intended to help the heterogeneous collection of people classified as poor have to be very carefully designed. Some policies will benefit some poor people while leaving others unaffected. Minimum wages, for example, will help the poor who are already employed in organised urban labour markets, but they will not help the poor who are employed in unorganised labour markets where the policy cannot be enforced or the unemployed. Other policies will help some poor people while harming others. Higher producer prices of wage goods, for instance, will be of benefit to those poor people who produce wage goods for the market, but they will harm those poor people who purchase wage goods in the market. Still other policies will benefit not only some poor people but also some rich ones. The provision of free universal primary education is an example of a policy in which many of the benefits are bound to accrue to middle and upper-income households as well as to the poor.

The problem of leakages, of benefits being captured by people outside the target group, is likely to be particularly severe in an investment transfer strategy. This can be illustrated by considering some of the examples given by the World Bank itself. Investment in irrigation and drainage may indeed be of great benefit to poor farmers, but in the absence of a land redistribution programme within the irrigation perimeter it will be impossible to prevent the large farmers from benefitting as well. Moreover on grounds of efficiency it would be desirable that they should benefit. Similarly, public investment in access roads and other infrastructure will be helpful to the poor, but it would be neither possible nor desirable to exclude the non-poor from the use of such facilities. In practice, moreover, the non-poor often gain disproportionately from public investments because the distribution of benefits reflects not the distribution of the population but the distribution of ownership and control over economic resources. The value of a farm-to-market road, for example, is likely to be greater the larger is a farmer's marketable surplus. Since big farmers have a larger marketable surplus than small ones, it is the big farmers who will reap most of the benefits. It is difficult to see how this problem can be overcome, given the impracticability of levying tolls on just the rich, if the distribution of productive assets and the primary distribution of income (before transfers) is unequal.

The implication of widespread leakages and the unintended negative effects of some policies on some sections of the poor is that a gross transfer to the poor of much more than 2 per cent of GNP will be needed to achieve a net transfer of 2 per cent. The scale of the annual transfers, in other words, will have to be much larger than the magnitudes envisaged in the World Bank's study. A marginal redistribution of income (be it consumption or investment) will require much more than a marginal reallocation of resources and a marginal adjustment to government priorities and policies. A major effort will be necessary even to achieve a modest improvement in the standard of living of the poor.

Third, there is the problem created by the self-equilibrating nature of a market economy. Given the distribution of productive assets among the various social classes and the primary distribution of income that flows from it, there is relatively little governments can do to alter the distribution of income among households. The reason for this is that most government policy interventions designed to change the distribution of income simultaneously set in motion economic forces which counteract and in the long run largely neutralise the intended effects of the policy. For example, minimum wage legislation if enforced, creates incentives to substitute capital for labour. This results both in more unemployment and ultimately, once all substitution effects have worked themselves out, possibly in a higher share of profits in value added. The net effect is to leave the distribution of income between wages and profits roughly unchanged.

Something similar occurs when governments intervene in commodity markets. Suppose a government attempts to raise the real income of the poor by depressing the price of the most important wage good, food. Several things will then happen. Initially, poor farmers who happen to grow food will be worse off and rich consumers of food will be better off. Hence the net impact effect of the policy will depend on comparing the benefits received by (*i*) poor food buyers and (*ii*) rich food buyers on the one hand, with the losses of (*iii*) poor food producers and (*iv*) rich food producers on the other. It is evident that the policy intervention will not necessarily always favour the poor on balance. However even if in a particular case it does, the long-run effects will not necessarily be positive. Lower food prices will encourage farmers to switch their land from food to non-food crops. This will reduce the supply of food and exert upward pressure on food prices, thereby undermining the policy. If government attempts to compensate for the decline in domestic food supplies by increasing food imports, this will put pressure on the balance of payments. Ultimately the exchange rate may have to be devalued and this will raise the local currency price of imported food, again undermining the policy. The original distribution of income will tend to reassert itself.

Government transfer and expenditure programmes, as we have seen, harm some poor people and benefit some rich people. Land improvement projects raise the rental value of land and consequently benefit landowners, large and small alike. Construction projects generate wages for poor, unskilled workers, but they also provide wages for relatively highly paid skilled workers, salaries for professional and managerial staff and profits for the owners of the enterprise. Even if one chooses labour-intensive projects and tries to direct them toward the poor, the ultimate effect on the overall distribution of income is unlikely to be significant. Given the distribution of land, the ownership of enterprises and the distribution of skills and other forms of human capital, government price and expenditure policies are unlikely to be powerful enough to prevent the self-equilibrating mechanisms of a market economy from continuously recreating the initial distribution of income.

Irma Adelman has made the same point this way:

> "Once the choice of development strategy has jelled, policies and programs aimed at changing the primary distribution of income can accomplish very little. This is true of both transfer programs and poverty-oriented projects. The size distribution of income tends to be quite stable around the trend established by the basic choice of development strategy. Following any intervention, even one sustained over time, the size distribution of income tends to return to the pre-intervention distribution" [24].

Thus for all these reasons – the necessity of sustaining policy for a very long time, the need to avoid leakages of benefits to the non-poor, the need to prevent policies intended to help the poor from in fact harming some of them, and the difficulty of preventing market forces from undermining policies by re-establishing the initial configuration of incomes – it seems unlikely that redistribution on the margin represents a practical strategy for reducing mass poverty. Something else in most cases will be required.

Redistribution of productive assets

The focus of attention shifted quickly from redistribution of the increments of growth to strategies which promised a bold "direct attack on mass poverty" [25]. The spirit of the discussion was captured by the phrase "redistribution before growth" [26] but much of the

171

analysis and debate centred on the advocacy by the ILO of a "basic needs" approach to development[27]. The former was of course a shorthand description of a strategy of development which highlighted the key variable ("redistribution") and indicated its place in a sequence of events ("before growth"). "Basic needs" in contrast underlined not the means of development but the ends and thereby signaled a change in priorities and an urgency to put "first things first" [28].

Thus basic needs, strictly speaking, is not a strategy for development but an approach to development. It specifies objectives but not the methods, which in principle are many, to achieve the objectives [29]. As Paul Streeten says, "Basic needs reminds us of ... the end of the development effort, which is to provide all human beings with the opportunity for a fuller life" [30]. The basic needs approach as advocated by the ILO, however, was modest in its targets. It did not hold out an immediate hope of providing all human beings with a full life but merely indicated what would be required to attain "a minimum objective of society" within the lifetime of one generation [31]. In a sense the ILO followed in the footsteps of the Indian Planning Commission which as early as 1962 prepared a paper on the "Implications of Planning for a Minimum Level of Living" [32].

The ILO defined basic needs to include the "minimum requirements of a family for private consumption", notably food, shelter and clothing, and "essential services provided by and for the community at large, such as safe drinking water, sanitation, public transport, and health and education facilities" [33]. Some writers have interpreted the basic needs approach to consist essentially of a shopping list of desirable private consumption goods and public services or as a list of production priorities. It has been said, for example, that the "distinct contribution" of basic needs "consists in ... adding physical estimates of the particular goods and services required to achieve certain results, such as adequate standards of nutrition, health, ..." [34]. This however is misleading and makes the basic needs approach vulnerable to charges of ignoring consumer sovereignty and imposing planners' preferences on households, of setting arbitrary and indefensible standards for minimum levels of consumption, of emphasizing consumption at the expense of production and growth and of advocating a strategy of consumption transfers to the poor.

Nothing could be further from the truth. Basic needs is not really about things at all – either gross domestic product (aggregate things) or food, health, education (a bundle of specific things). It is about giving priority in development to the needs and desires of poor people. This is reflected in three features of the approach which effectively convert it into a strategy: a preoccupation with ensuring that essential public services are available to the poor, an emphasis on the participation of the poor in the development process and recognition of the centrality of a major redistribution of income and wealth in favour of low-income groups. Let us consider each of these features briefly in turn.

In the majority of Third World countries a range of public services exists and often government outlays on the public services are considerable. The problem is that the benefits of public expenditure accrue not to those most in need but to the middle and upper-income groups. Expensive public hospitals concentrating on curative medicine in the metropolitan areas are emphasized at the expense of preventive medicine, of widely dispersed clinics, of paramedical personnel, of clean drinking water and proper sanitation and of the rural areas in general where most of the poor are to be found. University education for a tiny elite absorbs vast funds that could better be spent on providing universal primary and secondary education and on establishing a large number of vocational and technical training centres. In Pakistan, for instance, only 16 per cent of the age group attends secondary school, yet over 20 per cent of current public expenditure on education is allocated to the university sector, which caters to only 2 per cent of those aged 20-24. In Côte d'Ivoire, 19 per cent are enrolled in secondary school, yet an elite of 3 per cent of the age group goes to university and absorbs over 15 per cent of all public funds spent on education. Similar patterns can be found in public expenditure on housing. The rural areas receive nothing, while in Mexico City, Santiago and Bogota public housing standards are set at a level which excludes the poorer half of the population from the programme [35]. That is, housing subsidies benefit the rich.

The basic needs approach is concerned to reverse this, to ensure that housing subsidies, education expenditure and programmes intended to reduce morbidity benefit the poor. This does not necessarily imply greater expenditure on public services at the expense of public savings, investment and growth, but it does imply a reallocation of public consumption and a radical redesign of many government programmes.

The ILO has always stressed that "a basic-needs oriented policy implies the participation of the people in making the decisions which affect them" [36]. Far from being paternalistic and highly centralised and of imposing planners' preferences on an unwilling and unco-operative population, the basic needs approach to development depends for its success on government being able to redefine its purposes and adapt its administrative structures accordingly and on the ability of the poor to become organised so that they can articulate their interests and share in the exercise of political power.

There is no presumption that giving priority to the satisfaction of basic needs requires more government, a larger public administration. Indeed in a number of Third World countries central government expenditure already accounts for a relatively high proportion of GNP, as can be seen in Table 7.1, and additional public resources often are channelled through lower levels of government (state, provincial and local) as well as through state-owned enterprises. What is required by an effective redistributive strategy for development is a change in the composition of expenditure and in the organisation of government.

Table 7.1 **CENTRAL GOVERNMENT EXPENDITURE AS A PER CENT OF GNP, 1983**

Asia:	
India	14.9
Pakistan	17.8
Bangladesh	9.3 a
Malaysia	27.7 a
Philippines	11.8
Sri Lanka	33.6
Africa:	
Botswana	44.7
Egypt	39.0
Ghana	7.8 b
Kenya	26.6
Tanzania	19.7 a
Latin America:	
Argentina	22.3
Brazil	21.4
Chile	34.8
Colombia	13.0 a
Mexico	27.9
Peru	18.6

a) 1972.
b) The percentage in Ghana in 1972 was 19.5.
Source: IBRD, *World Development Report 1986*, New York, Oxford University Press, 1986, Table 22, pp 222-3.

173

In many countries the public administration is not well suited to implementing a development strategy which focuses on the elimination of poverty [37]. One reason for this is that the administrative systems introduced in the colonial period or imported and adopted in the post-independence period were based on Western precepts of public administration. Milton Esman makes the point very well:

> "These western precepts of public administration produced emphasis on written rules, precedent, predictability, consistency, equity, routine, efficiency and technique. They depoliticized administration, deemphasized program outputs, and relegated the public to the status of subjects. They put policy initiatives, programmatic innovation, and clientele involvement outside the legitimate purview of administrative personnel" [38].

The people who were "relegated ... to the status of subjects" often came to fear and distrust government and particularly in rural areas, and above all among the poor, government officials were seen more as coercive than as persuasive agents.

Thus the relationship between the state and the poor is unconducive to the mobilisation of large numbers of people for development. The hierarchical structure of government makes it difficult to identify and implement the myriad of small, labour-intensive projects implicit in basic needs development at the local level. And the style of administration means that government lacks flexibility and sensitivity to the needs and wishes of those in poverty. At the very least, a redistributive strategy of economic development requires decentralised administration to the local level and administration at that level by officials who enjoy the confidence and support of the great majority of the population. This is most likely to occur if the officials actually are recruited from the local population.

Beyond this is the need to organise the various groups in poverty. Participation, or the opportunity to participate if one wishes, is of course an end in itself, but participation also has a number of instrumental values which make it an important feature of a redistributive strategy of development. First, participation in representative community-based organisations can help to identify local priorities, to determine which needs are essential or basic and which of secondary importance, and to define the content of development programmes and projects so that they reflect accurately local needs, aspirations and demands. Next, having identified priorities and designed the programmes which incorporate them, participation in functional organisations (service co-operatives, land reform committees, irrigation societies, women's groups) can be used to mobilise support for national and local policies and programmes and local projects. Last, participation can be used to reduce the cost of public services and investment projects by shifting responsibility from central and local government (where costs tend to be relatively high) to the grass roots organisations (where costs can be low). In some cases, for example, it may be possible to organise the beneficiaries of an investment project and persuade them to contribute their labour voluntarily to help defray construction costs. In other cases some of the public services (clinics, nursery schools) can be organised, staffed and run by local groups rather than by relatively highly paid civil servants brought in from outside. Thus in an appropriate context participation can flourish and in so doing contribute much to development.

It must be said however that the appropriate context is a society characterised by a high degree of equality. Participation cannot flourish in a rigidly stratified society in which wealth and income are unequally distributed. In such a society local politics are almost certain to be dominated by a powerful minority of the rich and relations within such a community are likely to be conditioned by actual conflict or the threat of conflict rather than by co-operation and widespread recognition of the potential mutual advantages of participation. This is another sense in which "redistribution before growth" is the best way to proceed.

Unfortunately the distribution of income and wealth is very unequal in many Third World countries. This was shown in Chapter 1 (see Table 1.6). More relevant for present purposes however is the fact that within the rural areas the degree of inequality often is exceptionally high. Poverty in the Third World is largely a rural phenomenon and it is particularly acute among the landless and near-landless and hence the distribution of landed wealth is a key determinant of the overall incidence of poverty.

Scattered evidence on the extent of landlessness and on the degree of concentration of land ownership is assembled in Table 7.2. The data refer to various years between 1961 and 1985 and in most cases are unlikely to describe precisely the present situation. Our measure of landlessness is a very restrictive one, namely, landless farm workers as a percentage of the active agricultural population. This measure excludes landless persons who are not wage workers but instead are tenants (sharecroppers and leaseholders) and hence the extent of true landlessness is understated in the Table. In countries where tenant farming is the most common mode of production, as in Pakistan and the Philippines, the underestimate of landlessness is considerable.

It is even more difficult to obtain accurate measures of land ownership. Census data seldom contain such information and even when they do, the information may not be wholly accurate since large landowners often are reluctant to report the size of their holdings. Still, we have managed to find estimates of the distribution of land among landowners for eight countries in the Table. Note that those who own no land at all are disregarded when calculating the concentration ratio. The Gini coefficient in the Table purports to measure the degree of inequality of landed wealth among those who own at least some land however little. If the landless were included in the measure of inequality, as arguably they should, the Gini coefficients would of course be much higher.

Measures of the distribution of operational holdings are more readily obtained. The distribution of land among all cultivators, be they landowners or tenants, is usually much more equal than the distribution of land ownership. The reason for this is that large ownership holdings commonly are broken up into many small cultivated holdings that are farmed by tenants. This is particularly common in Asia. As a result, the distribution of operational holdings may be relatively equal even when the concentration of land ownership is great. Of course cases can be found of small peasant landowners renting out their land to large landowners and to the extent that this happens the distribution of operational holdings will tend to be less equal than the distribution of ownership holdings, but in general small peasants rent in more land than they rent out whereas the reverse is true of large landowners. One can therefore be confident that measures of the distribution of operational holdings understate the degree of inequality in the ownership of land.

In the case of three countries – Malaysia, Sri Lanka and Kenya – we have included estimates of the concentration of operational holdings in the Table. This is far from ideal, but the figures do indicate the lowest possible estimate of the degree of inequality in the distribution of land ownership. To that extent they are not without interest.

The data on landlessness in Table 7.2 indicate that in Asia a large number of people effectively own no productive assets. In Bangladesh, India and Malaysia between a quarter and a third of the population active in agriculture are wage earners. In Sri Lanka, because of the large plantation sector, over half are landless. The situation in Pakistan and the Philippines also is serious although this is disguised in the Table because of the large number

Table 7.2 **LANDLESSNESS AND THE CONCENTRATION OF LAND OWNERSHIP**

	Year a	Landless farm workers (per cent of active agricultural population)	Land ownership (Gini coefficient)
Asia:			
Bangladesh	1981	25	n.a.
India	1961	32	0.61
Malaysia	1957	34	0.48 b
Pakistan	1985	11	0.61
Philippines	1983	15	0.58
Sri Lanka	1981	54	0.58 b
Africa:			
Botswana	1981	7	n.a.
Egypt	1977	26	0.53
Kenya	1969	18	0.54 b
Latin America:			
Argentina	1970	49	0.87
Brazil	1970	26	0.85
Chile	1983	44	n.a.
Colombia	1964	42	0.87
Mexico	1980	21	n.a.
Peru	1981	20	0.95

a) The year refers to the date of the estimate of landlessness. This does not usually coincide with the date of the estimate of land concentration.

b) The figure refers to the distribution of operational holdings.

Sources: ILO, *Yearbook of Labour Statistics*, various issues; IBRD, *The Assault on World Poverty*, Baltimore, Johns Hopkins University Press, 1975, Table 1, p. 214 and Table 1-11, p. 250; Samir Radwan and Eddy Lee, *Agrarian Change in Egypt: An Anatomy of Rural Poverty*, London, Croom Helm, 1986, Table 4.7, p. 60 and p. 64; ILO, *Employment, Incomes and Equality: A Strategy for Increasing Productive Employment in Kenya*, Geneva, ILO, 1972, p. 33; S.M. Naseem, "Rural Poverty and Landlessness in Pakistan", in ILO, *Poverty and Landlessness in Rural Asia*, Geneva, ILO, 1977, p. 47; Nguyen T. Quan and Anthony Y.C. Koo, "Concentration of Land Holdings: An Empirical Exploration of Kuznets' Conjecture", *Journal of Development Economics*, Vol. 18, No. 1, May-June 1985, Table 3, p. 108.

of landless tenant farmers in those countries. In Latin America, between a fifth and a quarter of the population active in agriculture are landless workers in Brazil, Mexico and Peru, and the proportion rises to over 40 per cent in Argentina, Chile and Colombia. There are in addition large numbers of tenant farmers in most Latin American countries.

In Africa the evidence is sparse and the situation less uniform. Landlessness is low in Botswana because the rural economy is based on cattle raising on natural pastures rather than on farming. This does not necessarily imply however that the distribution of income in rural areas is relatively equal. In Kenya in 1969 about 18 per cent of the agricultural population consisted of landless farm workers; the proportion probably is higher today. In Egypt about a quarter are landless. These figures, while not low, suggest that the problem is not quite as serious as in parts of Asia and Latin America. Elsewhere in Africa however there are very large numbers of landless workers, as in Côte d'Ivoire, where most are migrants from other countries. Unfortunately it has not been possible to quantify the extent of international migration of landless agricultural workers in Africa, but it is considerable.

At the other extreme, there is a very high concentration of property in the hands of a few people. In Latin America the distribution of land among the minority of the rural population that owns any land at all is grotesque. The Gini coefficient varies between 0.85 in Brazil and 0.95 in Peru. Even in Asia concentration ratios are very high, the Gini coefficient varying between 0.48 in Malaysia (for the distribution of operational holdings) and 0.61 in India and Pakistan. In Sri Lanka, again because of the large plantation sector, even operational holdings are distributed very unequally. In Africa the situation is unclear, but most observers believe that land is more equitably distributed than in most other parts of the Third World although it is widely thought that the degree of inequality is increasing in many countries.

The general picture that emerges from these considerations is one of great inequality. An obvious manifestation of this is the high incidence of landlessness. In some countries this is reflected in large numbers of landless agricultural wage workers and in others in the prevalence of tenant farming, but regardless of the form it takes a high proportion of the population is virtually propertyless. The unequal distribution of productive assets is a major cause of widespread poverty and it is for this reason that strategies that give priority to the satisfaction of basic needs tend to emphasize land reform and other measures to improve the distribution of income and wealth. It is possible to imagine alternative ways of reducing mass poverty and satisfying basic needs within a reasonable period of time, but the historical record indicates that the countries which have been successful in this respect have in common an equitable distribution of productive assets, especially land. It is "an empirical fact that the only societies that have been successful in meeting basic needs are those that have also reduced inequalities" [39].

Alternative paths to satisfying basic needs

It can readily be demonstrated why a "redistribution of income and wealth ... is at the centre of a basic needs model" [40] or of any effective strategy to reduce poverty quickly. Assume, following the ILO, that the key needs are 2 180 to 2 380 kilocalories per head per day (depending on the region), 98 per cent school enrolment for all children aged 7-16 and 5.25 to 7.50 square metres of living space per person (again depending on the region).[41]. Assume further that the initial objective is to ensure that these needs are met on average by the poorest 20 per cent of households, implying that some people in the bottom two deciles of the population will fail to meet their basic needs. Assume finally that the objective is to meet these basic needs within one generation, i.e., 30 years.

One way to achieve these targets would be through rapid growth alone. In making its calculations the ILO used 1970 as the benchmark year. It assumed fertility rates and hence the overall rate of growth of the population would decline rapidly. It also assumed, contrary to much experience, that accelerated growth would not worsen the distribution of income but leave it unchanged. Under these rather optimistic assumptions the required rate of growth of output was estimated for seven broad regions of the Third World (see Table 7.3).

In China the required rate of growth is 6.0 per cent, which is less rapid than the rate actually experienced in the last 20 years. China therefore can achieve the basic needs targets in less than a generation provided it is able to sustain its long-run trend rate of growth. The required growth rates in arid and tropical Africa are more than 11 per cent and given that this is more than five times faster than the rate of growth actually achieved since 1973, it is evident that a growth strategy cannot be relied upon to reduce mass poverty in Africa. Curiously the oil-producing countries of the Middle East and Africa, because of the great inequality in the distribution of income, also will have to grow more than 11 per cent a year to satisfy basic needs within one generation, and the experience of the last two decades suggests that this is highly unlikely. Required growth rates in Latin America and Asia are between 8.7 and 9.7 per cent a year. Again, it is clear that these rates of growth are not feasible over a 30-year period. If poverty is to be reduced, the distribution of income will have to become much more equal.

Table 7.3 **REQUIRED RATES OF GROWTH TO SATISFY BASIC NEEDS WITHIN 30 YEARS**

Per cent per annum

Africa (arid)	11.2
Africa (tropical)	11.1
Asia (medium and low-income, excluding China)	9.7
China	6.0
Latin America (low-income)	9.4
Latin America (medium-income)	8.7
Middle East/Africa (oil-producing)	11.3

Source: ILO, *Employment, Growth and Basic Needs,* Geneva, ILO, 1976, Table 6, p. 41.

Just how much more equal depends of course on the rate of growth: the faster the average rate of growth of GNP, the less redistribution is required to achieve the basic needs targets within a generation. This is why it has always been "stressed that a rapid rate of economic growth is an essential part of a basic-needs strategy" [42]. For the purposes of calculation the ILO assumed an annual rate of growth of 6 per cent and a population that grew in accordance with the "low" estimate of the United Nations. The share in total income of the poorest 20 per cent of households that is required for the poor to be able to satisfy their basic needs then was estimated (see Table 7.4).

Table 7.4 **REQUIRED CHANGES IN THE DISTRIBUTION OF INCOME
TO SATISFY BASIC NEEDS WITHIN 30 YEARS**
Percentage share in total income of the poorest 20 per cent of households

	Initial year	At end of 30 years
Africa (arid)	5.5	12.4
Africa (tropical)	4.9	16.5
Asia (medium and low-income, excluding China)	5.3	14.3
China	11.3	11.3
Latin America (low-income)	4.3	11.9
Latin America (medium-income)	4.5	9.7

Source: ILO, *Employment, Growth and Basic Needs,* Geneva, ILO, 1976, Table 7, p. 42.

Apart from China, where as we have seen no further redistribution is necessary, the share of the poorest 20 per cent of the population would have to more than double in 30 years if the objectives are to be met. In the case of tropical Africa the share of the poor would have to increase 3.4 times. Moreover, in every region represented in the Table except medium income Latin America, the share of the poorest quintile of the population at the end of the period would have to be higher than it is currently in China. Clearly redistributions of this magnitude are unlikely, since they imply a greater degree of equality than is found in China, one of the most egalitarian countries, but the calculations do underline the fact that even under optimistic assumptions about the long-run rate of growth, very radical redistributive measures are necessary to reduce poverty quickly and substantially. This is an inescapable conclusion of the analysis – and one that is strongly supported by the historical evidence.

If policy is concerned only with the level of income of the poor at the end of one generation, policymakers should be indifferent as between an initial redistribution of income and wealth, annual redistributions accompanying the growth process and a massive redistribution in the terminal year of the programme. It has already been argued, however, that a strategy which places the entire burden of redistribution on the margin is likely to fail. All the comments made about the World Bank's model apply to the ILO's model with greater force if, that is, the ILO's model is interpreted to be an example of redistribution of the increments of growth. The reason the criticisms apply with even greater force is that the ILO's model postulates a more substantial redistribution of income in favour of the poor.

Having rejected an incremental approach we are left with the necessity of undertaking a major redistribution either at the beginning or at the end of the planning period. Given this choice, it obviously is preferable to choose a strategy which begins the development process with a redistribution of income and wealth because under that strategy the level of consumption of the poor in every year of the 30-year planning period will be higher than under the alternative. Once again, "redistribution before growth" makes more sense. Indeed it is hard to avoid the conclusion that redistributive strategies of economic development imply "the necessity of an *initial redistribution of assets*" [43]. To suggest the contrary is to ignore logic and fact and would be very misleading.

Redistributive strategies in practice

Although several countries have introduced one or another of the components of a redistributive strategy of development, few regimes have adopted the strategy in full. Two that have come close are Taiwan and South Korea. On the surface this may seem to be an odd statement since in both cases the government is right wing and right wing governments are not noted for giving priority to a direct assault on mass poverty. Upon reflection, however, it will be seen that the elements of a redistributive strategy that have been stressed in the previous discussion are present in these two cases.

Taiwan began with a redistribution of assets. The infant industrial sector at the end of the Second World War was largely in the hands of the Japanese. Indeed the Japanese owned more than 90 per cent of the larger scale operations and 78 per cent of all the industrial capital on the island [44]. These assets were transferred to the Taiwanese, and to the Chinese who immigrated from the mainland. Even more important was the redistribution of land. At the end of the Japanese colonial period in 1945 the poorest 40 per cent of agricultural households owned less than a tenth of the land while the wealthiest 2 per cent owned more than a third of the land. About 44.1 per cent of households were utterly landless [45]. This was changed by the land reforms that were introduced between 1949 and 1953.

Nearly a quarter of the cultivated land was redistributed to the poorest 47.9 per cent of farm households [46]. As a result by 1960 tenant cultivators accounted for only 14.4 per cent of all farm families [47]. The redistribution of wealth that occurred as a consequence of the reforms was massive and is estimated to have been equivalent to about 13 per cent of Taiwan's GNP [48]. The landlord and moneylender class was virtually eliminated by the reforms and their share of total farm income fell from 25 to 6 per cent [49]. By the end of this process – which took less than ten years – Taiwan had created an egalitarian farming system based on small peasant owner-operators.

179

A broadly similar process of asset redistribution occurred in South Korea.

Particularly in Taiwan, the rural population was organised and participated actively in economic affairs. Responsibility for implementing the land reforms was devolved by central government to the village. After the reforms, in 1952, the government promoted multipurpose farmers' associations, membership of which was restricted to farmers. These associations provide credit and extension services and facilities for purchasing inputs, marketing farm produce, crop storage and agricultural processing. In addition, the farmers themselves have been made responsible for the management of the irrigation systems through their autonomous irrigation co-operatives. The irrigation co-operatives have several advantages. They ensure that water is allocated efficiently; they substitute local management personnel for central government officials and thereby reduce the costs of administration; and by involving the people in the management of the most important capital assets in the agricultural sector, they ensure that irrigation schemes are designed with the needs of farmers in mind and then are operated efficiently.

Next, in both Taiwan and South Korea much emphasis has been placed on human capital formation and on providing essential public services to the entire population. Education in particular has always been important and families have been willing to spend a significant part of their own income to supplement the education and training provided by the state. In 1940 just over 21 per cent of the population of Taiwan were literate, and in South Korea the figure in 1945 was even lower, namely, 13.4 per cent. "Since then, illiteracy has been almost completely eradicated in both countries, and today Taiwan provides 9 years and Korea 6 years of free and compulsory schooling" [50]. Enrolment in primary school is universal and the secondary school enrolment figures are very high: 80.3 per cent in Taiwan [51] and 89 per cent in South Korea. This of course reflects a tremendous expansion of the educational system in both countries.

The health indicators are equally impressive [52]. The crude death rate is 5 per 1 000 in Taiwan and 6 per 1 000 in South Korea. Life expectancy at birth is 70.5 years for males and 75.5 for females in Taiwan and 65 and 72 for males and females respectively in South Korea. Taiwan in particular seems to have done significantly better than other Third World countries at a comparable level of per capita income.

Employment intensity is an important component of any successful redistributive strategy of development. This feature of South Korea's development was discussed in Chapter 5, but if anything, Taiwan did even better. The average size of firm in the manufacturing sector in Taiwan is much smaller than in South Korea. Indeed Tibor Scitovsky reckons "the average Taiwanese firm in 1976 was only half as big as the Korean, with 34.6 employees compared to 68.8 in Korea" [53]. Moreover, this calculation ignores firms with less than five employees, which in Taiwan account for 43 per cent of all manufacturing enterprises.

Growth in the manufacturing sector in Taiwan was very labour intensive and unlike most countries, growth occurred as a result of a rapid rise in the number of small enterprises as opposed to an increase in output and employment in already existing enterprises. Firms remained numerous, small and highly competitive. Between 1952 and 1985 employment in manufacturing increased from 12.4 to 33.5 per cent of the labour force, or between 5.7 and 6.3 per cent a year. Real wages also grew rapidly, namely, 4.2 per cent per annum in 1953-68 accelerating to 10.8 per cent per annum in 1968-78 [54]. Average real monthly earnings in manufacturing accelerated yet again in 1979-85, rising by about 12.4 per cent a year.

The distribution of income in Taiwan improved dramatically between 1953 and 1964 (see Table 7.5). The Gini coefficient just before the end of the land reform period was 0.56.

180

It then fell sharply to 0.32 in 1964. At that point the distribution of income in Taiwan was more equal than in South Korea and it remains so to this day. (Compare the data in Table 7.5 with the data for South Korea in Table 5.11.) Even after 1964 the distribution of income continued to improve slightly in both the farm and non-farm sectors as well as overall [55]. Indeed it is quite possible that the distribution of income in Taiwan now is the most equal in the world.

Finally, Taiwan did not neglect domestic savings and investment or forget the importance of growth. Capital formation increased rapidly, gross investment rising from 15.4 per cent of GDP in 1952 to a peak of 34.3 per cent in 1980. In the 1950s approximately 40 per cent of total investment was financed by capital imports, but since 1964 domestic savings on average have exceeded domestic investment and Taiwan has accumulated foreign assets. Taiwan, unlike South Korea, has not relied on foreign loans and foreign aid to finance its development; for nearly a quarter of a century it has been financially self-reliant. For instance, between 1964 and 1984 gross investment on average was 26.7 per cent of GDP, but gross savings were 28.7 per cent of GNP. The difference of two percentage points represents roughly the proportion of total product that has been used to increase foreign exchange reserves and to finance investment abroad.

Table 7.5   **THE DISTRIBUTION OF HOUSEHOLD INCOME IN TAIWAN, 1953-1978**
Gini coefficients

1953	0.558
1959	0.440
1964	0.321
1966	0.323
1968	0.326
1970	0.293
1972	0.290
1974	0.300
1976	0.289
1978	0.289 a

a)   Excludes Taipei city.

Source: Shirley W.Y. Kuo, Gustav Ranis and John C.H. Fei. *The Taiwan Success Story: Rapid Growth with Improved Distribution in the Republic of China, 1952-1979,* Boulder, Westview Press, 1981, Table 3.1, p. 45 and Table 5.1, p. 92.

Growth has been consistently rapid. Over the entire period for which data are available, 1952-85, real GNP increased 8.6 per cent per annum and real GNP per head 6.0 per cent per annum. This of course is very much faster than the rise in per capita income experienced in most other Third World countries and demonstrates conclusively that there is no inherent conflict between rapid growth and an equitable distribution of income. Taiwan (like South Korea) has combined an exceptionally equal distribution of income and wealth with exceptionally fast growth. As a result, poverty as it is known in the rest of the Third World has virtually disappeared.

The flawed strategy in Sri Lanka

The benefits of a redistributive strategy of development can be reaped in full only if all five of the major components of the strategy are implemented. This is well illustrated by the experience of Sri Lanka.

Sri Lanka became independent in 1948. It had however obtained powers of internal self-government under the Donoughmore constitution in 1931 and from that date enjoyed the benefits of a universal adult franchise. Thus even as a colony the people of Sri Lanka were able to exercise some control over domestic affairs. Primary education, formally compulsory since 1901, became free in 1942, and as a result by 1948 the literacy rate was unusually high for a Third World country, being 70 per cent for males 10 years old and over and 44 per cent for females [56]. Food rationing was introduced in 1942 and thus began Sri Lanka's tradition of rice rations, food subsidies and food stamps. In consequence, despite the very low average income per capita, the incidence of malnutrition on the island at the time of independence was well below average for a poor country. Public health measures also were introduced, the most famous being the malaria eradication programme that reduced the death rate from 20 per thousand in 1946 to 14 per thousand in 1947. The combined effect of all these programmes was to raise life expectancy for the entire population. By 1950 this had increased to 56.5 years [57], a level still to be reached by the average low-income economy other than China.

Sri Lanka was poor in 1948 and it still is poor. In 1984 the 16 million people on the island had an average income of only $360 a year, placing it among the 36 poorest countries in the world. The country was and remains predominantly agrarian. In 1981 only 22 per cent of the population lived in urban areas; 6 per cent lived in the estates sector on tea, rubber and coconut plantations and the great majority, viz. 72 per cent, in the rural areas. Socially, the country is divided into four groups: the Sinhalese (70 per cent of the population), Sri Lankan Tamils (13 per cent), Indian Tamils brought to the island during the colonial period to work on the estates (11 per cent) and Muslims, Malays and Burghers of European descent (6 per cent).

These social divisions have historically been associated with ethnic tension and in recent years with increasingly frequent social and ethnic conflict. The majority Sinhalese felt themselves to be (and no doubt were) "a deprived sector of the community, both politically and culturally" [58], during the colonial era. Moreover in a colonial economy in which avenues for advancement of the indigenous people were limited, competition between the Sri Lankan Tamils and the Sinhalese for access to education, government employment and entry into the professions was intense. The Indian Tamils, on the other hand, were kept on the sidelines, despised and isolated on the estates. The nationalist and independence movements were affected by these divisions and in the case of the Sinhalese, protest took the form of a revival of Buddhism and a sharpening of communal boundaries. This "vicarious nationalism" enabled the Sinhala Buddhists "to find succour in racist myths and legends" which unfortunately quickly led to "violence against ethnic and religious minorities" [59].

The Indian Tamils were disenfranchised in 1948, as soon as independence was achieved and the Sinhalese majority had full power. The Indian Tamil plantation workers remained "neglected, abused, ostracized and exploited" [60]. They lacked mobility and were unable to leave the estates; they were physically and culturally isolated; they had inferior education and health programmes; and of course they had no political power [61]. The Sri Lankan Tamils also found themselves to be under political attack after independence. In 1956 the government attempted to downgrade the Tamil language by imposing the use of Sinhalese as the sole official language and thus to make Sinhalese the language of instruction in all schools and the university and the language of government. The Sinhala Only Act served "to deprive thousands of Tamils of employment in the public sector" [62] and to restrict the educational opportunities and hence future employment prospects of their children. In 1971 the government introduced new admissions procedures to the University that were designed to increase the representation of the Sinhalese at the expense of the Tamils. Yet even by 1967 the share of Sinhalese Buddhists in university admissions was greater than their share in the population as a whole [63]. Finally, "in the course of dry-zone colonization, Sinhalese settlers were introduced into predominantly Tamil (though scantily populated) regions .... These moves were construed as deliberate attempts ... to dilute and weaken the political control the Sri Lankan Tamils exercised over these areas" [64].

Investment in colonisation schemes in the dry zones was an alternative to land reform in the Sinhalese areas of the wet zone. Yet the economic returns on the investments were low (including the huge Mahaweli project) and the consequences for growth were therefore unfavourable. The political consequences were a serious aggravation of ethnic conflict between the Sri Lankan Tamils and Sinhalese coupled with a neglect of landlessness and inequality among the Sinhalese peasantry. Major violence erupted in 1958, 1971, 1977, 1981 and 1982. Guerrilla warfare began in 1983 and since then more than 5 000 lives have been lost [65].

This is the background against which Sri Lanka's development policies should be viewed. Let us begin with the critical issue of the distribution of assets. In 1958 a Paddy Lands Act was passed which attempted to regulate tenancy arrangements, reduce rents and increase the security of tenants. The attempt however was unsuccessful; insecurity of tenure actually increased and large numbers of small tenants were evicted and converted into landless workers. No effort was made to alter the pattern of ownership or to introduce a "much needed land reform in the wet zone" [66].

Land reform legislation was however passed in 1972 and 1975. The former set a ceiling on ownership holdings of 25 acres in the case of paddy land and 50 acres in the case of other crops. These ceilings were so high however that virtually no land became available for redistribution to the peasantry. The 1975 legislation was more effective and provided for the nationalisation of the tea, rubber and coconut plantations. In principle the estates could have been sub-divided and turned over to the workers thereby creating a smallholder export crop sector, but this option would have benefitted the despised Indian Tamils (most of whom were not even citizens of Sri Lanka) and was rejected. Instead nearly all of the estates, representing 18-20 per cent of the country's cultivated land, were turned into public corporations. Virtually the only transfer of assets that occurred was from wealthy, largely foreign companies to the state. The poor did not benefit directly from a redistribution of land although real wage rates of plantation workers did rise sharply in the years immediately after nationalisation. Between 1975 and the peak in 1979, real wages increased by perhaps as much as 90 per cent, but by 1983 they had fallen back again by at least 14 per cent [67].

Turning to the question of participation, an effort was made under the 1958 Paddy Lands Act to create an effective village-level institution, the Cultivation Committee. The Committees were supposed to implement the tenancy reforms and in addition encourage the adoption of improved techniques of cultivation and generally promote paddy production. In practice, however, they were weak and ineffective and were dominated by landlords. Hence there was no institutional mechanism for local participation in tenancy reform, land redistribution or local initiatives to encourage development. The Committees were in fact disbanded in 1979. Commenting on the general situation during the entire post-independence period, Wickramasekara observes that "the lack of participation of the rural poor in programmes" that affect them is a major cause of "the inefficiency of such programmes. A feature of all programmes undertaken by the government has been the top-down approach and local level participation was often confined to rhetoric" [68].

The area in which Sri Lanka undoubtedly has had great success and is famous for its achievements is in human capital formation, food distribution programmes and the provision of essential public services. Health and education in the state system are free, although the quality of the services is perhaps rather low and this possibly accounts for the rapid expansion of private educational and health facilities. In education, there undoubtedly has been an excessive emphasis on the social sciences and more literary subjects to the relative neglect of science, engineering and management, and a case can be made for a less academically oriented curriculum in general. Be that as it may, however, literacy rates for men and women have increased to very high levels since independence, namely 91 per cent for men and 82 per cent for women [69], and enrolment rates in primary and secondary education for both males and females are well above average for low-income countries. Inequalities between the city and the countryside are not as great as in many countries although there is obvious discrimination against the estate sector. The literacy rate in 1978/9, for example, was 65.6 per cent in the estate sector, 87.3 per cent in the rural sector and 90.7 per cent in the urban areas [70].

The food distribution schemes did much to ensure that most people had enough to eat most of the time. They also played an important role in reducing inequality in the distribution of income. Indeed it has been estimated that the lower income groups "received as much as 16 per cent of their real incomes from the rice ration" [71]. Generally adequate nutrition combined with preventive and curative health measures had a dramatic effect on health indicators. The infant mortality rate fell from 141 per thousand in 1946 to 37 in 1984, the lowest of any low-income country except China; the death rate fell from 19.8 per thousand in 1946 to 6 in 1984, the lowest of any low-income country; the birth rate fell from 37.4 per thousand in 1946 to 26 in 1984, again the lowest of any low-income country except China [72]. By 1984, life expectancy for men was 68 years and for women 72 years. The latter was unmatched by any low-income country and the former was matched only by China. The sole blot on this remarkable record was the evident discrimination against the Indian Tamils, among whom death rates and infant mortality rates were twice as high as in the country as a whole [73].

The social and economic policies adopted in Sri Lanka between independence in 1948 and the radical change in government orientation in 1977 resulted in a relatively low degree of inequality in the distribution of income (see Table 7.6). The Gini coefficient fell from 0.50 in 1953 to 0.41 in 1973 and then rose sharply to 0.52 in 1981/2 in response to the curtailment of public expenditure on food subsidies, health and education [74]. Broadly similar patterns are observed in the urban and rural sectors: inequality diminished in both sectors between 1963 and 1973 and then rose again. In the estate sector, however, the pattern is reversed. Inequality increased between 1963 and 1973 and then declined.

The high degree of equality reported on the estates sector is partly an illusion. Income differentials are narrow because the resident population consists of a small number of managers and a sizeable and largely undifferentiated labour force. Profits generated in the sector do not accrue as income in the sector but are recorded elsewhere. Both men and women work on the estates but the minimum wage for women is 25 per cent below that of men [75]. Thus dependency ratios and the sexual composition of the household affect the distribution of income among workers. The important point, however, as Bernard Swan states, is that the egalitarianism of the plantation sector is "based not on shared prosperity, but on shared poverty, hardship, abandonment and rejection" [76]. In 1969/70, for instance, average incomes in the estate sector were about 14 per cent below those in the rural sector and nearly 48 per cent below average incomes in the urban areas [77].

Table 7.6 **THE DISTRIBUTION OF INCOME IN SRI LANKA, 1953–1981/82**
Gini coefficients

	Entire island	Urban	Rural	Estates
1953	0.50	n.a.	n.a.	n.a.
1963	0.49	0.49	0.44	0.27
1973	0.41	0.40	0.37	0.37
1978/9	0.49	0.51	0.49	0.32
1981/2	0.52	0.54	0.49	0.32

Sources: Based on Consumer Finance Surveys of the Central Bank. 1953: Piyasiri Wickramasekara, "Strategies and Programme for Raising the Productivity of the Rural Poor in Sri Lanka", in Swapna Mukhopadhyay, ed., *The Poor in Asia: Productivity-raising Programmes and Strategies,* Kuala Lumpur, UN Asian and Pacific Development Centre, 1985, Table 5-6, p. 377. All other years: W.D. Lakshman, "State Policy in Sri Lanka and its Economic Impact 1970-85: Selected Themes with Special Reference to Distributive Implications of Policy", *Upanathi,* Vol. 1, No. 1, January 1986, Table 7, p. 26.

Public expenditure on education, health and nutrition (food subsidies) can be regarded as human capital formation. In Table 7.7 we compare public expenditure on human capital formation with public expenditure on physical investment. It can be seen from the Table that between 1950 and 1977 human capital formation accounted for roughly 33 per cent of total government recurrent and capital expenditure and physical investment for rather less, namely, 22 per cent. After 1977, however, policy priorities were reversed and by 1980 human capital formation accounted for only 11 per cent of government expenditure whereas physical investment had soared to nearly half of the total. This change in the composition of public expenditure also was accompanied by a change in its relative magnitude. Prior to 1977 government expenditure only once rose above 30 per cent of GDP (in 1972) whereas in the three years following the economic reforms, public spending averaged 35.7 per cent of GDP.

In other words, during the period 1950-77 when Sri Lanka followed a redistributive strategy of development based on consumption and investment transfers, the size of the public sector actually was smaller than in the subsequent period of liberalisation and growth-oriented development. The rise in public expenditure had nothing to do with greater fiscal effort – current revenues in 1983 were 20.2 per cent of GNP, the same as in 1972. The rise was made possible by a massive inflow of foreign aid. In 1984, for example, official development assistance was equivalent to 8 per cent of the country's GNP. Thus foreign aid, in the name of structural adjustment and liberalisation, contributed to an enlargement of the public sector and a sharp reduction in human capital formation.

One of the flaws in Sri Lanka's development strategy was its lack of employment intensity. Indeed unemployment was persistently high, ranging from 11.7 per cent in 1981/2 to what is widely regarded as an implausibly high 24 per cent in 1973 [78]. The unemployed tend to be young, looking for their first job, disproportionately women and relatively well educated in the sense that the great majority have at least some schooling beyond the primary level [79]. In fact it has been argued that the cause of much of the unemployment is a mismatch between the education and aspirations of the large numbers of new entrants to the labour force and the scarcity of jobs, particularly in the public sector, that require academically trained people [80]. Given a labour market that is segmented, with earnings in the public sector much higher than in other occupations, and social programmes (food rations and free health) which reduce the cost of waiting, it is sensible from the point of view of an individual and his family to refuse low wage jobs and remain unemployed in the hope eventually of obtaining secure, high wage employment in the public sector.

Table 7.7 **PUBLIC EXPENDITURE ON HUMAN CAPITAL FORMATION AND PHYSICAL INVESTMENT IN SRI LANKA, 1950-1980**

	Human capital formation	Physical investment	Total government expenditure
	(Per cent of total government expenditure)		(Per cent of GDP)
1950	19	28	21
1951	45	24	22
1952	31	26	30
1953	28	19	24
1954	22	17	19
1955	24	20	19
1956	79	16	24
1957	27	16	24
1958	26	18	26
1959	30	17	27
1960	33	17	27
1961	33	21	29
1962	20	23	29
1963	33	20	27
1964	33	18	29
1965	41	21	28
1966	40	22	29
1967	39	25	28
1968	40	25	27
1969	38	26	28
1970	37	23	25
1971	35	21	27
1972	31	20	35
1973	31	22	27
1974	32	22	24
1975	31	28	30
1976	25	33	28
1977	33	27	23
1978	23	34	37
1979	21	40	37
1980	11	49	33

Sources: Based on data in Piyasiri Wickramasekara, "Strategies and Programme for Raising the Productivity of the Rural Poor in Sri Lanka", in Swapna Mukhopadhyay, ed., *The Poor in Asia: Productivity-raising Programmes and Strategies,* Kuala Lumpur, UN Asian and Pacific Development Centre, 1985, Table 5-15, p. 423.

This does not imply however that unemployment is a luxury of the relatively prosperous members of the community who can afford to spend long periods in job search. Unemployment may be "voluntary" in a technical sense but it certainly isn't accepted willingly. Indeed the violent insurrection of unemployed Sinhalese youth in 1971 shows just how politically explosive unemployment can be. Moreover, analysis has shown that unemployment weighs most heavily on the poor. Particularly as regards male unemployment, the "general picture that emerges is that the poor have higher unemployment rates, that more of their unemployed are young, that the rich unemployed are more educated and that, whatever their level of education the poor have greater difficulty in finding employment" [81]. The failure to generate satisfactory employment for the young has been one of the serious weaknesses of the economy and has made poverty worse and inequality greater than they need have been. Unemployment has represented a great waste of human capital resources and thus has been a major source of inefficiency as well. Given that "any move towards full employment should benefit the poor more than the rich" [82], a more employment-intensive strategy of development would contribute to greater equity, efficiency and growth.

It has often been said that the rate of economic growth in Sri Lanka has been slow and that the slow growth is a consequence of excessive expenditure on education, health and food subsidies. Neither statement is correct. The rate of growth of GDP per head in Sri Lanka during the period 1960-77 was 1.9 per cent a year. This was faster than the average rate of growth of low-income countries other than China. Thus Sri Lanka grew relatively quickly compared to other poor countries and its performance was far from bad even when compared with some of the middle-income countries. It is however true that the rate of growth slowed down appreciably in the 1970s. It is also true that Sri Lanka's growth was inadequate compared to the rates of growth indicated in Table 7.3 as necessary to satisfy basic needs within 30 years. Of course many basic needs were being satisfied through consumption transfers and public expenditure programmes, but even so it must be recognised that the overall rate of growth was not satisfactory. Finally, it is true that the pattern of growth in Sri Lanka was biased against the alleviation of poverty and in this sense growth policies were in conflict with the country's social policies.

Until 1977 Sri Lanka's priorities, as far as growth was concerned, centred on industrialisation. Manufacturing was protected by tariffs, exchange rates were overvalued, foreign exchange controls were pervasive. Import substitution occurred, but despite this there was a great shortage not only of imported goods but also of domestically produced alternatives. Exporting was discouraged and in particular, the plantation sector was given no incentive to replant old stock and as a result Sri Lanka's comparative advantage in tea, rubber and coconut was severely eroded. The ratio of exports to GDP fell and the rate of growth of per capita export earnings was negative. Agricultural output per head stagnated. Finally, as we have seen, the employment intensity of growth was low.

Thus it was poor economic policies rather than excessive expenditure on the public services and consumption transfers that accounts both for the unfortunate pattern of growth and for the unsatisfactory rate of growth. In 1977 a number of policy reforms were introduced. The exchange rate was devalued, imports were liberalised and greater incentives to export were introduced. Foreign aid and private foreign investment were encouraged. Prices, wages and interest rates were decontrolled, food subsidies were sharply curtailed and government expenditure on education and health reduced. As can be seen in Table 7.8, there was an acceleration in the rate of growth of GDP and of GDP per head. This was accompanied by a better balance in the sectoral pattern of growth, with much faster expansion of value added in agriculture and a slight slowing down of the growth of value added in industry. The acceleration in the rate of growth of agricultural value added is particularly encouraging, although this may be due as much to the maturity of the huge Mahaweli irrigation project as to the policy reforms. More generally, there is the danger that the recently achieved rapid growth may not be sustainable if the reforms aggravate social tensions and if political stability proves to be elusive.

187

Table 7.8 **GROWTH RATES IN SRI LANKA, 1960-1985**
Per cent per annum

	1960-77	1977-85
Agriculture	2.4	3.9
Industry	5.5	5.0
Services	4.2	6.8
GDP	3.9	5.7
GDP per capita	1.9	4.0

Sources: World Bank tapes and Central Bank of Ceylon, *Monthly Bulletin*, Colombo, November 1986.

There is, alas, a dark side to the new economic policies. Between 1978 and 1983 the real wages of workers employed in industry and commerce declined 19.4 per cent and the wages of government teachers fell 9.5 per cent [83]. Between 1973 and 1978 the real income of the poorest 10 per cent of the population declined by 12 per cent, although the losses were fully recovered by 1981 [84]. The reduction in food subsidies led, not surprisingly, to an increase in undernutrition. Between 1969/70 and 1980/1, for instance, the incidence of households with less than 2 200 calories per day per person rose 35.6 per cent in the rural sector, 67.5 per cent in the estates sector and 37.7 per cent in the urban areas [85]. Finally, as we saw earlier, inequality in the distribution of income almost certainly increased after the economic reforms were introduced.

In switching from a flawed redistributive strategy of development to a growth-oriented strategy, Sri Lanka appears to have lost the features of the former which distinguished it so favourably from most other Third World countries. Whether the advantages of the new strategy will fully compensate for what has been lost remains to be seen, but the experience so far leaves room for doubt. Above all, the ethnic conflict between the Sinhalese and Sri Lankan Tamils – which is partly economic and social – has not been resolved, the discrimination against Indian Tamils on the plantations has not been removed and the inequalities among the rural Sinhalese in the wet zone have been largely ignored. These are problems which growth alone is unlikely to solve and hence the merits of a less flawed redistributive strategy in Sri Lanka are likely to remain under discussion for the foreseeable future.

Summary

Redistributive strategies of development represent a genuine alternative to growth-oriented strategies in countries which attach priority to reducing quickly the most acute forms of poverty and to creating an egalitarian society. Problems of consistency in policy design must not be overlooked, however. Nor must the political preconditions for redistributive measures be ignored.

Policies which concentrate on the creation of more productive employment, or on redistributing the increments of growth or on satisfying basic needs are really sub-strategies within a more comprehensive redistributive strategy of economic development. This comprehensive strategy includes five central elements, the absence of any one of which is likely to lead to disappointment with the ultimate results. These five central elements are:

i)   An initial redistribution of productive assets, particularly land;

ii) The creation of local institutions which permit participation by the people in the selection, design and management of social and economic projects and programmes [86];

iii) Investment in human capital – particularly in education, nutrition and health programmes – and the provision of essential social services and economic infrastructure;

iv) The choice of an employment intensive pattern of development, led either by the export of labour-intensive manufactured goods or by rapid growth of agricultural output [87]; and

v) Sustained rapid growth of aggregate income per head.

Between them, these elements ensure an equal distribution of income and wealth, rapid accumulation of human and physical capital, and fast growth of output and income.

The strategy does not necessarily require an exceptionally high rate of domestic savings. Nor does it necessarily require an unusually large state sector. It certainly is compatible with a capitalist system of production and exchange, although obviously not with *laissez faire*. The strategy's point of departure is an even distribution of the ownership of the means of production. Since most Third World countries are predominantly agrarian, the implication is that development under this strategy usually will be based on a system of small peasant agriculture.

The emphasis on human capital formation serves several purposes. First, the development of human resources contributes directly to the well being of the poor. Second, it helps to create a more equal distribution of income. Third, it creates an environment in which equality of opportunity is not likely to lead to great inequality of outcome. Fourth, by providing comprehensive health, nutrition and educational services, complementarities between the various services can be exploited. For example, better health for the poor (as a result of primary health care services) increases the efficiency with which the body transforms calories into improved nutrition (the calories possibly obtained from a grain rationing programme); and improved nutrition, in turn, leads to increased attendance at school (funded by the state) and improves the ability of children to learn. Similarly, there are linkages between women's health, life expectancy, education and fertility; between literacy and health; between education, literacy and labour productivity, etc. [88]. Finally, there are complementarities between physical and human capital which a redistributive strategy can exploit. Investment in modern industry requires skilled labour; agricultural mechanisation requires people who can, for example, operate and repair irrigation equipment; modern services (banking, tourism, public administration) require a literate and numerate labour force. Thus an emphasis on human capital formation can in principle yield high returns in the form of an increase in the marginal productivity of investment in physical assets. Principle can be converted into practice, however, only if the pattern of development is labour intensive.

The importance of rapid growth is by now perhaps self-evident. Redistribution alone can go part way towards eliminating the worse forms of poverty but it cannot go all the way. Sustained growth of per capita income is essential. Moreover, if poverty is to be eliminated within one or at most two generations, the rate of growth must be rapid. Beyond that, it is important that the pattern of growth reinforces the other components of a redistributive strategy. This is most likely to occur when policies ensure that the available labour force is fully utilised, there is no bias against peasant agriculture and the pattern of international trade reflects the country's resource endowment and comparative advantage.

189

1. Data on the level and rate of growth of GDP in Central and South America in this period are available in Miguel Urrutia, "Latin America and the Crisis of the 1980s", in Louis Emmerij, ed., *Development Policies and the Crisis of the 1980s*, Paris, OECD Development Centre, 1987, Tables III.1 and III.2.

2. See the Appendix on "Is Economic Growth Desirable?" in W. Arthur Lewis, *The Theory of Economic Growth*, London, Allen and Unwin, 1955, p. 431.

3. *Ibid.*, p. 421.

4. *Ibid.*, p. 422.

5. *Ibid.*, p. 423.

6. D. Turnham assisted by I. Jaeger, *The Employment Problem in Less Developed Countries: A Review of Evidence*, Paris, OECD Development Centre, 1971.

7. Albert Fishlow, "Brazilian Size Distribution of Income", *American Economic Review*, Vol. LX, No. 3, May 1972, pp. 391-402.

8. On Pakistan see Keith Griffin and Azizur Rahman Khan, eds., *Growth and Inequality in Pakistan*, London, Macmillan, 1972. On Peru see Keith Griffin, *Underdevelopment in Spanish America*, London, Allen and Unwin, 1969.

9. Irma Adelman and Cynthia Taft Morris, *Economic Growth and Social Equity in Developing Countries*, Stanford, Stanford University Press, 1973, p. 179.

10. ILO, *Poverty and Landlessness in Rural Asia*, Geneva, ILO, 1977. Also see Keith Griffin and Azizur Rahman Khan, "Poverty in the Third World: Ugly Facts and Fancy Models", *World Development*, Vol. 6, No. 3, March 1978.

11. See Keith Griffin, *International Inequality and National Poverty*, London, Macmillan, 1978, Ch. 7.

12. Mahbub ul Haq, *The Poverty Curtain: Choices for the Third World*, New York, Columbia University Press, 1976, pp. 24-5.

13. ILO, *Towards Full Employment: A Programme for Colombia*, Geneva, ILO, 1970; ILO, *Matching Employment Opportunities and Expectations: A Programme of Action for Ceylon*, Geneva, ILO, 1971; ILO, *Employment, Incomes and Equality: A Strategy for Increasing Productive Employment in Kenya*, Geneva, ILO, 1972; ILO, *Sharing in Development: A Programme of Employment, Equity and Growth for the Philippines*, Geneva, ILO, 1974; ILO, *Towards Self-Reliance: Development, Employment and Equity in Tanzania*, Addis Ababa, JASPA, 1978.

14. For an extreme statement of the urban bias thesis see Michael Lipton, *Why Poor People Stay Poor: Urban Bias in World Development*, London, Temple Smith, 1977.

15. See Keith Griffin and Jeffrey James, *The Transition to Egalitarian Development: Economic Policies for Structural Change in the Third World*, London, Macmillan, 1981. Nutrition-based poverty lines were widely used after they were employed by Dandekar and Rath in their pioneering study. See V.M. Dandekar and Nilakantha Rath, *Poverty in India*, Bombay, Economic and Political Weekly, 1971.

16. I remember as a graduate student in Oxford listening to Thomas (later Lord) Balogh discuss this possibility in his lectures on development economics in 1961.

17. Hollis Chenery, Montek S. Ahluwalia, C.L.G. Bell, John H. Duloy and Richard Jolly, *Redistribution with Growth*, London, Oxford University Press, 1974, p. xvii.

18. *Ibid.*, Table XI.5, p. 228.

19. *Ibid.*

20. *Ibid.*, p. 227.

21. *Ibid.*, p. 228.

22. *Ibid.*, pp. 234-5.

23. *Ibid.*, p. 228.

24. Irma Adelman, "A Poverty-Focused Approach to Development Policy" in John P. Lewis and Valeriana

Kallab, eds., *Development Strategies Reconsidered*, New Brunswick, N.J., Transaction Books for the Overseas Development Council, 1986, p. 56.

25. Mahbub ul Haq, *op. cit.*, p. 27.

26. Irma Adelman, *op. cit.*, p. 57.

27. ILO, *Employment, Growth and Basic Needs: A One-World Problem*, Geneva, ILO, 1976. The satisfaction of basic human needs was advocated earlier in the 1975 Dag Hammarskjold Report on Development and International Cooperation, *What Now*, a special issue of *Development Dialogue*, 1975, No. 1/2.

28. Paul Streeten with Shahid Javed Burki, Mahbub ul Haq, Norman Hicks and Frances Stewart, *First Things First: Meeting Basic Needs in the Developing Countries*, New York, Oxford University Press, 1981.

29. See Frances Stewart, *Basic Needs in Developing Countries*, Baltimore, Johns Hopkins University Press, 1985, p. 2.

30. Paul Streeten, *Development Perspectives*, London, Macmillan, 1981, p. 331.

31. ILO, *Employment, Growth and Basic Needs*, p. 33.

32. See Pitambar Pant, "Perspective of Development, India 1960-61 to 1975-76: Implications of Planning for a Minimum Level of Living", in T.N. Srinivasan and P.K. Bardhan, eds., *Poverty and Income Distribution in India*, Calcutta, Statistical Publishing Society, 1974. Pant believed that the minimum level of living could be achieved only by an acceleration in the rate of growth and hence should not be classified among those who believe in "redistribution before growth".

33. ILO, *Employment, Growth and Basic Needs*, p. 32.

34. Paul Streeten with Shahid Javed Burki *et al., op. cit.*, p. 3.

35. See Jose-Pablo Arellano, "Meeting Basic Needs: The Trade-Off Between the Quality and Coverage of the Programs", *Journal of Development Economics*, Vol. 18, No. 1, May-June 1985.

36. ILO, *Employment, Growth and Basic Needs*, p. 32.

37. See Keith Griffin and Jeffrey James, *op. cit.*, Chapter 5, from which much of what follows is taken.

38. Milton J. Esman, "Administrative Doctrine and Developmental Needs", in E. Philip Morgan, ed., *The Administration of Change in Africa*, Dunellen, 1974, p. 7.

39. Paul Streeten with Shahid Javed Burki *et al., op. cit.*, pp. 20-1.

40. Louis Emmerij, "Basic Needs and Employment-Oriented Strategies Reconsidered", *Development and Peace*, Vol. 2, Autumn 1981, p. 158.

41. ILO, *Employment, Growth and Basic Needs*, Table 5, p. 40.

42. *Ibid.*, p. 33.

43. Louis Emmerij, "Basic Needs and Employment-Oriented Strategies Reconsidered", *loc. cit.*, p. 158, emphasis in the orginal.

44. John C.H. Fei, Gustav Ranis and Shirley W.Y. Kuo, *Growth with Equity: The Taiwan Case*, New York, Oxford University Press, 1979, p. 25.

45. *Ibid.*, pp. 23-4.

46. *Ibid.*, Table 2.1, p. 41.

47. *Ibid.*, Table 2.3, p. 43.

48. *Ibid.*, p. 43.

49. *Ibid.*, p. 44.

50. Tibor Scitovsky, "Economic Development in Taiwan and South Korea, 1965-1981", in Lawrence J. Lau, ed., *Models of Development: A Comparative Study of Economic Growth in South Korea and Taiwan*, San Francisco, ICS Press, 1986, p. 140.

51. *Ibid.*, Table 4, p. 141.

52. The data for Taiwan come from Council for Economic Planning and Development, Republic of China, *Taiwan Statistical Data Book 1986*, June 1986. The data for South Korea were taken from IBRD, *World Development Report 1986*, New York, Oxford University Press, 1986.

53. Tibor Scitovsky, *op. cit.*, p. 146.

54. Shirley W.Y. Kuo, Gustav Ranis and John C.H. Fei, *The Taiwan Success Story: Rapid Growth with Improved Distribution in the Republic of China, 1952-1979*, Boulder, Westview Press, 1981, Table 2.5, p. 20.

55. Data on the distribution of income in the farm and non-farm sectors are available in *ibid.*, Table 5.2, p. 98.

56. United Nations Department of International Economic and Social Affairs, *Socio-Economic Development and Fertility Decline in Sri Lanka*, New York, United Nations, 1986, Table 3, p. 10.

57. Surjit S. Bhalla and Paul Glewwe, "Growth and Equity in Developing Countries: A Reinterpretation of the Sri Lankan Experience", *World Bank Economic Review*, Vol. 1, No. 1, September 1986, Table 1, p. 41. The Table contains numerous social indicators going as far back as 1881.

58. Kumari Jayawardena, "Aspects of Class and Ethnic Consciousness in Sri Lanka", *Development and Change*, Vol. 14, No. 1, January 1983, p. 9.

59. *Ibid.*, p. 16.

60. Bernard Swan, "Sri Lanka: Constraints and Prospects in the Pursuit of Rural Development", in David A.M, Lea and D.P. Chaudhri, eds., *Rural Development and the State*, London, Methuen, 1983, p. 150.

61. Piyasiri Wickramasekara, "Strategies and Programme for Raising the Productivity of the Rural Poor in Sri Lanka", in Swapna Mukhopadhyay, ed., *The Poor in Asia: Productivity-raising Programmes and Strategies*, Kuala Lumpur, UN Asian and Pacific Development Centre, 1985, p. 428.

62. Netherlands Institute of Human Rights, *Ethnic Violence, Development and Human Rights*, The Hague, CIP-gegevens Koninklijke Bibliotheek, 1985, p. 98.

63. Peter Richards and Wilbert Gooneratne, *Basic Needs, Poverty and Government Policies in Sri Lanka*, Geneva, ILO, 1980, Table 13, p. 30.

64. Bernard Swan, *op. cit.*, p. 150.

65. *New York Times*, 23 April 1987.

66. Piyasiri Wickramasekara, *op. cit.*, p. 429.

67. W.D. Lakshman, "State Policy in Sri Lanka and its Economic Impact 1970-85: Selected Themes with Special Reference to Distributive Implications of Policy", *Upanathi*, Vol. 1, No. 1, January 1986, Table 10, p. 30. W. Gooneratne and D. Wesumperuma estimate the rise in rural wages on tea and rubber estates was 77.4 per cent between 1975 and 1979 and that they fell by 22.5 per cent in the very next year. See W. Gooneratne and D. Wesumperuma, "Plantation Agriculture in Sri Lanka – An Overview of Employment and Development Prospects", in W. Gooneratne and D. Wesumperuma, eds., *Plantation Agriculture in Sri Lanka*, Bangkok, ILO-ARTEP, 1984, Table 4, p. 11.

68. Piyasiri Wickramasekara, *op. cit.*, p. 431.

69. United Nations Department of International Economic and Social Affairs, *op. cit.*, Table 3, p. 10.

70. Piyasiri Wickramasekara, *op. cit.*, p. 424.

71. *Ibid.*

72. The figures for 1946 are from Paul Isenman "Basic Needs: The Case of Sri Lanka", *World Development*, Vol. 8, No. 3, March 1980, Table 1, p. 238. The figures for 1984 are from IBRD, *World Development Report 1986*.

73. UNICEF reports that the crude death rate on the estates in 1980 was 12.4 per thousand (as compared to 6.2 for Sri Lanka as a whole) and the infant mortality rate on the estates in 1979 was 80 per thousand (as compared to 38 for the entire country). See UNICEF, *The Social Impact of Economic Policies During the Last Decades*, Colombo, UNICEF, June 1985, p. 31.

74. It has been argued by Paul Glewwe that inequality declined between 1969/70 and 1980/1. His data show however that income inequality increased whereas only expenditure inequality diminished, but he chooses to disregard the income data in reaching his conclusions. See Paul Glewwe, "The Distribution of Income in Sri Lanka in 1969-70 and 1980-81: A Decomposition Analysis", *Journal of Development Economics*, Vol. 24, No. 2, December 1986.
Note, too, that the data in Table 7.6 are not comparable with the data for Sri Lanka in Table 1.6. The data were obtained from different sources and the Gini coefficient calculated in different ways.

75. See Rachel Kurian, *Women Workers in the Sri Lanka Plantation Sector*, Geneva, ILO, 1982, p. 70.

76. Bernard Swan, *op. cit.*, p. 150.

77. Paul Glewwe, *op. cit.*, Table 1, p. 261.

78. UNICEF, *op. cit.*, Table 3.1, p. 7.

79. The pioneering study of unemployment in Sri Lanka is ILO, *Matching Employment Opportunities and Expectations: A Programme of Action for Ceylon, loc. cit.*

80. *Ibid.* Also see Paul Isenman, *op. cit.*, pp. 249-51.

81. Peter Richards and Wilbert Gooneratne, *op. cit.*, p. 65.

82. *Ibid.*, p. 66.

83. W.D. Lakshman, *op. cit.*, Table 10, p. 30.

84. *Ibid.*, Table 8, p. 27.

85. Calculated from data in Piyasiri Wickramasekara, *op. cit.*, Table 5-1, p. 370.

86. Academic research on local participation is woefully inadequate. See however G.V.S. de Silva, Niranjan Mehta, Md. Anisur Rahman and Ponna Wignaraja, "Bhoomi Sena: A Struggle for People's Power", *Development Dialogue*, 1979:2 and the 1984:2 issue of *Development* (the journal of the Society for International Development).

87. A case has been made, because of the slowing down in the growth of world trade, for favouring agriculture-led over export-led growth. See Irma Adelman, "Beyond Export-Led Growth", *World Development*, Vol. 12, No. 9, September 1984.

88. Linkages or complementarities among basic needs are underlined by Paul Isenman, *op. cit.*, pp 242-3.

193

Chapter 8

SOCIALIST STRATEGIES OF DEVELOPMENT

The previous chapters have been concerned with economic development essentially within a capitalist framework. All of the strategies analysed so far rely on the market mechanism and competitive processes to allocate resources, i.e., to determine what is produced, how it is produced and for whom it is produced. Market forces may be tempered by government regulation or intervention, by controls, taxes and subsidies, but however *dirigiste* some of the strategies may seem, all have as their point of departure a commitment to a market economy. Similarly, private property and specifically the private ownership of the means of production, i.e., of productive assets, is seen as an integral part of a market economy. Economic actors are free to save and invest, to buy and sell financial and physical assets, to innovate, take risks and earn high rewards when the risks pay off. Specific property rights may be extinguished occasionally when the wider public interest requires it, as during a redistributive land reform, but the principle of private property is not brought into question by any of the strategies previously considered.

Private enterprise – the initiative of numberless farmers, manufacturers and traders – is assumed to drive the system, to determine the structure of production and the pace of expansion. Again, wide variation is possible and the different strategies may, for example, envisage different roles for government enterprise. In some strategies state investment and state ownership of industrial enterprises may be prominent whereas in others, the state may own and manage few enterprises. In none of the strategies so far considered, however, is the state given exclusive or even primary responsibility for running the economy. All of the economies are mixed economies – the mix varying considerably from one strategy to another and from one sector of the economy to another – but within the mixture the private sector is dominant in terms of ownership and control of productive assets. The state plays a supportive and regulatory role in the economy, not a commanding one. In other words, however large the public sector may be, in the other strategies the state does not run the economy, it merely intervenes in it.

This chapter, in contrast, is concerned with development within a very different framework, a socialist framework. Property relations, prices and the role of government are fundamentally different in socialist as compared to capitalist societies. For a start, the means of production are socialised rather than privately owned. Typically, all large industrial enterprises are owned by the state although in some socialist countries small and medium-sized enterprises may be organised as co-operatives and some enterprises, particularly in the services sector, may be in private hands. In agriculture, most farming is done within a co-operative framework. The land is owned collectively and often managed and cultivated collectively too, although in China farming is done on small peasant holdings (which in theory still are collectively owned but which for practical purposes are hard to distinguish from privately-owned farms). In a few socialist countries, notably Poland and Yugoslavia, there is a large private sector in agriculture. In most of the other socialist countries there are also state farms which operate with wage labour in a manner similar to state-owned factories.

Socialist economies are centrally planned economies. Enterprises are given targets and quotas, usually specified in physical terms, and are allocated the inputs needed to reach the targets directly by the state. Profits and prices play a subsidiary role in resource allocation. Indeed, prices usually are set by the planners, not determined by market forces. There are of course exceptions in all socialist economies, but only in Yugoslavia does the price system as it is known in the West operate relatively freely. In Hungary, economic reforms have enlarged the role of the market and in China tentative steps have been taken in that direction, but in the other socialist countries, central planning and quantitative controls are used to determine the output of commodities, the level of investment and the rate of growth. Thus the state in a socialist economy tends to be pervasive: it does more than intervene in the economy, it runs it.

The governments of many countries describe themselves as socialist. In some countries the claim to be socialist is largely rhetorical whereas in others it must be taken seriously. It is hard to know where to draw the line. In this chapter, however, the boundary has been drawn tightly and only fifteen countries which indisputably are socialist have been so classified. These include the Soviet Union and eight countries in Eastern Europe, namely, Albania, Bulgaria, Czechoslovakia, East Germany, Hungary, Poland, Romania and Yugoslavia. Also included are six countries from the Third World: China, Cuba, Kampuchea, Mongolia, North Korea and Vietnam.

It could be argued that the boundary has not been drawn tightly enough. Our minimal requirement for a country to be considered socialist is simply that the means of production are socialised, but this is compatible with state ownership and operation of all farms and factories and with governance by a bureaucratic "new class". This is not what most socialist thinkers envisaged when they advocated socialism and some analysts might claim that several of the countries on our list of fifteen are not in fact socialist but rather state capitalist or else something which is neither capitalist nor socialist [1]. The argument has force, but at the risk of being a bit arbitrary we prefer to leave the list as it stands. Otherwise there is a danger of classifying as socialist only those countries that conform to an ideal which is rarely attained and then attempting unfairly to compare an ideal socialism with less than ideal capitalism.

Excluded from our list of socialist countries are countries such as Angola, Ethiopia, Mozambique, Nicaragua and South Yemen which have had a radical nationalist revolution and which have many socialist features but which have not adopted a fully socialist strategy of development. Several of them in fact are struggling with civil wars and against external threats and intervention; their economies are on a war footing and in a sense they have not been able to adopt any long-run strategy of development. Their self-description as socialist states does indicate however that in parts of the Third World the attractions of socialist development strategies may be increasing. This makes it all the more important to understand the economic and political implications of these strategies.

The fifteen countries on our list account for 32.3 per cent of the world's population. The list includes the world's largest country, China, as well as one of the smallest, Mongolia. It includes countries which by any standard are prosperous, e.g., East Germany, and one which recently was one of the most wretched on earth, Kampuchea. The list includes countries from East and Southeast Asia, the Caribbean and Europe. Thus the fifteen countries are diverse in terms of size, geographical location, climate, resources, language, culture and average standard of living. About the only thing they have in common is that all of them have adopted, or have had thrust upon them, a socialist strategy of development.

Table 8.1 contains information on GNP per capita in 1980 and the size and rate of growth of the population [2]. The Table is divided into two sections, the upper half containing six Third World countries and the lower half the Soviet Union and eight European countries. This division corresponds roughly to a division between poor and rich socialist countries although Albania clearly should be classified with the former.

Table 8.1 **POPULATION SIZE AND AVERAGE INCOME IN FIFTEEN SOCIALIST COUNTRIES**

	GNP per capita, 1980 (US dollars)	Population, 1984 (million)	Population growth, 1973-84 (per cent per annum)
China	290	1 029.2	1.4
Cuba	1410 a	9.9	0.7
Kumpuchea	n.a.	7.1	3.2 b
Mongolia	780 a	1.9	2.8
North Korea	1130	19.9	2.6
Vietnam	n.a.	60.1	2.6
Albania	840 a	2.9	2.0
Bulgaria	4 150	9.0	0.3
Czechoslovakia	5 820	15.5	0.5
East Germany	7 180	16.7	−0.1
Hungary	4 180	10.7	0.2
Poland	3 900	36.9	0.9
Romania	2 340	22.7	0.8
U.S.S.R.	4 550	275.0	0.9
Yugoslavia	2 620	23.0	0.8

a) 1979.
b) 1980-85.
Sources: IBRD, *World Development Report*, Oxford University Press, 1981, 1982, 1986; United Nations, *World Population Prospects: Estimates and Projections as Assessed in 1984*, New York, 1986.

The socialist world, like the capitalist world, is not monolithic. Economic structure differs considerably from one country to another, as does the rate of growth. Let us consider first the structure of production and the distribution of the labour force across sectors (see Table 8.2).

As one would expect, agriculture accounts for a modest proportion of GDP in all the European socialist countries (except Albania, for which there are no data). It is also a relatively small sector in Cuba, Mongolia and North Korea. One the other hand, in China, Kampuchea and Vietnam (for the last two of which data are missing) output from agriculture remains a significant proportion of GDP. There is no evidence that the agricultural sector is relatively small in socialist countries compared to capitalist countries

196

at a comparable level of per capita income. If anything, the reverse may be the case: agriculture tends to account for a relatively high proportion of GDP in socialist countries, perhaps reflecting a different pattern of demand and distribution of income.

Table 8.2 **THE STRUCTURE OF PRODUCTION AND EMPLOYMENT, 1980**
(percentages of GDP and total employment)

| | Agriculture | | Industry | | Services | |
	Output	Employment	Output	Employment	Output	Employment
China	31	71	47	17	22	12
Cuba	13 a	23	31 a	31	56 a	46
Kampuchea	n.a.	n.a.	n.a.	n.a.	n.a.	n.a.
Mongolia	15	55	29	22	56	23
North Korea	20 b	49	65 b	33	15 b	18
Vietnam	n.a.	71	n.a.	10	n.a.	19
Albania	n.a.	61	n.a.	25	n.a.	14
Bulgaria	17	37	58	39	25	24
Czechoslovakia	8	11	75	48	14	41
East Germany	9	10	70	50	21	40
Hungary	14	15	59	53	27	32
Poland	15	31	64	39	21	30
Romania	11	29	64	36	25	35
USSR	16	14	62	45	22	41
Yugoslavia	12	29	43	35	45	36

a)   1981, net material product.
b)   1970, national income.
Sources: IBRD, *World Development Report 1982*, Oxford University Press, 1982; United Nations, *Statistical Yearbook 1983/84*, New York, 1986; John Halliday, "The North Korean Enigma", in Gordon White, Robin Murray and Christine White, eds., *Revolutionary Socialist Development in the Third World*, Brighton, Wheatsheaf Books, 1983.

It is widely believed that in socialist countries the productivity of labour in agriculture is much lower than the national average. Agriculture is thought to be a technologically backward sector characterised by low returns to labour. This belief, however, obscures the diversity among socialist countries and in general is not correct. Indeed in the Soviet Union the productivity of labour in agriculture is slightly above the national average while in Czechoslovakia, East Germany and Hungary it is broadly comparable. In Cuba, where output per worker in the non-agricultural sectors is not quite twice that in agriculture, there is structural distortion but the degree of structural distortion is lower than one typically finds in the Third World [3]. Structural distortion is evident, however, in Poland and Yugoslavia (in both of which agriculture is largely private) and in Bulgaria and Romania. But far worse than any of these is Mongolia where the ratio of output per worker in non-agriculture to agriculture is seven. Mongolia, of course, is a special case: agriculture consists largely of nomadic grazing of cattle on semi-arid rangelands and although half of the labour force in 1980 is reported to have been engaged in agriculture, just over half the population lived in urban areas! [4].

Turning to industry, the common perception of the socialist countries as placing emphasis on industrialisation and the development of the manufacturing sector is confirmed by the data. Industry accounts for a much higher proportion of output and employment in socialist countries than in capitalist countries of a comparable per capita income. For example, in China, industry accounted for about 47 per cent of gross domestic product in 1980 whereas in India it accounted for 26 per cent. In North Korea industry accounted for 65 per cent of GDP as early as 1970 whereas in South Korea, industrial output in 1980 was only 41 per cent of the total. A similar pattern is found when one looks at the economically more advanced economies. For instance, in East Germany in 1980, industrial output was 70 per cent of GDP; in West Germany in 1984 it was 46 per cent. In 1980, industrial production represented about 62 per cent of gross domestic product in the Soviet Union and 34 per cent in the United States. These differences in the structure of GDP almost certainly are exaggerated by differences in relative prices – since in socialist countries the prices of industrial goods tend to be relatively high and the prices of agricultural goods relatively low – but even at comparable prices, differences in the composition of output would be significant.

Even in industry, however, there are a few surprises. Thus in Yugoslavia the share of industry in total output is much lower than in the other European socialist countries and rather similar to what one would expect to find in a capitalist economy of a comparable level of income. Industrial output in Cuba is relatively low. Indeed industry accounts for a smaller proportion of output (but not of employment) than in the average middle-income Third World country. In Mongolia, too, industrial output is below the average of middle-income countries while industrial employment is identical to the average.

The services sector is almost the mirror image of the industrial sector. That is, in those countries where the industrial sector is large and output per worker is high, the services sector tends to be small and labour productivity in services tends to be relatively low [5]. This is the pattern one has come to expect in socialist countries. Once again, however, the pattern is not uniform. In Yugoslavia, Cuba and Mongolia the services sector accounts for a large proportion of total product – indeed it is the largest sector – and, moreover, output per worker in services is higher than in either of the other two sectors. In Yugoslavia and Cuba, tourism plays an important role in the economy whereas in Mongolia trading activities are important.

The significant point to emerge from all this is that the structure of output and employment do vary among socialist countries. Differences in the level of development, natural resources, comparative advantage, etc., do affect the composition of production and the pattern of employment. Socialist countries are not all alike and the path of development is not wholly determined by the choice of a socialist strategy of development. The pace of development also varies among socialist countries. Data on rates of growth in socialist countries are scarce and unreliable but such data as exist on the rate of growth of GNP per capita during the twenty-three years beginning in 1960 are included in Table 8.3.

There are a number of points that can be made about growth rates in the socialist countries. First, on the whole, growth rates of income per head have been quite high. They compare favourably with growth rates of capitalist economies, whether highly advanced or underdeveloped. As we shall see later when discussing Hungary, care must be taken in interpreting the data, and particularly in drawing welfare implications, but there is little doubt that in general physical output has increased quite rapidly in most socialist countries. Second, three of the 15 countries have performed poorly, namely, Cuba, Vietnam and Kampuchea. Vietnam, of course, was engaged in a major war and it is surprising there was any rise in output per head during the 1960s, the period for which we have data [6]. Under the circumstances the growth performance must be regarded as remarkable. Kampuchea did not become a socialist country until 1975 when the Khmer Rouge captured the capital in the aftermath of the Vietnam War. Since then the country has suffered a series of afflictions: civil war, famine and, in 1977-8, military conflict with the Vietnamese. Although no figures are available on the rate of growth of total output, it is unlikely that per capita income has regained the level, say, of 1970. Cuba is a bit of a puzzle. There is no obvious explanation for its poor performance and it is possible that the estimated growth rate is inaccurate. We have used a CIA source, but a careful study by the World Bank came to the conclusion that it was impossible to make a reliable estimate of the rate of growth in Cuba [7].

Third, there is no evidence from the data of any slowing down of growth during the course of the first two decades covered in the Table. In fact growth accelerated between the 1960s and 1970s in all of the Soviet bloc countries of Eastern Europe except the Soviet Union itself (where it declined marginally). In Yugoslavia there was a slight acceleration of the growth rate, in China a moderate acceleration and in Mongolia a sharp acceleration. Only in Albania and North Korea did growth rates decline significantly, and even then they remained exceptionally rapid [8]. Fourth, in the 1980s, however, there has been a very sharp slowing down of growth in almost all socialist countries except China. In some cases, such as in Poland, Yugoslavia and North Korea, the falling growth rate has been accompanied by debt crises and severe balance-of-payments problems. The socialist countries, in other words, have not been immune to the effects of the general recession in the world economy and like the capitalist economies, both rich and poor, they have experienced cyclical fluctuations in growth rates.

Table 8.3 **GROWTH OF GNP PER CAPITA, 1960-1983**
Per cent per annum

China	5.1
Cuba	1.0 a
Kampuchea	n.a.
Mongolia	3.0 b
North Korea	2.9
Vietnam	0.7 c
Albania	4.2 b
Bulgaria	3.5
Czechoslovakia	2.3
East Germany	3.0
Hungary	2.5
Poland	2.9
Romania	4.1
USSR	3.0
Yugoslavia	4.9

a) 1959-78.
b) 1960-79.
c) GDP per capita, 1960-70.
Source: US Central Intelligence Agency, *Handbook of Economic Statistics,* Washington, D.C., 1984; US Central Intelligence Agency, *The Cuban Economy: A Statistical Review,* Washington, D.C., 1981; IBRD, *World Development Report,* Oxford University Press, 1981 and 1984.

Finally, if one examines the fragmentary evidence covering the 35 year period, 1950-1985, there does appear to have been a slowing down of the long-run rate of growth in the Soviet Union and most of its Eastern European allies, but this is due at least in part to the unprecedentedly fast growth in the first half of the 1950s combined with the unprecedentedly slow growth in the first half of the 1980s [9]. Both sub-periods may turn out to have been truly exceptional. It is quite certain, however, that whatever the long-run trend rate of growth of output, there has been a tendency in many socialist economies for the capital-output ratio to rise. This reflects not shifts in the sectoral composition of output but a fall in the marginal productivity of capital and that, in turn, probably is due to technological obsolescence in plant and equipment. The socialist economies have grown rapidly as a result of very high rates of capital accumulation, but the pace of technical change has been relatively slow and consequently more and more investment has been required to achieve a given rate of growth.

There are particular problems that arise in trying to assess or evaluate socialist strategies of development. One problem is that development within a socialist framework first began in the Soviet Union, a European country which even at the time of the revolution was far more advanced economically than the countries of Asia, Africa and Latin America with which we are primarily concerned. Thus it is not obvious that the Soviet experience is directly relevant to economic development in the contemporary Third World [10]. Next, there is the problem of time scale. Capitalist development has been occurring in some countries for two centuries or longer and hence the secular or long-run tendencies of capitalism are reasonably well understood. The socialist experience, in contrast, is recent, the first efforts dating from the Bolshevik revolution of 1917. For nearly forty years in fact the Soviet Union was almost unique in being one of only two socialist countries in the world – the other was Mongolia – and it is only since the end of the Second World War that there have been a number of other examples of socialist strategies of development which can be studied. Even now, however, the number of socialist countries is relatively small and this small size of sample makes it difficult to generalise. Furthermore, as Carl Riskin has pointed out, not all of the observations in the sample can be regarded as independent [11]. A particular model of socialism was imposed upon most of the Eastern European countries by the Soviet Union. The Eastern Europeans did not freely choose the strategy that was adopted. Indeed it can be argued that their choice was so constrained by the Soviet Union that for some purposes the Soviet bloc countries should be regarded as a single observation of socialist development. That is, instead of eight examples from the Soviet bloc, there is only one.

In addition to the above problems, there is the international context in which socialist development has taken place. The reaction of the world to the Bolshevik revolution was uncompromisingly hostile and repeated attempts were made from outside to undermine the regime and frustrate its policies. The implantation of socialism in Eastern Europe came at the end of the Second World War and at the beginning of a period of ideological and military confrontation – the Cold War – that continues to the present day. None of the Eastern European countries, with the exception of Yugoslavia, was given an opportunity to develop its economy and society unthreatened by the West. And Yugoslavia had to contend with threats from the Soviet Union. China after the revolution was isolated economically and politically. Indeed, the regime was denied international diplomatic recognition for a quarter of a century while the fiction was maintained in the United Nations and elsewhere that the administration on the island of Taiwan represented the Chinese people. Korea was divided by external powers and a war for reunification (the Korean War) failed. The socialist regime in the northern half of the country found itself on the frontline in the conflict between the Soviet Union and the United States, where it still remains. Vietnam also was divided; it too fought a war for reunification and after a ferocious struggle reunification was achieved and a socialist administration installed throughout the country. Cuba was and remains subjected to a trade embargo by the United States and hostility from many of its neighbours. An attempted invasion at the Bay of Pigs was repulsed in 1961.

Thus socialist countries have encountered unrelenting hostility, economic embargoes, diplomatic isolation and military invasion from the non-socialist world. This external environment inevitably has exerted a strong influence on policy and strategy. Indeed the influence has been so strong that sometimes it is impossible to know whether a particular feature of a socialist strategy of development arose because of the external environment or is an inherent aspect of the strategy itself.

Lastly, there is the political dimension of socialist strategies of development. All of the countries in our sample are one party states. All are governed by a Marxist-Leninist party that is intolerant of other philosophies and even of alternative interpretations within the dominant view. All tend to suppress dissent of whatever sort on whatever topic. All are totalitarian. None shows any tendency of becoming a social democratic state of the type common in Western Europe, although one would hesitate to say that such an evolution is impossible. The historical evidence, however, is clear: socialist economic systems in practice have been accompanied by totalitarian political systems [12]. And the system as a whole has political as well as economic objectives, namely, to transform society and prepare the foundations for utopian communism, to abolish private property and material incentives, to create a new socialist man. The system is a package and one must accept that it has not been possible to open the package and select from its contents only those items that are most attractive. It is all or nothing and hence it is artificial and probably impossible to attempt to evaluate socialist economics while ignoring socialist politics.

Four strategies

In theory there can be more than one socialist strategy of economic development and a number of authors have given careful thought to what an ideal socialist strategy would be [13]. The approach adopted in this chapter, however, is to consider not the ideal but the real, the actual experience of socialist countries under alternative development strategies. Four such alternative strategies can be identified: the classic Soviet (or Stalinist) model, the workers' self-management model of Yugoslavia, the Chinese (or Maoist) model and the self-reliant model of North Korea. We shall describe each of these briefly in turn.

The Soviet model of development is a strategy for industrialisation in a country with a large agricultural sector. As in much Western thought [14], it is taken for granted that the key to growth is the expansion of the manufacturing sector and the objective of the Soviet model is to achieve this expansion as fast as possible. The problem is how to finance the massive investment in industry that alone will make rapid growth possible given that the initial size of the industrial sector is small and hence that the volume of profits available for reinvestment is low. This problem was solved by the Russian economist Evgeny Preobrazhensky who argued that in a backward economy the state sector (industry) must be nourished by surpluses generated outside the state sector (i.e., in agriculture) until such time as the state sector was able to finance its own expansion out of profits generated within the state sector itself [15]. This is the famous "law of primitive socialist accumulation".

This then immediately gives us three features of the Soviet model, namely, (*i*) an emphasis on rapid industrialisation, (*ii*) a squeeze on agriculture and (*iii*) unusually high rates of capital accumulation at the expense of current consumption. The problem then arose as to how to translate a reduction in consumption into investment goods, i.e., in effect how to transform grain into machines. The obvious way would have been to export the grain and import the machines, but this avenue was closed to the Soviet Union by an economic embargo. Instead a policy of unbalanced growth was adopted in which investment in industry was concentrated on capital goods (broadly, heavy industry) to the neglect of consumer goods (broadly, light industry) [16]. Machines were used to make machines *ad infinitum*. The model thus acquired two additional general features: (*iv*) a presumption of autarky and a neglect of comparative costs even when the assumption of an autarkic economy no longer was necessary and (*v*) a tendency to create and perpetuate immense imbalances, not just of heavy over light industry, but of production over consumption, work over leisure, education over housing, etc.

It was not until about 1925 that the Soviet model began to be developed and applied in the Soviet Union. It was in that year that Stalin began to speak of "socialism in one country", of the need to become economically self-reliant, of the urgency (partly for military reasons) of developing the metal industries (particularly steel) and engineering (especially machine tools). Allocations via the market mechanism came to an end. Tight central planning was installed, prices and wages were fixed by the state and detailed allocations to state enterprises in quantitative, physical terms were introduced. The command economy was born. The state became all-powerful and coercive [17]. Grain shortages, however, emerged in urban areas and in 1928 Stalin argued in favour of large-scale farming in order to produce "the maximum quantity of marketable grain". The following year the Soviet model was completed by forced collectivisation of agriculture. Grain production fell, much hardship was inflicted upon the Russian peasantry and starvation occurred, but the marketable surplus was increased and industrialisation progressed. The model worked. Indeed, during the period when it was most fully implemented, 1928-37, and when the West was suffering from the Great Depression, GNP in the Soviet Union increased at least 6.2 per cent per annum. This is not spectacular growth, but it certainly was very rapid by the standards of the time.

The Soviet model no longer is fully applied in the Soviet Union and when it was introduced in Eastern Europe after the Second World War it varied slightly from one country to another. In broad terms, however, the strategy developed in the USSR during the 1920s and 1930s was adopted by all the Soviet bloc countries. Nonetheless, attempts have been made from time to time to reform the strategy and eliminate its worst features. None of the reforms has been wholly successful but the so-called "new economic mechanism" introduced in Hungary in 1968 deserves mention [18]. In a number of steps, some going forward, others backward, Hungary has ended compulsory planned output targets and administered allocations of materials. It has decentralised the economy and given factory managers much greater power over investment and production decisions. It has allowed private enterprise to develop and the country now has a substantial private sector consisting of shops, small manufacturing firms, construction teams, etc. Private hiring of wage labour even is allowed, although no more than, say, half a dozen employees are permitted in any one enterprise. Most important, many price controls have been abolished and the market mechanism has been given room in which to operate.

A great many problems remain to be solved. Domestic prices are not integrated with international (or border) prices. Incompatibilities have arisen between Hungary's trade regime and that of her Comecon neighbours. The reforms have not been fully and consistently applied and in particular the rules have been changed frequently, thereby creating much uncertainty. The problem of how to control state monopoly enterprises in a decentralised, market-guided socialist economy has not been solved. Nor has the problem been successfully resolved of how to prevent unacceptable inequalities from emerging. Finally, there is a conflict between the need (on grounds of efficiency) to allow unprofitable enterprises to go bankrupt and the desire (on social grounds) to prevent the unemployment of labour.

Despite all this, several gains have been recorded. The choice of goods to buy has increased, the quality of goods and services has improved and queues have diminished in number and length. Consumer preferences have begun to determine the composition of output rather than planners' preferences. None of this is captured in output and growth statistics although the well being of the population obviously has risen. The rate of growth, ironically, actually has fallen since the late 1970s, but this cannot be blamed on the reforms. Growth rates have fallen throughout Eastern (and Western) Europe and in the particular case of Hungary there was a sharp deterioration of 17 per cent in the country's terms of trade between 1975 and 1979.

Hungary thus shows that some reform within the Soviet model is possible and that the reforms are beneficial. It still is not clear, however, whether major systemic change within the Soviet model is feasible. Yugoslavia, in contrast, shows that an entirely different socialist strategy of development is possible based on greater use of the price mechanism and workers' self-management [19].

In a sense the Yugoslav model is at the opposite extreme from the Soviet model. The economy is completely decentralised. There is effectively no central planning and no mechanism for co-ordinating investment projects, even major ones. Political and economic power are highly devolved and the authority of the centre is weak. This undoubtedly has many advantages in a country composed of nine mutually antagonistic nationalities, but in a small country it also has economic disadvantages. Unlike the Soviet model, where great stress is placed on economies of scale in industry and agriculture, the Yugoslav model proceeds on the assumption that small is beautiful, always and everywhere. As a result, even where they exist, the advantages of large-scale production are unexploited. Moreover, complementarities between projects tend to be ignored and externalities overlooked. As in the other socialist countries, the investment rate is high and growth above average, but the allocation of investment is poor and the return on capital low. Like the other socialist countries, but for quite different reasons, it takes an exceptionally high rate of investment for any given rate of growth.

The most distinctive feature of the Yugoslav strategy of economic development is not, however, its high degree of decentralisation and greater reliance on prices to guide the economy but its adoption in the early 1950s of workers' control of collective enterprise. The workers do not own the enterprise in which they work, nor did they take the decision to establish it in the first place, but they do have responsibility for managing it. The firms of course have professional managers who execute policy, but the workers through their workers' councils participate in decision making and in making appointments. No doubt the managers have a great deal of power, since they are the only ones who have all the information necessary for taking informed decisions, and no doubt the participation of many workers is rather perfunctory, since they would rather do something else in their leisure time, but at least in principle the workers can exercise considerable influence over many of the things that affect their daily lives.

In practice what most affects their daily lives is their income and it is here that workers' self-management has made a difference to the overall performance of the economy. In contrast to a capitalist enterprise that maximises profits, a workers' self-managed enterprise will tend to maximise net income per worker. As a consequence of this, there will be a tendency to economise on labour, to reduce the number of workers entitled to a claim on the income of the enterprise. This in itself is perhaps not undesirable, since for any given level of output it minimises the number of employees and thereby helps to reduce costs and raise productivity.

203

The problem, however, is that if the workers' councils continuously try to economise on labour, this will introduce a bias in favour of a relatively high degree of mechanisation. That is, capital-labour ratios in collective enterprises will tend to be relatively high, indeed higher than warranted by the relative availability of labour. Put another way, for any given level of investment, the number of jobs created will tend to be less than the number of persons seeking work. The inevitable outcome is unemployment, and unemployment in Yugoslavia, compared to other socialist countries, has in fact been a major problem, despite the high rates of growth achieved and widespread emigration of labour to Western Europe. Indeed, unemployment in Yugoslavia is systemic, not cyclical, and arises from the way the industrial sector is organised.

Not only will workers' councils attempt to maximise net income per worker in the enterprise, they will also tend to take a short-term view and favour a high distribution ratio. There is a conflict of interest between the managers who will tend to favour retention of profits for reinvestment and expansion of the enterprise and the labour force who are likely to favour higher current wages. That is, managers will be under pressure to distribute most of the firm's income to the workforce, with the result that relatively little will be retained for reinvestment. One might imagine that this would result in a low rate of investment, but that is not so. Instead the firms finance their investment not from retained profits but by borrowing from the banking system. High borrowing then leads to inflation (since *ex ante* savings are insufficient to finance desired investment) and this, in turn, leads to a rise in imports and balance-of-payments problems. If the balance of payments deficit is covered by foreign borrowing, a debt crisis sooner or later is inevitable.

The inevitable is in fact what happened. Workers attempted to protect their real incomes and demanded higher money wages. This pushed up costs and prices and led to generalised inflation. The government tried to prevent inflation from accelerating partly by allowing the exchange rate to become overvalued, partly by relying on some price controls and partly by borrowing abroad. The result was a disaster. Inflation rose from an average of 16.5 per cent a year in 1974-79 to 30 per cent in 1980 and 52 per cent in 1984. The rate of growth of GDP fell from an average of 6.3 per cent a year in 1974-79 to 2.2 per cent in 1980 and a low of –1.3 per cent in 1983. Foreign debt rose from $6.6 billion in 1975 to 18.9 billion in 1980 [20].

The crisis, although partly conjunctural, exposed a contradiction at the heart of the Yugoslav strategy of economic development. On the one hand, the economy is decentralised and there is no effective central planning. But on the other hand, government intervention has meant that the price system is seriously distorted and market discipline is weak. Relative commodity prices fail to reflect costs, interest rates frequently are negative in real terms, the exchange rate is not adjusted to compensate for rises in domestic prices and the banking system is too expansionist and accommodating. Yet if the banking system pursues a restrictive monetary policy, the tendency of self-managed enterprises to retain only a small portion of their net income creates a danger that investment and growth will be low. If instead, the banking system readily finances investment demand from self-managed enterprises, the pressure of aggregate demand on resources will be excessive. In practice, wage and price inflation have been endemic. Job scarcity in the self-managed sector is systemic and this is not counterbalanced by the private sector, which is so severely constrained by government controls that it cannot absorb the unemployed. Thus the Yugoslav strategy of development is unique among socialist strategies in combining generally high rates of growth with high unemployment and high inflation.

The Chinese challenge to Soviet orthodoxy, however, was far more important than the Yugoslav, partly because China is a much larger and more important country and partly because China's poverty places her firmly in the Third World. Yugoslavia, however much it insists it is non-aligned, will always be European (and takes part in some of the work of the OECD) and can never realistically aspire to leadership of the left in Asia, Africa or Latin America. China obviously has the potential to be a natural leader, provided the country is able to devise a successful strategy of socialist development. Debate about strategy in China, however, has been fierce and perhaps in no other socialist country have politics and economic policy been so visibly entwined or so vigorously argued.

It has been claimed by some that the Chinese strategy as designed by Mao does not differ fundamentally from the Soviet model [21]. But this, surely, is a mistaken view. First of all, the Chinese began with a redistributive land reform (1949-52) which resulted in a fairly even distribution of the cultivated area and laid the foundation for egalitarian development within the rural areas. Second, the subsequent institutional transformation of the countryside – the formation of co-operatives (1954-56) and then of communes (in 1958 and reformed in 1962) – was done with the consent if not always the enthusiasm of the great majority of poor peasants [22]. Third, the purpose of the institutional transformation in the countryside was not to extract the largest possible marketable surplus of grain from the peasantry for the benefit of the industrial proletariat, but to provide a framework for comprehensive rural development. This does not mean that production quotas and the compulsory delivery of grain at fixed low prices were not imposed – they certainly were – but the desire of the authorities to extract grain to promote urban industrialisation was tempered by the fact that the Chinese revolution was a peasant revolution, not one led by an industrial proletariat. The political base of the regime thus was in the countryside and this put some constraints on the extent to which the livelihood of the huge rural population could be compressed. Even so, there was a huge famine in the early 1960s. Fourth, notwithstanding the famine, it was never part of the Chinese strategy to reduce the level of consumption of the population in order to achieve high rates of capital accumulation. On the contrary, the commune system was designed to put a floor under rural incomes and to bring about a high degree of equality in the distribution of income at the local level, i.e., within the production teams. In all these ways the Chinese model differs from the Soviet to such a degree that it becomes a difference in kind.

Consumption in China rose between 1949 and 1957 in both rural and urban areas. This was due in part to a massive redistribution of property income in favour of the poor. Land rents were transferred to landless agricultural labourers, tenants and small peasant farmers through the land reform. Profits on industrial and financial assets were transferred to the state and thence to the urban population through the nationalisation programme. Of course, some of the profits were used to increase investment but the level of consumption in the cities rose too. Consumption also rose, however, because of a massive increase in resource utilisation in rural and urban areas. The degree of capacity utilisation rose in industry and urban unemployment virtually disappeared until the new economic reforms were introduced after 1979; seasonally available "surplus" labour in the countryside was mobilised for a host of productive activities. Total output therefore increased and with it, aggregate consumption. Investment increased too of course. Indeed, investment grew much more rapidly than consumption and consequently the investment ratio rose and the consumption ratio fell, but average consumption per head was intended to rise and did so.

Mao Tse-Tung was in fact highly critical of the Soviet approach of "draining the pond to catch the fish", i.e., of squeezing consumption in agriculture in order to raise investment in industry.

The Chinese strategy, while giving priority to capital goods and intermediate industries, as in the Soviet model, envisages a much more balanced expansion of agriculture and industry. Furthermore, industrial growth is seen as interacting with agricultural growth in a mutually beneficial way, industry supplying agriculture with improved means of production and agriculture supplying raw materials and wage goods. This was made clear by Mao in 1955 when he wrote as follows:

> "Heavy industry, the most important branch of socialist industrialisation, produces for agricultural use tractors and other farm machinery, chemical fertilizer, modern means of transport, oil, electric power, etc., and all these things can be used, or used extensively, only on the basis of an agriculture where large-scale co-operative farming prevails. ... We must on no account regard industry and agriculture, socialist industrialisation and the socialist transformation of agriculture, as disconnected or isolated things, and on no account must we emphasize the one and play down the other" [23].

The Maoist ideal was never achieved, but compared to the Soviet model China did achieve more balanced growth.

The planning system in China, on the surface, was similar to that of the Soviet Union. Decisions about state-owned industry were taken at the centre and resources were allocated in physical, non-price terms within a set of material balances. However, comprehensive centralised planning based on material balances has never played the role in China that it does in the Soviet Union. First, for long periods targets were set not by economic planners but were determined politically and were restricted to a relatively small number of objectives. Comprehensiveness was replaced by selectivity. Second, during such periods the use of material balances was replaced by mass mobilisation of labour and orchestrated mass political campaigns. Economics gave way to politics. Third, during these periods the authority of the central bureaucracy declined and decision taking shifted to the local level, to self-sufficient and relatively autonomous localities, i.e., to counties and communes. The power of the central elite occasionally was countered by the power of local elites who had a better understanding and perhaps sympathy for the needs of the mass of the population.

At times – as in the great Leap Forward (1958-9), the famine that followed (1960-62) and during the Cultural Revolution (1966-76) – this utopian, romantic and "radical" streak [24] in the Maoist strategy led to disaster [25]. The core of good sense in the strategy, however, was in recognising the need to decentralise the economy and reduce the rigidities inherent in a system of quantitative allocation of resources by central planners. The Chinese, like the Yugoslavs, perceived the problem, but unlike the Yugoslavs, they attempted to decentralise while denying a significant role to the market [26]. That is, they attempted, unsuccessfully, to devise a decentralised system of planning. What they got instead, in the form of the rural communes, was an institution in which local self-reliance could be encouraged and in which local initiatives, experiments and decentralised decision making could in principle and sometimes did in practice take place.

The Chinese strategy of development "walked on two legs", not just in the original sense of simultaneously adopting advanced, capital-intensive technology and traditional, labour-intensive technology, but also in the sense of simultaneously encouraging the expansion of the state and collective sectors. The rural commune was much more than a large Soviet collective farm. It was both an agricultural unit and an institution designed to industrialise the countryside. It had responsibilities for production and for providing basic social services. It was charged with ensuring that minimum standards of consumption were maintained by every household and with mobilising resources for investment, including unemployed and underemployed labour. Finally, it acted not only as an economic institution but also as the instrument of local government. In practice of course its full potential seldom was realised, but in favourable circumstances it could produce remarkable results.

The incentive structure incorporated into the Chinese strategy of development was egalitarian. Rural-urban income differentials were not as great as in many other Third World countries. Within the urban areas, wage differentials in industry were narrow and the income differential between "manual" and "mental" workers was remarkably small. Indeed "manual" workers often were paid more than "mental" workers such as teachers and university professors and research workers. Within the commune, the work point system of payment ensured that inequalities of income were low. Material incentives were of course used, but they were supplemented by non-material rewards and penalties, exhortation and social pressure. Mao believed that socialism, by ending the major class conflicts and by creating an equal and fair society, would create an environment in which ordinary people would act together with a unity of purpose impossible under capitalism. The energy, enthusiasm, selflessness and creativity of the people would be released and development would proceed by leaps and bounds.

At times, it must be said, Mao's vision came close to being a reality. In extended bursts the people made enormous sacrifices and much good was achieved. But the effort could not be sustained indefinitely, nor could it always be channelled efficiently. There was much waste of energy and resources. In the end it was acknowledged by the authorities that the incentive system was defective, that resources were being misallocated and that a greater use of material incentives and the price mechanism would help to increase the well being of the Chinese people. An ambitious economic reform programme was launched in 1978, two years after Mao's death, which continues still.

The reformers have a difficult problem of how to overcome the inherent systemic flaws in the Chinese model. The weaknesses of comprehensive centralised economic planning are recognised and the Chinese have attempted to resolve these weaknesses in various ways. Sometimes planning has ceased to be comprehensive but instead has been selective. At other times it has ceased to be centralised but instead power has been devolved to the provinces or decentralised in other ways. Sometimes it has ceased to be economic, the authorities relying instead on political campaigns, ideological controls and mass mobilisation. Sometimes all of this has occurred at once and the country has fallen into anarchy. Always, however, as Carl Riskin has emphasized, the authorities have avoided relying on the market [27]. As a result, in periods when planning was discredited or failed to work as intended, the government had few economic instruments that could be used to achieve its objectives; it had no choice but to rely on political instruments and these proved to be ineffective and in the long run unacceptable. The reforms begun in 1978 thus can be seen as an attempt to move away both from political controls as a tool to guide the economy and from quantitative centralised planning, and instead to introduce the price mechanism and other indirect means of guidance. This represents a radical departure from nearly 30 years of socialist experience in China and the success of this important initiative is far from certain.

Our fourth example of a socialist strategy of development is that of North Korea. The Soviet Union under Stalin pursued a policy of "socialism in one country", but that was relatively easy to do because the USSR is a country of continental dimensions. North Korea, on the other hand, with a population of about 20 million, is a medium-sized country, yet it too has chosen to go it alone and pursue a policy of self-reliance (or as they call it, *juche*). Moreover, unlike, say, Burma, it appears to have been successful [28].

It is possible that North Korea's determination to be self-reliant arises from its intense nationalism. The nationalism, in turn, almost certainly is a product of Japanese colonialism. This is not to say that the Koreans did not have a strong sense of national identity prior to the Japanese occupation of the country in 1910, but the harshness of the Japanese regime and the attempt by the Japanese to suppress the Korean language and culture led to a vigorous reassertion of Korean nationalism at the time of liberation in 1945 and again at independence in 1948. In contrast to many Third World countries, independence in North Korea was not the culmination of a nationalist movement but a signal for a renewed nationalist struggle. Independence, far from being a joyful occasion, was a bitter one. Korea became a pawn in the politics of the Cold War, the ideological confrontation between the United States and the Soviet Union, and the country was divided in two along the 38th parallel.

The struggle for reunification began almost immediately and finally in June 1950, North Korea took the fateful decision to send its troops across the 38th parallel and try to reunify the country by force. There were popular uprisings throughout the South, the army of the southern government (Republic of Korea) disintegrated and within three months all of the country except for a perimeter around the port of Pusan was in northern hands. At that point the United States and its South Korean ally counterattacked under the banner of the United Nations.

The rest is history. The south was recovered, 90 per cent of the territory of the north was occupied for about three months by United Nations troops and the whole of North Korea was laid waste. Chinese forces intervened and after fierce fighting the *status quo ante* was restored. The legacy of the Korean War for North Korea was defeat, devastation and a great sense of vulnerability. The country withdrew into isolation determined to cultivate its own garden and build a strong industrial sector.

North Korea had in fact experienced rapid growth of mining and manufacturing during the Japanese colonial period. Investment in communications also had occurred. The agricultural sector, however, was relatively weak because the most fertile land was in the south and it was there that the Japanese concentrated their efforts to increase the production of rice for export. The Japanese took possession of large tracts of land throughout the country and after three decades of colonial rule the rate of tenancy for the whole of Korea was 77.2 per cent [29]. In North Korea, 4 per cent of farm households owned 58 per cent of the arable land at the time of liberation.

The North Korean development strategy, like the Chinese, began with a land reform. In October 1945 rents were forcibly reduced to 30 per cent of the harvest. This was followed five months later, in March 1946, with a radical redistributive programme. About 95 per cent of all land rented out was confiscated and this was equivalent to 54 per cent of all cultivated land. The confiscated land was then given to tenants and poor peasants and in the end 76 per cent of all peasant households received some land. Collectivisation of agriculture did not occur until after the Korean War, in the period 1953-58.

The industrial reforms followed the redistributive land reform. In August 1946, industrial and other assets equivalent to 80.2 per cent of gross industrial output value were confiscated and used to form the basis of state-owned industry. Thenceforward North Korea clearly had a socialist economy, but at that stage the economy was of the conventional Soviet type. *Juche* had not yet been articulated as an alternative development strategy within a socialist framework. Nor had the extraordinary cult of Kim Il Sung appeared.

In fact it was not until 1955, after the Korean War, that *juche* as a strategy of economic development was properly formulated and achieved primacy. Prior to that time, as Gordon White argues, *juche* had been "an important component of modern Korean nationalist ideology, shared by communists and non-communists alike" [30]. The notion of self-reliance had played a role in "psychological decolonization" [31], but it was not until after defeat in the Korean War produced a reaction against relying further on the Soviet Union, a reaction that was entirely predictable given its proven unreliability as an ally during the war, that *juche* became the basis for government policy.

Three basic aspects of North Korea's strategy of self-reliance have been identified [32]. First, the resources to finance a high rate of capital accumulation should be generated internally. The country should not rely on foreign aid, although moderate amounts are acceptable. Foreign direct investment should be avoided, but some foreign borrowing is permissible. In practice the rate of domestic savings has been quite high, between 25 and 35 per cent of total product, and hence the country has been able to finance its own growth. It did, however, borrow heavily after the sharp increase in world oil prices in 1973 and ran into a severe repayment problem in the mid-1970s.

Second, the country should seek to develop a comprehensive, diversified and integrated national economy. The principle of specialisation along the lines of comparative advantage was explicitly rejected on grounds that it would result in a lopsided economy. North Korea did not wish to be without a modern manufacturing sector and feared that too close an integration into the world economy, or even into the socialist trading system of Comecon, inevitably would result in external dependence and vulnerability. It did not for that reason agree to become a full member of Comecon. Instead it deliberately reduced the share of foreign trade in total product and then kept it low, although it is impossible to make accurate estimates of the share of trade in GNP. Furthermore, North Korea has tried to avoid becoming dependent on any one trading partner. It remained neutral during the Sino-Soviet dispute and trades with both China and the Soviet Union. When the political climate in the West improved, North Korea diversified its trading partners and in particular developed important trading links with Japan. In 1970 about 83 per cent of North Korea's trade was with other socialist countries, but by 1975 the proportion had fallen to 57 per cent [33].

Self-reliance in the manufacturing sector began with the Three-Year Plan (1954-56). Heavy industry was given priority over light industry which in turn was given priority over agriculture. The disproportions in North Korea were not however as great as in the early period of industrialisation in China (1953-57). North Korea followed a sectorally more balanced development path. The result was a highly diversified industrial sector which was geographically dispersed. The country is 98 per cent self-sufficient in machine tools and exports a wide range of industrial products, e.g., rolled steel, electric motors and transformers, as well as of course the traditional mineral ores. Employment in industry increased from 12 per cent of the labour force in 1946 to 23 per cent in 1965 to 30 per cent in 1980. The proportion of the labour force engaged in industrial activities in North Korea is now about twice that in other Third World countries of a comparable per capita income. Parallel to the rise in industrial employment was an increase in urbanisation. Between 1953 and 1980 the urban population increased from about 18 per cent of the total to 63 per cent, again well above the average of comparable Third World countries.

The third basic aspect of the country's strategy of development is reliance on domestic sources of food, raw materials and fuel. We saw earlier that the development strategy began with a land reform. Agriculture was then supported with massive investment in irrigation and later in machinery. As a result, agricultural production grew rapidly and North Korea was able to compensate for the loss of the main food growing areas to South Korea. Indeed the country became self-sufficient in food grains in 1969.

A more difficult problem was how to be self-reliant in fuels given that North Korea has no oil and that modern industrial economies tend to be based on oil. The approach adopted was to minimise the demand for petroleum products and concentrate on developing the country's resources of coal. The approach succeeded and as a result North Korea's energy profile is very different from that of most countries. In the world as a whole in 1980, petroleum and natural gas acounted for about 72.6 per cent of energy consumption; in North Korea they account for 5-10 per cent, all of which is imported. Conversely, in the world as a whole, solid fuels account for 18.4 per cent of total energy consumption whereas in North Korea 70-80 per cent of the country's commercial energy comes from coal [34].

Not only has North Korea become self-reliant in fuels, it has done so while developing a very energy-intensive economy. Average per capita consumption of energy in the country in 1984 was 2 058 kilograms of oil equivalent. This compares with an average of 743 kilograms in the middle-income economies and only 288 kilograms in the low-income economies! [35]. Evidently self-reliance in fuels has not been obtained at the cost of restricted consumption.

In summary, North Korea shows that economic self-reliance in a medium-sized country is possible. The particular strategy followed in North Korea probably was historically determined and then strongly influenced by the political ambitions and style of the leadership. It therefore is unlikely to be copied by other countries. Even so, North Korea's experience is interesting because it demonstrates how far from an open economy it is possible to go. Self-reliance is not autarky, but it does imply developing a broadly-based and well-integrated economy. Provided domestic resources are mobilised for a high rate of capital formation such an economy is capable of rapid growth. In the short term there are bound to be costs in terms of lower allocative efficiency but this may be more than compensated by the long-term rise in per capita income. Such a strategy can increase the autonomy and economic independence of medium-sized countries, and possibly give them more room for political manoeuvre in a turbulent world, although it cannot insulate a country completely from disturbances originating in the international economy.

Investment and industrial production

We have seen that without exception socialist strategies of development have aimed for high rates of capital formation and high rates of growth of industrial output. The data in Table 8.4 will help us to see to what extent they have been successful in attaining these objectives. The Table is divided into four sections corresponding to the four distinct socialist strategies that have been identified, China, North Korea, the USSR (and six Eastern European countries following the Soviet model) and Yugoslavia.

The first column of the Table contains information on gross domestic investment. As can be seen, gross investment in 1979 represented a high proportion of gross domestic product in all of the countries included in the Table. Indeed in China, North Korea and

Yugoslavia the rate of investment was more than 30 per cent; in the Soviet Union it was 24 per cent and in Eastern Europe it varied between 24 per cent in Czechoslovakia and 37 per cent in Hungary. These figures can be compared with investment coefficients of 24 per cent in India; 18 per cent in the other low-income countries; 26 per cent in the middle-income countries and 23 per cent in the advanced capitalist economies [36]. It is evident therefore that the strategies of development adopted by the socialist countries have indeed resulted in comparatively high rates of capital formation.

Table 8.4 **CAPITAL FORMATION AND INDUSTRIAL GROWTH**

	(1) Gross domestic investment, 1979 (Per cent of GDP)	(2) Gross industrial output, 1963-85 (Per cent per annum)
China	31	10.4 c
North Korea	32 a	14.4 d
USSR	24	6.2
Bulgaria	35 b	8.1
Czechoslovakia	24	5.5
East Germany	31 b	5.7
Hungary	37	4.6
Poland	26	6.3
Romania	35	10.8 c
Yugoslavia	38	6.6

a) 1978.
b) Gross fixed capital formation as percentage of net material product, 1976-81.
c) 1963-84.
d) 1965-82.
Sources: Col. (1): IBRD, *World Development Report 1981*, Oxford University Press, 1981; UNECE, *Economic Survey of Europe in 1985-1986*, New York, 1986; M. Bienefeld and M. Godfrey, eds., *The Struggle for Development*, Chichester, John Wiley, 1982, Appendix Table 5, p. 359.
Col. (2): UN, *Monthly Bulletin of Statistics*, various issues; UN, *Statistical Yearbook*, various issues; UNECE, *Economic Survey of Europe in 1985-1986;* M. Bienefeld and M. Godfrey, eds., *op.cit.;* Government of China, *Statistical Yearbook of China*, 1985; US Central Intelligence Agency, *Handbook of Economic Statistics 1984*, Washington, September 1984.

They have also resulted in high rates of growth of industrial output. The second column of the Table shows this clearly. The period covered includes for almost all the countries the first half of the 1980s, when industrial output actually fell for a while in Hungary and Poland and when in most other socialist countries the rate of growth of output was well below previous trends. Nonetheless, the performance of the industrial sector over the twenty years or so included in the Table is impressive. In China the growth rate of industry was 10.4 per cent per annum; in North Korea, 14.4 per cent. Among the major Third World countries only Indonesia and South Korea can compare. Industrial growth in India, Pakistan, Egypt, Nigeria and Brazil (and even Hong Kong but not Singapore) was noticeably below these rates.

Industrial growth in Yugoslavia (6.6 per cent per annum) and the Soviet Union (6.2 per cent) was more rapid than the average of the Third World and much more rapid than the average of the advanced capitalist economies, but it was of the same order of magnitude as the rate of growth achieved in, say, Sri Lanka, the Philippines and Mexico. Similarly, gross value of output in industry increased 6.3 per cent a year in Cuba during 1965-84 [37]. The growth rates in Eastern Europe varied between 4.6 per cent a year in Hungary (which was a mediocre performance by world standards) and 10.8 per cent in Romania. The unweighted average of the rate of growth in the six Eastern European countries is 6.8 per cent a year, which is good by world standards.

The problem in the socialist countries has not been slow rates of growth of industrial output. Rather it has been a slow pace of technical change and consequently a tendency for the productivity of capital to decline. For example, during the period 1976-84 the ratio of gross industrial output to fixed capital declined on average each year by the following percentages [38]:

USSR	−2.9
Bulgaria	−2.5
Czechoslovakia	−2.0
East Germany	−1.1
Hungary	−3.2
Poland	−3.3
Romania	−2.9

Although it cannot be documented so neatly, it appears that the productivity of capital in the industrial sector also has been falling in China [39].

In addition to problems of capital productivity, the industrial sector of many socialist countries has suffered from a lack of flexibility and an inability to match supply to demand. As a result, there are surpluses of some products (and an unplanned accumulation of unsold stocks) and great shortages of others (as reflected in long delivery dates and, for final consumers, queues). Finally, there are problems of low quality and lack of variety in all branches of industry, not just in consumer goods. It is for these reasons, and not because of slow growth, that many socialist countries are seeking ways to improve the performace of their industrial sector.

Socialist agriculture in practice

It is widely believed that the performance of the agricultural sector in socialist countries has been poor and that therefore socialist agricultural organisation has been shown to be a failure. These statements however are misleading for a number of reasons. First, there are in principle several different forms of socialist agricultural organisation, e.g., state farms, small producer co-operatives, large collectives, communes. There is no single arrangement that one can identify as typical of socialist agriculture. Second, in practice socialist countries have adopted a variety of institutional forms, not all of them socialist. For example, state farms now predominate in the Soviet Union; elsewhere they tend to be of relatively minor significance. Large collectives, as in Hungary, have been characteristic of most Eastern European countries, but even there the precise institutional arrangements have varied considerably from one country to another. The co-operative was dominant in Vietnam from 1958 to the late 1970s and the commune was dominant in China from 1958 until 1979. Small peasant holdings farming collectively-owned land under contract are now almost universal in China and similar arrangements are increasingly common in Vietnam. In Poland and Yugoslavia agriculture is largely a private sector activity.

212

Table 8.5 **TREND RATES OF GROWTH OF AGRICULTURAL OUTPUT, 1966-1985**
Per cent per annum

	Total agricultural production	Per capita agricultural production
China	3.7	1.6
Cuba	2.2	0.9
Kampuchea *a*	1.2	−2.0
Mongolia	1.6	−1.4
North Korea	5.0	2.3
Vietnam *a*	5.2	2.3
Albania	3.1	0.8
Bulgaria	1.5	1.0
Czechoslovakia	2.5	2.1
East Germany	1.5	1.6
Hungary	2.9	2.7
Poland	1.0	0.2
Romania	3.5	2.5
USSR	1.5	0.6
Yugoslavia	2.1	1.3

a) 1974-85.
Sources: FAO, *Production Yearbook 1985*, Vol. 39, 1986 and *Production Yearbook 1977*, Vol. 31, 1978.

Third, in practice the long-term rate of growth of agricultural output in socialist countries has exhibited a wide range. The first column of Table 8.5 indicates that over the period 1966 to 1985, virtually two decades, the trend rate of growth varied from a low of one per cent per annum in Poland to 5 per cent in North Korea. Vietnam did even better, viz., 5.2 per cent a year, but the period covered by the data is relatively short (1974-85) and may contain a large element reflecting a recovery from the Vietnam War. Fourth, the unweighted average rate of growth of total agricultural output of the 15 countries in the Table is 2.6 per cent a year. A weighted average would of course be substantially higher because the rapid growth in China of 3.7 per cent a year would exert a very large influence. Fifth, if one focuses on the six Third World countries in the upper portion of the Table, the unweighted average rate of growth is a quite impressive 3.15 per cent per annum.

The well being of the population, however, depends more on the rate of growth of agricultural output per head than it does on the rate of growth of total agricultural output. The second column in the Table contains per capita growth rates. Again it is clear, sixth, that performance has varied enormously within the group of socialist countries. At one extreme is Hungary where per capita agricultural output has grown 2.7 per cent a year for two decades. This is the great agricultural success story of Eastern Europe. The co-operatives are autonomous entities, free to make their own decisions, and guided not by quotas but by prices. They have done very well. At the other extreme are Kampuchea and Mongolia where the trend rate of growth per head has been sharply negative. Kampuchea and Mongolia, however, are special cases: Kampuchea has yet to recover from a devastating war and Mongolia is traditionally a nomadic country where agriculture in the narrow sense of crop cultivation is of little significance. Seventh, the unweighted average of the rate of growth of agricultural production per head of the 15 countries is 1.1 per cent per annum. This is a far higher rate of growth than the average achieved by the capitalist Third World countries. And again, a weighted average of per capita growth rates would make the contrast between the two groups of countries even sharper. Finally, if one considers the six Third World countries in the Table and calculates an average of their rates of growth, then agricultural performance in the Third World socialist countries (0.6 per cent per annum per capita) approximates that of the capitalist Third World countries. Note, however, that this comparability of results can be obtained only by not excluding the two small socialist countries that clearly are special cases (Kampuchea and Mongolia) and by not taking a weighted average [40]. That is, the results can be made to appear to be similar for the two groups of countries only if the calculations are strongly biased against the socialist countries. On any reasonable calculation it must be concluded that per capita growth in the socialist Third World countries has been faster than the average in the capitalist Third World countries.

The problem in the socialist countries is not that agriculture has grown slowly compared to the non-socialist countries, but that it has grown slowly compared to the rate of growth of the non-agricultural sector in socialist countries [41]. That is, the problem arises from a development strategy which gives excessive priority to industry over agriculture. Pronounced unbalanced growth in favour of manufacturing has resulted in chronic food shortages. Income per head has risen rapidly and agricultural output per head also has risen, but it has not risen fast enough to eliminate an excess demand for food.

Imagine a simple economy [42] consisting of a food sector (f) and a non-food or manufacturing sector (m). Assume that the f-sector accounts for 30 per cent of total product and is growing 2.5 per cent a year. The m-sector accounts for the remaining 70 per cent of total product and let us assume is growing 7.0 per cent a year. The rate of growth of total product (g) is a weighted average of the sectoral growth rates. Thus

$$g = af + (1-a)m,$$

where a = the share of food in total output.

Under our assumptions g = 5.65.

Next assume that the population growth rate (p) is 1.5 per cent a year. The growth of per capita income (y) = (g-p) is therefore 4.15 per cent a year. And the growth of food output per head (f-p) is one per cent a year.

The rate of growth of the demand for food (f*) depends upon the rate of growth of the population, the rate of growth of per capita income and the income elasticity of demand for food (e). Specifically,

$$f* = p + ey.$$

Let us be relatively conservative and assume that e = 0.5. Under these assumptions f* = 3.6. That is, the demand for food grows 44 per cent faster than the supply notwithstanding the fact that per capita food production is rising steadily year by year. There is a major structural disequilibrium in the economy.

There are basically three ways in which the disequilibrium can be eliminated. First, the country can satisfy the demand for food by importing supplies from abroad. This is the solution the Soviet Union has adopted. Provided exports from the m-sector expand fast enough, this is a perfectly viable solution. If exports do not grow rapidly, however, the country will encounter balance-of-payments difficulties which in the long run will be aggravated if the short-term deficit is covered by foreign borrowing. A second alternative is to raise the relative price of food paid by consumers, thereby cutting off demand and redistributing income to those who spend a below average proportion of their income on food. This is the policy that was attempted in Poland. The danger is that those who spend a high proportion of their income on food, i.e., the relatively poor, will resist the cut in their real incomes. Either civil disorder or a general wage-push inflation could then result. The third way to eliminate the disequilibrium is by changing development priorities, increasing the emphasis given to agriculture in the hope that this will result in an acceleration in the sector's rate of growth. This is the solution that has been followed in China, so far with considerable success [43].

There are reasons to believe that socialist co-operatives, collectives and communes can make a major contribution to rural development [44]. They can organise the purchase of material inputs, help in marketing output, provide credit and purchase and maintain agricultural machinery for the general benefit of the agricultural community. They can take on the responsibility for managing large and complex irrigation systems. They can mobilise seasonably available labour for investment in public works projects. They can promote small-scale rural industries. And they can provide an institutional framework for the delivery of basic public services – primary education, preventive and simple curative medicine, family planning services and creches for infants of working mothers. All of these tasks can be efficiently organised on a collective basis.

Experience of the socialist countries indicates, however, that collective farming in the narrow sense is unlikely to be efficient. There are few economies of scale in cultivation, weeding, harvesting, threshing, etc., particularly in Third World countries where factor proportions favour labour-intensive methods of farming. Thus there are few if any advantages from large-scale cultivation as such. Moreover in practice collective farming has encountered serious problems of allocative inefficiency. In the majority of countries the connection between individual effort and reward has been weak. Worker incentives have been poor and in consequence the quality of effort as well as the amount of effort has been disappointing. Where governments have responded to a defective incentive system by dictating instructions to collectives or communes that has only made matters worse. Agriculture does not respond well to commands from bureaucrats who are unable to take into account such things as daily changes in the weather or variations in soil fertility from one field to another.

Very serious problems can arise if the commands from policy makers cause widespread disruption of agricultural production. A horrific example is the great famine in China of 1960-62. It is now believed that the famine was a product not just of nature but of bad government policies [45]. First, the food production system was severely damaged during the Great Leap Forward when labour was reallocated away from farming toward capital construction projects and rural industrialisation. The authorities apparently were not aware that "surplus" labour was largely a seasonal phenomenon and any permanent withdrawal of labour from farming on a large scale would affect production. Second, despite the falling production, the government increased the pressure on food producers by raising grain procurements absolutely (and also of course relatively to total supply). Third, the government then distributed these higher grain procurements to the cities. As a result the peasantry starved by the millions. Indeed, 15 million people may have died in the famine.

Since 1979, however, the Chinese government has moved away from "commandism" in the rural areas and has almost completely abandoned collective cultivation of the land. Instead a small peasant farming system has been created which is not so different from the system that prevailed prior to the formation of the first co-operatives in 1954. But in some regions at least, e.g., in Xinjiang, some collective organisations have been retained [46]. In fact there is scattered evidence from several parts of China that collective activities in capital construction, irrigation management, reafforestation and in the pastoral economy are still very important. But in many areas even essential collective activities have been run down or dismantled in the rush to establish the household as the dominant economic unit in rural areas, and this is beginning to be recognised as causing problems for the success of the reforms. It may be that the Chinese are still seeking a way to combine the advantages of co-operation in investment and in the management of certain assets with the undoubted advantages of small peasant farms.

Social services and the distribution of income

A feature of the development strategy followed by all socialist countries is an emphasis on collective services as opposed to private ones: good public transport but few private automobiles, child care centres but very scarce housing, an equitable public food distribution system but relatively few private restaurants. Moreover within the public services emphasis tends to be placed on providing benefits for the mass of the people rather than on catering to the specific needs and wishes of individuals considered one by one: preventive medicine as opposed to heart transplant surgery, large primary and secondary education sectors but a relatively small university sector, good public sports facilities but few ladies' hairdressers. In practice the urban population has been better served than the rural, but the rural population has been better served than their counterparts in most other Third World countries.

This emphasis on the provision of basic social services to the entire population has enabled the socialist countries to score highly on many indicators of the quality of life (see Table 8.6). For example, infant mortality rates and maternal death rates tend to be much lower in socialist countries than in the average Third World country. Only Kampuchea has an infant mortality rate similar to that of the least developed capitalist Third World countries. Medical care in the socialist countries is given high priority and this is reflected in the large number of nurses, paramedical personnel, barefoot doctors and physicians per 10 000 population. It is also reflected in concern to provide a healthy environment (clean water, proper drainage) and in the widespread geographical distribution of medical facilities. Health care is not concentrated in the major cities to the neglect of the countryside. In the average Third World country there are about 5 000 people per physician, but no socialist country on our list has a ratio as high as that. Vietnam comes fairly close and data on Kampuchea are missing, but China, Cuba and Mongolia have many fewer persons per physician than is typical of countries at their level of average income per head. As a result, life expectancy at birth in the socialist countries tends to be between 60 and 70 years whereas in the Third World in general it tends to be between 50 and 60. That is, on average people in the socialist Third World countries tend to live ten years longer or more than people in other Third World countries.

Turning to education, it can be seen from the fourth column of the Table that primary education is virtually universal in the socialist countries. It also is virtually universal in the middle-income economies, but in the low-income Third World countries only about three-quarters of the children of primary school age actually go to school. The contrast is even more marked in secondary education. Cuba and Mongolia provide a secondary education to 74 and 86 per cent respectively of the relevant age group, whereas less than half of the children of secondary school age in the average middle-income economy actually go to school. In the low-income economies roughly a quarter go to secondary school as compared to 35 per cent in China and 48 per cent in Vietnam.

Table 8.6 INDICATORS OF THE QUALITY OF LIFE IN SOCIALIST COUNTRIES

	Infant mortality, 1980-85 (Per 1 000 births)	Population per physician, 1981	Life expectancy at birth, 1980-85 (Years)	Primary school enrolment, 1983 (Per cent of age group)	Secondary school enrolment, 1983
China	39	1730	67.8	104	35
Cuba	17	600	73.4	108	74
Kampuchea	160	n.a.	43.4	77 b	9 b
Mongolia	53	440	62.0	106	86
North Korea	30	n.a.	67.7	n.a.	n.a.
Vietnam	50 a	4310	58.8	113	48
Albania	45	n.a.	70.9	101	67
Bulgaria	18	400	71.6	101	85
Czechoslovakia	16	350	71.0	88	45
East Germany	11	490	72.1	95	88
Hungary	20	320	70.3	101	74
Poland	20	550	71.2	101	75
Romania	26	650	70.2	99	63
USSR	25	260	70.9	106	99
Yugoslavia	30	670	70.7	101	82

a) 1984.
b) 1965.

Sources: United Nations, *World Population Prospects: Estimates and Projections as Assessed in 1984*, New York, 1986; IBRD, *World Development Report 1986*, Oxford University Press, 1986.

The generous provision of social services – not just health and education, but also family planning and public food distribution programmes – helps to set a floor to the incomes of the least well-off households. Policies to provide employment to the unemployed also play an important role.

One of the characteristics of some socialist countries is an apparent scarcity of labour. This is due in part to the slow growth of the population and labour force, but more significant are government measures which ensure full employment. With the exception of Yugoslavia, where unemployment is relatively high, urban unemployment in most socialist countries is low. Indeed in several countries it is common for workers to have more than one job. From a production point of view it can be argued that in many state enterprises there is excessive employment in the sense that there is featherbedding and many workers contribute little to output. Thus the productivity of labour is relatively low. But from an income point of view these jobs provide a livelihood to people who might otherwise be unemployed. In China the economic reforms have eased controls on rural to urban migration and within the state enterprise sector greater flexibility has been introduced into the labour market. The result has been a rise in urban unemployment. The authorities have responded, however, by encouraging the neighbourhood committees to assist the "job-waiting youths", i.e., the unemployed, to establish small co-operative as well as private enterprises of their own. Most of these small enterprises are in service activities – restaurants, repair shops, etc. – and provide goods and services for which there is much demand.

In the countryside, the co-operatives and collectives of socialist countries have absorbed underemployed labour in a host of activities: capital construction projects, small-scale rural industry and "sideline" occupations of various sorts. As a result, the economy of the rural areas is more diversified than it otherwise would be and the amount of seasonal unemployment is relatively small. The rural economy is no longer synonymous with agriculture.

The combination of all these policies has helped to reduce and in some countries eliminate the worst forms of poverty and degradation. The implication is that the share of the lowest income groups in socialist countries must be higher than in the typical non-socialist country. Moreover, because most productive assets are either collectively owned or owned by the state, income from property is not a major source of inequality. The implication is that the share of the very rich in socialist countries (say, the top 5 per cent of the population) is likely to be lower than in non-socialist countries. The net effect of a higher share for the very poor and a smaller share for the very rich should be a more equal distribution of total income.

Unfortunately, there is very little data on the distribution of income in socialist countries and hence it is impossible to be certain that the degree of equality is greater there than in the typical Third World country. Some evidence, however, has been assembled in Table 8.7. This evidence must be interpreted with great caution since some of it refers to the distribution of income among individuals while some refers to the distribution among households and is uncorrected for the size of household. Some of the data represent income before taxes and some after the payment of direct taxes. Some takes account of the non-monetary income of the elite but none accurately reflects transfers in kind (public expenditure on health, education, etc.) or the incidence of indirect taxation. The data in the Table probably overstate the degree of inequality in living standards rather than the reverse, but one cannot be sure of this [47].

Several interesting points arise from the Table. First, from column (2) one can see that the share of the poorest 20 per cent of the population varies from 6.6 per cent in Yugoslavia to 11.2 per cent in Czechoslovakia. The average seems to be about 8.5 per cent. This is a much higher share for the poor than one normally finds in Third World countries, and is higher than the share in Sri Lanka, a country which has followed at least in part a redistributive strategy of development [48]. Second, the two socialist countries where the share of the poor is lowest, namely Yugoslavia and Hungary, are countries which have gone furthest in allowing market forces to determine the allocation of resources and incomes. The share of the poor in those two countries is not noticeably different from that in several Asian countries such as Bangladesh, India and Indonesia.

Table 8.7 **THE DISTRIBUTION OF INCOME IN SOCIALIST COUNTRIES**

	(1) Year	(2) Poorest 20%	(3) Middle 60%	(4) Richest 20%	(5) (4)/(2)	(6) Gini coefficient
China	1979	n.a.	n.a.	n.a.	n.a.	0.33
Cuba a	1973	7.8	57.2	35.0	4.5	0.27
Czechoslovakia b	1973	11.2	54.5	34.3	3.1	0.22
East Germany a	1972	9.6	51.0	39.4	4.1	0.28
Hungary a	1982	6.9	57.3	35.8	5.2	0.28
Poland b	1975	8.4	50.9	40.7	4.8	0.31
Romania-Bulgaria a	1970	9.3	53.8	36.9	4.0	0.27
USSR b	1973	8.5	50.6	40.9	4.8	0.31
Yugoslavia a	1978	6.6	54.7	38.7	5.9	0.31

a) Households.
b) Per capita individual income.
Sources: US Central Intelligence Agency, *The Cuban Economy: A Statistical Review*, Washington, D.C., 1981; IBRD, *World Development Report 1986*, Oxford University Press, 1986; Christian Morrisson, "Income Distribution in East European and Western Countries", *Journal of Comparative Economics*, Vol. 8, 1984; IBRD, *China: Socialist Economic Development*, Baltimore, Johns Hopkins University Press, 1983, p. 64.

Third, turning to the share of the richest 20 per cent of the population in column (4), one can see that the range is from a low of 34.3 per cent in Czechoslovakia to a high of 40.9 per cent in the USSR. The average for the eight countries for which there are data is 37.7 per cent. This is a much smaller share for "the rich" than one finds in a typical Third World country, even in a relatively egalitarian one such as Sri Lanka. The abolition of large private incomes from property seems indeed to make a difference. Fourth, in column (5) we present the ratio of the share of income received by the upper quintile, i.e., "the rich", to that received by the lower quintile, "the poor". The smallest ratio is 3.1 in Czechoslovakia, indicating that the incomes of the rich on average are just over three times larger than the incomes of the poor. At the top end of the range is Yugoslavia where the ratio is 5.9, indicating that the rich receive on average just under six times as much as the poor. These ratios are considerably lower than those found in most Third World countries, although the ratio in Sri Lanka is actually fractionally lower than that in Yugoslavia.

Lastly, in column (6) we present Gini coefficients in order to provide an overall measure of the degree of inequality. The most equal distribution of income is in Czechoslovakia, where the Gini coefficient is only 0.22. The greatest inequality is in Poland, the USSR and Yugoslavia where the coefficient is 0.31, and in China where the coefficient is 0.33. Again, these coefficients are very low by the standards of non-socialist Third World countries. Only Taiwan, with a Gini coefficient of 0.29 in 1976, can match the socialist countries. The next best capitalist country, Sri Lanka, had a coefficient of 0.34, placing it outside the range bound in socialist countries. The Gini coefficient in South Korea, another relatively egalitarian non-socialist country, was 0.38 in 1976, substantially higher than in any of the socialist countries for which we have data [49].

There is almost no evidence on changes in the extent of inequality in socialist countries over time. In the Soviet Union there are fluctuations in the degree of inequality in response to changes in government policy, but apparently no trend is discernible [50]. In Hungary it is likely that the economic reforms have led to some increase in inequality although it is not possible to document this fully. In China there is a great debate about the effects of the reforms on the distribution of income. Most observers, including the Chinese authorities, expect income differentials to widen, but it is conceivable that this may turn out not to be correct. The urban reforms have resulted in higher incomes in the collectives and a reduction in wage differentials between workers in the state enterprises and in the collective sector. Thus urban inequality probably has diminished. The improved agricultural terms of trade have certainly reduced rural-urban inequality. Within the rural areas the introduction of the "responsibility system" may by now have led to increased inequality, but in the short run there are reasons to believe that inequality actually declined, at least at the local level [51]. Indeed, a recent study by the World Bank indicates that the Gini coefficient for the distribution of rural income fell in the years immediately after the economic reforms were introduced [52]:

1979	0.26
1980	0.24
1981	0.23
1982	0.23

If subsequent research confirms this finding and contrary to expectations shows that it has continued, it will have major implications for our understanding of the consequences of economic reform in socialist Third World countries. For the time being, however, there still are doubts about overall trends in the distribution of income in China.

Conclusions

There is more than one strategy of socialist economic development and each differs from the others in non-trivial ways. All of them, however, differ in fundamental ways from capitalist strategies of development. An assessment of socialist strategies cannot be based purely on internal factors since the strategies were strongly affected by the international context and the military situation at the time they were adopted. Moreover the strategies cannot be assessed purely in economic terms since politics and economics under socialism are inextricably intertwined. Some sections of the population clearly found the creation of a socialist state in their country intolerable and in Cuba, for instance, about 10 per cent of the population emigrated after the socialist revolution. This cannot be disregarded.

Similarly, one cannot ignore the fact that in China since 1979 and more recently in the Soviet Union the leadership has been trying to introduce major economic and political reforms. Pressure for reform also exists in Vietnam and several of the Eastern European countries. This is strong *prima facie* evidence of discontent with the way the system has been functioning. Certainly Stalinist tactics have been repudiated in the majority of socialist countries; Albania and North Korea are exceptions. None of this implies, however, that socialism has been repudiated or that some socialist countries want to become capitalist. There is no evidence of that.

The growth performance in socialist countries has been good and on the whole better than in the non-socialist countries. Social policies have resulted in relatively slow population growth and hence the growth of income per head has been quite high. It can be argued that economic performance has not been good enough given the high costs of growth (in both economic and political terms), but it cannot reasonably be argued that aggregate rates of growth under socialism tend to be lower than under other systems.

A primary objective in most socialist countries has been rapid industrial expansion and in general this objective has been achieved. Technical change, however, has been disappointingly slow and in consequence the productivity of industrial investment has tended to fall. The implication of this is that unless the proportion of total product allocated to capital formation rises from its already high level, the rate of growth of industrial output will gradually decline. Agricultural growth has been rapid by world standards, but even so it has expanded too slowly to satisfy the demand created by rapidly rising incomes per head. Agriculture has performed poorly given the high rate of growth in the non-agricultural sectors and this suggests that in most socialist countries a structural disequilibrium will persist unless priorities are changed to favour accelerated growth of agricultural production.

The experience of the socialist countries indicates that collective farming tends to be inefficient and particularly in low-income socialist countries a case can be made for small-scale cultivation based on the peasant household. This does not mean, however, that communal, collective or co-operative institutions have no role to play. On the contrary, the socialist experience shows quite clearly that strong rural organisations can contribute much to rural development, both in terms of achieving acceptable rates of growth in rural incomes and in ensuring that the fruits of growth are equitably distributed.

It is widely believed that the socialist economies are essentially closed economies and that they ignore opportunities to exploit their comparative advantage by engaging in international trade. This is at best only a half-truth. First, the ratio of exports to gross domestic product in socialist countries varies enormously, viz., from 5 per cent in the USSR to 30 per cent or more in Cuba, Hungary and Yugoslavia (see Table 8.8). Secondly, the export ratio in socialist countries sometimes is higher than in comparable non-socialist countries. The ratio of exports to GDP is much higher in China than in India, for example. Similarly, the Cuban ratio is higher than that of the average middle-income economy. Third, a major difference, however, is that a high proportion of socialist trade tends to be with other socialist countries and hence is not genuinely multilateral as in the West. But this feature of socialist trading patterns is gradually changing and in the last fifteen years socialist trade with the non-socialist world has expanded more rapidly than intra-socialist bloc trade.

Fourth, in the period 1973-84, the quantity of exports from socialist countries has grown more rapidly than the 3.2 per cent rate of growth of the volume of total world trade. That is the share of the socialist countries in the volume of world trade is tending to rise slowly. Only Poland and Romania have experienced a decline in their share of world trade although Hungary has experienced great difficulty because of a deterioration in its terms of trade. Finally, the available evidence in the final column of Table 8.8 suggests that in recent years the socialist economies have become more open. Only in Romania has the quantity of exports grown less rapidly than total product. In the Soviet Union exports have expanded at the same rate as output, but in the other countries exports have increased between 20 per cent (Yugoslavia) and 140 per cent (Hungary) faster than GDP or NMP. The socialist countries no longer are as inward looking as perhaps they once were.

Turning now to the distributive aspects of economic development, the conclusion is unavoidable that the socialist countries have been remarkably successful in providing social services to the entire population. The record in public health is outstanding and in education

221

Table 8.8 **FOREIGN TRADE IN SOME SOCIALIST COUNTRIES**

	Export ratio, 1984 (per cent of GDP)	Export growth, 1973-84 (% per annum)	Export growth as multiple of GDP growth, 1973-84
China	10	10.1	1.5
Cuba	34 *a*	3.3	n.a.
Bulgaria	24 *b*	11.5	2.2 *c*
Czechoslovakia	14 *b*	5.5	2.1 *c*
East Germany	16 *b*	6.5	1.5
Hungary	40	8.4	2.4
Poland	18	2.6	*e*
Romania	10 *b*	n.a.	0.6 *d*
USSR	5 *b*	4.1	1.0
Yugoslavia	31	4.9	1.2

a)   1978.
b)   1983.
c)   Export growth, 1973-84 divided by NMP growth, 1976-84.
d)   Export growth as multiple of NMP growth, 1983-85
e)   The growth of NMP was negative over the period 1976-84.

Sources: IBRD, *World Development Report 1986,* Oxford University Press, 1986; US Central Intelligence Agency, *The Cuban Economy: A Statistical Review,* Washington, D.C., 1981, Table 53, p. 47; US Central Intelligence Agency, *Handbook of Economic Statistics,* Washington, D.C., 1984; UNECE, *Economic Survey of Europe in 1985-1986,* New York, 1986.

too the performance is far superior to the average in non-socialist Third World countries. The socialist countries also have been more successful than most others in providing employment to the entire labour force. The productivity of labour is not always as high as it could be, but at least a very high proportion of the working population is gainfully employed. Finally, income in socialist countries tends to be more evenly distributed than elsewhere. Inequalities, privilege and unfairness do of course exist, but they are less conspicuous than in the average Third World country.

NOTES AND REFERENCES

1. The Soviet Union, for example, is said by some analysts to be a type of capitalist society: Martin Nicolaus, *Restoration of Capitalism in the USSR,* Chicago, Liberator Press, 1975 and   Charles Bettelheim, "The Specificity of Soviet Capitalism", *Monthly Review,* Vol. 37, September 1985. Others claim that the Soviet Union is in "transition" from capitalism to socialism and hence is neither one nor the other: Ernest Mandel, "The Class Nature of the Soviet Union", *Review of Radical Political Economy,* Vol. 14, Spring 1982 and Paul Sweezy, "After Capitalism, What?", *Monthly Review,* Vol. 37, July-August 1985. Rudolf Bahro describes the Soviet Union and Eastern Europe as "actually existing socialism" which differs from the genuine thing. See his *The Alternative in Eastern Europe,* New York, Schocken, 1981. The problem with all this literature is that if socialism is defined in idealised terms, then no evidence from any actual country can be used to evaluate (positively or negatively) how a socialist economy functions in practice. Socialism, by definition, becomes denuded of empirical content.

2. Data on GNP per capita were taken from the World Bank because it is a reputable Western source. However in 1983 the World Bank ceased to report estimates of GNP per capita for non-market economies that are not members of the Bank. Thus in the 1986 edition of the *World Development Report* figures for Poland and

Hungary only are reported for Soviet bloc countries. The quality of the data reported in the first column of Table 8.1 clearly leaves much to be desired and no particular significance should be attached to the figures.

3. See Chapter 6.

4. The 1986 *World Development Report* indicates that by 1984 the proportion of the labour force engaged in agriculture in Mongolia had fallen to 40 per cent. Without knowing the proportion of output generated in agriculture that year it is impossible to calculate the ratio of output per worker in non-agriculture to agriculture, but it is obvious that the degree of structural distortion in the economy is falling rapidly. The urban population in 1984 was 55 per cent of the total.

5. An exception is Bulgaria. The services sector is small but labour productivity in the sector is equivalent to the national average. Another exception is China, where the services sector is small but labour productivity is well above the national average. The reason for this of course is the very low relative productivity in agriculture.

6. The insurgency in what was then South Vietnam began in 1959. The United States became involved in the war in 1961 and the war continued to escalate until 1973 when the United States withdrew and the war officially ended. Hostilities in Vietnam continued, however, until 1975.

7. See Carmelo Mesa-Lago and Jorge Perez-Lopez, *A Study of Cuba's Material Product System, Its Conversion to the System of National Accounts, and Estimations of Gross Domestic Product per Capita and Growth Rates*, World Bank Staff Working Papers No. 770, 1985. Andrew Zimbalist and Susan Eckstein suggest that gross social product per head grew on average 2.9 per cent a year during the period 1962-83. (See their "Patterns of Cuban Development: The First Twenty-five Years", *World Development*, Vol. 15, No. 1, January 1987, p. 8.)

8. According to World Bank sources the average annual percentage rate of growth of GDP in the two countries was as follows:

	1960-70	1970-79
Albania	7.3	6.8
North Korea	7.8	6.2

(*Source:* IBRD, *World Development Report 1981*, Oxford University Press, 1981.)
Other sources give different rates of growth but the pattern is the same.

9. See Wladimir Andreff, "Déclin ou mutation du modèle planifié d'industrialisation lourde : quels enseignements pour le Tiers-Monde?", paper presented to a conference on Economie industrielle et stratégies d'industrialisation dans le Tiers-Monde, ORSTOM, Paris, 26-27 February 1987.

10. See however Charles Wilber, *The Soviet Model and Underdeveloped Countries*, Chapel Hill, University of North Carolina Press, 1969.

11. Carl Riskin, "A Comment on Professor Brus' Paper", in Louis Emmerij, ed., *Development Policies and the Crisis of the 1980s*, Paris, OECD Development Centre, 1987.

12. The opposite of course is not true. There have been a great many right wing totalitarian regimes, in the Third World and elsewhere, which have ruled over capitalist economies. There is thus no historical link between capitalism and freedom, contrary to what is sometimes thought.

13. See, for example, Wlodzimierz Brus, *Socialist Ownership and Political Systems*, London, Routledge and Kegan Paul, 1975; Wlodzimierz Brus, *The Market in a Socialist Economy*, London, Routledge and Kegan Paul, 1972; Ota Sic, *The Third Way*, London, Wildwood House, 1976; Alec Nove, *The Economics of Feasible Socialism*, London, George Allen and Unwin, 1983.

14. See Chapter 5.

15. Evgeny Preobrazhensky, *The New Economics*, London, Oxford University Press, 1965 (originally published in Russian in 1926).

16. The formal basis for the policy was presented in a paper by G. Feldman in 1928 and later published in English. See G. Feldman, "On the Theory of Economic Growth Rates", in Evsei Domar, *Essays in the Theory of Economic Growth*, London, Oxford University Press, 1957.

17. See M. Ellman, *Socialist Planning*, Cambridge, Cambridge University Press, 1979 and Robert Bideleux, *Communism and Development*, London and New York, Methuen, 1985, Ch. 7.

18. See Alec Nove, *op. cit.*, Part 3.

19. For a favourable assessment of the Yugoslav model see Robert Bideleux, *op. cit.*, Ch. 11.

20. United Nations Economic Commission for Europe, *Economic Survey of Europe in 1984-1985*, New York, 1985, Ch. 3.

21. See for example Robert Bideleux, *op. cit.*, Ch. 8 and Wlodzimierz Brus, "Experience of the Socialist Countries", in Louis Emmerij, ed., *Development Policies and the Crisis of the 1980s*, Paris, OECD Development Centre, 1987.

22. Vivienne Shue, *Peasant China in Transition: The Dynamics of Development Toward Socialism, 1949-1956*, Berkeley, University of California Press, 1980.

23. Mao Tse-Tung, "On the Cooperative Transformation of Agriculture", *Selected Works*, Beijing, Foreign Languages Press, Vol. 5, 1977, p. 197.

24. Gordon White, "Chinese Development Strategy After Mao", in Gordon White, Robin Murray and Christine White, eds., *Revolutionary Socialist Development in the Third World*, Brighton, Wheatsheaf Books, 1983.

25. It also led, in 1958, to the collapse of the alliance with the Soviet Union.

26. See Carl Riskin, *China's Political Economy: The Quest for Development Since 1949*, New York, Oxford University Press, 1987.

27. *Ibid.*

28. Little information is available about the North Korean experience. I have relied on the work of John Halliday. See his "The North Korean Enigma", in Gordon White, Robin Murray and Christine White, eds., *op. cit.*; "The North Korean Model: Gaps and Questions", *World Development*, Vol. 9, No. 9/10, September-October 1981.

29. In Japan at that time (1940) 26.8 per cent of the farmers were full tenants and 42.1 per cent part tenants, or 68.9 per cent in all. The tenancy rate in Japan was therefore lower than in Korea but not dramatically so.

30. Gordon White, "North Korean Juche: The Political Economy of Self-reliance", in Manfred Bienefeld and Martin Godfrey, eds., *The Struggle for Development: National Strategies in an International Context*, Chichester, John Wiley, 1982, p. 325.

31. *Ibid.*, p. 326.

32. *Ibid.*, p. 335.

33. *Ibid.*, p. 347.

34. The data on global energy consumption were taken from IBRD, *World Development Report 1983*, Oxford University Press, 1983, p. 29.

35. IBRD, *World Development Report 1986*, Oxford University Press, 1986, p. 195.

36. The figures for India and the other low-income countries include of course investment financed by foreign capital. The gross domestic savings rates in 1979 were 20 per cent in India and 15 per cent in the other low-income countries.

37. Andrew Zimbalist, "Cuban Industrial Growth, 1965-84", *World Development*, Vol. 15, No. 1, January 1987, Table 3, p. 87.

38. United Nations Economic Commission for Europe, *Economic Survey of Europe in 1985-1986*, New York, 1986, Table 3.3.5, p. 159. Part of the decline may reflect changes in arbitrary prices and in the composition of industrial output, but there can be little doubt that the decline in the productivity of capital is genuine.

39. A World Bank study estimates that the productivity of capital declined 29 per cent between 1957 and 1978 and by another 14 per cent between 1978 and 1983. See G. Tidrick, *Productivity Growth and Technological Change in Chinese Industry*, World Bank Staff Working Paper No. 761, Washington, 1986, Table 2, p. 4.

40. If one excludes Kampuchea and Mongolia from the calculation, the unweighted average rate of growth of the four remaining socialist Third World countries is 1.8 per cent per annum per head. If one calculates an average weighted by size of population for the six countries, the rate of growth is 1.6 per cent per annum per head. Both figures are more than twice as high as the average rate of growth of agricultural output per head in the capitalist Third World countries.

41. See Z. Kozlowski, "Agriculture in the Economic Growth of the East European Socialist Countries", in Lloyd Reynolds, ed., *Agriculture in Development Theory*, New Haven, Yale University Press, 1975.

42. The model is borrowed from M. Kalecki, *Essays on Developing Economies*, Brighton, Harvester Press, 1976, Ch. 7.

43. Nicholas Lardy argues in his *Agriculture in China's Modern Economic Development* (Cambridge, Cambridge University Press, 1983) that in several respects the priority given to agriculture actually declined after the introduction of the reforms. While this is true if one focuses on state investment, it ignores the sweeping institutional reforms, the greatly improved agricultural terms of trade and the new incentive structure facing farmers.

44. See Keith Griffin, *World Hunger and the World Economy,* London, Macmillan, 1987, Ch. 3.

45. Carl Riskin, "Feeding China: The Experience since 1949", paper presented to a conference on Hunger and Poverty – The Poorest Billion, World Institute of Development Economics Research, Helsinki, Finland, 21-25 July 1986.

46. Keith Griffin, *op. cit.,* Ch. 6.

47. For excellent discussions of the problems of interpreting data on income distribution in socialist countries see Abram Bergson, "Income Inequality Under Soviet Socialism", *Journal of Economic Literature,* Vol. XXII, No. 3, September 1984 and Christian Morrisson, "Income Distribution in East European and Western Countries", *Journal of Comparative Economics,* Vol. 8, 1984.

48. For data on the distribution of income in non-socialist Third World countries see Chapter 1, Table 1.6.

49. The Gini coefficients for Taiwan and South Korea were obtained from Tibor Scitovsky, "Economic Development in Taiwan and South Korea, 1965-81", in L.J. Lau, ed., *Models of Development: A Comparative Study of Economic Growth in South Korea and Taiwan,* San Francisco, ICS Press, 1986, p. 139.

50. Abram Bergson, *op. cit.*

51. See Keith Griffin, ed., *Institutional Reform and Economic Development in the Chinese Countryside,* London, Macmillan, 1984.

52. IBRD, *China: Long Term Development Issues and Options,* Baltimore, Johns Hopkins University Press, 1985, Table 1.2, p. 29.

Chapter 9

THE STRATEGIES COMPARED

We approach the end of our journey. Six broad strategies of economic development have been identified and their features discussed. Five of these strategies apply to capitalist countries and one to the socialist countries. The first five we have called Monetarism, the Open Economy, Industrialisation, the Green Revolution and Redistributive strategies of development. The sixth strategy, the Socialist strategy, has been divided into four sub-strategies which we have called the Soviet or Stalinist strategy, the Yugoslav self-management strategy, the Chinese or Maoist strategy and the self-reliant strategy of North Korea. Although for purposes of analysis we have treated these six strategies as discrete, some of the features overlap or, if one prefers, some of the strategies combine together rather naturally. This is the case, say, of the redistributive and green revolution strategies as well as the open economy and monetarist strategies. These combinations cohere in a way that many assemblages of economic policies do not. In this chapter, however, we shall concentrate on our six "pure" strategies and attempt to compare these different paths to development.

Before doing so, however, let us pause for a moment to consider whether countries really have a choice of strategy and if they do, what makes them choose one strategy rather than another. In Chapter 2 it was argued that many states do not choose a development strategy at all. It certainly would be foolish to imagine that strategies are arrayed before policymakers in the same way that dishes are displayed before customers in a cafeteria. Policymakers are not free to select whichever strategy strikes their fancy; their choices and their actions are heavily constrained. There is sometimes a contradiction between what is demanded by a coherent development strategy and what is required to maintain the cohesion of a fragile society. There is, moreover, the limited capacity of the machinery of government. This constitutes in some countries a major constraint on what a government can effectively do. In many African states this point was unacknowledged and governments sought to accomplish vastly more than they had the capacity to implement successfully. Particularly in countries where administrative capacity is low, the leadership should be wary of selecting a path of development that is too "government-intensive". Policymakers must make choices for the public sector and they must establish priorities for government activities. The most fundamental choice of all – that between a capitalist and socialist organisation of the economy – is hardly analogous to choosing between shrimp cocktail or tomato soup as the first course at dinner. Men and women have died, many in vain, while attempting to make that fundamental choice for themselves and for others, including of course others not yet born.

Even when such awesome issues are not on the political agenda, policymakers do not have a free hand to select just any old economic policy. Very small countries, for example, are constrained by their size and this tends to rule out certain strategies while highlighting the advantages of others. In particular, very small countries run serious risks if they close their economies and in effect they have little choice but to follow a more or less open economy strategy of development, however modified the strategy might be. All countries, however, not just the small ones, are subject to international influences and pressures. Some of these pressures, for example those emanating from the International Monetary Fund, are directed towards encouraging countries to adopt a particular development strategy, in the case of the IMF, a monetarist one. Other countries have been even more unfortunate and have been outright victims of external politics and have had their development strategy imposed upon them. The adoption of the Soviet strategy of development in Eastern Europe is a case in point.

The influence of bilateral aid donors and the World Bank has been an important determinant in some countries of the strategies selected. This was especially true in the early years of many newly independent countries but was also true in Latin America, where independence was achieved in the nineteenth century. The United States Agency for International Development, for example, tried in Latin America in the 1960s to steer economic development in a redistributive direction under the Alliance for Progress programme; today it is trying to steer development in a monetarist direction. In neither case has success been conspicuous. The World Bank has had a much larger impact in Africa. Ghana, Uganda, Kenya, Tanzania, Zambia and Malawi, for instance, began with economic programmes prepared by expatriate economists and these programmes were heavily influenced by World Bank national studies that were prepared shortly after independence. This is conveniently forgotten now that the Bank is highly critical of economic policy in much of Africa.

The legacy of history, a people's memory of their colonial experience, also affects the strategy adopted. In the minds of many, external domination is closely associated with a colonial division of labour in which the centre specialises on manufactured goods and the periphery on agriculture and other primary products for export. Political independence, in contrast, is associated with industrialisation and partial delinking from the world economy. That is to say, a country's political history may rule out some strategies for economic development and predispose policymakers to favour others. One does not quickly forget the lessons of the past even if, as sometimes happens, the significance of events is incorrectly interpreted. The widespread adoption in the 1950s and early 1960s of strategies for import-substituting industrialisation almost certainly was due in part to a reaction to what was perceived by the governments of newly independent countries to be disadvantageous and even exploitative economic arrangements during the colonial era.

But perhaps above all, the choice of development strategy is strongly influenced by the ideology and material interests of a country's governing groups. It would be surprising if a country dominated by a mercantile class were to turn its back on foreign trade; the natural thing would be to pursue policies consistent with an open economy strategy of development. Similarly, a country ruled by an urban-based elite could be expected to promote industrialisation while one dominated by large agricultural landowners would be more likely to see the advantages of a green revolution strategy. On the other hand, reformist and revolutionary regimes based on mass political movements in which the urban labour force and the peasantry have a strong voice are more likely to choose redistributive or socialist strategies for economic development. This is all pretty obvious: governments are inclined to adopt policies which benefit their supporters and disinclined to adopt policies which hurt them.

The point should not be exaggerated however. The choice of strategy is not wholly determined; there is some freedom for manoeuvre; governments can and do make policy. In the first place, political power is seldom the monopoly of a single group or class. Not even a powerful dictatorship is literally totalitarian: it is subject to pressures, influence, demands and claims from competing groups. No government, in other words, can singlemindedly adopt policies which favour exclusively the material interests of a single class. Hence strategy never need be and in practice is unlikely ever to be determined by the interests of just one ruling group. Second, the dominant group in a country is unlikely to be homogeneous. Intra-class conflict and factional strife are almost always present and these give the policymaker some freedom of action. One must not push this point too far, since the dominant classes rarely allow internecine struggles to undermine their control of the state. And of course the policymakers themselves have their class allegiances. The state is not autonomous and above politics. But even so, groups can be played off against one another or alternatively coalitions and alliances can be formed; compromises can be made. The ease with which this can be done varies from one country to another depending upon such things as the amount of freedom enjoyed by the press and the extent of political oppression. Also relevant is the extent to which the civil service has distinct interests of its own and has the power to make its interests felt. The set of policies that emerges from such a process may lack coherence and hence fails our test of what constitutes a strategy for development, but it would be wrong to say that the policies that do emerge were wholly determined by the class composition of the society. Finally, the balance of political power in a society can and does change over time, although in some societies the change is very slow. New social formations develop, new domestic political forces come to the surface, new currents of power and influence appear on the international scene. These periods of change, these times of transition, create opportunities for policymakers and increase their degrees of freedom. It is then perhaps that it is easiest to change direction and introduce consistent and mutually reinforcing policies which in retrospect can be recognised as forming a distinct strategy for economic development. In this sense, strategy should be seen as a process rather than a blueprint for development.

Countries thus do have a choice although some countries have more choice than others and in no country is choice unlimited. But even if countries had no choice it would be interesting to know what difference the absence of choice makes to economic performance. That is, we would still want to be able to compare development strategies even if we were certain that a country's strategy was wholly determined by, say, its domestic class composition and the external environment. In the pages that follow we shall attempt to compare our six strategies under six broad headings: resource utilisation and the level of income; savings, investment and growth; human capital formation; poverty and inequality; the role of the state; and participation, democracy and freedom.

Resource utilisation and the level of income

Perhaps the first question to ask of a country's economic policies is whether they permit that country to use the resources at hand efficiently. This question in turn can be divided into two parts: are resources fully utilised and is the composition of output optimal? It is of

228

course possible to utilise resources fully, to have no idle capacity or unemployed labour, and yet produce the wrong things in the wrong way. Similarly, it is possible to get factor proportions right and to get the balance of output right and yet to have much waste and inefficiency in the form of unused resources.

The monetarist strategy of development, for example, places high priority on using the price mechanism to allocate resources efficiently. Under ideal circumstances of full employment and perfect competition this should result in optimal factor combinations in production and the most efficient composition of output. But because the strategy tends to neglect macroeconomic policy, monetarist approaches to development policy are likely to lead to high unemployment of labour and low utilisation of installed capacity, i.e., to macroeconomic inefficiency due to inadequate aggregate demand. This in turn is likely to lead to microeconomic inefficiency because of the inability of key prices (real interest rates, wage rates and the exchange rate) to adjust fast enough to clear the market. The ideal circumstances required for a monetarist strategy to work properly are in practice unreal.

At the other extreme are socialist strategies of development. Central planning and in particular the use of quantitative controls tends to be associated with an inefficient allocation of resources. Prices often are arbitrary and irrational and fail even to approximate to opportunity costs. As a result, techniques of production do not reflect factor scarcities and the composition of output does not reflect the pattern of intermediate and final demand. Shortages and gluts are common. On the other hand, central planning is quite effective in ensuring that resources are fully utilised. Equipment tends to operate near to full capacity and high unemployment of labour is rare, although disguised unemployment and featherbedding of labour in industry are common. The result is that socialist strategies tend to suffer from microeconomic inefficiency while enjoying quite high macroeconomic efficiency.

A similar outcome but less exaggerated also is characteristic of some variants of the industrialisation strategy. That is, industrialisation based on the production of consumer goods for the domestic market or on the production of capital goods tends to suffer from allocative inefficiency (but not as great as under a socialist strategy) and to benefit from macroeconomic efficiency (but again, not as great as under a socialist strategy). A particular problem with such strategies is that industry tends to be monopolistically organised and sheltered from foreign competition. Hence competitive pressures are weak, costs tend to be high and the quality of output low.

The most successful strategy of development as regards resource utilisation and the level of income is the open economy. The open economy has the virtues of relying on the price mechanism (and hence benefitting from allocative efficiency), of being exposed to international competition (and hence being under continuous pressure to cut costs and improve quality) and of using exports as a leading sector (and in this way being able to ensure adequate aggregate demand). Of course one cannot guarantee that external demand always will be sufficient to provide full employment and a high degree of capacity utilisation, but fears that demand elasticities for exports are low appear so far to be unfounded. The open economy also has an advantage over some of the other strategies of development in being in a good position to exploit economies of large-scale production and opportunities for intra-industry specialisation.

Export-oriented industrialisation enjoys many of the same advantages as the open economy. It tends to produce relatively few price distortions and to allocate resources quite efficiently and it tends to generate a high level of aggregate demand. The degree of competition also is quite high, although some industries may be oligopolistically organised.

The green revolution and redistributive strategies, because of the high labour intensity of their development paths, also tend to be relatively efficient in their use of resources.

In assessing a development strategy one wants resources to be fully utilised and to be efficiently allocated. Planning seems to be better able to ensure a full utilisation of resources, competition to ensure that they are efficiently utilised. If one chooses to rely on competition, then the government must assume responsibility for maintaining a high level of aggregate demand. It must also ensure, ideally by exposing producers to international market forces, that domestic industry is in fact competitive and not oligopolistically or monopolistically organised. If instead of competition one relies on planning, then it is better to use planned prices rather than quantitative controls. Finally, if one is forced to choose between microeconomic inefficiency and macroeconomic inefficiency, it is better to choose the former. A misallocation of resources almost always is less serious than leaving resources idle. Indeed, the costs of allocative inefficiency typically are low – just 1 or 2 per cent of GNP – whereas the costs of operating capital equipment for only one instead of two or three shifts and the costs (both material and moral) of widespread unemployment of labour can be very high indeed. Thus, everything else being equal, those strategies that use resources fully are likely to enjoy a relatively high level of income and rate of growth.

Savings, investment and growth

A deficiency of aggregate demand is likely to be associated with a low level of savings and investment and a slow rate of growth of output and average incomes. It is for this reason that the macroeconomic performance of the monetarist strategies has been poor. Countries following a socialist strategy of development, in contrast, usually have high rates of domestic savings and investment. These are the extreme cases; savings rates in countries following one of the other strategies tend to fall somewhere in between the monetarist and socialist strategies, although very high rates of savings are not unknown in countries which have adopted the open economy model.

Capital accumulation need not of course be financed entirely by domestic savings. It is possible to obtain capital from abroad in the form of direct foreign investment, loans from overseas banks and foreign aid. The superiority of domestic over foreign savings as a means of financing development is widely recognised and the perils of falling into a debt trap, for example, are now well known. In practice not all foreign capital imports are used to increase investment – some foreign capital is used to raise private consumption, some to finance higher current public expenditure (including expenditure on armaments) and some may be used to facilitate capital flight – but insofar as part of the imported capital is used to finance capital formation, the average level of investment will rise and the aggregate rate of growth should increase. The question then becomes whether there is a connection between the ability of a country to attract foreign capital and use it wisely and the strategy for economic development that is followed.

As regards using foreign capital wisely, countries following a socialist strategy of development are more likely to be able to prevent leakages into private and public consumption and into expenditure on armaments; they are also more likely to be able to prevent capital flight. Central planning gives them a distinct advantage in ensuring that capital imports do raise the level of investment. On the other hand the socialist countries are likely to be at a disadvantage when it comes to attracting foreign capital. Most foreign aid is provided by the advanced capitalist countries and they are unlikely to be willing on a large scale to help finance the development of socialist countries. Similarly, most private direct investment is likely to flow to capitalist countries and although investing in socialist countries certainly is a possibility, in practice direct foreign investment is unlikely to make a major contribution to their overall rate of investment. In particular cases, however, as in Fiat's investment in the Soviet Union, foreign private investment can be a vehicle for the transfer of improved technology and make a significant difference in a specific sector. Apart from such rather isolated contributions, which usually take the form of joint ventures, we are left with borrowing from overseas financial institutions as potentially the most important source of external finance in socialist countries. The possibilities in this case depend on the country's ability to service a foreign debt, and since most countries following a socialist strategy of development have a relatively small export sector, their ability to service foreign loans is likely to be limited.

Thus countries following one of the five capitalist strategies of development are likely to be more successful in attracting foreign capital. In the short run there is little reason to choose one of the five strategies in preference to another, but in the long run a country with an open economy probably has an advantage. One reason for this is that it will have less difficulty servicing foreign loans. A second reason is that foreign investors will in principle be able to produce either for the domestic or for the export market and thus they will derive potential benefits from an option that is denied them by countries pursuing a more inward-oriented strategy. Once again, similar advantages are likely to be enjoyed by countries following an industrialisation strategy oriented towards exports.

The green revolution and redistributive strategies of development may encounter some difficulties in attracting foreign direct investment. The reason for this is that both strategies place emphasis on labour-intensive methods of production, small-scale and widely-dispersed enterprises and on the output of consumer goods for a large but low-income market. These are not things in which foreign investors typically excel. On the contrary, foreign investors, apart from some agri-businesses, are more likely to have a comparative advantage in using capital-intensive methods of production, in relatively large enterprises using standardised production techniques which exploit economies of scale and producing relatively sophisticated or technologically advanced products for middle and upper-income groups. It is partly for this reason that most foreign investment in the last quarter century has been concentrated in the urban manufacturing, petroleum and minerals sectors and not in agriculture or in the production of wage goods for a mass market. However even if this is so, even if the green revolution and redistributive strategies are at somewhat of a disadvantage when it comes to attracting direct investment, there is no reason in principle why they should be less able to attract foreign aid or obtain foreign loans.

Whatever source of finance is used, a high rate of investment is essential for expanding the stock of capital and, in addition, is highly desirable because it is a vehicle for introducing technical change, i.e., product and process innovations. A high rate of investment, however, is not sufficient to ensure a rapid rate of technical progress; a country must also either have access to foreign technology or it must itself engage in research and development. In the short run it may be sensible, because it is cheaper, to rely on foreign research and development, but in the long run those countries which develop local capabilities to undertake applied research are likely to enjoy a better economic performance than those which remain dependent on importing technology from abroad. Two of our strategies score high marks for technical change and innovation and they do so for diametrically opposite reasons. The open economy tends to be technologically progressive because it is receptive to foreign influences, sensitive to changes in demand in overseas markets and aware of product innovations and improvements in quality that are introduced by competitors. But above all it is technologically progressive because it has a tendency actively to seek improved technology overseas – through joint ventures with foreign companies, licensing agreements, sending students abroad for technical training, etc. International competitive forces provide a strong incentive to the open economy to be always on the look-out for improved technology that lowers costs and raises quality. The green revolution strategy, on the other hand, is unique in that it places technical change at the centre of the stage. Moreover, unlike the open economy, emphasis is placed on generating technical improvements (in agriculture) at home through domestically financed and organised research institutes. Foreign technology may also be imported of course, particularly technology produced at the various international agricultural research centres, but the nature of agricultural production is such that a green revolution strategy inevitably requires a major domestic research effort.

At the other end of the spectrum are countries following a socialist strategy of development. One of the problems associated with this strategy is its technological unprogressiveness. Techniques of production often are obsolete, product design and quality often are poor, and new products and processes are introduced relatively infrequently. Similar problems frequently bedevil countries which have chosen a strategy of industrialisation via the production behind tariff barriers of consumer goods or of capital goods produced in state enterprises. On the other hand, where industrialisation has been based on production for export, technical change usually has been very rapid. In this respect the strategy is quite similar to the open economy model. The reason of course is the presence of competitive pressure.

An advantage of rapid technological change is that it raises the marginal product of investment. Those countries which are technologically progressive receive a stimulus to growth through low or falling incremental capital-output ratios. Conversely, those countries which are technologically unprogressive require a high and rising rate of investment to achieve any given rate of growth. Socialist countries and those basing their industrialisation on the capital goods sector have suffered from this problem, although in the case of the socialist countries, the rising incremental capital-output ratios have been offset at least in part by very high rates of capital accumulation. The cost of course has been a smaller than average proportion of output devoted to consumption.

Aggregate growth rates have been highest in countries following an export-led industrialisation strategy (as in South Korea), or in countries following a redistributive strategy of development with a strong emphasis on exports (as in Taiwan), or in countries with an open economy which have enjoyed rapid expansion of exports (as in Botswana) or in countries following a socialist strategy of development. There are, in other words, a number of development strategies which are capable of producing above average rates of growth of total product and per capita income. The sectoral pattern of growth is more dependent on the specific strategy pursued. Agricultural growth rates are likely to be higher in countries following a green revolution or, surprisingly to some people, a socialist strategy of development. The rate of growth of agricultural output should in principle also be quite high under a well-conceived redistributive strategy of development. Industrial growth tends to be most rapid in the socialist countries and in those capitalist countries following an industrialisation strategy. This is of course what one would expect.

Human capital formation

There is more to growth than capital accumulation, the introduction of new processes and products and the expansion of the employed labour force. The quality of the labour force as reflected in its health and nutrition, skills and education also is important. Indeed, they are important for four reasons.

First, a healthy and educated population is an end in itself; it is one of the goals of development.

Second, human capital is a direct input into the production process. For example, a high incidence of morbidity lowers the productivity of labour and reduces the number of days worked. Hence programmes which result in improved health are likely to have a positive impact on the level of output. Similarly, the more skilled is the labour force, the higher its productivity will be. Skilled labour is likely to be able to work faster, with less supervision, with fewer errors and to produce goods and services of higher quality.

Third, human capital is complementary to physical capital. Machines require skilled workers to operate them and mechanics to repair them. Modern agriculture requires a literate farm population: people who can read instructions on a fertilizer bag, absorb information contained in simple literature distributed by extension agents and understand the contents of a repair manual for agricultural equipment. Modern services (banking, insurance, tourism) require numeracy: people who can make simple calculations quickly and accurately. A country that emphasises physical capital formation while neglecting its human capital will soon discover that the returns on physical capital are low.

Moreover, fourth, human capital formation is necessary for technical change. It is difficult to introduce improved methods of production, new ways of doing things and more complex and sophisticated products unless the labour force (and indeed the buyers and consumers) have sufficient training and education to enable them to understand what is being asked of them (or offered to them). Investment, human capital and technical change are closely interlinked.

The great majority of Third World countries have made enormous advances in education and training. Literacy rates have increased sharply, primary education is virtually universal in many countries, the proportion of the relevant age group enrolled in secondary schools has risen, the number of institutions providing technical training has begun to grow and many countries now are able to offer a university education to at least some of their most promising young people. This is all very encouraging. None the less, education and training have figured more prominently in some development strategies than in others.

A case can be made that the prominence of education in some Third World countries reflects their cultural values as much as the strategy for economic development they have adopted. It has often been said, for example, that countries in the Chinese sphere of cultural influence, namely, China itself, Taiwan, North and South Korea, Hong Kong and Singapore, have historically attached great importance to education and this has continued to the present irrespective of their strategy of development or political orientation. While this may be true, it is also true that mass education and training are an integral part of the redistributive and socialist strategies of development and one would expect, as in fact is the case, that countries following one or the other of these two strategies would do particularly well in this field. The socialist countries, as is well known, have an enviable record in education and even countries such as Tanzania and Sri Lanka which have followed flawed redistributive strategies have done very well. Countries such as Brazil and Pakistan, in contrast, which have emphasized industrialisation, have done much less well. These examples, once again, suggest the importance of the link between strategy choices and the interests of the dominant classes of the countries concerned.

Broadly the same conclusions apply to health. There has been an enormous improvement in health standards throughout the Third World. Life expectancy has risen dramatically, infant and maternal mortality rates have fallen precipitously, infectious diseases have been brought under control and in some countries have virtually disappeared, and morbidity rates have declined everywhere. Once again, however, those countries which for ideological or other reasons have pursued either a redistributive or socialist strategy of development have done better than average. The explanation in the case of health is the same as that in education: human capital formation is expected to play a greater role in those two strategies than in the monetarist, open economy, industrialisation and green revolution strategies.

Perhaps the litmus test for the importance attached by policymakers to human capital formation are policies in the field of nutrition and food distribution. Just as literacy, longevity and infant mortality are imperfectly correlated with per capita income, so too the incidence of hunger and malnutrition are imperfectly correlated with per capita income[1]. That is, they can be of similar orders of magnitude in countries at very different levels of income per head. Some countries have been remarkably successful in providing the entire population with enough to eat despite a very low average income, whereas other countries have many people suffering from chronic hunger despite a much higher average income.

The difference in outcome reflects differences in development strategy. Those countries which have pursued a redistributive or socialist strategy of economic development have tended to include among their policies food distribution schemes of various sorts – special programmes for infants and nursing mothers, school feeding programmes, factory canteens with subsidised food or general food rationing systems – and these have helped to ensure that the poor and other vulnerable groups have had access to food at prices they can afford. Countries which have followed other development strategies tend to have been less successful in providing minimum adequate nutrition to the entire population except in those cases (as in South Korea) where policies have resulted in a relatively equal distribution of wealth and income. Not even the green revolution strategy, which emphasizes food production, is capable of ensuring adequate nutrition unless a land reform and other policies have led to a high degree of equality. This proposition is well illustrated by the experience of the Philippines.

Poverty and inequality

The extent of poverty and inequality in a country depends on a great many things. We shall select just four items for brief comment: (*i*) the level and composition of state expenditure, (*ii*) the employment intensity of the path of development, (*iii*) the average level of income and its distribution and (*iv*) the distribution of productive assets.

Certain types of public expenditure can have a significant impact on reducing the incidence of poverty and creating a more egalitarian society. These include expenditure on the various categories of human capital formation that were discussed in the previous section: basic preventive health measures and simple curative medical facilities, universal primary and secondary education and widespread technical training centres, food distribution and nutrition programmes. Also included on a list of poverty alleviating public expenditures are basic social services: adequate drainage, the provision near households of sources of water (preferably safe to drink), a reliable system of public transportation serving both rural and urban areas. More ambitious are transfer policies which ensure that everyone has an adequate income during their old age.

Most Third World countries have adopted some of these policies, particularly those policies that can be justified as yielding a positive rate of economic return, but only those countries which have followed a redistributive or socialist strategy of development have consistently given high priority to the full range of these types of public expenditure. Countries pursuing other strategies implement fewer of these policies and in addition tend to lag behind, although they do not always lag so very far behind.

Another way to reduce poverty, at least among the economically active population and members of their households, is to follow a labour-intensive pattern of growth. This is feasible under a number of different strategies. Employment creation is a particularly prominent feature of the green revolution and redistributive strategies; it is common in countries following an open economy strategy, except in those countries where exports consist primarily of petroleum or mineral products; and it is characteristic of countries pursuing a strategy of export-led industrialisation.

On the other hand, the employment intensity of growth is likely to be somewhat lower in countries following a monetarist strategy because of the high rate of unemployment that seems to accompany that strategy. Perhaps surprisingly, it also is likely to be somewhat lower under a socialist strategy. The reason for this is that although socialist countries typically have low rates of open unemployment, they tend to adopt highly mechanised methods of production. Visible unemployment is prevented by excessively high manning rates and in effect disguised unemployment and featherbedding are created in the industrial sector. The high manning rates do of course ensure that almost every member of the labour force has a job and hence an income, and consequently the system does help to reduce poverty, but the excessively mechanised investment pattern has the paradoxical effect of reducing the long-run rate of growth of labour productivity and average earnings.

It is obvious that the higher the average level of income, the lower is likely to be the incidence of poverty, everything else being equal. Therefore countries which use their resources fully and allocate those resources efficiently are likely to have less poverty than others. More important, however, is the distribution of income. Even if one rejects the view presented in Chapter 1 that the concept of poverty is closely linked to perceptions of inequality, and concentrates instead on the irreducible absolutist core to the notion of poverty, it is still the case that the lower the degree of inequality, the lower is likely to be the incidence of poverty[2]. This will be true unless it can be shown that in the short run those policies which reduce inequality also reduce the level of output substantially and in the long run, policies which reduce inequality also reduce the trend rate of growth substantially. Neither of these propositions is supported by the empirical evidence.

Indeed the contrary position is closer to the truth. The distribution of income tends to be more equal among countries following a socialist strategy for economic development than among countries following other strategies. Yet the socialist countries, as we have seen, have enjoyed above average rates of growth of income per head. The reasons for the high degree of equality in socialist countries are partly their low wage and salary differentials and partly the virtual absence of income from property, and above all, the absence of large incomes from inherited wealth. Countries following a redistributive strategy of development also have an unusually even distribution of income and as the case of Taiwan demonstrates, they can achieve very fast rates of growth. Socialist and redistributive strategies of development are not the only strategies, however, that are consistent with a relatively equal distribution of income. The export-led industrialisation strategy of South Korea also has been associated with less inequality than in most Third World countries, thanks in part to the implementation of a land reform before the strategy began. Similarly, an open economy strategy based on the export of labour-intensive goods and services is likely to exhibit less inequality than average.

On the other hand, above average income inequality is likely to be present under (*i*) monetarist strategies, (*ii*) open economy strategies based on the export of petroleum and mineral products, (*iii*) open economy strategies based on the export of agricultural products in countries where landownership is highly concentrated, and (*iv*) under industrialisation strategies, particularly those based on producing consumer goods for the domestic market. The effects of a green revolution strategy are less certain. Much depends on the factor bias (if any) of the technology introduced, the degree of labour intensity of production and the distribution of landownership. The experience so far, however, suggests that the strategy is not likely to be effective in reducing poverty and inequality unless it is accompanied by a land reform.

Indeed, the distribution of productive assets, especially land, is fundamental. Those countries which have had a land reform (China, North Korea, South Korea, Taiwan) have succeeded in reducing poverty and inequality quite considerably, while most of those countries which have not (such as Brazil and the Philippines) have continued to have large numbers of people living in poverty even when they have managed to achieve rapid rates of economic growth. There are of course exceptions – Sri Lanka has not had a land reform but has introduced other policies which have resulted in a remarkably even distribution of income – but the exceptions are not numerous and the general tendency is readily apparent.

There are two broad ways of achieving a relatively equal distribution of productive wealth. One way is to socialise the means of production, transferring income generating assets to the state, to collectives or to co-operative enterprises. The other is to retain private ownership while ensuring that ownership is widely dispersed, e.g., by distributing land evenly among the rural population, by encouraging small-scale industrial enterprises (as in Taiwan), by adopting stringent anti-monopoly legislation, and by using tax incentives (including inheritance taxation) to promote a wide distribution of share ownership among the entire population. And of course the two broad approaches can be combined or mixed. The essential point, however, is that experience shows that if the distribution of wealth is relatively equal, this will result in a relatively equal distribution of income and that, in turn, will lead to a low average incidence of poverty.

The role of the state

Different strategies for economic development impose different demands upon the state. These demands affect not only the overall size of the state but also and more importantly the functions the state is required to discharge. Indeed it is not primarily how much the state does but what it does that distinguishes one strategy from another. Nearly all of the development related functions performed by the state can be classified under five headings as follows:

i) Normal recurrent expenditure. This includes provision for such things as the judiciary, police and armed forces; the diplomatic corps; the post office; central bank, council of economic advisors and the central statistical bureau. Most of the expenditure under this heading is on the wages and salaries of servants of the state, and includes everyone from archivists and customs officials to tax collectors and weathermen;

ii) Capital expenditure on social and economic infrastructure: schools, clinics, ports, highways, bridges, power stations, water supply, etc.;

iii) Economic regulation. Included under this heading is tax policy, accounting regulations, rules governing accelerated depreciation allowances, minimum wage legislation, foreign exchange controls, investment licenses, banking regulations, and so on;

iv) Transfer payments. Several government programmes may entail taxing one group of people in order to provide cash incomes or payments in kind to other groups of people. Traditional welfare services (unemployment compensation, supplementary income benefits, state pensions) are obvious examples. In some countries food distribution programmes are an important transfer payment;

v) Investment in directly productive activities. This includes state ownership and management of manufacturing enterprises, petroleum companies and mines, and state farms; banks and other financial institutions; air, railroad, shipping and trucking companies; irrigation works, etc.

The monetarist strategy of development has two distinctive features. First, it implies a very small state sector and an attempt to provide as much room as possible for the growth of the private sector. Second, it tries to limit the functions of the state as much as possible to those that come under the heading of normal recurrent expenditure. Of course some investment on infrastructure is unavoidable and a minimum amount of economic regulation is inescapable, but the strategy envisages very few transfer payments and no participation by the state in directly productive economic activities. Thus the state under a monetarist strategy is small in size and specialised in its functions.

In practice, however, countries attempting to follow a monetarist strategy have encountered great difficulties in reducing the overall size of the state and restricting the range of its activities. Recurrent expenditure has tended to remain high, partly because many of the activities under this heading are analogous to fixed overhead costs of government, partly because it has been politically difficult to reduce the number of civil servants and partly because the social tensions created when the strategy was introduced have forced governments to increase expenditure on the police and armed forces. Moreover, it has not been possible to switch responsibility for the provision of economic infrastructure from the public to the private sector: the return on such investments is in general not high enough to attract private initiative and the level of private savings has in general not been large enough to provide the finance needed for major infrastructure projects. Governments following a monetarist strategy have however been more successful in reducing public capital expenditure on social infrastructure, notably on schools, universities, public housing and hospitals.

Monetarist strategies have also been successful in reducing government regulatory activities. Economic controls and regulations have been abolished or simplified and, in addition, state enterprises have been turned over to the private sector. But as we saw in Chapter 3, the success tends to be short-lived. The private banking sector in particular has encountered severe difficulties and the government has been forced to reimpose tight regulations and often to absorb private financial institutions into the state sector. When major industrial and commercial enterprises have verged on bankruptcy the government has felt it had no alternative but to step in and either nationalise the enterprise or provide massive subsidies (a form of transfer payment). Finally, contrary to the sprit of the strategy, the state also has been forced to make transfer payments to labour and to provide employment on emergency relief works in order to temper the effects of unemployment. Thus the force of circumstances has meant that the role of the state under a monetarist strategy has in practice diverged considerably from its role in theory.

The role of the state in an open economy strategy is not nearly so restricted as in a monetarist strategy. The state in this strategy as in all others is of course responsible for its normal recurrent expenditure. In addition, it is required to make a major investment in infrastructure, above all in those activities such as power and transport needed to support the foreign trade sector. That is, it is the task of the state to remove bottlenecks in economic and social overhead capital or, better still, to anticipate them by providing capacity in plenty of time.

The management of foreign trade policy is a prime task of a government pursuing an open economy strategy. In the initial stages this may imply deregulation of certain aspects of the economy in order to ensure that the effective exchange rate is the same for both exports and imports. This is not necessarily a hands-off policy, however. Government may take it upon itself to provide trained labour and ensure that the skills needed in the export sector are readily available. Alternatively it may subsidise from tax revenues the training schemes of private enterprise. Such a subsidy would of course be a form of transfer payment. Equally, the government could finance market research and trade missions; it could help in negotiating with foreign investors; it could be active in seeking appropriate technologies from abroad. And of course it is perfectly compatible with an open economy strategy for the government to own and operate directly productive activities, including such things as petroleum and mining enterprises engaged in exporting. None the less, because of the general attitudes that tend to accompany advocacy of an open economy, the role of the state is likely to be more modest under an open economy strategy than under any of the four remaining strategies to be considered.

Indeed the role of the state under an industrialisation strategy is likely to be quite pervasive, i.e., the state is almost certain to be large in size and its activities broad in scope. It may even engage in formal planning. Whether industrialisation is based on replacing imported consumer goods or developing a domestic capital goods sector, the thrust of state activity is likely to shift from normal recurrent expenditure and investment in infrastructure to economic regulation and investment in directly productive activities.

Industrialisation strategies imply urbanisation and that, in turn, implies massive investment in urban social and economic infrastructure. Beyond that, import-substituting industrialisation places heavy demands on government regulatory activities: tariff policy, foreign exchange allocation, tax subsidies, investment licences, and so on. The development of the capital and intermediate goods industries, in addition, almost certainly will require large state subsidies to the private sector or more likely, direct investment by the state in the desired activities. Furthermore, the state is likely to find that the finance of industrialisation necessitates either the creation of public sector financial institutions or detailed regulation of the private banking system. Even an industrialisation strategy based on exporting manufactured goods, as we saw in Chapter 5 when examining the case of South Korea, probably will require active intervention by the state in support of private industry.

The green revolution strategy also places heavy demands upon the state, although the specific demands are quite different from those of an industrialisation strategy. First, the strategy requires major expenditure and scientific endeavour on agricultural research. This inevitably is a public sector activity. Second, the strategy depends for its success on assured supplies to farmers of irrigation water and in some countries this means that the state will have to invest massively in large-scale irrigation projects. Third, accelerated agricultural growth will be impossible unless the rural areas have an adequate infrastructure. A good road and transport network is essential, as is the provision of power for the development of small-scale industries and other non-agricultural rural activities. Government investment in transport and energy is therefore likely to be considerable. Indeed it is probable that the amount of infrastructure investment needed to support a green revolution strategy is greater than the amount of infrastructure investment needed for an industrialisation strategy. The reason for this is that the infrastructure needed for an industrialisation strategy can be concentrated in a few major urban areas whereas the infrastructure needed for a successful green revolution strategy must be spread evenly throughout the rural areas. Unit capital costs of transport and power are likely therefore to be relatively high.

A redistributive strategy of development can take several forms provided only that it is not biased in favour of capital intensity and hence is anti-egalitarian. In practice, however, a redistributive strategy is almost certain to take one of two broad forms. It can be based on producing labour-intensive manufactured goods for export or it can be based on rapid agricultural growth. If the former route is pursued, the state will have to assume most of the tasks required by an industrialisation strategy. If the latter route is followed, the state will have to assume many of the tasks required by a green revolution strategy. Regardless of which route is taken, the state in addition will have to ensure that the distribution of income and wealth is equitable and in many countries this probably means that in the initial stages a land reform will be required. A land reform will of course place considerable demands upon the public administration even if administration at the village level is left to local organisations.

The strategy also requires substantial state expenditure on human capital, notably education and health programmes, and in common with the green revolution strategy, it may be thought by government to be desirable to introduce a family planning programme. In addition, a public food distribution system and other nutrition programmes may possibly form part of the strategy. Thus the state is certain to have heavy responsibilities for administering welfare programmes and transfer payments. On the other hand, it is less likely to be deeply involved in investments in directly productive activities in industry and agriculture (apart from irrigation).

Redistributive strategies depend for their success on mobilising the population for grass-roots development, on exploiting the myriad opportunities at the local level for small-scale investment projects and on organising the various groups in the community around effective institutions so that they can articulate their demands, establish priorities and work together for the common good. This approach to development implies a different style of public administration and a different relationship between the leaders and the led. The strategy is more likely to be successful, consequently, in countries where authority is devolved to the regions, where administration is highly decentralised and where participation is actively encouraged and promoted.

This style of governance, these characteristics of the state, may emerge more readily from some historical experiences than others. For example, the struggle for independence in some Third World countries occasioned an extensive mobilisation of the population by the nationalist movement. Where once the capacity to mobilise the people was channelled towards the political struggle, it could now be turned to development ends, at least in principle. Admittedly, few governments attempted to exploit this possibility, but where the leadership was inclined to favour a redistribtive strategy, as in Tanzania, structures existed in embryo for a different kind of state.

Lastly, there is the socialist strategy of economic development. The state under this strategy is all-embracing. It is large in size – indeed much larger than under any other strategy – and its scope is almost unlimited. Its most distinguishing characteristic, however, is its direct responsibility for investment in and management of productive activities, particularly in industry but often including large parts of agriculture as well. Under no other strategy is the private sector so small. As a result, the centre of gravity of the state under this strategy shifts to the state economic enterprises. The other developmental functions listed at the beginning of this section are present, and they loom large in comparison with many other strategies, but they pale into relative insignificance when compared with the state's role in the production of goods and services.

Transfer payments and welfare programmes also are prominent and of course economic activity of state, collective, co-operative and private enterprise is subject to detailed regulation. Investment in social and economic infrastructure, while not perhaps wholly the responsibility of the state, is certainly predominently the responsibility of the state. The most important exception is provision by collective enterprises in some rural areas of health and educational facilities and small-scale overhead and infrastructure works. Thus the state in a socialist strategy for economic development is at the opposite end of the spectrum from the state in a monetarist strategy. It is neither small in size nor specialised in function but on the contrary, tends until checked by reforms to take over all economic activities (in pursuit of "ownership by the whole people") and to extend its influence into all aspects of life (in an attempt to create a "new socialist man").

Participation, democracy and freedom

It would be tidy if a close correspondence could be found between a country's strategy for economic development and the degree of freedom and democracy its citizens enjoy. But, alas, the world is an untidy place and there appears to be no correlation between economic policy and the nature of the political regime. Except perhaps at the extremes.

Monetarism is an extreme economic doctrine and it is not surprising that extreme political measures have been necessary wherever it has been adopted. Military dictatorship, severe repression of dissent and opposition, massive violence by the state against the civilian population invariably have accompanied the monetarist strategy of development. The correlation is perfect. Unfortunately, however, there are only three observations (Chile, Argentina and Uruguay) and thus one cannot be certain that there is a causal connection between the two. Common sense rather than statistics must be our guide. But what does common sense tell us? Can one imagine the people of a nation willingly and peaceably accepting a strategy that turns the price mechanism loose and lets market forces rule regardless of the hardships that result, the injustices that are created and the inequality that emerges? I confess that I cannot imagine such a strategy being tolerated for long if it produces such results and my common sense tells me that if policymakers nevertheless insist on following such a strategy, they will have to do so by force. Repression, violence and dictatorship are inevitable.

What about the other extreme, the socialist strategy of development? Are people's democracies democratic? Certainly not. Then is the lack of democracy an inherent feature of a socialist strategy? Once again, certainly not. There is no reason in principle why a democratic socialism should be impossible and indeed there are millions of people in Europe, Australia, New Zealand and elsewhere who regularly vote for democratic socialist political parties. But in practice socialist strategies of development have been adopted in countries ruled by the communist party and as long as the communist party continues to monopolise political power in the name of the dictatorship of the proletariat, the historical record will show - or be interpreted by many as showing - that socialism and democracy are incompatible.

Quite apart from democracy, the high degree of centralisation in most countries that have followed a socialist strategy is bound to reduce popular participation in development and possibly some freedoms as well. There are of course examples of decentralised socialism (notably in Yugoslavia) and there have been many attempts to reform the system, to devolve authority, to spread power and responsibility, to increase artistic freedom and civil rights, but the results so far in countries ruled by the communist party are not terribly encouraging. None the less, one must not overstate the case. Participation of a sort does exist in socialist countries, not usually in the electoral sense but quite commonly through involvement at the local level in structures taking economic decisions[3]. Participation is of course substantial in the co-operative and collective sectors, but it is not confined to them. Indeed, the extent of participation by the poor probably is greater under the socialist strategy than under any other except the redistributive strategy of development[4]. And the redistributive strategy is in a sense the Third World equivalent of Western social democracy. Moreover, despite the authoritarianism that is characteristic of the socialist strategy of development, the extent of day-to-day repression of ordinary people is relatively low, much lower in fact than in most other Third World countries.

The political consequences of an open economy strategy are equally ambiguous. Free trade neither requires democracy, political freedom and participation nor does it necessarily promote it. Much depends, I suspect, on what happens to the distribution of income. If an open economy strategy results in greatly increased inequality, this will lead to social tension and then political violence is likely to follow. The government then has a choice between introducing policies to reduce economic inequality or introducing political repression. If it chooses the latter, an open economy strategy will go hand-in-hand with authoritarianism. But this outcome is far from inevitable, particularly since in many circumstances the strategy may lead to less rather than more inequality.

Much the same can be said about the implications of an industrialisation strategy. If the particular policies adopted to promote the manufacturing sector result in a substantial worsening of the distribution of income and wealth, the government at some stage probably will have to abandon or modify its policies or else become authoritarian. Where there are unfavourable initial conditions of great inequality, industrialisation based on import substitution does seem to have a tendency to accentuate income disparities and social conflict and this may account in part for the association in Latin America between repressive regimes and an industrialisation strategy of development. The essence of the problem, however, is the initial conditions, not industrialisation as such, and the same policies pursued in another region with different initial conditions could lead to quite different results.

We seem to be saying in effect that if a development strategy succeeds in reducing poverty and at least does not accentuate inequality, then it will be compatible with a free and democratic political system. It will not necessarily promote democracy but nor will it be an obstacle to it. On the other hand, if a development strategy fails to reduce poverty and also accentuates inequality, then the basis for participation; freedom and democracy will be weakened and the probability of an authoritarian regime emerging will increase.

Take the case of a green revolution strategy. If fully implemented, the strategy should result in a labour-intensive path of development and this certainly will reduce absolute poverty and possibly inequality as well. If the strategy is accompanied by a redistributive or communal land reform, inequality at the local level is sure to decline sharply. There will then be a platform on which to build institutions which promote participation at the village level. Moreover, because of the employment intensity of development and the equitable distribution of productive assets, social cleavages based on economic differences will be small, and provided conflicts based on other factors (race, ethnicity, language, religion) are not too severe, the environment for a workable political democracy should be favourable. On the other hand, if the technology introduced under a green revolution strategy is landlord biased, or if the incidence of landlessness is high and the concentration of landownership is great, or if policies discriminate in favour of the relatively better-off groups, then social tension and political violence are likely to increase. A situation like that in the Philippines may emerge, a situation unfavourable to the preservation of democracy and freedom.

Participation is of course a central component of a redistributive strategy of development and it therefore has an advantage over all other strategies in this respect. Redistributive strategies also emphasize a labour-intensive pattern of growth and a relatively egalitarian distribution of the ownership of land and other assets. Thus the incidence of absolute poverty should be low and the degree of equality should be high under this strategy. Everything else being equal, these features should help to reduce social stratification and class conflict and make it easier to introduce and maintain democratic institutions and political freedoms. But of course everything else never is equal and it is always possible that even in a relatively egalitarian society, intense conflicts will be present that have relatively little to do with economic policy and the class composition of society or have only an indirect connection. The political divisions in Sri Lanka are a case in point.

Those who believe in historical materialism may be disappointed by the open-ended nature of these findings. There is no best path to development and there is no close correspondence between development policy or development strategy on the one hand and the resulting political system on the other. One cannot predict the shape of the superstructure knowing only the materials from which the base is constructed. It does not follow from this that economics has no influence on politics. That would be going too far. Nor does it follow that politics has no influence on economics. Indeed, if anything, the causal influences flowing from politics to economic policy are stronger than those flowing in the reverse direction. None the less we have argued that the strategy of economic development pursued by a country can predispose it towards authoritarianism or democracy although it seldom is the sole determining factor. Thus, while economists can't solve the politicians' problems for them, they can make them slightly easier or somewhat more difficult to solve.

NOTES AND REFERENCES

1. See Amartya Sen, "Development: Which Way Now?", *Economic Journal,* Vol. 93, No. 372, December 1983.

2. It is logically possible, however, for some statistical measurements of inequality, e.g. the Gini coefficient, to show a reduction in inequality (arising, say, from a redistribution of income from the rich to the middle-income groups) without there being any reduction (and possibly even an increase) in poverty.

3. See for example, Willem F. Wertheim and Matthias Stiefel, *Production, Equality and Participation in Rural China,* Geneva, UNRISD, 1982, Part III.

4. Studies of participation in the Third World are beginning to appear, including a major series sponsored by the United Nations Research Insitute for Social Development. See, for example, Andrew Turton, *Production, Power and Participation in Rural Thailand,* Geneva, UNRISD, 1987; Fernando Calderon and Jorge Dandler, eds., *Bolivia: La Fuerza Historica del Campesinado,* Geneva, UNRISD, 1986; Leon Zamosc, *The Agrarian Question and the Peasant Movement in Colombia,* Cambridge, Cambridge University Press, 1986.

BIBLIOGRAPHY OF WORKS CITED

ADELMAN, Irma
"A Poverty-Focused Approach to Development Policy", in John P. Lewis and Valeriana Kallab, eds., *Development Strategies Reconsidered*, New Brunswick, NJ., Transaction Books for the Overseas Development Council, 1986.

"Beyond Export-Led Growth", *World Development*, Vol. 12, No. 9, September 1984.

ADELMAN, Irma and Cynthia Taft MORRIS
Economic Growth and Social Equity in Developing Countries, Palo Alto, Stanford University Press, 1973.

AHLUWALIA, Isher Judge
Industrial Growth in India: Stagnation Since the Mid-Sixties, Delhi, Oxford University Press, 1985.

AHLUWALIA, Montek S.
"Inequality, Poverty and Development", *Journal of Development Economics*, Vol. 3, No. 3, September 1976.

"Rural Poverty, Agricultural Production and Prices: A Re-examination", in John W. Mellor and Gunvant M. Desai, eds., *Agricultural Change and Rural Poverty: Variations on a Theme by Dharm Narain*, Delhi, Oxford University Press, 1986.

AHLUWALIA, Montek S., Nicholas G. CARTER and Hollis B. CHENERY
"Growth and Poverty in Developing Countries", *Journal of Development Economics*, Vol. 6, No. 3, September 1979.

AHMED, R.
Agricultural Price Policies Under Complex Socioeconomic and Natural Constraints: The Case of Bangladesh, Washington, D.C., International Food Policy Research Institute, Research Report 27, 1981.

ANDRADE, Regis de Castro
"Brazil: The Economics of Savage Capitalism", in Manfred Bienefeld and Martin Godfrey, eds., *The Struggle for Development: National Strategies in an International Context*, Chichester, John Wiley, 1982.

ANDREFF, Wladimir
"Déclin ou mutation du modéle planifié d'industrialisation lourde: quels enseignements pour le Tiers-Monde?", paper presented to a conference on Economic industrielle et stratégies d'industrialisation dans le Tiers-Monde, ORSTOM, Paris, 26–27th February 1987.

ANON.
"Bangladesh: Where the Right Policies Get No Credit", *The Economist*, 18th October 1986.

"The Peasants' Revolt", *The Economist Development Report*, November 1985.

ARELLANO, José-Pablo
"Meeting Basic Needs: The Trade-Off Between the Quality and the Coverage of the Programs", *Journal of Development Economics,* Vol. 18, No. 1, May–June 1985.

ARMSTRONG, Warwick
"Imperial Incubus: The Diminished Industrial Ambitions of Canada, Australia and Argentina: 1870–1930", paper presented to a conference on Economic industrielle et stratégies d'industrialisation dans le Tiers-Monde, ORSTOM, Paris, 26–27th February 1987.

ARROW, Kenneth and Gérard DEBREU
"Existence of an Equilibrium for a Competitive Economy", *Econometrica*, Vol. 22, No. 3, July 1954.

ASIAN DEVELOPMENT BANK
Emerging Asia: Changes and Challenges, Manila, Asian Development Bank, 1997.

BAHRO, Rudolf
The Alternative in Eastern Europe, New York, Schocken, 1981.

BALASSA, Bela
Change and Challenge in the World Economy, London, Macmillan, 1985.

"Exports and Economic Growth: Further Evidence", *Journal of Development Economics*, Vol. 5, No. 2, June 1978.

BALASSA, Bela, ed.
Development Strategies in Semi-Indusirial Economies, Oxford, Oxford University Press, 1982.

BALASSA, Bela *et al.*
The Structure of Protection in Developing Countries, Baltimore, Johns Hopkins University Press, 1971.

BARDHAN, Kalpana
"Economic Growth, Poverty and Rural Labour Markets in India: A Survey of Research", Geneva, International Labour Office, World Employment Programme Working Paper WEP 10-6/WPS4, March 1983.

BARKER, Randolph and Robert HERDT with Beth ROSE
The Rice Economy of Asia, Washington, D.C., Resources for the Future, 1985.

BARRO, Robert
"Economic Growth in a Cross Section of Countries", *Quarterly Journal of Economics*, Vol. 106, May 1991.

BASU, Kaushik
"One Kind of Power", *Oxford Economic Papers*, Vol. 38, No. 2, July 1986.

BERGSMAN, Joel
Brazil: Industrialization and Trade Policies, London, Oxford University Press, 1970.

BERGSON, Abram
"Income Inequality Under Soviet Socialism", *Journal of Economic Literature*, Vol. XXII, No. 3, September 1984.

BERRY, Albert, François BOURGUIGNON and Christian MORRISSON
"Changes in the World Distribution of Income Between 1950 and 1977", *Economic Journal*, Vol. 93, No. 370, June 1983.

BERRY, Albert and W.R. CLINE
Agrarian Structure and Productivity in Developing Countries, Baltimore, Johns Hopkins University Press, 1979.

BETTELHEIM, Charles
"The Specificity of Soviet Capitalism", *Monthly Review*, Vol. 37, September 1985.

BHAGWATI, J.N.
"Rethinking Trade Strategy", in John P. Lewis and Valeriana Kallab, eds., *Development Strategies Reconsidered*, New Brunswick, N.J., Transaction Books for the Overseas Development Council, 1986.

"The Generalized Theory of Distortions and Welfare', in J.N. Bhagwati, N.W. Jones, R.A. Mundell and J. Vartek, eds., *Trade, Balance of Payments and Growth: Essays in Honour of Charles P. Kindleberger*, Amsterdam, North Holland, 1971.

244

BHAGWATI, Jagdish and Padma DESAI
India: Planning for Industrialization, London, Oxford University Press, 1970.

BHAGWATI, Jagdish and T.N. SRINIVASAN
Foreign Trade Regimes and Economic Development: India, New York, Columbia University Press for the National Bureau of Economic Research, 1975.

BHAGWATI, J.N., N.W. JONES, R.A. MUNDELL and J. VANEK, eds.
Trade, Balance of Payments and Growth: Essays in Honour of Charles P. Kindleberger, Amsterdam, North Holland, 1971.

BHALLA, Surjit S. and Paul GLEWWE
"Growth and Equity in Developing Countries: A Reinterpretation of the Sri Lanka Experience", *World Bank Economic Review*, Vol. 1, No. 1, September 1986.

BHATTACHARYA, A., P.J. MONTIEL and S. SHARMA
Private Capital Flows to Sub-Saharan Africa: An Overview of Trends and Determinants, unpublished paper, World Bank, Washington, D.C., 1996.

BIDELEUX, Robert
Communism and Development, London and New York, Methuen, 1985.

BIENEFELD, Manfred and Martin GODFREY, eds.
The Struggle for Development: National Strategies in an International Context, Chichester, John Wiley, 1982.

BOYCE, James
Agrarian Impasse in Bengal: Institutional Constraints to Technological Change, Oxford, Oxford University Press, 1987.

"Irrigation Development in Asian Rice Agriculture: Technological and Institutional Alternatives", paper prepared for the World Institute for Development Economics Research, Helsinki, May 1986.

"Kinked Exponential Models for Growth Rate Estimation", *Oxford Bulletin of Economics and Statistics*, Vol. 48, No. 4, November 1986.

BRUNNER, Karl and Allan H. MELTZER, eds.
Economic Policy in a Changing World, Amsterdam, North Holland, 1982.

BRUS, Wlodzimierz
"Experience of the Socialist Countries", in Louis Emmerij, ed., *Development Policies and the Crisis of the 1980s*, Paris, OECD Development Centre, 1987.

Socialist Ownership and Political Systems, London, Routledge and Kegan Paul, 1975.

The Market in a Socialist Economy, London, Routledge and Kegan Paul, 1972.

BULL, Hedley
The Anarchical Society: A Study of Order in World Politics, London, Macmillan, 1977.

BURAWOY, M.
"The Functions and Reproduction of Migrant Labor: Comparative Material from Southern Africa and the United States", *American Journal of Sociology*, Vol. 81, 1976.

BUSTAMANTE, LA.
"Mexican Migration: The Political Dynamic of Perception", in C.W. Reynolds and C. Tello, eds., *U.S.-Mexican Relations: Economic and Social Aspects*, Stanford, Stanford University Press, 1983.

CALDERON, Fernando and Jorge DANDLER, eds.
Bolivia: La Fuerza Historica del Campesinado, Geneva, UNRISD, 1986.

CARDOSO, F.H. and E. FALETTO
Dependency and Development in Latin America, Berkeley, University of California Press, 1983.

CASSEN, Robert
Does Aid Work?, Oxford, Oxford University Press, 1986.

CASTILLO, Gelia T.
All in a Grain of Rice, Laguna, Philippines: Southeast Asian Regional Centre for Graduate Study and Research in Agriculture, 1975.

CHENERY, Hollis
"Patterns of Industrial Growth", *American Economic Review*, Vol. 50, No. 4, September 1960.

CHENERY, Hollis and Lance TAYLOR
"Development Patterns: Among Countries and Over Time", *Review of Economics and Statistics*, Vol. 50, No. 4, November 1968.

CHENERY, Hollis, Montek S. AHLUWALIA, C.L.G. BELL, John H. DULOY and Richard JOLLY
Redistribution With Growth, London, Oxford University Press, 1974.

CHENERY, Hollis and Moshe SYRQUIN
Patterns of Development 1950–1970, Oxford, Oxford University Press, 1975.

CHENERY, Hollis, Sherman ROBINSON and Moshe SYRQUIN
Industrialization and Growth: A Comparative Study, Oxford, Oxford University Press, 1986.

CHRISTIAN MICHELSEN INSTITUTE
Bangladesh: Country Study and Norwegian Aid Review, Bergen, Christian Michelsen Institute, 1986.

CLARK, Colin
The Conditions of Economic Progress, London, Macmillan, 1940.

COLLIER, D., ed.
The New Authoritarianism in Latin America, Princeton, Princeton University Press, 1979.

COMMITTEE FOR DEVELOPMENT PLANNING
Human Resources Development: A Neglected Dimension of Development Strategy, New York, United Nations, 1988.

CORDEN, W.M.
"The Costs and Consequences of Protection: A Survey of Empirical Work", in Peter B. Kenen, ed., *International Trade and Finance: Frontiers for Research*, Cambridge, Cambridge University Press, 1975.

"The Effects of Trade on the Rate of Growth", in J.N. Bhagwati, R.W. Jones, R.A. Mundell and J. Vanek, eds., *Trade, Balance of Payments and Growth: Essays in Honour of Charles P. Kindleberger*, Amsterdam, North Holland, 1971.

"The Structure of a Tariff System and the Effective Protective Rate", *Journal of Political Economy*, Vol. LXXIV, No. 3, June 1966.

CORNIA, G.A.
"Farm Size, Land Yields and the Agricultural Production Function: An Analysis for Fifteen Developing Countries", *World Development*, Vol. 13, No. 4, April 1985.

COTLEAR, Daniel
"The Effects of Education on Farm Productivity", in Keith Griffin and John Knight, eds., *Human Development and the International Development Strategy for the 1990s*, London, Macmillan, 1990.

DANDEKAR, V.M. and Nilakantha RATH
Poverty in India, Bombay, Economic and Political Weekly, 1971.

DE SILVA, G.V.S., Niranjan MEHTA, Md. Anisur RAHMAN and Poona WIGNARAJA
"Bhoomi Sena: A Struggle for People's Power", *Development Dialogue*, No. 2, 1979.

DIAZ-ALEJANDRO, Carlos
"Good-Bye Financial Repression, Hello Financial Crash", *Journal of Development Economics*, Vol. 19, No. 1/2, September–October 1985.

DOMAR, Evsei
Essays in the Theory of Economic Growth, London, Oxford University Press, 1957.

EDWARDS, Sebastian
"Stabilization with Liberalization: An Evaluation of Ten Years of Chile's Experiment with Free-Market Policies, 1973–1983", *Economic Development and Cultural Change*, Vol. 33, No. 2, January 1985.

EICHER, Carl K. and John M. STAATZ, eds.
Agricultural Development in the Third World, Baltimore, Johns Hopkins University Press, 1984.

ELLMAN, M.
Socialist Planning, Cambridge, Cambridge University Press, 1979.

EMMERIJ, Louis
"Basic Needs and Employment-Oriented Strategies Reconsidered", *Development and Peace*, Vol. 2, Autumn 1981.

EMMERIJ, Louis, ed.
Development Policies and the Crisis of the 1980s, Paris, OECD Development Centre, 1987.

Economic and Social Development into the XXI Century, Washington, D.C., Johns Hopkins University Press for the Inter-American Development Bank, 1997.

ENOS, John
"Korean Industrial Policy", *Prometheus*, Vol. 4, No. 2, December 1986.

ESMAN, Milton J.
"Administrative Doctrine and Developmental Needs", in E. Philip Morgan, ed., *The Administration of Change in Africa*, Dunellen, 1974.

EVANS, Peter
Dependent Development: The Alliance of Multinational, State and Local Capital in Brazil, Princeton, Princeton University Press, 1979.

FEI, John C.H., Gustay RANIS and Shirley W.Y. KUO
Growth with Equity: The Taiwan Case, New York, Oxford University Press, 1979.

FELDMAN, Ernesto V.
"La Crisis Financiera Argentina: 1980–1982. Algunos Comentarios", *Desarrollo Economico*, Vol. 23, No. 91, October–December 1983.

247

FELDMAN, G.
"On the Theory of Economic Growth Rates", in Evsei Domar, *Essays in the Theory of Economic Growth*, London, Oxford University Press, 1957.

FERNANDEZ, Roque B.
"La Crisis Financiera Argentina: 1980–1982", *Desarrollo Economico*, Vol. 23, No. 89, April–June 1983.

FFRENCH-DAVIS, Ricardo
"The Monetarist Experiment in Chile: A Critical Survey", *World Development*, Vol. 11, No. 11, November 1983.

FIELDS, G.S.
"Employment, Income Distribution and Economic Growth in Seven Small Open Economies", *Economic Journal*, Vol. 94, No. 373, March 1984.

FISHLOW, Albert
"Brazilian Size Distribution of Income", *American Economic Review*, Vol. LX, No. 3, May 1972.

FOUQUIN, Michel
"L'inégalité des pays en développement face au commerce internationale", paper presented to a conference on Economie industrielle et stratégies d'industrialisation dans le Tiers-Monde, ORSTOM, Paris, 26–27th February 1987.

FOXLEY, Alejandro
Latin American Experiments in Neo-Conservative Economics, Berkeley, University of California Press, 1983.

FRIEDMAN, Milton
Capitalism and Freedom, Chicago, University of Chicago Press, 1952.

FRIEDMAN, Milton and R. FRIEDMAN
Free to Choose, Penguin, 1980.

GERSCHENKRON, Alexander
Economic Backwardness in Historical Perspective, Cambridge, Mass., Harvard University Press, 1962.

GHAI, Dharam
"Successes and Failures in Growth in Sub-Saharan Africa: 1960–82", in Louis Emmerij, ed., *Development Policies and the Crisis of the 1980s*, Paris, OECD Development Centre, 1987.

GHAI, Dharam and Lawrence SMITH
Agricultural Prices, Policy and Equity in Sub-Saharan Africa, Boulder, Colorado, Lynne Rienner Publishers, 1987.

"Food Policy and Equity in Sub-Saharan Africa", Geneva, ILO World Employment Programme Working Paper WEP 10-6/WPS5, August 1983.

GIOVANNINI, Alberto
"Saving and the Real Interest Rate in LDCs", *Journal of Development Economics*, Vol. 18, Nos. 2–3, August 1985.

GLEWWE, Paul
"The Distribution of Income in Sri Lanka in 1969–70 and 1980–81: A Decomposition Analysis", *Journal of Development Economics*, Vol. 24, No. 2, December 1986.

GOONERATNE, W. and D. WESUMPERUMA, eds.
Plantation Agriculture in Sri Lanka, Bangkok, ILO-ARTEP, 1984.

GREENWALD, B. and J.E. STIGLITZ
"Externalities in Economies With Imperfect Information and Incomplete Markets", *Quarterly Journal of Economics*, Vol. Cl, No. 2, May 1986.

GRIFFIN, Keith
"Culture, Human Development and Economic Growth", Geneva, UNRISD/UNESCO Occasional Paper Series on Culture and Development, No. 3, 1997.

"Economic Policy During the Transition to a Market Oriented Economy", unpublished report prepared for UNDP, 1998.

"Globalization and the Shape of Things to Come," keynote address delivered to the Macalester International Roundtable on Globalization and Economic Space, Macalester College, 8–10 October 1998.

World Hunger and the World Economy, London, Macmillan, 1987.

International Inequality and National Poverty, London, Macmillan, 1978.

"On the Emigration of the Peasantry", *World Development*, Vol. 4, May 1976.

The Political Economy of Agrarian Change, London, Macmillan, 1974.

Underdevelopment in Spanish America, London, Allen and Unwin, 1969.

GRIFFIN, Keith, ed.
Institutional Reform and Economic Development in the Chinese Countryside, London, Macmillan, 1984.

GRIFFIN, Keith and A.K. GHOSE
"Growth and Impoverishment in the Rural Areas of Asia", *World Development*, Vol. 7, No. 4/5, April/May, 1979.

GRIFFIN, Keith and John GURLEY
"Radical Analyses of Imperialism, The Third World and the Transition to Socialism: A Survey Article", *Journal of Economic Literature*, Vol. XXIII, September 1985.

GRIFFIN, Keith and Jeffrey JAMES
The Transition to Egalitarian Development: Economic Policies for Structural Change in the Third World, London, Macmillan, 1981.

GRIFFIN, Keith and Azizur Rahman KHAN, eds.
Growth and Inequality in Pakistan, London, Macmillan, 1972.

"Poverty in the Third World: Ugly Facts and Fancy Models", *World Development*, Vol. 6, No. 3, March 1978.

GRIFFIN, Keith and John KNIGHT, eds.
Human Development and the International Development Strategy for the 1990s, London, Macmillan, 1990.

GRIFFIN, Keith and Terry McKINLEY
Implementing a Human Development Strategy, London, Macmillan, 1994.

HABERLER, G.
"Some Problems in the Pure Theory of International Trade", *Economic Journal*, Vol. 60, No. 2, June 1950.

HALLIDAY, John
"The North Korean Enigma", in Gordon White, Robin Murray and Christine White, eds., *Revolutionary Socialist Development in the Third World*, Brighton, Wheatsheaf Books, 1983.

"The North Korean Model: Gaps and Questions", *World Development*, Vol, 9, No. 9/10, September–October 1981.

HAQ, Mahbub ul

Reflections on Human Development, New York, Oxford University Press, 1995.

The Poverty Curtain: Choices for the Third World, New York, Columbia University Press, 1976.

The Strategy of Economic Planning: A Case Study of Pakistan, Karachi, Oxford University Press, 1963.

HARBERGER, Arnold C.

"Observations on the Chilean Economy, 1973–1983", *Economic Development and Cultural Change*, Vol. 33, No. 3, April 1985.

"Using the Resources at Hand More Effectively", *American Economic Review*, Vol. XLIX, May 1959.

HAYAMI, Yujiro and Vernon RUTTAN

Agricultural Development: An International Perspective, Baltimore, Johns Hopkins University Press, rev. ed, 1985.

HAYEK, F.A.

The Road to Serfdom, London, Routledge and Sons, 7th ed., 1946.

HELLEINER, G.K.

"Outward Orientation, Import Instability and African Economic Growth: An Empirical Investigation", in S. Lall and F. Stewart, eds., *Theory and Reality in Economic Development*, London, Macmillan, 1986.

HELLER, P.S. and R.C. PORTER

"Exports and Growth: An Empirical Reinvestigation", *Journal of Development Economics*, Vol. 5, No. 2, June 1978.

HICKS, J.R.

Capital and Growth, Oxford, Clarendon Press, 1965.

HIRASHIMA, S.

"Poverty as a Generation's Problem: A Note on the Japanese Experience", in John W. Mellor and Gunvant M. Desai, eds., *Agricultural Change and Rural Poverty: Variations On A Theme by Dharm Narain*, Delhi, Oxford University Press, 1986.

HIRSCHMAN, Albert

"The Political Economy of Import-Substituting Industrialisation in Latin America", *Quarterly Journal of Economics*, Vol. LXXXII, No. 1, February 1968.

"The Turn to Authoritarianism in Latin America and the Search for its Economic Determinants", in D. Collier, ed., *The New Authoritarianism in Latin America*, Princeton, Princeton University Press, 1979.

HOSSAIN, M.

"Employment and Labour in Bangladesh Rural Industries", *Bangladesh Development Studies*, Vol. XII, Nos. 1 and 2, 1984.

HUGUET, J.W.

"International Labour Migration from the ESCAP Region", mimeo., Paris, OECD Development Centre, January 1987.

IBRD

China: Long Term Development Issues and Options, Baltimore, Johns Hopkins University Press, 1985.

China: Socialist Economic Development, Baltimore, Johns Hopkins University Press, 1983.

The Philippines: Recent Trendy in Poverty, Employment and Wages, Washington, D.C., June 1985.

World Development Report, New York, Oxford University Press, various issues.

ILO

Employment, Growth and Basic Needs: A One-World Problem, Geneva, 1976.

Employment, Incomes and Equality: A Strategy for Increasing Productive Employment in Kenya, Geneva, 1972.

Matching Employment Opportunities and Expectations: A Programme of Action for Ceylon, Geneva, 1971.

Poverty and Landlessness in Rural Asia, Geneva, 1977.

Sharing in Development: A Programme of Employment, Equity and Growth for the Philippines, Geneva, 1974.

Towards Full Employment: A Programme for Colombia, Geneva, 1970.

Towards Self-Reliance: Development, Employment and Equity in Tanzania, Addis Ababa, ILO-JASPA, 1978.

IMF

World Economic Outlook, Washington, D.C., October 1986.

ISENMAN, Paul

"Basic Needs: The Case of Sri Lanka", *World Development,* Vol. 8, No. 3, 1980.

ISHIKAWA, S.

Economic Development in Asian Perspective, Tokyo, Kinokuniya, 1967.

JAYAWARDENA, Kumari

"Aspects of Class and Ethnic Consciousness in Sri Lanka", *Development and Change*, Vol. 14, No. 1, January 1983.

JENKINS, Rhys

"Latin American Industrialization and the New International Division of Labour", paper presented to a conference on Economie industrielle et stratégies; d'industrialisation dans le Tiers-Monde, ORSTOM, Paris, 26–27th February 1987.

JOHNSON, L.L.

"The Problems of Import Substitution: The Chilean Automobile Industry", *Economic Development and Cultural Change*, Vol. 15, No. 2, Pt. 1, January 1967.

JOHNSTON, Bruce F. and Peter KILBY

Agriculture and Structural Transformation: Economic Strategies in Late-Developing Countries, New York, Oxford University Press, 1975.

KALDOR, Nicholas

"Limits On Growth", *Oxford Economic Papers*, Vol. 38, No. 2, July 1986.

KALECKI, M.

Essays on Developing Economies, Brighton, Harvester Press, 1976.

KEARNEY, Michael

"From the Invisible Hand to Visible Feet: Anthropological Studies of Migration and Development", *Annual Review of Anthropology*, 1986.

KENEN, Peter B., ed.

International Trade and Finance: Frontiers for Research, Cambridge, Cambridge University Press, 1975.

KHAN, Azizur Rahman

"Poverty and Inequality in Rural Bangladesh", in ILO, *Poverty and Landlessness in Rural Asia*, Geneva, 1977.

KHAN, Azizur Rahman and Eddy LEE, eds.
Poverty in Asia, Bangkok, ILO-ARTEP, 1985.

KIM, Jang-Ho
Wages, Employment and Income Distribution in South Korea: 1960–83, New Delhi, ILO-ARTEP, March 1986.

KIRKPATRICK, C.H.
"Export Led Development, Labour Market Regulation and the Distribution of Income in Asian NICs: The Case of Singapore", paper presented to a conference on Economic industrielle et stratégies d'industrialisation dans le Tiers-Monde, ORSTOM, Paris, 26–27th February 1987.

KIRKPATRICK, C.H., N, LEE and F.I. NIXSON
Industrial Structure and Policy in Less Developed Countries, London, Allen and Unwin, 1984.

KOZLOWSKI, Z.
"Agriculture in the Economic Growth of the East European Socialist Countries", in Lloyd Reynolds, ed., *Agriculture in Development Theory*, New Haven, Yale University Press, 1975.

KRAVIS, Irving B.
"Comparative Studies of National Incomes and Prices", *Journal of Economic Literature*, Vol. XXII, March 1984.

KRAVIS, Irving B., Alan W. HESTON and Robert SUMMERS
"Real GDP Per Capita for More Than One Hundred Countries", *Economic Journal*, Vol. 88, No. 350, June 1978.

KRINKS, Peter
"Rectifying Inequality or Favouring the Few? Image and Reality in Philippines Development", in David A.M. Lea and D.P. Chaudhri, eds., *Rural Development and the State*, London, Methuen, 1983.

KRUEGER, Anne O.
"Comparative Advantage and Development Policy 20 Years Later", in Moshe Syrquin, Lance Taylor and Larry Westfall, eds., *Economic Structure and Performance: Essays in Honor of Hollis B. Chenery*, Orlando, Academic Press, 1984.

Liberalization Attempts and Consequences, Cambridge, Mass., Ballinger Publishing Co., 1978.

"Trade Policy as an Input to Development", *American Economic Review*, Vol. 70, No. 2, May 1980.

KUO, Shirley W.Y., Gustav RANIS and John C.H. FEI
The Taiwan Success Story: Rapid Growth With Improved Distribution in the Republic of China, 1952–1979, Boulder, Colorado, Westview Press, 1981.

KURIAN, Rachel
Women Workers in the Sri Lanka Plantation Sector, Geneva, ILO, 1982.

KUZNETS, Simon
"Economic Growth and Income Inequality", *American Economic Review*, Vol. 49, March 1955.

Economic Growth and Structure: Selected Essays, London, Heinemann, 1966.

Modern Economic Growth: Rate, Structure and Spread, New Haven and London, Yale University Press, 1966.

LAKSHMAN, W.D.
"State Policy in Sri Lanka and its Economic Impact 1970–85: Selected Themes with Special Reference to Distributive Implications of Policy", *Upanathi*, Vol. 1, No. 1, January 1986.

LAL, Deepak
The Poverty of Development Economics, London, Institute of Economic Affairs, Hobart Paper No. 16, 1983.

LALL, S. and F. STEWART, eds.
Theory and Reality in Economic Development, London, Macmillan, 1986.

LAPIERRE, Dominique
The City of Joy, Bungay, Suffolk, Richard Clay (The Chaucer Press), 1985.

LARDY, Nicholas
Agriculture in China's Modern Economic Development, Cambridge, Cambridge University Press, 1983.

LAU, L.J., ed.
Models of Development: A Comparative Study of Economic Growth in South Korea and Taiwan, San Francisco, ICS Press, 1986.

LEA, David A.M., and D.P. CHAUDHRI, eds.
Rural Development and the State, London, Methuen, 1983.

LEE, E.L.H., ed.
Export-Led Industrialisation and Development, Bangkok, ILO-ARTEP, 1981.

LEIJONHUFVUD, Axel and Christof RÜHL
"Russian Dilemmas", *American Economic Review*, Vol. 87, No. 2, May 1997.

LEWIS, John P. and Valeriana KALLAB, eds.
Development Strategies Reconsidered, New Brunswick, N.J., Transaction Books for the Overseas Development Council, 1986.

LEWIS, Jr., Stephen R.
"Development Problems of the Mineral-Rich Countries", in Moshe Syrquin, Lance Taylor and Larry Westphal, eds., *Economic Structure and Performance: Essays in Honor of Hollis B. Chenery*, Orlando, Academic Press, 1984.

LEWIS, W. Arthur
"Economic Development with Unlimited Supplies of Labour", *Manchester School*, Vol. 22, May 1954.

The Evolution of the International Economic Order, Princeton, Princeton University Press, 1978.

The Theory of Economic Growth, London, Allen and Unwin, 1955.

LINDER, S.B.
An Essay on Trade and Transformation, Stockholm, Almqvist and Wiksell, 1961.

LIPTON, Michael
Why Poor People Stay Poor: Urban Bias in World Development, London, Temple Smith, 1977.

LIST, Friedrich
Das Nationale System der Politischen Okonomie, Tubingen, Mohr-Siebeck Verlag, 1959 (1st ed., 1841).

LITTLE, Ian
'Small Manufacturing Enterprises in Developing Countries", *World Bank Economic Review*, Vol. 1, No. 2, January 1987.

"The Experience and Causes of Rapid Labour-Intensive Development in Korea, Taiwan Province, Hong Kong and Singapore; and the Possibilities of Emulation", in E.L.H. Lee, ed., *Export-Led Industrialisation and Development*, Bangkok, ILO-ARTEP, 1981.

LITTLE, Ian, Tibor SCITOVSKY and Maurice SCOTT
Industry and Trade in Some Developing Countries, London, Oxford University Press, 1970.

McKINNON, Ronald I.
Money and Capital in Economic Development, Washington, D.C., Brookings Institution, 1973.

"The Order of Liberalization: Lessons from Chile and Argentina", in Karl Brunner and Allan H. Meltzer, eds., *Economic Policy in a Changing World*, Amsterdam, North Holland, 1982.

MADDISON, Angus
"Economic Policy and Performance in Capitalist Europe", in Louis Emmerij, ed., *Economic and Social Development into the XXI Century*, Washington, D.C., Johns Hopkins University Press for the Inter-American Development Bank, 1997.

Two Crises: Latin America and Asia 1929–38 and 1973–83, Paris, OECD Development Centre, 1985.

"A Comparison of Levels of GDP Per Capita in Developed and Developing Countries, 1700–1980", *Journal of Economic History*, Vol. XLIII, No. 1, March 1983.

Economic Progress and Policy in Developing Countries, New York, W.W. Norton, 1970.

MAGEE, S.P.
"Factor Market Distortions, Production and Trade: A Survey", *Oxford Economic Papers*, Vol. 25, No. 1, March 1973,

MAHALANOBIS, P.C.
The Approach of Operational Research to Planning in India, London, Asia Publishing House, 1963.

MAIZELS, Alfred
Exports and Economic Growth of Developing Countries, London, Cambridge University Press, 1968.

MANDEL, Ernest
"The Class Nature of the Soviet Union", *Review of Radical Political Economy*, Vol. 14, Spring 1982.

MANOILESCU, M.
The Theory of Protection, London, King, 1931.

MAO TSE-TUNG
Selected Works, Vol. 5, Beijing, Foreign Languages Press, 1977.

MELLOR, John W.
"Agricultural Change and Rural Poverty", Washington, D.C., International Food Policy Research Institute, Food Policy Statement No. 3, October 1985.

"Agriculture on the Road to Industrialization", in John P. Lewis and Valeriana Kallab, eds., *Development Strategies Reconsidered*, New Brunswick, N.J., Transaction Books for the Overseas Development Council, 1986.

"Food Price Policy and Income Distribution in Low-Income Countries", *Economic Development and Cultural Change,* Vol. 27, No. 1, October 1978.

The New Economics of Growth: A Strategy for India and the Developing World, Ithaca, Cornell University Press, 1976.

"The Role of Government and the New Agricultural Technologies", Washington, D.C., International Food Policy Research Institute, Food Policy Statement No. 4, November 1985.

MELLOR, John W. and Gunvant M. DESAI, eds.
Agricultural Change and Rural Poverty: Variations On A Theme by Dharm Narain, Delhi, Oxford University Press, 1986.

MESA-LAGO, Carmelo and Jorge PEREZ-LOPEZ
A Study of Cuba's Material Product System, Its Conversion to the System of National Accounts, and Estimations of Gross Domestic Product per Capita and Growth Rates, Washington, D.C., World Bank Staff Working Papers No. 770, 1985.

MICHAELY, Michael
"Exports and Growth: An Empirical Investigation", *Journal of Development Economics*, Vol. 4, No. 1, March 1977.

MICHELL, Tony
"South Korea: Vision of the Future for Labour Surplus Economies?", in Manfred Bienefeld and Martin Godfrey, eds., *The Struggle for Development: National Strategies in an International Context*, Chichester, John Wiley, 1982.

MOORE, Jr., Barrington
Social Origins of Dictatorship and Democracy: Lord and Peasant in the Making of the Modern World, London, Allen Lane, 1967.

MORAWETZ, David
Twenty-five Years of Economic Development 1950 to 1975, Washington, D.C., The World Bank, 1977.

MORGAN, E. Philip, ed.
The Administration of Change in Africa, Dunellen, 1974.

MORRISSON, Christian
'Income Distribution in East European and Western Countries", *Journal of Comparative Economics*, Vol. 8, 1984.

MUKHOPADHYAY, Swapna, ed.
The Poor in Asia: Productivity-raising Programmes and Strategies, Kuala Lumpur, UN Asian and Pacific Development Centre, 1985.

MYINT, Hla
"Exports and Economic Development of Less Developed Countries", in Carl K. Eicher and John M. Staatz, eds., *Agricultural Development in the Third World*, Baltimore, Johns Hopkins University Press, 1984.

NASEEM, S.M.
"Rural Poverty and Landlessness in Pakistan", in ILO, *Poverty and Landlessness in Rural Asia*, Geneva, 1977.

NETHERLANDS INSTITUTE OF HUMAN RIGHTS
Ethnic Violence, Development and Human Rights, The Hague, CIP-gegevens Koninklijke Bibliotheek, 1985.

NICOLAUS, Martin
Restoration of Capitalism in the USSR, Chicago, Liberator Press, 1975.

NOGUES, Julio J.
Andrzej OLECHOWSKI and L. Alan WINTERS, "The Extent of Nontariff Barriers to Industrial Countries' Imports", *World Bank Economic Reivew*, Vol. 1, No. 1, September 1986.

NOVE, Alec
The Economics of Feasible Socialism, London, George Allen and Unwin, 1983.

NURSKE, Ragnar
Patterns of Trade and Development, Stockholm, Almqvist and Wiksell, 1959.

Problems of Capital Formation in Underdeveloped Countries, New York, Oxford University Press, 1953.

O'DONNELL, G.
Modernization and Bureaucratic Authoritarianism, Berkeley, Institute of International Studies, University of California, 1973.

OSMANI, S.R.
"The Food Problems of Bangladesh", paper presented to the Food Strategies Research Conference, World Institute of Development Economics Research, Helsinki, 21–25th July 1986.

OVERSEAS DEVELOPMENT INSTITUTE
Foreign Direct Investment Flows to Low-income Countries: A Review of the Evidence, Briefing Paper, London, September 1997.

PAINE, Suzanne
Exporting Workers: The Turkish Case, University of Cambridge, Department of Applied Economics, Occasional Paper 41, University of Cambridge Press, 1974.

PANT, Pitambar
"Perspective of Development, India 1960–61 to 1975–76: Implications of Planning for a Minimum Level of Living", in T.N. Srinivasan and P.K. Bardhan, eds., *Poverty and Income Distribution in India*, Calcutta, Statistical Publishing Society, 1974.

PARK, Y.C.
"Foreign Debt, Balance of Payments and Growth Prospects: The Case of the Republic of Korea, 1965–88", *World Development*, Vol. 14, No. 8, August 1986.

PAUKERT, Felix
"Income Distribution at Different Levels of Development: A Survey of Evidence", *International Labour Review*, Vol. CVIII, Nos. 2–3, August–September 1973.

PINSTRUP-ANDERSEN, Per
"Food Prices and the Poor in Developing Countries", *European Review of Agricultural Economics*, Vol. 12, Nos. 1/2, 1985.

PINSTRUP-ANDERSEN, Per and Peter R.B. HAZELL
"The Impact of the Green Revolution and Prospects for the Future", *Food Reviews International*, Vol. 1, No. 1, 1985.

POWER, John
"Import Substitution as an Industrialization Strategy", *Philippine Economic Journal*, Spring 1966.

"The Role of Protection with Particular Reference to Kenya", *Eastern Africa Economic Review*, Vol. 4, No. 1, June 1972.

PREBISCH, Raul
"Commercial Policy in Underdeveloped Countries", *American Economic Review*, Vol. XLIX, May 1959.

PREOBRAZHENSKY, Evgeny
The New Economics, London, Oxford University Press, 1965.

PSACHAROPOULOS, George
"Education and Development: A Review", *World Bank Research Observer*, Vol. 3, No. 1, 1988.

"Returns to Investment in Education: A Global Update", *World Development*, Vol. 22, 1994.

QUAN, Nguyen T. and Anthony Y.C. KOO
"Concentration of Land Holdings: An Empirical Exploration of Kuznets' Conjecture", *Journal of Development Economics*, Vol. 18, No. 1, May–June 1985.

QUIZON, Jaime and Hans BINSWANGER
"Modeling the Impact of Agricultural Growth and Government Policy on Income Distribution in India", *World Bank Economic Review*, Vol. 1, No. 1, September 1986.

RADWAN, Samir and Eddy LEE
Agrarian Change in Egypt: An Anatomy of Rural Poverty, London, Croom Helm, 1986.

RAJ, K.N., and A.K. SEN
"Alternative Patterns of Growth Under Conditions of Stagnant Export Earnings", *Oxford Economic Papers*, Vol. 13, No. 1, February 1961.

RAM, Rati
"Level of Development and Returns to Schooling: Some Estimates from Multicountry Data", *Economic Development and Cultural Change*, Vol. 44, No. 4, 1996.

"Exports and Economic Growth: Some Additional Evidence", *Economic Development and Cultural Change*, Vol. 33, No. 2, January 1985.

RAMOS, Joseph
"Stabilization and Adjustment Policies in the Southern Cone, 1974–1983", *Cepal Review*, No. 25, April 1985.

RAWLS, John
A Theory of Justice, Oxford, Clarendon Press, 1971.

REYNOLDS, C.W. and C. TELLO, eds.
U.S.-Mexican Relations: Economic and Social Aspects, Stanford, Stanford University Press, 1983.

REYNOLDS, Lloyd, ed.
Agriculture in Development Theory, New Haven, Yale University Press, 1975.

REYNOLDS, Lloyd
Economic Growth in the Third World, 1850–1980, New Haven, Yale University Press, 1985.

"The Spread of Economic Growth to the Third World: 1850–1980", *Journal of Economic Literature*, Vol. XXI, No. 3, September 1983.

RICARDO, David
Principles of Political Economy and Taxation, 1817; reprinted London, J.M. Dent and Sons, 1957.

RICHARDS, Peter and Wilbert GOONERATNE
Basic Needs, Poverty and Government Policies in Sri Lanka, Geneva, ILO, 1980.

RICHARDSON, George
Information and Investment, London, Oxford University Press, 1960.

RISKIN, Carl
"A Comment on Professor Brus' Paper", in Louis Emmerij, ed., *Development Policies and the Crisis of the 1980s*, Paris, OECD Development Centre, 1987.

China's Political Economy: The Quest for Development Since 1949, New York, Oxford University Press, 1987.

"Feeding China: The Experience Since 1949", paper presented to a conference on Hunger and Poverty – The Poorest Billion, World Institute of Development Economics Research, Helsinki, 21–25th July 1986.

SABATO, Ernesto, ed.
Nunca Mas, Buenos Aires: Report of the National Commission on the Disappeared, 1984.

257

SAHLINS, Marshall

Stone Age Economics, Chicago, Aldine-Atherton, 1972.

"The Original Affluent Society", *Development*, No. 3, 1986.

SAMUELSON, Paul

"International Factor Price Equalization Once Again", *Economic Journal*, Vol. 59, No. 2, June 1949.

"International Trade and the Equalization of Factor Prices", *Economic Journal*, Vol, 58, No. 2, June 1948.

SCHULTZ, T.W.

"Capital Formation by Education", *Journal of Political Economy*, December 1960.

"Investment in Human Capital", *American Economic Review*, March 1961.

Transforming Traditional Agriculture, New Haven, Yale University Press, 1964.

SCITOVSKY, Tibor

"Economic Development in Taiwan and South Korea, 1965–81", in L.J. Lau, ed., *Models of Development: A Comparative Study of Economic Growth in South Korea and Taiwan*, San Francisco, ICS Press, 1986.

SEN, Amartya

"Development as Capability Expansion", in Keith Griffin and John Knight, eds, *Human Development and the International Development Strategy for the 1990s*, London, Macmillan, 1990.

Resources, Values and Development, Oxford, Blackwell, 1984.

"Development: Which Way Now?", *Economic Journal*, Vol. 93, No. 372, December 1983.

"Poor, Relatively Speaking", *Oxford Economic Papers*, Vol. 35, No. 2, July 1983.

Poverty and Famines: An Essay on Entitlement and Deprivation, Oxford, Oxford University Press, 1981.

"Public Action and the Quality of Life in Developing Countries", *Oxford Bulletin of Economics and Statistics*, Vol. 43, 1981.

Choice of Technique, Oxford, Blackwell, 3rd ed., 1968.

SENGHAAS, Dieter

The European Experience: A Historical Critique of Development Theory, Leamington Spa, Berg, 1985.

SHARMA, J.S.

Growth and Equity: Policies and Implementation in Indian Agriculture, Washington, D.C., International Food Policy Research Institute, Research Report 28, November 1981.

SHAW, Edward S.

Financial Deepening in Economic Development, New York, Oxford University Press, 1973.

SHEAHAN, John

"Market-Oriented Policies and Political Repression in Latin America", *Economic Development and Cultural Change*, Vol. 28, No. 2, January 1980.

SHUE, Vivienne

Peasant China in Transition: The Dynamics of Development Toward Socialism, 1949–1956, Berkeley, University of California Press, 1980.

SIC, Ota

The Third Way, London, Wildwood House, 1976.

258

SINGH, Ajit
"The Interrupted Industrial Revolution of the Third World: Prospects and Policies for Resumption", paper presented to a conference on Economic industrielle et stratégies d'industrialisation dans le Tiers-Monde, ORSTOM, Paris, 26–27th February 1987.

SINGH, H. and K.W. JUN
Some New Evidence on Determinants of Foreign Direct Investment in Developing Countries, Policy Research Working Paper No. 1531, Washington, D.C., World Bank, 1995.

SMITH, Adam
An Inquiry into the Nature and Causes of the Wealth of Nations, 1776; reprinted New York, Random House, 1937.

SOLIGO, R. and J.J. STERN
"Tariff Protection, Import Substitution and Investment Efficiency", *Pakistan Development Review*, Vol. 5, No. 2, Summer 1965.

SRINIVASAN, T.N. and P.K. BARDHAN, eds.
Poverty and Income Distribution in India, Calcutta, Statistical Publishing Society, 1974.

STEPAN, A., ed.
Authoritarian Brazil, New Haven, Yale University Press, 1973.

STEWART, Frances
"John Williamson and the Washington Consensus Revisited", in Louis Emmerij, ed., *Economic and Social Development into the XXI Century*, Washington, D.C., Johns Hopkins University Press for the Inter-American Development Bank, 1997.

Basic Needs in Developing Countries, Baltimore, Johns Hopkins University Press, 1985.

STIGLITZ, J.E.
"The New Development Economics", *World Development*, Vol. 14, No. 2, February 1986.

STIGLITZ, J.E. and A. WEISS
"Credit Rationing in Markets with Imperfect Information", *American Economic Review*, Vol. 71, No. 3, June 1981.

STREETEN, Paul
Development Perspectives, London, Macmillan, 1981.

STREETEN, Paul with Shahid Javed BURKI, Mahbub ul HAQ, Norman HICKS and Frances STEWART
First Things First: Meeting Basic Needs in the Developing Countries, New York, Oxford University Press, 1981.

SUKHATME, P.
"Assessment of Adequacy of Diets at Different Income Levels", *Economic and Political Weekly*, Vol. 13, 1978.

"Measurement of Undernutrition", *Economic and Political Weekly*, Vol. 17, 11th December 1982.

"On Measurement of Poverty", *Economic and Political Weekly*, Vol. 16, August 1981.

"On the Measurement of Undernutrition: A Comment", *Economic and Political Weekly*, Vol. 16, 6th June 1981.

SUTCLIFFE, Robert
Industry and Underdevelopment, London, Addison-Wesley, 1971.

SWAN, Bernard
"Sri Lanka: Constraints and Prospects in the Pursuit of Rural Development", in David A.M. Lee and D.P. Chaudhri, eds., *Rural Development and the State*, London, Methuen, 1983.

SWEEZY, Paul
"After Capitalism, What?", *Monthly Review*, Vol. 37, July–August 1985.

SYRQUIN, Moshe, Lance TAYLOR and Larry WESTPHAL, eds.
Economic Structure and Performance: Essays in Honor of Hollis B. Chenery, Orlando, Academic Press, 1984.

TABATABAI, Hamid
"Economic Decline, Access to Food and Structural Adjustment in Ghana", Geneva, ILO World Employment Programme Working Paper WEP 10-61/WP80, July 1986.

THOMAS, Brinley
Migration and Economic Growth, 2nd ed., Cambridge, Cambridge University Press, 1973.

TIDRICK, G.
Productivity Growth and Technological Change in Chinese Industry, Washington, D.C., World Bank Staff Working Paper No. 761, 1986.

TIMMER, Peter
"Choice of Techniques in Rice Milling in Java", *Bulletin of Indonesian Economic Studies*, Vol. 9, July 1973.

TURNHAM, D., assisted by l. JAEGER
The Employment Problem in Less Developed Countries: A Review of Evidence, Paris, OECD Development Centre, 1971.

TURTON, Andrew
Production, Power and Participation in Rural Thailand, Geneva, UNRISD, 1987.

UN
Department of International Economic and Social Affairs, *Socio-Economic Development and Fertility Decline in Sri Lanka*, New York, 1986.

Economic Commission for Europe, *Economic Survey of Europe*, New York, various issues.

UNITED NATIONS
Demographic Yearbook, New York, various issues.

World Population Prospects, New York, 1986.

UNCTAD
Handbook of International Trade and Development Statistics, New York, 1985.

UNDP
Human Development Report, New York, Oxford University Press, various issues.

UNICEF
The Social Impact of Economic Policies During the Last Decades, Colombo, UNICEF, June 1985.

UNIDO
Handbook of Industrial Statistics 1984, New York, 1985.

Industry in a Changing World, New York, 1983.

Industry in the 1980s: Structural Change and Interdependence, New York, 1985.

US NATIONAL ADVISORY COUNCIL ON INTERNATIONAL MONETARY AND FINANCIAL POLICIES
Annual Report 1984, Washington, D.C., 1984.

URRUTIA, Miguel
"Latin America and the Crisis of the 1980s", in Louis Emmerij, ed., *Development Policies and the Crisis of the 1980s*, Paris, OECD Development Centre, 1987.

VAN ARKADIE, Brian
"Some Realities of Adjustment: An Introduction", *Development and Change*, Vol. 17, No. 3, July 1986.

WEBER, Eugen
Peasants into Frenchmen: The Modernization of Rural France, 1870–1914, London, Chatto and Windus, 1977.

WERTHEIM, Willem F. and Matthias STIEFEL
Production, Equality and Participation in Rural China, Geneva, UNRISD, 1982.

What Now
Dag Hammarskjold Report on Development and International Cooperation, a special issue of *Development Dialogue*, No. 1/2, 1975.

WHITE, Gordon
"Chinese Development Strategy After Mao", in Gordon White, Robin Murray and Christine White, eds., *Revolutionary Socialist Development in the Third World*, Brighton, Wheatsheaf Books, 1983.

"North Korean Juche: The Political Economy of Self-reliance", in Manfred Bienefeld and Martin Godfrey, eds., *The Struggle for Development: National Strategies in an International Context*, Chichester, John Wiley, 1982.

WHITE, Gordon, Robin MURRAY and Christine WHITE, eds.
Revolutionary Socialist Development in the Third World, Brighton, Wheatsheaf Books, 1983.

WICKRAMASEKARA, Piyasiri
"Strategies and Programme for Raising the Productivity of the Rural Poor in Sri Lanka", in Swapna Mukhopadhyay, ed., *The Poor in Asia: Productivity-raising Programmes and Strategies*, Kuala Lumpur, UN Asian and Pacific Development Centre, 1985.

WILBER, Charles
The Soviet Model and Underdeveloped Countries, Chapel Hill, University of North Carolina Press, 1969.

WORLD BANK
World Development Report 1997, New York, Oxford University Press, 1997.

ZAMOSC, Leon
The Agrarian Question and the Peasant Movement in Colombia, Cambridge, Cambridge University Press, 1986.

ZIMBALIST, Andrew
"Cuban Industrial Growth, 1965–84", *World Development*, Vol. 15, No. 1, January 1987.

ZIMBALIST, Andrew and Susan ECKSTEIN
"Patterns of Cuban Development: The First Twenty-five Years", *World Development*, Vol. 15, No. 1, January 1987.

INDEX

foreign aid, 27, 82, 83, 185, 187, 209, 230, 231
foreign capital, 82–5, 96, 123, 181, 230–1
foreign debt, 6, 28, 54, 55, 58–9, 61, 72, 79–81,
    82, 83, 96, 98n, 199, 230, 231
foreign investment, xxvi, 27, 28, 82–3, 117, 209,
    230, 231
foreign trade, 27
Fouquin, Michel, 129n
Foxley, Alejandro, 65n, 131n
France, xxiv, 2, 7, 13, 18, 38, 41, 86, 98n
freedom, 3, 42, 95, 128, 164, 228, 240–2
Friedman, Milton, 42, 66n
Friedman, R., 66n

Gabon, xvii
Georgia, xvii
Germany, 6, 37, 41, 86, 98n, 101, 102, 195, 196,
    197, 198
Gerschenkron, Alexander, 101, 129n
Ghai, Dharam, xxviiin, 98n, 161n
Ghana, 2, 4, 5, 33, 34, 69, 89, 90, 92, 93, 99n,
    102, 104, 105, 133, 134, 136, 137, 140–1,
    227
Ghose, A.K., 161n
Giovannini, Alberto, 66n
Glewwe, Paul, 192n
globalisation, xxiii–xxviin
Godfrey, Martin, 130n, 211t, 224n
Gooneratne, Wilbert, 192n, 193n
Greece, 98n
green revolution strategy of development, 29–30,
    33, 35, 132–60, 226, 227, 230, 231, 232,
    234, 235, 236, 238–9, 241–2
Greenwald, B., 66n
Griffin, Keith, xxi, xxviin, xxviiin, 22n, 23n, 96n,
    98n, 161n, 162n, 190n, 191n, 224n, 225n
growth, 3–6, 7, 16, 29, 31, 38, 47, 94, 164–7,
    189, 230–2, 235
  agricultural, 134–5
  and international trade, 69–70
  in Argentina, 59
  in Chile, 55–6
  in socialist countries, 198–9
  in Taiwan, 181
  of world trade, 77–9
Guatemala, 94
Gurley, John, 22n

Haberler, G., 96n
Halliday, John, 197t, 224n
Haq, Mahbub ul, xvi, xxviin, 129n, 166, 190n,
    191n

Harberger, Arnold, C., 55, 67n, 72, 97n
Hayami, Yujiro, 162n
Hayek, F.A., 66n
Hazell, Peter B.R., 161n, 162n
health, 10, 30, 31, 38, 180, 182, 184, 185, 189,
    216, 221, 233, 234, 239, 240
Helleiner, G.K., 76, 98n
Helier, P.S., 98n
Herdt, Robert, 162n
Heston, Alan W., 22n
Hicks, J.R., 66n
Hicks, Norman, 191n
Hirashima, S., 161n
Hirschman, Albert, 129n, 131n
Hong Kong, xxvi, 104, 106, 107, 113, 211, 233
Hossain, M., 163n
Huguet, J.W., 88t
human capital, 31, 180, 184, 185, 189, 232–4,
    239
human development index, xvi–xvii
human development strategy, xv–xix
Hungary, 195, 197, 198, 211, 212, 213, 219, 220,
    221
  economic reforms in, 202–3

illiteracy, 10
imperialism, 1, 2, 3
import-substituting industrialisation, 28, 45, 50,
    92, 95, 108–12, 126
  in Brazil, 114–8
income distribution, 13, 14–8, 27, 28–9, 30, 31,
    46, 49, 58, 64, 74–5, 76, 94, 113, 127, 145,
    160, 168, 175, 189, 234, 235–6, 239, 241
  in Brazil, 117–8
  in India, 120
  in socialist countries, 216–20, 221–2
  in South Korea, 125–6
  in Sri Lanka, 184
  in Taiwan, 180–1
  in the Philippines, 155–6
India, xxiii, xxiv, xxv, xxvii, 2, 4, 8, 10, 11, 12,
    15, 21, 33, 34, 35, 72, 87, 89, 92, 99n, 102,
    105, 107, 114, 131n, 132, 133, 136, 137,
    144, 146, 149, 150, 151, 154, 157, 160, 175,
    177, 198, 211, 219, 221
  agricultural growth in, 147–51
  industrialisation in, 118–21, 124, 126, 127,
    128
Indonesia, 2, 10, 11, 12, 15, 18, 21, 98n, 106,
    144, 211, 219
industrialisation, 4, 70, 100, 187, 227, 233
  and exports, 113

267

268